GREAT CAKES

Also by Carole Walter

YOUR FIRST LOAF

GREAT CAKES

Carole Walter

CLARKSON POTTER / PUBLISHERS

NEW YORK

Published by Clarkson N. Potter, Inc.,
201 East 50th Street, New York, New York 10022.
Member of the Crown Publishing Group.

Random House, Inc.
New York, Toronto, London, Sydney, Auckland
www.randomhouse.com

CLARKSON N. POTTER, POTTER, and colophon are
registered trademarks of Random House, Inc.

Reprinted by arrangement with
the Ballantine Publishing Group, a division of
Random House, Inc.

LIBRARY OF CONGRESS CATALOGING-IN-PUBLICATION DATA
Walter, Carole.
Great cakes / Carole Walter
p.   cm
Originally published: New York : Ballantine Books, 1991.
Includes bibliographical references and index.
1. Cake.   I. Title.
TX771.W287   1998   97-43589
641.8'653—dc21   CIP

Printed in the United States of America
Design by Beth Tondreau Design
ISBN 0-609-60307-8

For Fannie

my mother of beauty
my mother of generosity
my mother of patience
my mother of wisdom

THE WOMAN WHO
LET ME GROW

ACKNOWLEDGMENTS

··

My good fortune began when I received a phone call from my friend and colleague Anne Casale telling me that her editor, Joëlle Delbourgo, was looking for a teacher to write a book on cakes. I was thrilled. To have an opportunity to write a book on my favorite subject was a dream that I never thought would be fulfilled.

Six years have passed since that phone call and through those years many individuals have played a part in creating this book. Writing it has been a complete labor of love. To simply say "thank you" to those people hardly seems sufficient.

My literary agent, Amy Berkower, wisely guided me through the nitty-gritty of negotiating a book contract. I have spent four years with Ginny Faber, my editor, who carefully scrutinized every aspect of this book. Ginny has a keen literary sense, a grace with words, and is incredibly patient.

I feel a great indebtedness to my dear friend Joanna Pruess, whose knowledge of food history was invaluable and helped me find the true origin of the quotation "Let them eat cake." Thanks to my gifted photographer, Matthew Klein, my food stylist, Rick Ellis, and my prop stylist, Linda Cheverton, the team responsible for the realistic and mouthwatering photographs in this book. Thanks also to Jimmy Harris and Carole Lowenstein for their great work on the jacket, to Nancy Sheppard for writing copy that says everything about the book I wanted to say, and to Laura Maestro for the wonderful illustrations. Copy editor Jane Mollman, did an outstanding job tying up loose ends in the manuscript.

A special thank you goes to my talented colleague Nick Malgieri for his generous words of praise in the foreword. Nick is an esteemed master baker, author, and teacher, with an incredible wealth of knowledge about baking. His faith in me and sincere friendship touches me more than I can say.

Thank you to Sylvia Lewis, who sat with me for two years at the word processor coaxing me to find the words.

Linda Bogan and Charleen Henwood, two loyal friends gave generously of their time over two years testing recipes. I am enriched by their dedication to this book. And thank you to Judith Bernhaut, my "jack-of-all-trades," who can and did do anything asked of her, to Dolores Cameron and Christina Dean, who were there in the beginning, and special thanks to my part-time teaching teammate, Kathleen Sanderson, for her input and words of encouragement.

A special thank you to Sue Torgersen who left no stone unturned when I needed product information, to Alex Marin, Margarete Grimm, and Shirley Grey for their help preparing art references.

Thank you to the dear friends who found time during the busy Christmas season to help with the tedious job of proofing my galley pages: Jacques Burdick, Annellen Guth, Joan Rothbell, Audrey Ruda, June Seligman, my daughter, Pamela Winston, and my husband, Gene.

For helping me with the technical and historical information, my sincerest thanks to:

MASTER CHEF ALBERT KUMIN, the International Pastry Arts Center, Elmsford, N.Y., for advice on pound cakes and almost anything I could ever need to know about making pastries.

CHEF DIETMAR FERCHER, renowned pastry chef from Vienna, Austria, for the technique of glaze application.

NANCY SILVERTON, author of *Desserts*, whose clever idea it was to cream butter with citrus rinds to achieve the best flavor.

CHEF ALEX MILES, of The Cakery, Dumont, N.J., for an informative session on creaming butter.

HELEN CHARDACK, talented New York pastry chef, for researching technical information on mascarpone cheese.

JOSEPH G. COSTA and FRANCIS LACLAIR, of Sorrento Cheese Company, Inc., in Little Ferry, N.J., and Buffalo, N.Y., for educating me about ricotta cheese.

NAHUM WAXMAN, owner of Kitchen Arts & Letters in New York City, one of America's leading culinary bookstores.

DONNA D'AMATO, a highly knowledgeable nutritionist, who shared valuable information and advised me in the selection of cakes to index for healthy eating.

SHIRLEY CORRIHER, who generously gave so much information from her vast background in food science.

JOANNE HOFF, a food scientist well-versed in baking, and Mary Lantz, home economist, for their research on baking powder.

Special appreciation goes to two technicians, Antoinette Hartman, a representative of Wilton Enterprises, and Elaine Gonzales, author of *Chocolate Artistry*. Tony, an accomplished, award-winning cake decorator, helped refine my information on cake decorating. Elaine, a wizard when it comes to chocolate, scrutinized the chocolate information in *Great Cakes* with a fine tooth comb.

Heartfelt thanks to my many students whose help was invaluable when I hit a stumbling block. Sincere appreciation also goes to Arlene Sarappo and the staff and assistants from Kings Cookingstudios at Kings Supermarkets, Inc., in New Jersey for their support and encouragement. Thank you also to colleagues and friends who shared favorite recipes.

And most of all to Gene, my husband and best friend, to my children, Pam and Andy, Frank and Marla, plus my grandson, Zachary, and to my family and close friends, thank you for sharing me with *Great Cakes*.

Acknowledgments

"*Let them eat cake*"

—Erroneously attributed to Marie Antoinette; actually by Jean Jacques Rousseau, 1712–1778

Recipe of Martha Washington's Great Cake

"TAKE 40 EGGS and divide the whites from the youlks and beat them to a froth start work 4 pounds of butter to a cream and put the whites of eggs to it a spoon full at a time till it is well work'd then put 4 pounds of sugar finely powderd to it in the same manner then put in the Youlks of eggs and 5 pounds of flower and 5 pounds of fruit 2 hours will bake it add to it half an ounce of mace 1 nutmeg half a pint of wine and some frensh brandy."

THE WOMENS COMMITTEE
VALLEY FORGE HISTORICAL SOCIETY
VALLEY FORGE, PA. 19481
783-0535

CONTENTS

Contents

Part Three

SPECIAL OCCASION CAKES

Contents

Part Four
. . . .

SWEET ENDINGS

Contents

xvii

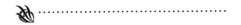

CAKES WITH REDUCED CHOLESTEROL
(Substitute margarine for butter and skimmed milk for whole milk)

CAKES WITH LESS FAT

Contents

Contents

CHOLESTEROL FREE–FAT FREE
SAUCES, TOPPINGS AND GARNISHES

Contents

X X

FOREWORD

·····················

The appearance of a book such as *Great Cakes* is no everyday event. Never before has the complex subject of cake making been treated with so great a degree of practicality, clarity, originality, and downright common sense. All the information necessary to create beautiful and delicious cakes is expressed here in the most accessible terms, by a true master of the art and science of cake making.

Carole Walter is known and respected among the cooking teachers and other food professionals of the United States as a careful and meticulous teacher and baker. Aside from her more than twenty years of experience in teaching baking and cooking, she draws upon a lifetime both as a consultant to industry and as a renowned hostess. Her ability to combine the strict professional principles of her work with the practical needs of home cooks gives *Great Cakes* a unique perspective and makes it the only cake cookbook appropriate for both beginners and advanced bakers.

Carole's credentials as a food professional would fill a small book of their own. She holds the coveted Certified Culinary Professional distinction conferred by the International Association of Culinary Professionals and currently serves as the President of the New York Association of Cooking Teachers. Her generosity is unstinting—she often and willingly shares with friends and colleagues the information from her vast baking experience; now she shares it for the first time in book form with you.

In *Great Cakes* you'll find the complete range of cakes, from easy coffee cakes to delicate creations in the French and Viennese styles. It is the result of Carole's lifelong passion for baking with the result that every technique and recipe, every hint and bit of extra advice, have been tested and honed to perfection over the years.

I have been fortunate on many occasions to enjoy the cakes and pastries that Carole prepares to the delight of her friends and students. Now those wonderful treats will reach a far wider audience who will discover the excellence of her flair for flavoring and the practicality of her methods. *Great Cakes* is a book that both home bakers and professionals will use and enjoy for many years to come.

Nick Malgieri

PREFACE

....

What makes a great cake? Is it the luxurious combination of flavors and textures? Is it aroma, color, eye appeal? The answer is any and all of these qualities. Each of us has our own criteria for measuring greatness, whether we are judging a Viennese Sachertorte, a cheesecake or a sour cream bundt.

Cakes are here to stay. It is true that we live in a diet-conscious society; we are swamped with information on sound health and the "do nots" of dining. Yet, indulgence in a little something sweet continues to be the reward for foods passed by. I believe in nutrition, well-balanced meals, and exercise. I also believe in moderation; I want the best, but it does not have to be the greatest amount.

It is encouraging to me that in spite of the prevalence of a double-income society, interest in home baking has not waned. For many, baking has become a creative outlet from the pressures of a nine-to-five job. Women holding full-time jobs care enough to attend baking classes at night, and enrollment of men wanting to learn how to bake has noticeably increased.

Home entertaining can offer a delightful respite from the daily pressures of earning an income. Drop-in guests or last-minute plans often require a quick adjustment, and foods on hand can be a boon. Many of the recipes in this book can be made ahead and frozen.

Baking is the most satisfying of the culinary arts. Unlike meal preparation, it can be done at your leisure. It is easy, relaxing, and fun. I bake for my family, for friends, and professionally. With good planning you can bake a cake with pure, natural ingredients in less time than you would imagine. By investing in some tools of the trade and a supply of basic ingredients, with minimum effort you, too, will soon be making great cakes.

Carole Walter
1991

INTRODUCTION

....

Cakes are just one variety of the category of sweets known as pâtisserie, or pastry. They differ from other forms of pastry in the complexity of their internal chemistry and by the great variety of blending techniques that result in different cake styles. Anyone who has ever attempted to bake from scratch with less than perfect results knows that in cake baking there are more steps, more stages at which things can go wrong, than in other kinds of baking. Achieving a perfect cake with wonderful flavor and texture can give you an unparalleled sense of creative satisfaction. The techniques for making cakes require some learning, but once you have mastered them, you have at your disposal an almost infinite variety of dessert possibilities for every mood and occasion.

And that is what *Great Cakes* is all about. This is a teaching book. I've chosen the recipes to present as easy-to-understand, straightforward an approach to cake baking as possible, while at the same time giving you all the information you need to get perfect results in your own kitchen. My goal throughout has been to keep it simple—and clear.

My passion for baking began as a child and has persisted over twenty years of teaching students of all levels of expertise. Working with students has taught me just how much the home baker often doesn't understand about technique, based on the conventional ways recipes are written. I've learned a great deal from my own failures, from those of other bakers, from my students, and from great professionals. When I encounter a problem, I work to solve it, retesting a recipe a dozen or more times if necessary until I get the results I want. In *Great Cakes* I've tried to share with you all that I've learned. In all the recipes I've been very specific about the time it takes to perform various procedures, because proper execution guarantees success. However, these time frames are meant to provide approximate guidelines. Watch your ingredients for the desired result. Over time, you will learn to judge for yourself when creamed butter is properly lightened in color or when a batter is sufficiently blended. Until that time, the time-frames can be a valuable learning tool. I hope you'll find my recipes especially clear and explicit.

The recipes in *Great Cakes* are divided into four main sections. Part I deals with ingredients, equipment, procedures, and techniques. Part II, "Quick and Easy," contains pound cakes, plain butter cakes, cakes with crunch, and cakes made with fruits and vegetables, as well as sponge, angel food, and chiffon cakes and jelly rolls and roulades. These cakes are in tune with today's style of eating. Most can be made in less than an hour and are not too rich. They are not meant to leave you feeling guilt-ridden for reasons of calories or health. Angel food cakes, made without butter, should hold special appeal for the cholesterol-conscious. These cakes often need no embellishment other than confectioners' sugar, fresh fruits, sorbets, or ice creams—if they need embellishment at all.

Part III, "Special Occasion Cakes," focuses on more elaborate confections. American party cakes are wonderful filled and frosted creations. You'll also find cheesecakes, European tortes and gateaux for very festive occasions, and a selection of Passover cakes. Needless to say, some of these cakes take longer to prepare because they need frostings and fillings.

Part IV, "Sweet Endings," contains ideas for fruit toppings, glazes, fillings, and frostings, as well as a section on the basics of cake decorating.

Each chapter opens with a description of the cake type (butter, chiffon, genoise, and so on) followed by a "Before You Begin" section containing information pertinent to that cake type, plus tips for achieving good results and solving problems that may arise. Do take the time to read through this section before you start a recipe.

The Twelve Most Common Mistakes Made in Cake Baking

1. Failure to read the recipe in its entirety before starting.
2. Failure to assemble all ingredients and equipment before proceeding.
3. Inaccurate measurement of ingredients.
4. Failure to presift when necessary and measure flour correctly.
5. Allowing "room-temperature" ingredients to become too warm.
6. Improper creaming of butter and sugar.
7. Underbeating egg yolks and overbeating egg whites.
8. Improper folding.
9. Overheating chocolate when melting.
10. Failure to temper ingredients before combining.
11. Overmixing batters after the flour has been added.
12. Failure to match proper pan size, capacity, and material with appropriate batter.

Trouble Shooting

Even the most experienced bakers sometimes have failures. There are times when your finished cake does not measure up to standard, or even worse, flops. The information below will help you zero in on the problem.

IF THE CAKE DID NOT RISE WELL:

The baking powder was old.
The butter was too soft for creaming.
The batter contained either too much or too little fat.
The sugar was too coarse.
The batter did not contain enough sugar.
The batter contained too little or too much liquid.
The batter was overmixed.
The oven temperature was too hot.

IF THE CAKE SINKS IN THE CENTER:

....

The batter contained too much fat.

The cake contained too much sugar.

The sugar was too coarse.

The batter contained too much or the wrong kind of
leavening.

IF THE SIDES OF THE CAKE COLLAPSE:

....

The batter contained too much liquid.

The batter did not contain enough flour.

IF THE TEXTURE IS TOUGH:

....

The batter did not contain enough fat.

The batter did not contain enough sugar.

The batter contained too many eggs.

The batter was overmixed after the flour was added.

IF THE TEXTURE IS TACKY OR STICKY:

....

The sugar was too coarse and did not completely melt during
baking.

The batter contained too much sugar.

IF THE CAKE IS CRUMBLY
AND HAS LARGE HOLES:

....

The batter contained too much sugar.

The batter contained too much leavening.

IF THE CAKE IS DRY AND STALES QUICKLY:

The batter did not contain enough fat.
The batter did not contain enough sugar.
The batter did not contain enough liquid.
The oven temperature was too low causing the cake to bake
  too long.
The cake was not stored properly.

IF A DENSE LINE FORMED AT THE BASE OF THE CAKE:

The batter contained too much fat.
The batter contained too much liquid.
The batter was not made with the proper flour.

IF THE CAKE HAS A MOIST LINE UNDER THE TOP CRUST:

The cake was underbaked.
The cake was jarred while baking.
The oven temperature was too hot.

IF THE CAKE HAS TUNNEL-LIKE HOLES:

The batter did not contain enough fat.
The batter was overmixed.
The flour contained too much gluten.

IF THE CAKE HAS STREAKS OF UNEVEN COLOR:

The batter was not properly mixed.
The baking powder was old.

IF THE CRUST OF THE CAKE HAS POOR COLOR OR IS TOO DARK:

The batter contained too much leavening.
The batter contained too much sugar.
The batter did not contain enough fat.
The oven temperature was not hot enough or too hot.

IF THE SURFACE OF THE CAKE HAS BROWN SPOTS:

The sugar was too coarse.

IF THE SURFACE OF THE CAKE PEAKED OR CRACKED:

The batter did not contain enough fat.
The batter did not contain enough sugar.
The batter contained too much flour.
The batter was overmixed.
The flour contained too much gluten.
The oven was too hot.

Part One

INGREDIENTS, EQUIPMENT, PROCEDURES, and TECHNIQUES

INGREDIENTS

..........✿..........

🌾 FLOURS, MEALS, AND STARCHES

Supermarkets today stock the largest selection of flours ever available. Most common are those grown from wheat, but flours made from such grains and cereals as rye, rice, corn, oats, and barley are now a familiar sight as well. There are also nongrain flours made from potatoes, buckwheat, soybeans, and nuts. Flour, along with eggs, forms the major framework of most baked products.

Some thirty thousand varieties of flour are grown all over the world. Wheat flours are classified by two seasonal categories, winter and spring, and are often described by the colors white, yellow, and red. Winter wheat is sown in the fall and harvested in the spring or summer; spring wheat is planted in the spring and harvested in the fall before the harsh winter weather. Generally, the most delicate flours are made from winter wheat and are known as "soft," and the strong flours from spring wheat are classified as "hard." These categories sometimes overlap depending upon climate and soil conditions in the part of the world where the wheat is grown.

Each stalk of wheat contains many tiny kernels called wheat berries. Each wheat berry consists of three parts, the bran or outer shell, the endosperm or starchy center, and the germ or embryo. White flour is made from the starch while whole wheat is made from the entire wheat kernel.

After flour is milled, it undergoes aging, which controls the liquid absorption and conditions the flour for better baking qualities. Flour is bleached naturally from oxygen in the air as it ages; however, some flours are bleached further with benzoyl peroxide or other chemical agents. Whether you choose bleached or unbleached flour

3

is a matter of personal preference. They may be used interchangeably in recipes. All white wheat flours are fortified with malted barley flour, niacin, reduced iron, thiamine mononitrate, and riboflavin according to standards set forth by the Federal Drug Administration, and are labeled "enriched."

Flours contain many kinds of protein, but white and whole wheat flours are the only ones that contain the proteins gliadin and glutenin. These proteins, which are insoluble, form gluten when they come into contact with liquid, soaking it up the way a sponge soaks up water. The higher the protein content of the flour, the more liquid it will absorb. For this reason, high-protein flour forms a stiffer batter than one made with a low-protein flour, even though both batters were made with the same measurements of flour and liquid. For bread baking, high protein is an advantage because it gives dough body. For cake baking it can be a deterrent as it toughens the crumb and reduces the volume.

Gliadin gives batters and doughs elasticity, while glutenin adds strength and stability. Along with egg proteins, they form the cellular structure or web that traps the carbon dioxide gas needed for the rising of the batter in the heat of the oven. As the batter bakes, the gas bubbles expand until the batter reaches an internal temperature of 140°, at which point it coagulates or stabilizes and becomes a leavened cake. Only wheat flour is able to perform this function. Although rye flour contains a small amount of gluten, it is a different kind. It is wheat flour that makes possible the rising of baked products.

Protein information, usually based on the amount in grams per 4-ounce or about a 1-cup measurement rather than the percentage per pound, is printed under the nutritional guidelines on the outside of every bag or box of flour. Soft wheat white flours start at 7 grams per cup and are suitable for cakes. Hard wheat white flours, used for bread baking, reach up to 15 grams, while some whole wheat flours contain as much as 16 grams of protein per 4 ounces. All-purpose flour averages somewhere in the middle of this 7- to 16-gram range.

Most popular brands of bleached all-purpose flours such as Gold Medal and Pillsbury have a protein content of 11 to 12 grams per cup. Unbleached flour like Heckers or Ceresota has a protein content of 12 to 13 grams. Unfortunately, package labeling sometimes creates confusion. Two exceptionally fine flours sold in the United States give an example. They are White Lily, a soft wheat flour, milled in Knoxville, Tennessee, and King Arthur Flour, a hard wheat flour milled in Norwich, Vermont. While both these flours are labeled all-purpose, White Lily has a protein value of 9 grams per 4 ounces and King Arthur 13 grams per 4 ounces. Despite the similar labeling, they are not interchangeable. White Lily, popular for making biscuits and pie pastry, is closer to cake flour, while King Arthur is best for breads. White Lily may be used successfully in any recipe in this book that calls for cake flour. When all-purpose flour is specified, *increase* the White Lily flour by two tablespoons per cup. If using King Arthur, *decrease* the flour by two tablespoons per cup.

When buying flour, take note of the amount of protein listed on the bag. A difference of only one or two grams can affect the consistency of the batter and the quality of a finished cake. It is also possible that bags from the same manufacturer will vary in protein strength and moisture content because of such variables as climate and soil conditions among particular crops. For cake baking choose all-purpose flour with the lowest protein content when you have a choice. Understanding the differences in flour proteins and moisture absorption should help you solve many of your baking problems.

When storing flour, keep in mind that it reacts to temperatures. If stored near heat, it dries out, so it will absorb more of the liquid in a batter. If stored in a humid place, it picks up moisture, which gives the batter a more liquid consistency. Small bugs called weevils or grubs may also develop under damp storage conditions. To keep flour fresh, store it in an airtight container at room temperature and use it within a few weeks. For longer storage, refrigerate for about 3 months or freeze for up to a year. Always bring the cold flour to room temperature before using.

The following is a list of commonly available flours, meals, grains, and starches. It does not include flours produced by smaller companies, as their protein ranges are too variable. The gram measurements are per 4-ounce portions.

BLEACHED ALL-PURPOSE FLOUR (11 to 12 grams): an enriched pure white all-purpose flour made from hard and soft wheats, milled from the center or starchy part of the wheat kernel. Bleaching is a chemical process manufacturers use to whiten the flour and to balance the liquid absorption.

UNBLEACHED ALL-PURPOSE FLOUR (11 to 13 grams): an enriched unbleached all-purpose flour made from hard and soft wheat flours and occasionally from only hard wheat flour. It contains all the natural vitamins and minerals of the wheat and is slightly maize in color. While unbleached flour contains no chemical bleaching agents, the flour is bleached naturally by oxygen in the air. Unbleached and bleached flours may be used interchangeably in recipes.

CAKE FLOUR (8 grams): an enriched bleached flour made from high-quality soft wheat. Cake flour is specially milled for cakes and delicate pastries. If you have trouble finding cake flour in the flour section, look for it in the cake mix section, where it is sometimes stocked instead. (Unbleached cake flour is sold in some specialty food shops and health food stores.) Be sure to buy plain cake flour, not the type labeled "self-rising," which contains leavening and salt.

SELF-RISING FLOUR (8 to 9 grams): an enriched bleached soft wheat flour that contains leavening and salt and is used for biscuits, quick breads, and cakes. Self-rising flour is best when used in recipes specially developed by the manufacturer. The proportion of leavening and salt in self-rising flour is 1½ teaspoons of leavening and ½ teaspoon salt per cup of flour. If you must substitute self-rising flour in a recipe, reduce the baking powder and salt proportionately. Avoid using self-rising flour if your recipe calls for baking soda.

INSTANT FLOUR (11 grams): a specialty granular all-purpose flour that pours like salt and dissolves easily in cold water. Instant flour is useful for making quick gravies. While it may be used as a substitute for all-purpose flour, it should not be used for recipes in this book because it makes the consistency of the batter grainy instead of smooth.

PASTRY FLOUR (9 to 10 grams): a specially blended flour that is not quite as delicate as cake flour, but softer than all-purpose. This product is used for making pie pastries, cookies, and sweet doughs, and also in some European recipes. It is generally sold in bulk to commercial bakers; however, some specialty food shops do sell it for home use. You can make your own by using a ratio of 2 parts all-purpose flour to 1 part cake flour. As an example, to make 2 cups of pastry flour, use 1⅓ cups of all-purpose flour combined with ⅔ cup cake flour.

WHOLE WHEAT OR GRAHAM FLOUR (15 to 16 grams): a nutritious and flavorful hard wheat flour made from the entire wheat kernel, the shell, the starch, and the germ. Whole wheat flour is milled into textures ranging from fine to quite coarse. Graham flour is a specially milled whole wheat flour developed by Dr. Sylvester Graham. Both whole wheat flour and graham flour may be used in place of white flour. However, if substituting whole wheat flour for white, it is best to use no more than 50 percent whole wheat flour in the batter or the cake will be too heavy because whole wheat flour contains less starch than white flour.

STONE-GROUND WHOLE WHEAT FLOUR (15 to 16 grams): usually manufactured by smaller mills from high-quality wheats. The wheat is ground to a powder between two huge stones commonly propelled by water. The water keeps the flour cool during milling and as a result vitamin B and all the natural nutrients are retained. Whole wheat stone-ground flour is less refined and more flavorful than commercial whole wheat flour. It should be blended with no less than 50 percent white flour to give greater volume to the baked product.

Both stone-ground and whole wheat flours should be stored in the refrigerator or freezer as they contain wheat germ and can go rancid quickly. They will keep up to three months in the refrigerator and up to one year in the freezer.

CORNMEAL: native to the western hemisphere, available in both yellow and white varieties. Yellow cornmeal is more nutritious than white, but their baking properties are the same. Cornmeal is sometimes used with wheat flour in cakes for flavor and texture.

CORNSTARCH: 100 percent refined starch made from the endosperm of the corn kernel. For baking purposes, cornstarch is used to make a form of cake flour. It is sometimes used in small quantities in place of white wheat flour to give cakes a smooth, velvety texture. For nonbaking purposes, cornstarch serves as a thickening agent for fillings and sauces.

POTATO STARCH: a dried flourlike substance made from cooked potatoes. Potato starch is one good substitute for flour in Passover sponge cakes. It is also used in small amounts by itself or combined with wheat flour in tortes. Cakes made with potato starch generally have a very smooth and velvety texture. Potato starch is also used as a thickening agent in the preparation of sauces.

❧ LEAVENINGS

Leavening is the ingredient in cakes that makes them rise. The most common forms of leavening used in cake baking are the chemical ones, baking powder and baking soda, though cakes can also be leavened with yeast or air.

Chemical and yeast leavenings form carbon dioxide gas when exposed to liquid and heat. As the gas is released, small bubbles form throughout the batter, causing it to rise. Fast-acting chemical leavenings form carbon dioxide in combination with an acid such as cream of tartar and an alkaline like baking soda. Yeast is slow-acting and is desirable for soft batter doughs and sweet breads. Air is the leavening in a cake made with many beaten eggs, such as sponge, angel food, and genoise cakes. The air is whipped into the eggs, forming tiny cells that fill with steam when heated and force the batter to expand.

The recipes in this book call for double-acting baking powder. Purchase it in small quantities and be sure to date the bottom of the can because it picks up moisture easily and becomes lumpy. Fresh baking powder should be soft and powdery. It should be replaced at least two or three times a year and discarded sooner if lumpy. To test baking powder for freshness, stir 1 teaspoon into a glass of hot water. If the baking powder is fresh, the water will shimmer and bubble gently.

DOUBLE-ACTING BAKING POWDER: Double-acting baking powder releases gas in two stages. The first is released when the baking powder comes into contact with the liquid. The second and strongest boost comes from the oven heat while the cake is baking. This two-stage action enables batters to stand without losing all their gases or leavening power. This is especially helpful if you must stagger baking time due to insufficient oven space.

Commonly available brands such as Royal and Calumet are made from cornstarch or potato starch (which prevent lumping), sodium bicarbonate, calcium acid phosphate, and sodium aluminum sulphate. Some cooks prefer Rumford, a double-acting baking powder sold in health food stores, because it is made without sodium aluminum sulphate, a chemical that sometimes leaves an aftertaste.

SINGLE-ACTING BAKING POWDER: Single-acting baking powder releases all gas as soon as it comes into contact with liquid. It is no longer mass-produced, but brands made by small manufacturers such as Featherweight are available in health food stores. Some purists prefer single-acting baking powder because it contains less salt and no sodium aluminum sulphate. You can make your own; see Substitutions, page 521. Bake batters made with single-acting baking powder as soon as possible; they lose rising power as they stand.

BAKING SODA: also known as bicarbonate of soda. Because of its neutralizing action, it is used with batters containing acid ingredients such as molasses, fruits, chocolate, buttermilk, sour cream, and yogurt. Like baking powder, it acts as a leavening, but less is required. One-half teaspoon baking soda has about the same leavening power as 1 teaspoon baking powder.

CREAM OF TARTAR: A by-product of wine making, cream of tartar is made from the residue that forms on the inside of wine vats. It is most commonly used to stabilize beaten egg whites and to prevent crystallization of sugar during various stages of heating. Cream of tartar is one of the acid ingredients in single-acting baking powder.

YEAST: Although not used in this book, yeast is the major leavening for breads, sweet breads, and coffee cakes. It is manufactured in two forms: fresh compressed cakes, and packets of either active-dry or the new fast-rising granules. Fresh yeast is highly perishable and must be stored in the refrigerator. It may be frozen for longer keeping. Dried yeast, which has an expiration date listed on the package, can be stored on the pantry shelf for many months.

❧ SUGAR AND OTHER SWEETENERS

Sugar is a carbohydrate that comes from the roots, stems, or sap of plants, most commonly sugar cane and beets. The juice or sap is extracted from the plant and undergoes a lengthy refining process. Sucrose and granulated sugar are by definition the same ingredient and are classified as disaccharides. Sugar furnishes energy to the body faster than any other food.

Sugar serves many purposes in cake baking. It adds sweetness and contributes moisture. It also provides volume, tenderness, smooth texture, and color. If you wish to reduce the sweetness in a cake, be aware that the sugar must be in correct proportion to the other ingredients. Too little sugar results in a tough, dry cake with reduced volume. Excessive amounts of sugar give a cake a dark, crusty surface.

Liquid sweeteners such as honey, molasses, and maple syrup are not suitable sugar substitutes in cakes, since they cannot be aerated. Liquid sweeteners require baking soda to neutralize their acids. Without adjustments to the recipe, the cake will not rise properly and its texture will be heavy and too moist. Furthermore, the oven temperature must be reduced to avoid overbrowning.

GRANULATED WHITE SUGAR: an all-purpose sugar used for home sweetening purposes. Granulated white sugar is refined from sugar cane or sugar beets and is 99.94 percent pure. Try various brands of granulated white sugar until you find one with very small crystals. Granules that are too large do not hold enough air during the creaming process or when beaten with eggs, nor do they completely dissolve during baking. As a result, the surface of the cake will develop brown spots where the undissolved sugar has caramelized; the cake will be coarse-textured and will not rise as high, or it may even flop completely. Tiny crystals are especially important for butter, sponge, and chiffon cakes.

It has been my observation that granulated sugar sold in the southern and western sections of the United States is superior in quality to the sugar available in other parts of the country, especially the northeast. The size of the sugar crystal varies from manufacturer to manufacturer and sometimes from bag to bag. Try the supermarket house brands; some companies set their own specifications, which are often superior to those of the name brands.

Other alternatives are to substitute superfine sugar (sold in 1-pound boxes) or to strain sugar through a fine-mesh strainer before measuring. You can also grind table sugar in a food processor or blender. The granules will be uneven, but this is still preferable to having crystals too large.

SUPERFINE SUGAR: Often called "dessert" or "bar" sugar, this very fine-grain granulated sugar is used for delicate foam cakes, most creamed butter cakes, meringues, and whipped creams, because it holds air well and quickly dissolves. Although it is more costly, superfine sugar can be used in equal quantities as a substitute for granulated sugar. Because it is so fine, it lumps quite easily. Unless you have just opened the box, it should always be strained before measuring.

BROWN SUGAR: Brown sugar adds moisture and flavor to a cake, but produces a slightly heavier texture than a cake made with white sugar. Brown sugar is a combination of refined white sugar and molasses. The molasses is added before its sugar crystallizes. Although light and dark brown sugar may be used interchangeably in most recipes, light brown sugar has a more delicate flavor and is preferable for baking. Dark brown sugar contains more molasses and is better for other types of cooking. The intensity of the flavor is determined by the quality of molasses. A low-grade molasses gives a strong, sometimes bitter taste.

The moisture in brown sugar evaporates very quickly on exposure to air, causing it to harden. To prevent this, cooks often kept a wedge of fresh apple in the box. However, the new packaging in heavy plastic bags maintains freshness extremely well, so you don't need to use an apple if you observe a few simple precautions. Press the top of the bag to release all the air, turn it several times and secure tightly with a plastic tie or rubber band. Return the bag to the original box and store it in a cool place. See page 45 for instructions on measuring brown sugar.

GRANULATED BROWN SUGAR: a crystallized form of brown sugar that pours like salt. It can be substituted for regular brown sugar in equal amounts.

CONFECTIONERS' SUGAR: a combination of granulated sugar and 3 percent cornstarch, which is added to prevent lumping. Confectioners' sugar, also called 10X or powdered sugar, is made by processing the granules 10 times finer than granulated sugar. Commonly used in frostings, confectioners' sugar is not considered a substitute for granulated sugar. Because it is so fine, it lacks the ability to hold air. When confectioners' sugar is used in cake batters,

Ingredients,
Equipment,
Procedures
and Techniques

11

it yields a cake with a dense crumb and velvety texture. Confectioners' sugar must be strained before measuring.

MOLASSES: a thick, dark syrup made from the remnants of sugar crystals during the early stages of refining. Molasses for domestic use is sold in two forms: sulphured and unsulphured. Sulphured molasses has a rich, strong flavor and contains the sulphiting agent sulphur dioxide. Unsulphured molasses has a milder taste. Used in small quantities, molasses imparts flavor, color, and moistness to foods.

HONEY: a natural sweetener obtained from the nectar of such flowers as orange blossom, clover, and lavender. The flavor of honey varies according to flower source. Honey is 99.9 percent sugar and has almost the same sweetening power as sugar. In cakes, it is best used in small quantities to add flavor and moistness. Cake batters made with honey are baked at a lower temperature because heat caramelizes honey, causing the cakes to brown too quickly. Honey contains acid; therefore a small amount of baking soda must be added to neutralize the acid. Honey kept too long on the pantry shelf may crystallize, but it can be reliquefied easily; warm it on low heat until the crystals dissolve. Refrigerate for longer storage, then bring to room temperature by heating briefly.

LIGHT AND DARK CORN SYRUP: syrups made from cornstarch that has been converted into a liquid. Light corn syrup is more widely used than dark because it is flavorless. Used in small quantities, light syrup prevents liquid evaporation in shiny frostings. Light corn syrup also serves as a clear glaze and helps to prevent crystallization of sugar when making frostings, fondants, or candies. Dark corn syrup is flavored with caramel and is used when color and moistness are desired.

❦ FATS

Fats are enriching agents that add flavor, help maintain freshness, and tenderize the crumb of cakes. Four types of fats are used in home baking: animal fat in the form of butter or lard, margarine made from either animal or vegetable fat, solid or hydrogenated vegetable shortening, and oils, either bland or flavored.

Whether or not the fat can be aerated determines the type of cake it is used in and the manner in which it is incorporated into a batter. Solid fats such as butter, margarine, and vegetable shortening can be creamed and have the ability to draw in air to leaven or lighten a batter. These fats are the starting ingredient in batters for creamed butter cakes. Oils have no ability to draw in air and are therefore added at a later stage. Lard, which does not cream well, is used for pies and pastries.

A cake in which oil is the primary fat will be very moist. Melted butter must be treated as an oil when added to a batter, but the resulting cake will be less moist because butter solidifies upon cooling.

Plain cakes are best made with butter because of its pleasing flavor. However, margarine may be used as a substitute when health or kosher dietary restrictions are a consideration. Chocolate and spice cakes work especially well with butter substitutes because butter is not the dominant flavor. The more butter a batter contains, the heavier and finer-textured the cake will be. Vegetable shortening produces light cakes, but contributes no flavor. Do not substitute whipped butter or margarine; these products are aerated and the measurements will not be the same.

BUTTER: Butter contributes flavor, freshness, aroma, and richness. It contains at least 80 percent fat and from 10 to 16 percent water. The balance is curd and mineral matters. Salt is often used in butter as a preservative; the amount varies; at times it can overpower the natural sweet flavor for which butter is prized. In addition, salted butter contains more water than unsalted. Unsalted butter, labeled "sweet" by many packagers, is always preferable in baking. You may substitute salted butter in a pinch, but the flavor will not be as good. U.S. Grade AA unsalted butter is specified in the recipes in this book. If you must substitute salted butter for unsalted, taste it, then reduce the amount of salt in the recipe accordingly. Regardless of the expiration date on the package, if you don't plan to use the butter within a week or two after purchasing, store it in a deep freezer. Stored at zero degrees or below, butter will keep at least 6 to 8 months. Always keep opened butter well wrapped, as it picks up flavors and odors from other food in the refrigerator.

MARGARINE: Margarine was first introduced in France by Mege-Mouries in 1869, when butter was scarce due to wars and economic conditions. It is made from a blend of vegetable oils and hardened fat mixed with reconstituted skim milk or water. The oils give it a softer consistency than butter. Margarine has the same caloric value as butter. However, depending on the brand, it can be lower in cholesterol or cholesterol-free. Avoid reduced-calorie margarine as it contains too much water. Margarine may be substituted for butter in most baking, but it is best reserved for cakes where the good flavor of butter is not essential.

HYDROGENATED VEGETABLE SHORTENING: This is a flavorless, pure white, solid fat made from purified vegetable oils that are heated and pressurized with hydrogen. Unlike butter, vegetable shortening is 100 percent fat. It has the same number of calories as other fats, and since it contains palm oil, is high in saturated fat. Vegetable shortening may be substituted for butter, but it lacks the moisture content of butter so the substitution is not always desirable. Cakes made with vegetable shortening have a lighter crumb.

VEGETABLE OILS: Cakes made with oil are moister and maintain freshness longer than those made with solid fats, because oil does not resolidify after baking as do butter and other solid fats. Oil is most frequently used in chiffon cakes, some sponge cakes, and carrot or pumpkin cakes. My favorite oil for baking is safflower, although corn, soybean, canola, and rapeseed are good alternatives. Peanut oil has a slightly nutty taste, but is acceptable. Extra-virgin olive oil has a pronounced flavor and should be used only when specified. Such strong-flavored oils as sesame or walnut should be used very sparingly. They can be blended with a bland oil to create an interesting taste.

CREAM CHEESE: Cream cheese is a soft, unripened cheese made from pasteurized milk, cheese cultures, salt, and carob bean gum. It is delicious combined with butter in butter cakes and frostings, imparting a tangy flavor and giving the crumb a smooth, velvety texture. It is essential to bring cream cheese to room temperature before using it in cakes and frostings so that it will combine smoothly with the butter.

🍃 EGGS

Eggs are essential to the structure of a cake, because they bind all other ingredients together. A leavened cake can be made without a liquid, but it cannot be properly made without eggs. When eggs are added to creamed butter and sugar, they form cells that expand and multiply to lighten the mixture, and they help to form the structure of a cake as they coagulate in the heat of an oven. Beaten eggs are a major leavening agent, with or without a chemical leavener. Beating draws in air to create millions of tiny air cells, which expand in the heat of the oven to make the cake rise. Genoise and foam cakes such as sponge, chiffon, and angel food rely on these air cells for leavening.

Eggs add color, enrichment, flavor, and moistness to cakes. In cooked fillings, they are also an important thickening agent. The quality of the egg is reflected by its grading: AA, A, or B. Grade AA is the best and most commonly available to the consumer. A large egg weighs about 2 ounces in the shell. Egg yolks, which are rich in fat, contribute tenderness and color to cakes. The whites, or albumen, are mostly protein and are a binder. While the proportion of white to yolk is about double, a whole egg is almost 75 percent water. I have specified U.S. AA "large" eggs for the recipes in this book. In fact, in the United States, when recipes are printed without specifying an egg size, you can assume it is large. There is no difference in flavor or food value between white and brown eggs. Which you choose is entirely a matter of preference.

Since egg shells are quite porous, eggs easily pick up bacteria and refrigerator odor, so it is best to store them rounded side up in their original carton, even when your refrigerator has a special shelf for storing eggs. Do not use cracked eggs because of the possibility of bacterial contamination. In fact, eggs have been the culprits in a number of recent cases of salmonella poisoning, so nowadays greater caution is advised in handling eggs. Many older cookbooks advise bringing eggs to room temperature before using, since in this state they will draw in more air. Today it is felt that eggs should not stand at room temperature for more than 1 hour. After that, they begin to deteriorate and become a health risk (see page 45).

Once opened, whole eggs, covered tightly, will keep in the refrigerator for up to 2 or 3 days. Egg whites will keep up to four days refrigerated, or may be frozen for several months. Freezing them in individual plastic ice cube holders makes it easy to remember how many you have. The frozen cubes can be transferred to a plastic bag and stored up to 3 months. Frozen egg whites become slightly watery when thawed and do not hold their volume well, so they are not a good choice for angel food cakes and meringues. However, they are perfectly acceptable for use in recipes where they don't have to be whipped for leavening. Unbroken egg yolks can be covered with a small amount of water and stored in the refrigerator tightly covered for 2 or 3 days. If the yolks are broken, omit the water and just cover tightly. I do not like to freeze egg yolks, because they become grainy upon thawing.

❧ LIQUIDS

Liquid in a batter serves two essential purposes. It changes the protein in the flour to gluten and starts the chemical reaction of the leavening—baking powder and/or baking soda. These two actions, either singly or together, allow carbon dioxide gas to develop, which makes the cake rise. As the cake bakes, the liquid gives off steam, adding to the tenderness and fine texture of the cake.

The amount of liquid must be in correct proportion to the other ingredients. Too much liquid weakens the cake's structure and inhibits rising. Too little liquid results in a heavy cake with a dry crumb. Liquid substitutions do not always work. It is all right to substitute low-fat or skimmed milk for whole milk, but you should not substitute acid ingredients like fruit juices or purées or cultured products for milk without changing the leavening. These must be neutralized with the addition of a small amount of baking soda, and the baking powder will have to be reduced proportionately.

Milk is the liquid most commonly used in cakes. However, water, coffee, eggs, fruit juices or purées, sweet or sour cream, yogurt, buttermilk, and some soft cheese products containing high water levels (cream cheese, cottage cheese, and ricotta, for example) are also moistening agents.

MILK: Milk is 87 percent water and 13 percent milk solids. It gives cakes moistness, a tender crumb, sweet flavor, and good color, and is the usual moistener in creamed butter cakes. While all of the recipes in this book that call for milk refer to whole milk (3.5 percent milk fat or more), milk with a lower fat content may be used if you prefer. You can also use reconstituted powdered milk, canned evaporated skimmed milk, or canned evaporated milk diluted with 50 percent water. Condensed milk, containing sugar, is not the same product as evaporated milk and should not be substituted for whole milk.

CULTURED DAIRY PRODUCTS: Cultured dairy products such as sour cream, yogurt, and buttermilk have been soured with lactic acid or other bacterial cultures. They contribute delicious flavor to cakes, give fine texture, and extend shelf life. If you do not wish to purchase buttermilk by the quart, a cultured buttermilk powder is available at the supermarket and makes a satisfactory substitute. Crème fraîche (page 478), a cultured cream that can be whipped, is not commonly used in cake batters, but as a topping for cakes or in the preparation of refrigerated desserts.

COFFEE AND ESPRESSO: Coffee and espresso are wonderful flavorings for cakes, fillings, and frostings. They are especially complementary to chocolate, but are also delicious in spice or nut cakes. For a subtle coffee flavor, coffee can be used as the liquid in a cake. When more intense coffee flavor is desirable, I like to use highly concentrated coffee or espresso zest (page 58).

Arabica and robusta are the two major types of coffee beans from which hundreds of coffee blends are formulated. Coffee trees grow in temperate climates in such countries as Sumatra, Ethiopia, Kenya, Colombia, and Jamaica. After the dried hull of the berry is opened, the green beans are processed in various ways, then undergo roastings that range from light to dark. Lighter roasted beans are milder and less expensive, while the dark-roasted types are more oily, robust, and costly.

Espresso is made from dark-roasted coffee beans heated for a long period of time under very high temperatures so they exude rich oils and develop the characteristic bitter flavor. Its intense flavor makes espresso ideal for use in cake batters. Espresso beans should be more finely ground than coffee beans.

To maintain freshness, coffee and espresso should always be stored in well-sealed containers. Ground coffee can be refrigerated for up to 1 week or kept in the freezer up to a month if not used daily. I always store my coffee beans in the freezer, where they hold their freshness up to 3 months. Be sure to double-wrap the beans by placing the package in a tightly secured plastic bag.

🐚 CHOCOLATE

Stories about chocolate date back as far as the ancient civilization of the Mexican Aztecs, when the feathered serpent and god of peace, Quetzalcoatl, supposedly taught the Indians how to grow the *cacahuatl*, the cocoa tree. They learned to roast cocoa pods and ground them into a drink called *xocolatl* (bitter water), favored by the Emperor Montezuma as a stimulant and aphrodisiac.

When the Spanish conqueror Cortés landed in Mexico, he noted how much the Aztecs prized their cocoa beans and took them back to Spain, where at first they were used mostly for medicinal purposes.

As Spanish colonization of Mexico grew after the conquest, so did the chocolate plantations. The Spaniards began to blend sugar cane from the Canary Islands with the *xocolatl* to make a tasty drink they adored. Before long they were exporting it to Europe, where it became a luxury brew.

Around 1760, cocoa beans came to Colonial America through trade with the West Indies, and in 1765, the first chocolate factory was built in Massachusetts by the Englishmen John Hannon and James Baker, the latter a financier. In 1815, Coenraad van Houten established mills in Holland, where in later years "dutched" cocoa, a process that neutralizes the acid in the cocoa bean, was invented (page 22). In 1819, the first true chocolate factory was established in Switzerland by François Louis Cailler.

Cocoa trees, which grow in tropical climates near the equator, produce large pods containing up to fifty seeds, or beans. These are split open and scraped of their seeds, which are fermented and dried, then cleaned and roasted to develop flavor and soften the skin or husk. After roasting, the beans are crushed to separate the "nib" or meat of the bean from the husk and the germ.

The nibs are ground and then heated to liquefy the cocoa butter. This process transforms the dry nibs into a thick substance called "cocoa mass" or chocolate liquor. The liquor, which is about 55 percent cocoa butter and 45 percent chocolate liquor, is either formed into blocks of unsweetened chocolate or blended with sugar, milk solids, and other ingredients to make semisweet or milk chocolate. To make cocoa, the liquor is put under hydraulic pressure, which removes all but about 10 to 20 percent of the cocoa butter.

The remaining cocoa solids are formed into blocks called "press cakes" which are ground into cocoa powder.

In the final stages, the chocolate passes through huge rollers that smooth and refine the ingredients in a process known as "conching," a procedure that can last from a few hours to a few days. Chocolate that is conched only a short time will be gritty. The longer chocolate is conched, the smoother, richer, and more expensive it will be. After conching, the chocolate is tempered to stabilize the cocoa butter crystals and finally molded to be used for confectionery and baking purposes.

The recipes in this book specify the types of chocolate I like to use based on whether the cake is American or European and also on sweetness and the intensity of the chocolate taste desired. It is not always advisable to make substitutions because the quantity of sugar varies in many chocolates.

If you have difficulty finding premium or imported chocolates in the baking department of your supermarket, look for it in the candy section or in a department store. Imported semisweet is sold as eating chocolate and is usually packaged in 3- or 4-ounce bars. Mail order sources are listed on page 531.

UNSWEETENED (BITTER) CHOCOLATE: Also called baking chocolate, unsweetened chocolate contains approximately 45 to 47 percent chocolate liquor and 53 to 55 percent cocoa butter. Unsweetened chocolate was the primary baking chocolate in the United States until the culinary explosion of the 1970s, when appreciation of imported chocolates led to a whole new interest in using other varieties of chocolate. Unsweetened chocolate is used primarily for American-style cakes. It is not generally used in Europe.

It is not always advisable to substitute unsweetened chocolate for bittersweet and semi-sweet and vice versa. Not only is sweetneess affected, but the amount of cocoa butter in the chocolate changes the liquid absorption in the batter. This can change the texture of the cake. Substituting bitter-sweet or semi-sweet is of less consequence unless you are into fine chocolate work.

Popular brands of unsweetened chocolate are Baker's or Hershey's, packaged in eight 1-ounce molded squares. Also available are premium unsweetened chocolates manufactured by Ghirardelli of San Francisco, sold in 4-ounce bars, Callebaut, available in 11-pound blocks or 1.83-ounce packages from Maid of Scandinavia, and Wilbur, which can be ordered by mail in 5-pound blocks. These quality chocolates are more expensive, but they are worth the investment because of their fine flavor and texture.

BITTERSWEET AND SEMISWEET CHOCOLATES: These are authentic chocolates, which must, by federal regulation, contain at least 27 percent cocoa butter and no less than 35 percent chocolate liquor. Without the liquor, they are not "real" chocolates according to the United States Standards of Identity.

Each chocolate manufacturer has its own well-guarded formula. These formulas are blends of roasted cocoa beans (similar to coffee bean blends) that are processed into chocolates varying in degrees of chocolate intensity, sweetness, and smoothness. Semisweet and bittersweet chocolates are made of sugar, chocolate liquor, cocoa butter, lecithin (a natural soybean product), and vanilla or vanillin. They are sold under a wide variety of names such as semisweet, bittersweet, extra bittersweet, bitter, special dark, Eagle Sweet, dark sweet, and German's sweet. Unfortunately, there are no guidelines on package labels to indicate the amount of sugar added to a brand. This causes some confusion because a semisweet chocolate can be less sweet than a bittersweet. The only way you can tell is by tasting the chocolate.

Some semisweet chocolates are manufactured in the United States, but the most luxurious and costly chocolates are imported from Switzerland and Belgium. France, Holland, and England also make fine premium chocolates.

The easily recognized domestic brands of chocolates are: Baker's Semisweet chocolate, packaged in eight 1-ounce molded squares, Baker's German's Sweet, a special semisweet chocolate that is sweeter than a basic semisweet, packaged in 4-ounce bars, and Ghirardelli Semisweet, sold in 4-ounce bars. Bulk chocolate is sold in 10-pound blocks. The brand I prefer is Peter's (made by Nestlé). Another fine brand is Van Leer.

Imported brands are: Lindt Excellence or Surfin, sold in 3-ounce or 13-ounce bars, Tobler Tradition, available in 3-ounce or 13-ounce bars, and Callebaut Bittersweet, sold in 17.5-ounce bars or by mail in 5-pound blocks. Maillard Eagle Sweet Chocolate comes in 4-ounce bars and Poulain Bittersweet is available in 7-ounce bars.

The brand of chocolate you choose should be determined by the kind of chocolate the recipe calls for, how sweet you like the flavor of the chocolate to be, brand available, and budget.

COUVERTURE: Chocolates classified as couverture are "real" chocolates containing chocolate liquor and a very high cocoa butter content ranging from 36 to 40 percent or more according to the manufacturer. The additional cocoa butter makes the chocolate more fluid so it can be used to give thin glazes to cakes and for candy dipping, molding, or other confectionery purposes. This chocolate is ideal to use for making chocolate curls because the high amount of cocoa butter makes the bar less brittle. Most of the finest couverture comes from Europe. Couverture chocolate is more commonly used by professionals; however, for home use, Lindt Courante, Cacao Barry, Pupier Couverture, and Peter's Chocolat d'Or are excellent brands.

COMPOUND CHOCOLATE: an imitation chocolate primarily used for molding and novelty chocolate decorations, commonly found in cake decorating supply shops. Compound chocolate is also called confectionery coating and summer coating because it has a higher melting point than regular chocolate, holds its shape longer, and can be tinted in many colors. Chocolate-flavored compound coating is made from cocoa powder, dry milk solids, palm, coconut, or soya oil, and flavorings. Since it contains neither chocolate liquor nor cocoa butter, the United States Standards of Identity will not permit it to be labeled as "real" chocolate. Compound chocolate is the easiest chocolate to work with because it is made from vegetable fats, known as "stable fats," instead of cocoa butter, and therefore does not require tempering. A good brand is Nestlé's Icecap, which can be purchased in 10-, 5-, or 2½-pound blocks or by the pound in wafers from Maid of Scandinavia (page 532).

WHITE CHOCOLATE: White chocolate, not a real chocolate, is simply cocoa butter to which sugar, dry or whole milk, and vanilla or vanillin has been added. The amount of cocoa butter ranges from 30 to 55 percent, the higher percentages being couverture. White *compound* chocolates do not contain cocoa butter and have no chocolate flavor because they do not contain chocolate liquor.

White chocolate is very rich and should not be substituted for other chocolates because it reacts differently. It is tricky to use in cake batters because it contains so much cocoa butter that it lacks the ability to hold in air. This delicate chocolate is very sensitive to heat and is best used in frostings, mousses, ice creams, or in preparations where minimal heat is required. The brand I prefer is Tobler Narcisse. Other popular brands are Lindt Blancor and Lindt Swiss Confectionery Bar, found in the candy department of many supermarkets packaged in 3-ounce bars. Peter's Snowcap and Valrhona Ivoire may be purchased in bulk. White chocolate is more perishable than milk or dark chocolates because it contains about 30 percent milk. Unless you use it frequently, buy it in smaller quantities.

CHOCOLATE CHIPS OR DOTS: small pieces of molded chocolate that hold their shape during baking because they contain less cocoa butter. They are made in large and mini sizes, and are available in semisweet, bittersweet, milk, or white chocolate. Because of the reduced cocoa butter, the quality of these chocolates is generally not as fine. Mini chocolate bits, containing the smallest amount of cocoa butter, are less likely to sink in a batter because of their lighter weight. When purchasing chocolate bits, check the label to make sure it says "real chocolate" rather than "chocolate-flavored."

UNSWEETENED COCOA (Nonalkaline): A powder made from chocolate liquor, cocoa has a rich, robust chocolate flavor. It is recommended in recipes that use baking soda as the leavening agent because the baking soda neutralizes the acid in the cocoa.

To make cocoa, chocolate liquor is pressed to remove at least 75 percent of the cocoa butter. The remaining cocoa solids are formed into a solid mass called a presscake, which is further defatted and then ground into cocoa powder. Cocoa powder does contain cocoa butter, but in reduced quantities that range from 8 to 24 percent.

Hershey's brand cocoa is the most popular baking cocoa in the United States. It contains about 14 to 15 percent cocoa butter and is my favorite choice for American-style cakes. Other quality brands are Baker's, Ghirardelli, and Van Leer Family American Cocoa.

DUTCH-PROCESS UNSWEETENED COCOA: Similar to regular unsweetened cocoa, except that it is treated with an alkali to neutralize the acid in the chocolate liquor before processing. Neutralizing the acid gives the cocoa a milder flavor and makes it easier to dissolve in liquid. Dutch-process cocoa is darker in color than unsweetened cocoa, but the difference is hardly apparent in the finished product. It should only be used in recipes where baking powder is the primary leavening agent. Do not substitute regular unsweetened cocoa, which has a higher level of acid. Common brands of dutch-process cocoa are Droste, Poulain, Feodora, and Van Houten. Hershey's has introduced a domestic dutch-process chocolate packaged in a silver can.

🌿 SEASONINGS

SALT: Table salt, or sodium chloride, serves many purposes in cake baking. It is a flavor enhancer that also brings out the flavors of other ingredients. In this book the amount of salt has been kept to a minimum, but if you are on a salt-restricted diet, you may omit it altogether. Do not use kosher or sea salt for baking; the crystals are too large and do not dissolve well.

PEPPER: Pepper comes from the dried fruit of the pepper vine. It is a wonderful complement to chocolate, a flavor combination that has long been a staple in Mexican cuisine. Black pepper is unripened, while white pepper is ripe. The flavor of black pepper is slightly stronger than white, and I prefer it for baking.

Peppercorns are commonly sold preground, but for maximum flavor, grinding just before using is preferable. For baking purposes, I like to use a minichop rather than a pepper mill to grind the peppercorns as the grind will be more even. Grind the peppercorns to a medium to fine powder.

SPICES, GROUND AND WHOLE: The most commonly used spices in baking are cinnamon, nutmeg, mace (the flowery outer surface of the nutmeg), allspice, clove, ginger, and cardamom. Ground spices should be fresh and of fine quality. Store them in tightly covered containers in a cabinet away from heat and light. It is difficult to give an exact length of time spices will stay fresh, although most will keep for up to a year if properly stored. As the spice ages, test it by smelling—it should smell pungent—then taste a small amount to see if the flavor is still present. If the smell and taste are weak, replenish your supply.

Whole spices such as nutmeg, cloves, and cinnamon sticks stay fresh longer because they are exposed to less air, but, as with all spices, the more quickly they are used, the more flavorful they will be. Whole nutmeg, which is the hard seed of a fruit, is shaved in a grater. Whole cloves and cinnamon sticks release their flavors when the spices are steeped in liquid, such as in poaching fruits.

🌿 FLAVORINGS AND SPIRITS

VANILLA: actually the whole fruit of a tropical vanilla orchid. The finest-quality beans come from the islands of Madagascar, Reunion, and the Comoros, located in the Indian Ocean. These beans, referred to in the trade as "bourbon beans," are prized because they are rich in natural vanillin. Pure vanilla extract is the most frequently used flavoring in baking and dessert making. It is highly aromatic and can be used by itself or as a complement to other flavorings such as coffee, chocolate, liqueurs (cordials), and brandies. As tantalizing as the aroma is, however, the extract is bitter until combined with a sweetener.

The production of vanilla is very costly, which accounts for its high price in stores. The orchid blossoms are hand-pollinated, as they cannot come into contact with insects. The newly harvested bean looks like a long green pencil. After about six months of curing, it shrivels to about 6 inches and turns deep brown in color. *Pure vanilla extract* is made from vanilla beans, at least 35 percent alcohol, water, and often sugar, which acts as a preservative. *Vanilla flavor extract* is weaker in strength than pure vanilla extract; however, it is a natural product, as is *natural vanilla flavor*. A synthetic, commercially manufactured vanillin, a by-product of paper making, is less expensive and is often used as a substitute for pure vanilla. However, artificial or imitation vanilla flavorings do not compare with pure extract and should not be used in fine baking.

Whole vanilla beans can be used to infuse milk, cream, or sugar syrup for poaching fruits. The used bean can be dried and placed in a jar with granulated sugar to make vanilla sugar. Or you can split the bean down the middle, remove the tiny black seeds with the dull side of a paring knife, and add them to the heated milk or cream for custards, cake batters, or any preparation where you want a pronounced vanilla flavor. Do not add the seeds to such sweets as decorative frostings, as they give a peppery appearance. It is best to remove the seeds from a bean that has been softened. So if the bean was not softened in liquid, steam the bean for a minute in a vegetable steamer.

A whole vanilla bean is equivalent to about 2 to 3 teaspoons of extract, or you can estimate that about 2 inches of bean equals 1 teaspoon of extract.

FLAVORED EXTRACTS: Pure extracts of orange, lemon, and mint or peppermint are readily available. Imitation flavorings such as maple or coconut are acceptable, since no pure extracts are available in these flavors. At one time, pure almond extract was produced, but it has been discontinued by many of the major manufacturers. You may be able to find it in some specialty food stores; if not, use imitation almond extract. Extracts are highly concentrated; therefore they must be measured accurately and used sparingly.

LIQUEURS (CORDIALS) AND BRANDIES: Liqueurs and/or cordials are fruit alcohols that contain sugar and are therefore slightly syrupy. There are two general categories, those that are classified by flavor such as Grand Marnier, Cointreau, triple sec (orange), crème de cassis (currant), Kahlúa and Tía María (coffee), and crème de menthe (mint), and those based on formulas that have been passed on through generations, such as Benedictine and Chartreuse.

White fruit brandies, also called white fruit alcohols, are not syrupy because they are made from fermented fruits rather than sugar. For example, kirschwasser is made from fermented wild black cherries, framboise from raspberries, fraise from strawberries, and calvados from apples.

Liqueurs, brandies, and other spirits should be of a fine quality. The better the taste of the liqueur, the better the flavor it will give your cake. Inferior brands often impart a harsh or unpleasant taste.

🌿 NUTS AND SEEDS

Nuts most prevalent in baking are walnuts, pecans, hazelnuts (filberts), and almonds. Also used frequently are peanuts, pistachios, Brazil nuts, pine nuts (pignoli), chestnuts, macadamias, and coconut (page 58). Walnuts and pecans can be used interchangeably in most recipes since both are rich in oil and have similar textures. Harder nuts like hazelnuts and almonds can also be substituted for each other.

Nuts derive their delicious flavor from the natural oils they contain. These oils cause them to go rancid if not properly stored. Avoid exposure to light and heat and always keep the container well sealed. It is always preferable to purchase nuts in sealed packages or vacuum-packed cans, as exposure to air causes them to stale. When purchasing nuts in bulk from open containers, taste them to make sure they are fresh.

If you don't plan to use nuts within two to three weeks, store them in the refrigerator or freezer. Well wrapped, they will keep for several months refrigerated or up to one year in the freezer. To refresh nuts and enhance their flavor, heat them in a 325° oven for about 8 to 10 minutes before using.

Sesame, poppy, and caraway seeds are also popular in baking. They are generally sold in small jars or packages. I do not recommend purchasing them in bulk because they go stale quickly. As with nuts, they should be stored in tightly sealed containers in a cool, dark place. For longer storage, refrigerate or freeze.

❧ DRIED FRUITS

Quality should be your first concern when purchasing dried fruits. Premium dried fruits feel plump and have some degree of softness. Stale fruits weigh less because the moisture has evaporated. Avoid using precut smaller pieces; they dehydrate and lose their flavor quickly. Many varieties of dried fruits are available in bulk. Taste before you buy to determine freshness.

To store packaged dried fruits after they have been opened, reseal the package and tightly cover with plastic wrap or a plastic storage bag, pressing well to remove the air. Store dried fruits that have been purchased in bulk in a tightly sealed glass jar. If you don't plan to use them within two or three weeks, refrigerate. They will keep for several months. To refresh dried fruits before baking, refer to page 63.

❧ GELATIN

Plain unflavored gelatin is a high-protein granular substance obtained from cooked animal bones and hooves. It is colorless, odorless, and sugarless. Gelatin is packaged in small envelopes, each containing about 2¼ teaspoons of gelatin grains. Each packet will congeal 2 cups of liquid.

In cake baking, unflavored gelatin is most often used in fillings such as mousses and Bavarian creams that require refrigeration, and to stabilize whipped creams. Less gelatin is necessary for these purposes than when making more liquid preparations. Too much gelatin produces an unpleasant, rubbery consistency.

Gelatin must be rehydrated before it can be used. To dissolve the gelatin, put liquid, usually water, in a small heatproof custard dish. Sprinkle the specified amount of gelatin over the top of the water and let stand for about 5 minutes. The gelatin will turn opaque and thicken. Then put the custard cup in a small skillet filled with ½ inch of simmering water. As the mixture heats, the grains will dissolve and the liquid will become perfectly clear. Stir the gelatin occasionally to dissolve the crystals evenly. Do not let gelatin become too hot or it will lose its thickening power.

After the gelatin is melted, remove the custard cup from the water and cool *just to tepid*. This only takes about 2 to 3 minutes. Gelatin must be blended into cooler mixtures when tepid or it will form tiny lumps. If gelatin stands too long and becomes cold, it will solidify; however, it can be remelted and cooled down again to a pourable state. Once the gelatin has set a mousse filling or whipped cream, the mixture must be gently handled. Overmixing will cause the gelatin to thin down.

Equipment

The use of correct equipment radically reduces the amount of time and effort it takes to make a cake. Whipping eggs is effortless with an electric mixer, and removing lumps from a filling is simple with a few turns of a whisk. Baking a cake will be a joy if you use the tools of the trade.

Store shelves are brimming with all kinds of merchandise, but how to determine the right piece can be confusing. I have compiled a complete list of equipment that I consider useful. It is not necessary to begin with everything on the list, but over time you will want to stock your kitchen with these items. The essentials are marked with an asterisk. Seek out quality because kitchen gear receives a work-out! Your investment will reap wonderful returns.

Set of 4 high-quality stainless steel measuring cups, 1/4, 1/3, 1/2, and 1 cup*
8-ounce liquid measuring cup*
Set of 4 high-quality measuring spoons, 1/4, 1/2, and 1 teaspoon and 1 tablespoon*
Triple- or single-mesh sifter*
Kitchen spring scale, ounces and grams clearly marked
Electric stand mixer (page 32)*
Food processor*
Portable hand mixer
Small fine-mesh strainer*
Medium-mesh strainers, medium and large sizes*
Colander
Deluxe rotary egg beater
Thin-wired round French cake racks, 11- or 12-inch size*

Rectangular thin wire cake rack, at least 10 × 14 inches*
3 wooden bowl-shaped mixing spoons in graduated sizes*
Flat wooden spoon
2 standard size rubber spatulas*
1 small rubber spatula
1 wide rubber spatula, 2³/₄ × 4¹/₄ inches*
3 wire whisks in graduated sizes of 8, 10, and 12 inches*
12- to 14-inch balloon whisk, preferably with a wooden
   handle*
Pastry blender (with wires extending to the handle)
Minichop
Swivel-blade potato peeler*
Dough scraper, preferably with a wooden handle
1-, 2-, 3-, and 4-quart flat-bottom stainless steel mixing bowls*
1-, 2-, and 3-quart Pyrex mixing bowls
4-quart Pyrex mixing bowl*
Thermometers, gourmet (instant), oven, and candy (Taylor or
   Cooper)*
Kitchen timer*
Small hand grater*
Hand juicer
Steamer basket
Double boiler
Plastic-lined 8-inch and 14-inch canvas pastry bags, Ateco or
   Wilton (page 508)*
Assorted pastry tubes,* Ateco or Wilton (page 508)
Ateco or Wilton coupler*
Ateco decorating comb
Long serrated knife with at least a 9-inch blade*
4-inch Ateco or Wilton metal spatula
4-inch Ateco or Wilton offset metal spatula*
6-inch Ateco or Wilton metal spatula*
7⁵/₈-inch Ateco or Wilton offset metal spatula*
10-inch Ateco or Wilton offset metal spatula*
Square metal mini offset spatula, 2¹/₄ × 2¹/₄ inches
Two 1- or 1¹/₂-inch natural bristle pastry brushes*
18-inch metal artists' ruler (available in stationery stores)

❧ MEASURING EQUIPMENT

DRY AND LIQUID MEASURES

Measuring ingredients is done either by volume or by weight. Although measuring by weight is more consistently accurate and is the method commonly used worldwide, Americans still prefer to measure by volume. Unfortunately, the use of the metric system has only inched its way into our daily lives. For this reason, the recipes in this book use the American measurements set forth by the National Bureau of Standards.

Dry ingredients should always be measured with dry measures and liquid ingredients should always be measured with liquid measures. Dry measures are individual measuring cups that are filled to the brim and leveled with a straight blade. I prefer the stainless steel measuring cups made by Foley. These cups are sold in sets of four graduated sizes, 1/4-, 1/3-, 1/2-, and 1-cup capacities.

The measuring spoons I like the best are also made by Foley. They are made of stainless steel or plastic and are sold in sets of from four to six graduated sizes. The set I prefer is made of stainless steel and has four measurements, 1/4, 1/2, and 1 teaspoon and 1 tablespoon. Newer sets now being sold include a 1/8-teaspoon measure and a 1 1/2-teaspoon size (1/2 tablespoon).

The liquid measures I like are Anchor Hocking or Pyrex heatproof glass cups with a spout. They come in 1-, 2-, and 4-cup (1-quart) sizes, and are marked with lines that indicate various quantities. It's a good idea to check the position of the lines on the cup, as they are not always accurate. To test for accuracy, fill a dry measure to the top and pour it into the liquid measure. If the line is in the correct place, the cup should fill to the designated amount.

Foley, Anchor Hocking, and Pyrex measuring equipment is sold in most department and hardware stores or gourmet kitchen centers. I find aluminum and plastic measuring cups flimsy. Be wary of less expensive odd brands; the measurements are not always accurate.

KITCHEN SCALES

A scale is one of the most useful investments for a kitchen. Of the two types of scales sold, the balance scale and the spring scale, balance scales are the more accurate and also more expensive. For home use, a good-quality spring scale will do fine. Some of the ingredients I like to weigh on a scale are chocolate, nuts, fruits, and vegetables.

When purchasing a scale, look for one that can weigh at least 10 pounds with a basket on top that will hold about 2 cups and will not easily tip when it is filled. Also, when the basket is removed, if the surface of the scale is flat, a lightweight plastic container can be placed on top and used to measure quantities larger than 2 cups. Be sure to adjust the dial on the scale to take into account the weight of the substitute container.

❧ SIFTERS

Sifters are made in two different styles, triple-mesh and single-mesh. A triple-mesh sifter has three layers of wire mesh through which the dry ingredients pass. The advantage is that the flour need only be sifted once to aerate and remove lumps and a second time to combine it with the leavening and salt. A single-mesh sifter has one wire mesh layer. Therefore, the flour usually must be sifted and/or strained once before measuring and then three more times in order to blend the ingredients together thoroughly. A large strainer with medium-sized holes will do the same job as a single-mesh sifter, but both are more time-consuming to use.

Unlike strainers, sifters should never be washed, as small particles of flour inevitably stick in the wire mesh, turning to paste when the flour becomes wet. After each use simply shake the sifter well, giving it a few firm taps with your hand, then wipe the inside and outside with a dish towel or paper toweling. Store the sifter in a plastic bag.

It is not a good idea to use a sifter for confectioners' sugar (it is too dense to pass freely through the mesh) or for cocoa powder, which will soil the sifter. It is best to use a strainer.

Unfortunately, sifters sold on the market today do not hold up well. Both triple-mesh and single-mesh sifters are poorly constructed. The handles break easily under the stress of sifting and the mesh layers of the triple sifter easily clog. Rather than risk breaking the handle, I hit the side of the sifter with my hand to shake the dry ingredients through.

🌾 ELECTRIC APPLIANCES

An electric stand mixer is the most helpful piece of equipment in cake baking. While you can obtain satisfactory results by mixing a cake batter the old-fashioned way, by hand, you will save considerable time and labor by using the appliance, and consistently perfect results are easier to achieve. The two major considerations when purchasing a stand mixer are cost and storage space.

Moderately priced stand mixers such as Sunbeam give excellent results for the average baker. These mixers come with two bowls, a large one with a 14-cup capacity and a small one with a 7-cup capacity. The bowl rotates on a disk while two beaters aerate the batter. These mixers are good choices for those who have limited kitchen space because they are lightweight and small enough to fit under or in a cabinet.

Other desirable features are that the larger bowl is wide enough at the top to allow space for scraping the sides with a rubber spatula without stopping the mixer. Its shape is good for folding, too. The 7-cup bowl is very convenient for smaller amounts of batter.

For more serious bakers, I recommend the KitchenAid stand mixer, which is modeled after the professional mixers used in bakeries. It is designed to give maximum aeration and its stronger horsepower makes it ideal for beating stiff meringues and dense batters, and for kneading bread doughs. Unlike the less expensive stand mixers, KitchenAid mixers come with one bowl that remains stationary through beating, and three attachments: paddle, whisk, and dough hook. The paddle simulates the movement of a spoon beating against the bowl and is used for blending most basic batters. The whip attachment is used for aerating ingredients such as eggs and cream, and the dough hook is used for mixing bread doughs.

There are two models available for home use, a smaller unit with a narrow 4½-quart cone-shaped bowl and a larger one with a wider 5-quart rounded-bottom bowl.

The major advantage of the smaller unit is that it has a head that tilts to allow easy removal of the bowl. The head of the larger mixer does not tilt; instead, the bowl is moved up to the head with a hand crank. A disadvantage of both these units is that the paddle or whisk attachment does not always reach to the bottom of the bowl. This results in poor creaming of butter and sugar, which often cling to the bottom. Beating such whipped ingredients as eggs and cream is inadequate because the whisk does not lift the mixture from the bottom. To rectify this, do not lock in the attachment; just insert it into the notch. As the head of the mixer presses on the paddle or whisk, the weight holds the attachment in place and keeps it in contact with the bottom of the bowl. (I do not use this technique when I am using a dough hook. With very heavy doughs, it can put too much stress on the hook.)

If you plan to do a lot of baking, you may prefer the larger mixer because of the extra capacity of the bowl. I generally do not recommend mixers that can hold extremely large quantities because many kitchens do not have enough oven space to accommodate volume baking.

Portable or hand-held mixers will perform satisfactorily when batters are not too heavy, but mixing time increases dramatically, since it is difficult to perform other tasks while holding a mixer in your hand. These hand-held units are convenient for certain procedures, such as boiled frostings. If you plan to do a lot of baking, a stand mixer is a practical investment.

A food processor is a good choice when it is only necessary to blend ingredients together, not to aerate them. The unit also performs especially well for cheesecake recipes and dense cakes containing chopped nuts and fruits.

The mixing speeds used for the recipes in *Great Cakes* are only guidelines, because the power of electric mixers differs according to brand and/or style of unit, and sometimes from machine to machine. Very heavy batters or enlarged recipes also put stress on a motor, which can cause a reduction of speed. This especially applies to less powerful mixers. Regulate the speed settings according to the performance of your particular unit.

Cakes made with the KitchenAid mixer usually have greater volume because the machine draws more air into the batter. As a result, *reduce the mixing time on all recipes in this book by 20 to 25 percent when using this machine, to avoid overmixing.*

NOTE: When testing the recipes for *Great Cakes,* I decided against using the KitchenAid mixer. The recipes in this book were tested on the Sunbeam High Efficiency Electric Mixer, Model #01401, since most home kitchens are equipped with such mixers rather than the more expensive KitchenAid. I also used KitchenAid Electric Mixers, Model K-5S and Model K45SS. Because KitchenAid mixers draw in more air, they were used to compare the difference in the batter consistencies and volume, and the texture and height of the finished cake. The Cuisinart Food Processor Model DLC 7 Super-Pro was used to test procedures and recipes for and/or adapted to the processor.

🌿 BAKING PANS

For best results in cake baking, it is important to use high-quality baking pans of the correct size for the recipe. If the pan is too small the batter will overflow and collapse in the middle. If the pan is too large the cake will overbrown and dry. Good-quality pans conduct heat well and are heavy enough not to warp.

When purchasing baking pans, seek out a reliable manufacturer. Inferior brands are often not sized accurately. Generally, the more expensive the pan the better the quality and the more accurate the size. Baking pans imported from France and West Germany are of excellent quality. Because they are sized in metrics, there will be slight variations in size as compared to pans using the American National Bureau of Standard Weights and Measures, but the difference is not significant enough to affect results.

Aluminum baking pans are ideal for cake baking. Such brands as Magic Line, Village Baker, Wilton, Wearever, and Mirro perform very well. Imported tinned steel baking pans are also good choices. Tinned steel darkens with age, but this does not affect the pan's performance. Many fluted ring or kugelhopf pans imported from West Germany under the brand name Kaiser are made of tinned steel. Cast aluminum, which is commonly used for bundt pans, gives excellent results, though it is somewhat cumbersome to handle because of its weight. Ovenproof glass pans may be substituted for metal and are especially good for oblong or square cakes made with fruit. When substituting glass pans for metal ones, reduce the oven temperature by 25 degrees because glass is a powerful conductor of heat.

Stainless steel is easy to clean but it does not conduct heat well and is costly. Pans with nonstick coatings such as Teflon are acceptable, but avoid less expensive brands because they are too thin and the coating wears with age. Black or dark metal baking pans absorb a great deal of heat and are fine for breads and pies, but they cause cakes to overbake and brown excessively on the sides and bottom. These pans also rust over time if they are scrubbed with abrasive materials. Baking pans should always be cleaned thoroughly to prevent cakes from sticking to the pan. I like to use soapy steel wool for aluminum, tinned steel, and glass, but this harsh abrasive should be avoided for Teflon and black metal pans.

Purchasing a pan can be a confusing proposition because names are not standardized. Some manufacturers call kugelhopf pans bundt or bunt yet they all look exactly the same. Angel food cake pans are sometimes called tube pans and springform pans may be called cheesecake pans.

One of my favorite pans is a flat-bottomed 9-inch tube pan with a 3-quart capacity, a smaller version of the footed angel food cake pan. Until recently, this popular pan was manufactured by Wearever Aluminum, but it has now been discontinued. A good alternative is a slightly larger one that measures 9¾ × 3¾ inches with a 14-cup capacity. It can be ordered by mail from Bridge Kitchenware (page 531). While it is not footed, the pan is supported by a deeper and wider center tube, which allows air to circulate underneath when the pan is inverted.

I particularly like a 2-quart pan made by Hillwear. It comes with two removable 9-inch bottoms—one with a tube and the other flat. The flat bottom is nice to use for cheesecakes. Another handy pan is a round 9 × 1½-inch layer cake pan with a removable bottom, made by Wearever Aluminum. I like it because cakes can be removed without spoiling an attractive topping. It is best to purchase two of this size as they can be used individually or for layer cakes.

The following list of pans will answer almost every need in cake baking. Pans that are marked with an asterisk are those that I consider essential.

CAKE PANS
....

10-inch (12 cup) bundt pan*
9½-inch (12 cup) fluted ring or tube pan (kugelhopf)
9-inch (10 cup) fluted ring or tube pan (kugelhopf)*
8½-inch (8 cup) fluted ring or tube pan
Two 7½-inch (6 cup) fluted ring or tube pans (kugelhopf)
9-inch (3-quart) flat-bottomed tube cake pan*
8-inch (2-quart) flat-bottomed tube cake pan*
10 × 4½-inch (4-quart) angel food pan with removable
    bottom*

9³/₄ × 3³/₄-inch (3¹/₂-quart) flat-bottomed tube cake pan
    special order, Bridge Kitchenware (page 531)
10 × 3-inch round springform pan
9 × 3-inch round springform pan*
8 × 3-inch round springform pan
9 × 3-inch (11-cup) round deep layer pan
8-inch (2-quart) porcelain soufflé dish
Two or three 9 × 1¹/₂-inch (6-cup) round layer pans*
Two 9 × 1¹/₂-inch round layer pans with removable bottoms
Two or three 8 × 1¹/₂-inch (4-cup) round layer pans
10 × 2-inch (11-cup) round layer pan*
9 × 2-inch (8-cup) round layer pan
8 × 8 × 2-inch square pan
9 × 9 × 2-inch square pan*
9 × 13 × 2-inch oblong pan*
8 × 12 × 2-inch (2-quart) oblong ovenproof glass or Pyrex
    dish
10 × 15 × 1-inch jelly roll pan*
11 × 17 × 1-inch jelly roll pan*
9 × 4³/₄ × 2³/₄-inch (7-cup) large loaf pan
9 × 5 × 2³/₄-inch (8-cup) large loaf pan*
Two 8 × 4 × 2¹/₄-inch (5-cup) medium loaf pans*
Three 6 × 3¹/₄ × 2-inch (2¹/₃-cup) mini loaf pans
Two 12-cup muffin pans*

ALUMINUM FOIL PANS

Foil pans are useful for storing baked cakes in the freezer and/or refreezing leftover cakes. They are also handy to use when you wish to give cakes as gifts. Some are sold with lids, which makes packaging a cinch.

Foil pans can be substituted for your regular baking pans as long as the capacity is about the same. Creamed butter cake batters made with 2 to 2¹/₂ cups of flour will fill two 8 × 4 × 2¹/₂-inch medium-sized foil loaf pans. Two 8 × 8 × 2-inch square foil pans have a slightly larger capacity and will hold batters made with 2¹/₂ to 3 cups of flour.

When using these pans, grease them well with softened butter, using a pastry brush to reach into the crevices. Do not dust them with flour. Place the pans on a jelly roll pan or set them into a metal pan of similar size to bake. The double metal acts as a heat conductor, adds insulation, and supports the cake, making it less clumsy to handle.

BAKING PAN SUBSTITUTIONS

For creamed butter and genoise cakes it is easy to make baking pan substitutions as long as the capacity is the same as that of the pan in the recipe. On the other hand, cheesecakes, tortes, and foam cakes such as sponge, chiffon, and angel food are not good candidates for pan substitutions.

It is fun to experiment with specialty forms like heart-shaped pans, brioche bread pans, and some of the unusual imported designs from Europe.

Here are some guidelines to follow:

▶ Always select a pan as close as possible to the size called for in the recipe.

▶ Measure the size of baking pans by measuring across the inside of the top and vertically to calculate depth.

▶ To measure capacity, calculate how many cups or quarts of water it takes to fill the pan to the rim. While a pan may have different dimensions from the one called for, if the capacity is about the same it can be used.

▶ Fluted, bundt, Turk's head, and kugelhopf pans can generally be used interchangeably, provided the capacity is about the same. You may have to adjust the baking time if the height of the pan differs from the size called for in the recipe. If the pan is a little higher, the cake may take 5 to 10 minutes longer to bake. If the pan is lower than the one specified, the baking time will have to be reduced by about 5 to 10 minutes.

▶ Do not forget to reduce the oven temperature by 25 degrees if using oven-tempered glass such as Pyrex, as glass is a strong conductor of heat and the cake will otherwise brown too quickly on the bottom.

Ingredients, Equipment, Procedures and Techniques

37

CAKE RACKS

Cake racks are used for cooling cakes and when you want to apply a glaze. The best racks are those with thin wires, such as imported French racks. Cakes more readily stick to thick-wired racks, increasing the chance of tearing. For extra insurance, I often spray the rack with nonstick coating.

PROCEDURES and TECHNIQUES

🌾 INTRODUCTION—CAKE TYPES

Most cakes are made from four major ingredients: fat, sugar, eggs, and flour. They also sometimes contain chemical leavening, liquid, and a flavoring. Different methods of combining these ingredients, plus the proportions in which they are used, yield different kinds of cakes: butter, sponge, genoise, tortes, and so on. Here is a brief description of the major cake types and the techniques for making them.

Butter cakes are probably the most popular of the American-style cakes. Creamed butter cakes have a soft crumb with an even texture and good volume. To make them, butter is creamed first to draw in maximum air. Sugar is added gradually until it is well incorporated, then the eggs and flavorings are beaten in. Eggs, whether whole, yolks, or whites, help to form the framework of creamed butter cakes. They provide moisture, flavor, color, and nutritional value. They also help to aerate the batter, in addition to chemical leavening. The dry ingredients are added to the creamed butter, sugar, and eggs alternately with the liquid, and the final mixing is done briefly to avoid toughening the cake.

Another method for making butter cakes that has gained popularity in recent years is the one-bowl or double-quick method. This method dispenses with the preliminary creaming of the butter. Instead the dry ingredients are placed in a bowl, then very soft butter is added, along with a portion of the liquid. After thorough beating, the eggs, remaining liquid, and flavoring are added and the mixture is beaten well again. This technique yields a cake with a finer, more velvety crumb that is less aerated and therefore has slightly less volume. Of the two, I prefer the creamed butter method, because it yields a lighter cake. It is the technique I've used for the butter cake recipes in this book.

Foam-style cakes, such as sponge, angel food, and chiffon, are very light and airy and do not have much body because eggs are their primary ingredient. The major components of these cakes are aerated eggs and/or egg whites with the addition of flour, sugar, and sometimes a chemical leavening. Angel food and most sponge cakes contain no fat other than egg yolks. The classic way to make a sponge batter is to beat the yolks and sugar until the mixture is very light and thick, then add the flavorings and dry ingredients. Beaten egg whites are folded in last. Chiffon cakes are similar to sponge cakes except that they contain vegetable oil, which adds moistness to the crumb. Angel food cakes are also light but less tender than sponge cakes because they do not contain egg yolks. The relatively large amount of sugar in them helps to tenderize the crumb, but angel food cakes still have more "pull" or bounce than a sponge cake because the protein in the egg whites firms during baking.

Genoise is a very dry sponge cake. Beaten eggs are the framework of these cakes; flour, sugar, and a small amount of melted clarified butter are the other principal ingredients. No chemical leavening is required. They are rarely eaten plain; they are foundation cakes, from which one creates dozens of more elaborate concoctions. The thin genoise layers are moistened with a sugar syrup and/or a liqueur syrup and then embellished with pastry creams, buttercreams, whipped creams, or glazes. Although a genoise batter is sometimes called a "buttersponge," the method of making it is completely different from that used for a traditional sponge cake. To make a genoise batter, you warm eggs and sugar to dissolve the sugar, then whip the mixture until it cools and becomes very thick, creamy, and light in color. Gently fold in the flour and then add a small amount of melted clarified butter as an enrichment. The clarified butter gives the cake its unique flavor.

European tortes are rich, very flavorful cakes with dense textures. Since they contain little or no flour and no chemical leavening, they have less volume than American-style cakes. Many tortes use finely ground nuts, dried bread crumbs, or cookie crumbs in place of flour. Most tortes contain large amounts of butter and eggs, the latter most often separated and the beaten whites folded in to lighten and leaven the batter. Tortes often contain fruits, nuts, jams, and spirits. They have a long shelf life and usually taste better as they age.

Cheesecakes are dense, rich, smooth, and creamy. Their primary ingredients are cream cheese or curd cheese, sugar, eggs, and flavorings. Some recipes call for sour cream or heavy cream, and occasionally a small amount of flour or cornstarch. The ingredients are blended together rather than excessively beaten. As with tortes, cheesecakes mellow with age.

Each of these styles of cake is discussed in greater detail in the Before You Begin section of each chapter, and within the recipes themselves.

🍂 ALL ABOUT HANDLING BUTTER AND SOLID SHORTENING

Semisolid fats like butter are known technically as plastic fats. Unlike liquid oils, plastic fats can be worked to a smooth and malleable consistency so they incorporate air. Having butter at the correct temperature is crucial.

Many cookbooks specify that the butter should be at room temperature. But room temperature might be 68° in one kitchen and 78° in another. A better way to gauge proper temperature is as follows: Take a wrapped stick of butter in your hand. It should feel cool to the touch and leave a *slight* impression when pressed gently with your fingers. Ideally, the temperature of the butter should be 68° to 70°, about 30° cooler than body temperature. If you are unsure about the degree of coolness, test the temperature with an instant thermometer. The butter should be cool enough to cream without separating or breaking down. When you are creaming butter with an electric mixer, removing it from the refrigerator 20 to 30 minutes before using is generally sufficient to achieve the correct softness. If you are creaming the butter by hand, remove it from the refrigerator a little earlier.

The purpose of creaming is to incorporate air into the butter. As you cream, the volume of the butter should increase, the color become lighter, the texture smoother, yet the butter should retain the ability to hold its shape. At this point, it has reached the proper consistency, or plasticity, to accept the sugar. In butter-style cakes, bringing the fat to this stage is the *single* most important step toward successful cake baking.

If the butter is too soft, the milk solids will separate from the butterfat as you cream it. As the butter begins to deflate and becomes oily, it loses its ability to incorporate maximum air. If you continue to mix at this point, you will produce a flatter, heavier cake. You can correct this problem by refrigerating the bowl containing the butter for 5 to 10 minutes, or until it feels cool and begins to firm up. (Do not allow it to become too cold.) You can now continue with the creaming process.

HOW TO MEASURE SOLID SHORTENING AND STICK OR BAR BUTTER

Solid shortening is measured in dry measures. Using a tablespoon, pack the shortening into the required size cup to eliminate air pockets. Level with a pastry scraper or straight-edged knife and release the shortening with a rubber spatula. To get ⅔ cup, fill the ⅓-cup measure twice.

Butter and margarine come in premarked quarter-pound sticks, which is helpful, but the paper is not always aligned on the bar in the correct position. For accurate measurements, it is better to disregard the paper markings and cut the bars according to the following measuring charts. If you are starting with a 1-pound block of butter, divide the block into 4 quarters before measuring.

1 stick = ¼ pound = ½ cup = 8 tablespoons
⅔ stick = ⅓ cup = 5 ⅓ tablespoons

NOTE: Since 1 stick or 8 tablespoons equals ½ cup, ⅔ of a stick or 5⅓ tablespoons equals ⅓ cup. ⅔ of a cup is 1 stick plus ⅓ of a stick.

HOW TO CLARIFY BUTTER

Clarified butter is used in genoise and for other baking purposes where its distinctive flavor is advantageous and creamed butter is not required. (In general cooking it is used in preparing hollandaise sauce and it is an excellent medium for sautéing because it can be heated to a higher temperature without smoking.) The process of clarifying separates out the whey and milk solids, leaving a clear, golden fat. With these impurities removed, clarified butter has a long shelf life and can be stored in the refrigerator for months. It may also be frozen.

To achieve good clarification I like to melt the butter very slowly— over 30 to 40 minutes. As it cooks, the butter develops a sweet nutlike taste. With very long cooking the color continues to darken and the nutty flavor becomes more pronounced. The intensity of the flavor is a matter of personal taste. Since the volume of the butter is reduced by approximately 20 to 25 percent, it is a good idea to clarify a pound at a time.

To clarify butter: Place 1 pound of unsalted butter in a heavy, medium-sized saucepan. Cook on very low heat until the milky whey or white foam rises to the surface. Carefully skim off the foam with a spoon until it ceases to accumulate.

Continue to cook the butter slowly until the milk solids settle to the bottom of the saucepan, leaving the clear butter fat on the top. Cool in the saucepan undisturbed until tepid. Strain the clarified butter into a jar, using a fine-mesh strainer and taking care that none of the milk solids fall into the jar.

A *quick clarification method:* When you need only a small amount of clarified butter, the process can be done in a microwave oven. Place about 25 percent more butter than specified in a glass oven-proof dish. (For example, if you need 3 tablespoons of clarified butter, start with 4 tablespoons.) Melt on medium power in the microwave. Remove from the oven and skim the whey that forms on the surface. Set the butter aside briefly to allow the milk solids to settle. Microwave clarified butter will not be as pure as butter clarified by the traditional method, nor will it have the same nutty flavor, but it is satisfactory when you need it in a hurry.

ALL ABOUT HANDLING SUGAR

After proper creaming of the butter, the second most important factor in making a creamed butter cake is the adding of sugar. In order to maintain the suspension of the air cells achieved in the creaming, the sugar should be added to the fat very slowly, usually 1 tablespoon at a time over 4 to 10 minutes depending upon the amount of sugar the recipe calls for. Adding sugar to eggs alone, as in sponge cakes, requires from 2 to 5 minutes. For both procedures, use the medium-high speed of the mixer. Low speed will not draw in sufficient air and high speed may shock and break the air cells, just as an overblown balloon will burst.

Add brown sugar to a batter in small amounts, running the sugar through your fingers to break apart and soften the pieces before they go into the mixer. Discard any hard pebbly lumps that you may have missed when measuring. These will not melt during baking.

It is necessary to scrape down the sides of the mixing bowl with a rubber spatula to incorporate butter and sugar that stick to the side.

NOTE: The beaters of electric mixers do not always touch the bottom of the mixing bowl, which can result in a layer of butter or butter and sugar that never becomes incorporated into the batter even if you try to stir it in at the end. The texture of your cakes will suffer, and they will never reach optimal volume. This can often be corrected by a simple adjustment to the machine (page 33). Either check the manufacturer's handbook for directions or have the mixer repaired professionally.

HOW TO MEASURE SUGARS AND SWEETENERS

GRANULATED SUGAR: With a dry measure, you can measure granulated sugar by using either the dip-and-sweep method or spooning into a cup and leveling off. Since granulated sugar does not pack down to any significant degree, the way flour does, either method is acceptable. If your sugar develops lumps, as it sometimes does, pass it through a fine strainer before measuring.

SUPERFINE SUGAR: Superfine sugar, also called bar or dessert sugar, forms more lumps than granulated sugar and must always be strained through a fine strainer before measuring unless the box has been freshly opened. The technique for measuring is the same as for granulated sugar.

CONFECTIONERS' SUGAR: Confectioners' sugar is very lumpy and must be strained before measuring. Do not use a sifter; the sugar is too dense and will clog the screen of the sifter. The technique for measuring is the same as for granulated sugar.

BROWN SUGARS, LIGHT AND DARK: Before measuring, empty the approximate quantity to be used onto a sheet of waxed paper. Rub the sugar between your hands to soften and remove lumps. Depending on the degree of sweetness you desire, brown sugar may be either lightly or firmly packed.

To pack brown sugar lightly, press gently into a dry measure, running your hand across the top to level. When the measure is inverted, the sugar will hold its shape, but may have a few open spaces. To pack brown sugar firmly, press it tightly into a dry measure, running your hand across the top to level. When the cup is inverted the sugar will hold its shape without any open spaces.

THICK SYRUPS SUCH AS HONEY, MOLASSES, MAPLE, AND CORN: Measure these in dry measuring cups, even though they are liquids, because it is easier to scrape them out of such containers. Lightly grease the dry measuring cup first with vegetable shortening, oil, or butter, then pour in the sweetener, bringing liquid to the very top. Carefully hold the cup over the batter and pour in the syrup. Smaller quantities can be measured in greased measuring spoons. Scrape out the excess with a rubber spatula.

ALL ABOUT HANDLING EGGS
THE CORRECT TEMPERATURE OF EGGS

For most baking purposes eggs should be used at room temperature, since very cold eggs hold less air. However, because eggs deteriorate quickly and are a common cause of salmonella food poisoning, I find that removing them from the refrigerator about 20 to 30 minutes in advance is sufficient. The eggs will be cooler than room temperature, but I have had very good results when using them for creamed butter cakes. If they are to be used for whipping purposes, eggs should be warmer so they will have more volume. Eggs are easier to separate when they are cold, but afterward they should stand at room temperature for 20 to 30 minutes.

You can quickly remove the chill from eggs: Place the shelled eggs in a bowl, preferably stainless steel. Set the bowl in a sink filled with

Ingredients,
Equipment,
Procedures
and Techniques

45

1 to 2 inches of hot water, or hold the metal bowl about 8 inches above an open flame and stir the eggs constantly to prevent them from becoming too hot on the bottom. In seconds they will be ready to use.

There are times when eggs may be used directly from the refrigerator. Cold eggs will rescue a butter/sugar mixture that has separated from overbeating. In hot weather, cold eggs are especially helpful in creamed butter cakes if your kitchen is not air-conditioned. However, if the eggs are too cold when they are mixed into creamed butter and sugar, they may cause the mixture to become too firm. On the other hand, if they are too warm they will break down the butter/sugar mixture and cause it to separate.

For genoise, whole eggs and sugar are heated over warm water before beating, to dissolve the sugar crystals, so the starting temperature of the eggs does not matter.

HOW TO SEPARATE EGGS

Always separate eggs removing the white from the yolks, when eggs are cold. For recipes using whipped egg whites, select older eggs. As eggs age, the proteins strengthen and when whipped they form a stronger framework.

All eggs should be separated using 3 bowls. One for the initial cracking in case the yolk breaks. The second bowl to hold the separated yolk and the third, to hold the separated white.

The method that I prefer for separating eggs is the following; take a cold egg in your hand and hold over first bowl. With a sharp knife, give a firm tap across the shell. Turn egg so that the widest part is held in the palm of your hand. The shell forms a cup to hold the yolk. Now the white should flow freely into the bowl. Holding the empty shell in the opposite hand, alternate yolk, placing it from shell to shell until all the white is removed.

Place yolk into the second separate bowl. Pour white into the third bowl. It is crucial that *not one drop of yolk become mixed with the whites*. When beating egg whites, the presence of yolk and/or fat, no matter how small, will reduce the volume.

Defeathering is the process of removing the two twisted strands of white, known as the chalazae, that are attached to the yolk. The chalazae, according to Harold McGee, author of *On Food and Cooking*, is a Greek word that means, "hailstone" or "small lump." These strands of white or protein become hardened when heated either in the oven or on top of the stove. Its rubbery texture in such smooth mixtures as meringues or cooked fillings would be undesirable. Smaller strands are less significant in the finished product, therefore it is recommended that larger pieces be removed.

HOW TO BEAT AND ADD WHOLE EGGS AND EGG YOLKS

Eggs are generally added to a butter mixture one at a time at 1-minute intervals, unless you are using beaten whole eggs. Since eggs occasionally contain blood spots or have an undesirable odor, it is a good idea to open them into a separate saucer or small bowl before adding them to a batter. Small spots can be removed with a piece of eggshell, but discard any eggs containing larger blood spots. Cracking them into a bowl first also ensures that a piece of shell does not land in your batter, a nuisance to say the least. (The easiest way to remove a piece of eggshell from an opened egg is with half an eggshell.)

If you are making a creamed butter cake with an electric mixer, you add the shelled eggs directly to the batter. However, if you are beating the batter by hand or with a hand-held mixer, the cake will have better volume if the eggs are well beaten first.

Always beat whole eggs just before using. They will lose their aeration if they stand. For maximum volume, beat whole eggs and/or yolks on medium to medium-high mixer speed. Eggs whipped on high speed do not hold air well. When air is drawn into the eggs too rapidly, the air cells break and the mixture loses its volume.

Whip egg yolks until they are thick and lightened in color. Because they are thicker than beaten whole eggs or whites, whipped yolks can stand briefly before using. Egg yolks beaten with sugar can stand for an even longer period of time because the sugar stabilizes them.

When beating whole eggs, yolks, or whites with a KitchenAid mixer, always use the whip attachment, as the paddle does not aerate eggs well.

Ingredients, Equipment, Procedures and Techniques

HOW TO BEAT EGG WHITES

When beating egg whites you must be careful not to overdo it; whites go from being perfectly beaten to overbeaten very quickly. Overbeaten egg whites lose their smoothness and shine and look dry. It is always better to underbeat than to overbeat.

Recipes often call for the addition of salt or cream of tartar to the egg whites. Salt helps break up the albumin of the egg, making it easier to whip, and cream of tartar is used as a stabilizer, to whiten the whites and make them smooth. Beating egg whites in a copper bowl also helps stabilize them; they are stronger and maintain their foam longer than whites beaten in stainless steel or other materials.

Another way to stabilize beaten egg whites is to add a small amount of sugar. Sugar helps protect the whites from turning dry and grainy, makes them easier to fold, and prevents them from becoming watery as they stand. You can take the sugar from the base recipe and beat it into the whites. If your recipe calls for 1 cup of sugar, for instance, set aside about 2 tablespoons of the sugar and add it later to the beaten egg whites. Sugar may be used along with cream of tartar.

Here are some additional tips for beating egg whites:

▶ Make sure the bowl and beaters are clean, dry, and completely free of any fat. Rubbing the bowl with a little lemon juice or white vinegar will help clean it.

▶ Use bowls made of nonreactive metal, such as copper or stainless steel. Never use aluminum; it causes discoloration. You may use glass or pottery bowls if necessary, but these materials do not create as much friction as metal. Do not use plastic.

▶ Since eggs whites at room temperature or slightly warmish whip to their greatest volume, you may set the mixing bowl over a pot of hot water to warm them briefly before beating.

▶ Always begin beating egg whites on medium-low to medium speed of the mixer. This builds a stronger foundation because the air cells can hold longer without bursting. The mixer speed is increased to medium-high and finally to high when making stiff meringues.

▶ Always add sugar toward the side of the bowl to avoid deflating the whites.

▶ If you do overbeat the whites, add 1 unbeaten egg white to the bowl for every 4 to 5 whites you have used. Then rewhip to the desired peak stage. The additional white will not affect the recipe.

STAGES OF BEATING EGG WHITES: It is important to know how much to beat egg whites if you want your cakes to have good volume. Whites that are underbeaten or overbeaten result in cakes that either flop or do not rise as high as they should.

Most bakers think in terms of beating whites into one of three stages: frothy, soft peak, and stiff peak. I believe the stages are more clearly understood when you think of beating them into four stages: frothy, soft peak, firm peak, and stiff peak.

The firm peak stage is the stage referred to in most cookbooks as "stiff but not dry." If beating continues beyond this stage sugar must be added or within seconds the whites will turn dry, dull, and grainy and will not blend smoothly into batters or other mixtures. With the addition of sugar, they can be whipped to various degrees of stiffness with less risk of overbeating.

In cake baking, beaten egg whites are mostly used at the soft and firm peak stages.

When sugar is added to beaten egg whites, they become a form of meringue. The amount of sugar used, the time when it is added to the egg whites, and how long the mixture is beaten all determine whether the meringue will be soft or hard. Soft meringues usually contain less sugar and are used mostly for folding into batters for such cakes as sponge or chiffon, or to lighten such mixtures as fillings and frostings. Hard meringues contain more sugar, often in the form of a cooked sugar syrup. These meringues are very stiff and are generally used to make meringue-style pastries, desserts, confections, and frostings.

The following is a summary of the four stages of beaten egg whites:

▶ *Frothy*—the point where bubbles form and the whites look cloudy instead of clear. Salt or cream of tartar is added at this stage. The mixer speed is medium-low to medium.

▶ *Soft peak stage*—the mixer speed has gradually been increased from medium to medium-high, ridges begin to form on the surface, and when the beater is lifted, the peaks of the whites droop slightly. This is the optimum time to add sugar either to give the whites more body or to make a soft meringue. To make a soft meringue, the whites and sugar should be beaten for 60 to 90 seconds after the sugar is added. If beaten longer, they may become too firm to blend smoothly into other mixtures.

▶ *Firm peak stage*—the mixer speed remains at medium-high and the ridges on the surface are well defined and resemble waves. The whites are smooth, moist, and shiny, and when the beater is lifted, they stand in straight peaks. If you wish to make a stiff meringue, you add the sugar now.

▶ *Stiff peak stage*—the mixer speed has gradually been increased from medium-high to high. This is the stage that whites reach *after* the sugar was added at the firm peak stage. The whites are beaten until a very stiff and glossy meringue is formed. A word of caution: It is possible to overbeat stiff meringues. Some smoothness is lost and the volume can reduce.

HOW TO MEASURE EGGS

According to the United States Department of Agriculture, a carton of twelve eggs must weigh 24 ounces to be labeled "large." However, the size of individual eggs may vary within the same carton. Recipes in this book call for eggs graded AA Large. These should measure approximately 3 tablespoons after shelling (about 1 tablespoon of yolk and about 2 tablespoons of white). When using different size eggs, measure the shelled eggs in a liquid measuring cup to determine the amount. For example, four large eggs, which weigh approximately 2 ounces each, will measure less than 1 cup by capacity. To get a full cup of eggs, use 5 eggs instead of 4 eggs and select the larger ones from the carton until one cup is reached.

Since eggs are liquid, too much or too little at times can affect the quality of the cake, especially when large quantities are used. This is something to bear in mind if you are substituting extra-large for large eggs. Pay special attention to the size of the eggs when you are making foam-style cakes or genoise, because these are made with little flour and rely on eggs for their structure.

❧ HOW TO MEASURE FLOUR

It is essential that flour be measured accurately. Professional bakers measure by weight, according to the metric system used in Europe. While this is most accurate, in this country we generally measure by volume.

One of the most common mistakes that novice bakers make is to use liquid measuring equipment for dry ingredients, especially flour. The markings on a liquid measure end below the top, so to get a level measurement you must shake the cup, which packs the flour down. Use only dry measures for measuring dry ingredients. Spoon flour gently (I usually sift it first) into the measuring cup to over-flowing, then level with a straight-edged knife. Never bang, shake, or tap the cup, as the flour will pack. If you have a habit of shaking your measuring cup, try placing the cup on the counter as you measure instead of holding it.

The dip-and-sweep method is also very popular. Here you simply dip the measure into the flour and level with a knife. I believe that measuring this way packs the flour too densely. When there is too much flour in your batter, your cake may be heavy and will mound in the center. You may also sift flour directly into the measuring cup. This results in highly aerated flour, often too light in weight.

Measuring spoons should be used for less than 1/4 cup of flour and other dry ingredients. Dip the spoon into the flour and level with a knife. (With these smaller quantities, dipping is okay.)

❧ HOW TO MEASURE LIQUIDS

Use a liquid measuring cup and fill it exactly to the desired line. Check the measurement at eye level. Unless you are absolutely sure of your steady hand, it is not a good idea to measure liquid in a dry measuring cup. For accuracy the liquid must come all the way to the top, which is difficult to manage without spilling.

Ingredients,
Equipment,
Procedures
and Techniques

🌾 ADDING DRY INGREDIENTS WITH LIQUIDS

For creamed butter cakes, flour is sifted with leavenings, salt, and spices, then added to the batter alternately with the liquid, usually at a ratio of three parts dry ingredients to two parts liquid. For very thick batters, it is better to start with less flour, so the ratio would be 4 parts dry ingredients to 3 parts liquid.

If a recipe is increased, the flour should be divided into smaller quantities, usually four to five parts dry ingredients to three to four parts liquid. There is no need to be unduly exact when dividing ingredients, simply estimate the approximate amounts. The same applies to liquids.

The same method of alternating dry ingredients with liquid is also used for foam- or sponge-style cakes.

Most recipes specify that dry ingredients be added at low mixer speed. This not only prevents flour from scattering over the counter but helps avoid overbeating, which toughens the cake. As a rule, dry ingredients are blended into a batter just until they disappear, which should be in a matter of seconds. If it takes longer than that with your mixer set on low speed, increase the speed slightly. The entire procedure should not take more than a minute or two. When no liquids are called for, dry ingredients are occasionally added all at once to a batter. This procedure requires a slightly higher mixing speed because the weight of the flour can slow the machine. Over-mixing should still be avoided.

🌾 ADDING LIQUID FATS TO A BATTER

Since liquid fats are heavy and do not absorb air, they must be kept suspended by rapid mixing and quick handling or they will sink to the bottom of the bowl. Always pour liquid fat into a batter in a steady stream on medium speed. If dry ingredients are to be added and/or other mixing procedures are required, do so as soon as possible.

Do not attempt to stir fat that has settled on the bottom of the bowl into the batter. It will not blend in properly and the excess oil will inhibit rising.

🌿 HOW TO FOLD

The technique of folding is one of the most troublesome for bakers, yet the procedure is not difficult if you understand the principles involved.

When two substances of different densities are combined, the heavier one must first be lightened to avoid loss of air and ensure even blending without deflating the batter. The ingredients most frequently folded are beaten eggs and whipped cream, but you can also fold in flour or solid ingredients such as chocolate, nuts, and fruits when you want to avoid overmixing.

When you are working with egg whites or whipped cream, it is necessary to fold a small amount—usually ¼ to ⅓—into the batter first to lighten it. Then the rest of the whites or cream is folded in. The first folding will take about 20 turns with a wide rubber spatula. The second application will take about 40 turns. The recipes in this book indicate the approximate number of turns required. Always work quickly and avoid overfolding.

It is important to use a 2¾-inch-wide rubber spatula when folding in large amounts of egg whites. The larger spatula handles more batter in fewer strokes and less time. These spatulas are inexpensive and readily available at housewares stores and even some supermarkets. They are a wise investment that will serve you well if you plan to do a lot of baking. However, if you do not own a large spatula, you may fold in with your hand. Why not? Professional bakers do.

When working with smaller quantities such as 2 or 3 beaten egg whites or a cup of whipped heavy cream, I often *stir* in the first portion with a wire whisk. This technique is commonly used for cake fillings. I then fold in the remaining whites or whipped cream with a standard size spatula.

Here is the proper folding technique:

1. Hold the spatula in your hand with the curved side of the spatula away from you and cut down through the center of the batter.
2. Sweep the spatula toward you under the batter, running it along the bottom side of the bowl, then up the side to the top.
3. Flip the spatula over completely so that the curved side is facing the center of the bowl again. Hold the spatula loosely, so it will be easier to sweep with the spatula

1.

2.

3.

Ingredients,
Equipment,
Procedures
and Techniques

53

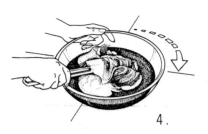

4.

across the top of the batter to the middle. You now have completed 1 turn.

4. Cut down through the center again as you begin the next turn, rotating the bowl slowly. Continue rotating with each turn. Occasionally run the spatula around the sides of the bowl. You may have to rotate the bowl in complete 360° circles 2 or 3 times to complete the process.

🐚 ALL ABOUT HANDLING CHOCOLATE

Chocolate is a complex blend of fat and solids held in suspension. Since it is somewhat temperamental, care should be taken when melting it. Because it burns easily, it should never be melted over direct heat. And it should never be heated beyond 120° to 125°, as overheating impairs its flavor and texture. To prevent overheating, cut or break it into small pieces so it will melt quickly and evenly, and stir it frequently as it melts. Finally, never expose chocolate to steam or moisture. Even a minute drop of liquid will cause it to "seize" or become hard and grainy, although you can salvage your chocolate if this happens by adding 1 teaspoon of vegetable short-ening for each ounce of chocolate. Do not add butter or margarine as they contain water, and even this small amount can cause seizing.

There are many ways to cut or break chocolate. You can easily break up bars with your fingers or a paring knife. One-ounce squares should be cut in half across the recessed portion with a chef's knife and then cut into ½-inch pieces. The simplest way to break block chocolate is by piercing it with an ice pick or a small screwdriver. When chocolate must be finely cut, I like to make thin shavings with a chef's knife or whirl the ½-inch pieces in a food processor until the chocolate is reduced to bits.

When working with a large amount of chocolate, I melt it in two steps. I reserve about 15 to 20 percent of the chocolate and warm the remaining amount until it is almost melted. Then I add the reserved unmelted chocolate and let it slowly soften, stirring it oc-casionally until all the chocolate is melted and the mixture is smooth and satiny. This method is called "seeding," a technique that is also used for tempering chocolate (see page 57). The unmelted chocolate immediately reduces the temperature of the melted chocolate, pre-venting it from becoming too hot.

Melted chocolate should be cooled to slightly tepid, about 100° to 105°, before being added to other ingredients. Chocolate that is too warm can make the consistency of a batter or frosting loose. If it is too cool, it will not blend in smoothly.

HOW TO MELT CHOCOLATE

A variety of methods may be used to melt chocolate. These apply to all chocolate except white and milk chocolate, which are more sensitive and require special handling (see below). Break the chocolate into 1/2-inch pieces and place it in an appropriate size heatproof bowl such as glass or stainless steel. Select one of the following melting methods.

Bain-marie: Set the bowl in a skillet filled with 1/2 inch of simmering water. Allow the chocolate to stand, with the heat off, stirring occasionally until it is melted and smooth. If the water gets too cool, turn on the heat to low. *Do not let the water boil or allow any steam to form.*

Double boiler: Boil 1 to 2 inches of water in the bottom of a double boiler, then turn off the flame. Place the chocolate in the top of the double boiler and set it over the hot water, letting it stand until the chocolate melts. Stir occasionally. Do not melt the chocolate with the heat on, as the steam that escapes from the sides can penetrate the chocolate, causing it to stiffen, and do not cover the double boiler for the same reason.

Microwave: Place the bowl in a microwave and melt the chocolate according to the manufacturer's instructions. Avoid high power settings as the chocolate will become too hot around the sides. Stir occasionally.

Oven: Place the bowl in a preheated 225° oven, then turn the oven off. Stir occasionally.

HOW TO MELT WHITE AND MILK CHOCOLATES

Break the chocolate into 1/2-inch pieces and place in a heatproof bowl. Set the container in warm (not hot) water and stir constantly until melted. White and milk chocolates should be melted at a lower temperature than dark chocolate as their flavor is extremely delicate and the milk solids will easily burn. These chocolates are softer than the dark varieties and will melt very quickly. The consistency should be smooth and creamy.

HOW TO MELT CHOCOLATE IN LIQUIDS

According to Elaine González of Chicago, one of the most knowledgeable chocolatiers in this country, "Chocolate has a love/hate
relationship with liquid; it loves a lot and hates a little." Solid bittersweet and semisweet chocolates may be melted in liquids such as
scalded heavy cream or milk, hot coffee, or water; however, the
amount of liquid must equal or exceed one-quarter of the amount
of chocolate to prevent the chocolate from seizing. For example, if
you are melting 1 ounce, or 2 tablespoons, of bittersweet or semisweet chocolate, you must use 1/4 ounce, or 1 1/2 teaspoons, of liquid.
When working with unsweetened chocolate, the ratio is one to one.
For each ounce of unsweetened chocolate, use 1 ounce, or 2 tablespoons, of liquid.

When you are combining melted chocolate with liquid, it is best
to add the melted chocolate to the liquid, not the other way around.
If a recipe does require adding liquid to chocolate, add it all at once,
not in small quantities, or the mixture will seize or lump.

If melted chocolate is too cool when added to a liquid, it will
resolidify, showing floating flecks of chocolate. You can correct this
by heating the mixture over a low flame and stirring it constantly
with a whisk until the chocolate melts completely and the mixture
is smooth.

TEMPERING CHOCOLATE

Tempered chocolate is used for coating truffles, for dipping candy,
and for making cake decorations like chocolate leaves. Only "real"
chocolate can be tempered because it contains cocoa butter crystals,
which contain unstable fats. Compound chocolate, also known as
confectionery coating and summer coating, is not tempered because
it does not contain cocoa butter crystals and is made with stable fats
like palm and coconut oil.

To temper bittersweet or semisweet chocolate, the chocolate is
heated to exactly 120°. This assures that all the cocoa butter crystals
are completely melted. The chocolate is cooled to 80°, then reheated until it reaches exactly 90°. The temperature is maintained
by placing the chocolate in a bain-marie or on a plastic-wrapped
heating pad at a low setting. If the temperature exceeds 90°, the
crystals scatter and the temper is lost. It is essential that the melted

chocolate be stirred occasionally during the tempering process to maintain an even temperature.

Milk chocolate is tempered at a slightly lower temperature (84° to 86°) than bittersweet or semisweet chocolate, because it contains milk solids, which are very sensitive. White chocolate is treated like milk chocolate, but is even more sensitive to heat because it does not contain chocolate liquor. Unsweetened chocolate is rarely tempered because it is used as a baking chocolate. If chocolate loses its temper it develops a grayish bloom and dulls, but it can be melted and tempered again.

Melted chocolate to which other ingredients have been added, such as a ganache glaze made with heavy cream or an icing that contains powdered sugar, does not require tempering.

HOW TO STORE CHOCOLATE
....

Wrap chocolate well in aluminum foil and then rewrap in plastic film. Chocolate easily picks up flavors from other ingredients because of the cocoa butter. Store it in a cool, dry place with low humidity and away from light. Ideally, the temperature should be about 65°.

Sometimes chocolate develops a bloom during storage. This is a sign that the cocoa butter has separated from the solids. There are two kinds of bloom, gray bloom, which comes from improper tempering, and sugar bloom, which has a milky yellow hue. Sugar bloom occurs when the chocolate is not properly wrapped to protect it from humidity or from extreme temperature changes, or if the chocolate melts and resolidifies. The bloom is harmless and will disappear when the chocolate is melted.

Ideally, chocolate should not be refrigerated for long-term storage because it picks up humidity. However, in very warm weather this is sometimes unavoidable. When weather is a problem, it is best to purchase chocolate in smaller quantities.

Proper storage conditions and the amount of cocoa butter in the chocolate determine its shelf life. Dark chocolates such as bittersweet and semisweet will keep for years without spoiling. In fact, as dark chocolates age, their flavor often improves. Milk chocolate will keep up to a year and white chocolate up to eight months.

Ingredients,
Equipment,
Procedures
and Techniques

🌰 HOW TO MAKE COFFEE AND ESPRESSO ZESTS

To make espresso and coffee zests, combine freeze-dried coffee crystals or instant espresso powder with a small amount of boiling water and stir until thoroughly dissolved to make a very concentrated flavoring. A larger quantity can be made ahead and stored refrigerated in a tightly covered jar. Use as you would any extract. The proportions of coffee to water are as follows:

Coffee zest—3 parts coffee crystals to 1 part boiling water

Espresso zest—2 parts espresso powder to 1 part boiling water

Most of the recipes in this book call for instant freeze-dried coffee crystals and instant espresso powder. These concentrated products are convenient to use and have a satisfactory flavor for baking. When you want a stronger coffee flavor, espresso zest may be substituted for coffee zest in most recipes.

🌰 ALL ABOUT HANDLING NUTS, COCONUT, SEEDS, AND FRUITS

HOW TO TOAST NUTS, COCONUT, AND SEEDS

Nuts are toasted to enhance their flavor and crispness. To toast skinned or unskinned nuts, spread them in a single layer on a heavy flat baking pan with sides such as a jelly roll pan or 9 × 12-inch oblong pan. Place them in a 325° oven. Bake skinned nuts until they turn a light golden brown. Bake unskinned nuts until they develop a sweet toasted smell. The time this takes varies: Whole almonds, hazelnuts, or filberts can take twelve minutes or longer. Oily nuts like walnuts and pecans will toast in eight to ten minutes. Six to eight minutes is usual for nuts that are sliced, slivered, or in smaller pieces, but if you crowd the nuts into the pan, it will take longer. Conversely, toasting fewer nuts takes less time. Seeds generally take less time still. Coconut should be toasted to a golden brown in about eight to ten minutes. Watch it carefully as it burns easily.

The first few whiffs of the pleasant aroma of the nuts roasting in the oven are an indication that they are almost ready. The nuts around the sides of the pan brown first, so stir the nuts after the first five minutes to ensure even baking. Watch the nuts carefully—they can go from done to burnt in less than a minute. Nuts can also be browned on top of the stove in a heavy, ungreased skillet over medium-low heat. Stir them often for even browning.

To remove skins and toast hazelnuts and filberts: Roast the nuts as described above. When the skins begin to pop and you smell the fragrance of toasted nuts, remove the pan from the oven. Empty the hot nuts onto several layers of paper toweling or a clean dish towel. Using the toweling to protect your hands, rub gently to release as much of the dark skin as possible (some skin may remain on the nuts). Work quickly while the nuts are still warm. If they become too cold, the skin is difficult to remove. If necessary, heat the nuts a second time to remove stubborn pieces of skin.

Almonds and pistachios can be blanched in boiling water to remove the skins; however, too much of the natural nut oils are lost. It is better to buy almonds already skinned. I rarely remove the skins on pistachios.

HOW TO CHOP NUTS

Different size nuts are used for specific purposes in cake baking. Some batters are too thin to hold large pieces of nuts, while others such as fruit cake batters are thick and hold big pieces well. Delicate sponge cakes must be made with nuts that are more finely chopped, and at times, nuts are ground into a meal and used in place of flour.

Many people chop nuts in a food processor for convenience, but if you use a processor, take great care not to overprocess. Overprocessed nuts become oily and tend to cling together. They can change the entire texture of a cake and occasionally ruin it. If nuts are processed for several minutes, they will turn into paste.

Here are tips to help you achieve success when using a processor.

▶ Never overload the bowl. Chop nuts in batches of no more than 1 to 1½ cups at a time. Use the pulse action at first to break up the nuts. Then process until you achieve the desired size.

▶ Add to the nuts 1 to 2 tablespoons of flour from the amount called for in the recipe. The flour will help to absorb the oils.

▶ To absorb the oil if nuts become overprocessed, add an additional 1 to 2 tablespoons of flour, not taken from the base recipe, and pulse 3 or 4 times to blend. It's better to add a little extra flour than to use nuts that are too oily.

▶ Adding a small amount of sugar to the nuts also helps to achieve a more even texture. As with flour, this can be taken from the base recipe or added additionally. Use up to 1 tablespoon of sugar for larger quantities such as 1 cup and 1 to 2 teaspoons for amounts under a cup.

▶ When chopping medium-sized nuts, try using the shredding disk instead of the steel knife. The texture of the nuts will be more even and powdery.

There are times when you want more uniform, larger pieces of nuts. In these cases, nuts must be chopped with a chef's knife or cut by hand with a paring knife because the processor chops them into irregular pieces.

The following list of the various sizes of nuts used in baking indicates how best to achieve the size. If you do not own a processor, you may use a chef's knife or hand nut chopper. Another method for chopping nuts is to place them in a small- or medium-sized plastic bag. Press out the air, twist the top to secure it, then crush the nuts to the desired size with the bottom of a small heavy pot or a meat pounder.

Finely chopped: Chop the nuts with a small amount of flour or sugar to the size of coarse bread crumbs in a food processor.

Medium-fine: the size of barley. Use a food processor.

Medium: the size of lentils. Use a food processor.

Medium-large: the size of baby peas. Use a food processor.

Large: the size of navy beans. Use a food processor.

Coarsely chopped: Cut the nuts the size of large peas, using a chef's knife.

Broken nuts: Break the nuts by hand into pieces the size of kidney beans.

HOW TO MEASURE NUTS: The baker often asks, "When are nuts measured, before or after chopping?" The answer is largely individual preference. One cup of whole nuts will measure less when they are chopped. If you prefer more nuts, as I do, start with a slightly brimming cup or measure them after chopping. Alternatively, you can weigh them. Eight ounces of whole nuts are equal to 8 ounces of chopped nuts.

HOW TO MAKE NUT FLOUR: Nut flour, made from very finely ground nuts, is used in place of or in addition to the flour in some recipes. For best results, oily nuts such as walnuts and pecans should be ground with a small French Mouli hand grater, which can reduce them them to a dry powder with little of the natural oils disturbed.

A food processor can be used, but it works best for less oily nuts such as almonds and hazelnuts. Add 2 tablespoons of flour for each cup of nuts, in addition to the flour used in the recipe, to help absorb the nut oils. Be sure to check the size of nuts frequently during the processing. It is also wise to scrape around the edge of the processor bowl as the nuts tend to accumulate there.

HOW TO PREPARE FRESH COCONUT AND COCONUT MILK

When purchasing a fresh coconut, choose one that feels heavy in your hand, then shake it and listen for the sound of liquid swishing. The weight and sound indicate that the center still contains the watery liquid and has not dried out.

To open the coconut, hold the coconut so it will not roll (a rubber dish drainer is an ideal place to do this). Turn the coconut so the three black dots or "eyes" are at the top. Using an ice pick or a small screwdriver, pierce the eyes completely through the flesh. Invert the coconut over the sink or a bowl and drain the juice. The watery liquid that comes out is not the coconut milk. It can be strained and used for a drink, but it is not recommended for cooking.

To crack the coconut in half, turn it on its side and draw a line around the middle of the coconut. Forcefully hit the coconut with a hammer along the line, turning the coconut until you have pounded all around its girth. Repeat 2 or 3 times or until the coconut splits.

Removing the barklike skin is optional. Use a small screwdriver to remove the flesh from the shell. If you want the coconut to be snowy white, then peel the thin skin with a small paring knife. Rinse the coconut to clean the surface of any small pieces of skin, then dry the meat with paper toweling.

Shred the coconut in a food processor fitted with a fine medium or shredding blade. If it is too coarse, chop it again with the steel blade, pulsing until you get the desired size. One coconut yields about 4 cups of shredded coconut. Fresh coconut is highly perishable. Refrigerate leftover coconut in an airtight container for up to 5 days or freeze for up to 3 months.

To prepare coconut milk: For every cup of coconut milk needed, use 1 cup of fresh, finely chopped coconut to 1 slightly brimming cup of boiling water. If you want a less rich milk, you may use up to 2 cups of boiling water to 1 cup of coconut, thus yielding about 2 cups of thin coconut milk.

Place the coconut in a bowl and pour the boiling water over it. Let stand for at least 30 minutes, then pour the milk through a double thickness of cheesecloth. Squeeze well to extract as much of the milk as possible, then discard the coconut. Refrigerate the milk in a covered container until ready to use. It will keep 2 to 3 days or it can be frozen for up to 3 months. A film of fat may form on the surface, and this should be discarded. Coconut milk is delicious for custard, rice pudding and other rice dishes, curries, and stews.

HOW TO GRATE AND MEASURE FRESH CITRUS RINDS

When the flavor of citrus is required in a recipe, nothing can equal the taste of freshly grated rind. Avoid dried rinds as they lack the rich, pungent oils that are present in fresh rinds. Always wash and dry the fruit before grating. (The brand imprint can easily be removed with a little warm soapy water.) Refrigerate the fruit but juice it within a few days as the surface turns moldy with age.

You may grate rinds ahead of time, but be sure to wrap them in plastic wrap. Exposure to air causes them to dry and lose their flavor.

There are three ways to grate citrus fruit:

▶ Rub the citrus fruits against a fine grater, grating only the colored surface of the fruit; avoid grating the bitter white membrane called the pith. The grated rind is called the zest. I especially like a small hand grater made by Foley.
▶ Remove thin strips of the colored rind from the fruit with a vegetable peeler, again avoiding the pith. Cut into 1-inch pieces. Place the rind in a minichop and grate fine. If you do not have a minichop, do not cut the rind into 1-inch pieces. Instead, make small stacks with the strips, cut them into thin slivers, and then finely chop the rind using a chef's knife.
▶ Remove threadlike strips of rind using a gadget called a zester. Chop finely using a chef's knife.

HOW TO PLUMP RAISINS, CURRANTS, AND DRIED CHERRIES

Raisins, currants, and dried cherries have more flavor and tenderness if they are plumped before baking. Plumping is also useful when these fruits have hardened with age. It can be done either by steaming the fruit or by immersing it in boiling water. The advantage of steaming is that the fruit retains its color and absorbs less moisture, but the water method is recommended when the fruit is especially hard. (The steaming method will also restore moistness to dried prunes, figs, and apricots.)

▶ *Steam method*—Steam the fruit over boiling water for about 1 minute or until softened. Spread out the fruit on several layers of paper toweling to dry, blotting as much moisture as possible with additional paper toweling.

▶ *Water method*—Place the fruit in a bowl and add boiling water to cover. Let stand 1 minute. Strain and spread out on several layers of paper toweling. Blot as much moisture as possible with additional dry paper toweling. The fruit should not be wet when you use it in the recipe.

ALL ABOUT PANS

The way in which pans are prepared varies according to batter type and what you plan to do with the baked cake. Butter cakes require greased pans, while pans for sponge, chiffon, and angel food, made without fat, are not greased. Pans are sometimes lined with waxed paper to prevent sticking, or, when greater strength is needed, with baking parchment.

Fluted or bundt-style pans are usually dusted with flour after they are greased. Sugar, seeds, finely chopped nuts, cookie crumbs, and stale bread crumbs can also be used. These coatings strengthen the sides of the cake and reduce the chance of the cake sticking to the ridges of the pan.

If a cake is to be stored in the pan and cut into serving pieces as needed, I omit the dusting of flour, since the moistness of the cake will turn the bottom of the cake pasty as it stands.

You may use butter, margarine, vegetable shortening, or oil to grease pans. I prefer butter for the flavor and nice finish it gives to

*Ingredients,
Equipment,
Procedures
and Techniques*

cakes. Be sure to use the proper amount of butter. It should not be spread so thin that it can barely be seen, nor so thick that you can't see the pan underneath. Apply it smoothly.

Vegetable cooking sprays such as Pam or Baker's Joy, a blend of fat and flour, are also satisfactory and are recommended for the cholesterol-conscious. However, use care when applying. Place the pan over a sink so that no spray falls on your kitchen floor. It's slippery. Read the label, and if the product is flammable, be sure to direct the spray away from any heat source.

HOW TO GREASE PANS

Place about 1 tablespoon of butter in the pan, break it into 2 or 3 pieces, and let it soften while you assemble the rest of the ingredients for the recipe. (A fluted pan may require a little more butter.) When the butter is soft, spread it on the pan using a piece of waxed paper or a pastry brush. If the pan is fluted, use a pastry brush; it reaches into the crevices. Be sure to butter the entire inside surface of the pan—there must be no bare spots.

If the pan is to be dusted with flour, use a medium-fine strainer or a flour shaker, a small metal shaker with large holes that is also useful for sprinkling confectioners' sugar. It can be purchased in most retail kitchen gadget departments. Grease the pan heavily with soft butter and sprinkle it with the flour. Then tip the pan and turn it 360° so the flour will cover the entire surface. Invert the pan over the sink and tap gently to remove the excess. Always use all-purpose flour for coating pans, not cake flour. Cake flour lumps and it is difficult to get a thin dusting.

Use the same technique to apply sugar, seeds, finely chopped nuts, bread crumbs, or cookie crumbs.

HOW TO LINE PANS WITH PAPER

Baking pans are lined with paper for easy removal of cakes, to prevent them from overbrowning, and to keep the sides soft. While it is strictly necessary to line only the pan bottoms, I like to line the bottom and sides of layer and flat-bottomed tube pans because lining helps keep the cake moist. This is more time-consuming, so the recipes in this book call for the more conventional bottom-only technique. If you wish to line the sides of the pan, see the instructions below.

The materials to use for lining pans are baking parchment, an all-purpose nonstick paper; waxed paper, for more delicate cakes; aluminum foil, which can be molded and is good for pans like loaf pans that are difficult to shape; and brown paper bags, for fruitcakes that require long slow baking. Lined pans require a preliminary light coating of butter to anchor the paper. For most pans, I spread the butter with a small piece of waxed paper or the wrapper from a bar of butter. Use a pastry brush for pans lined with aluminum foil.

Generally, baking parchment and waxed paper are interchangeable; however, parchment is preferable for heavily textured cakes. If the cake is very moist or heavy, the parchment should also be greased. Waxed paper must always be greased.

For more delicate cakes, such as fragile sponge types, use waxed paper to reduce the risk of tearing when the cake is removed. I also prefer waxed paper for lining the bottom and sides of layer pans and flat-bottom tube pans because it is lightweight and molds more easily than parchment.

▶ *To line the bottom and sides of a square or oblong pan*: Lightly butter the pan. Cut a strip of waxed paper at least 4 inches larger than the pan. Center the paper over the pan and press it into place. Press the paper into the corners, pleating it to mold it as smooth as possible. Trim the selvage with scissors. Butter the paper, taking care to flatten any folds in the corners.

▶ *To line the bottom only or the bottom and sides of a flat-bottomed tube pan*: Lightly grease the bottom and sides of the pan. Tear off a 12-inch square of waxed paper and place it on the counter. Set the pan on the paper and trace around the bottom and the inner tube. Fold the paper into quarters, aligning the traced lines, and cut around the outside arc, then around the inside arc. Open the paper and press the circle into the bottom of the pan.

If you wish to line the sides of the pan, tear off four 3-inch strips of waxed paper. Overlap the first 3 strips around the sides of the pan, securing the edges with butter. Cut 4 inches off the last strip and fit the remaining larger piece around the tube, then carefully regrease the entire paper-lined pan with very soft butter.

Ingredients, Equipment, Procedures and Techniques

65

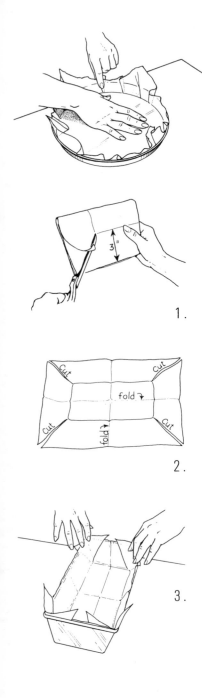

1.

2.

3.

Great Cakes

▶ *To line the bottom of a layer pan*: Lightly butter the bottom and sides of the pan. Line the pan on the bottom only with a parchment disk cut to the size of the pan. The parchment does not need to be buttered unless specified in the recipe. Waxed paper may be used as a substitute, but the paper must be greased.

▶ *To line the bottom and sides of a layer pan*: Lightly butter the bottom and sides of the pan. Center a 12-inch piece of waxed paper over the top of the pan and press it down smoothly into the bottom of the pan. Using the knuckle of your forefinger, press the paper into the sides of the pan. Pleat the paper around the sides of the pan with the folds all facing in the same direction. Regrease the paper with soft butter. The pleats will lie flat.

▶ *To line a springform pan*: Butter the bottom and sides of the pan. Line the pan on the bottom only with a parchment disk cut to the size of the pan. The parchment does not need to be buttered unless the recipe so instructs.

▶ *To line a loaf pan with aluminum foil*: Cut a strip of heavy-duty aluminum foil wide and long enough to allow for the depth of the pan. Turn the pan upside down on the counter and mold the foil snugly over the pan to form its shape. Lift off the foil, then turn the pan right side up. Lightly grease the pan and place the molded foil inside, pressing it carefully against the sides to avoid tearing. Grease the foil with soft butter, using a pastry brush.

▶ *To line a loaf pan with baking parchment, waxed paper, or brown paper*: Cut an oblong strip of paper wide and long enough to allow for the depth of the pan. Place the pan on the center of the paper and trace a line around the bottom of the pan. Remove the pan. Draw a second rectangle around the first rectangle, making it about 3 inches larger. Fold the paper into quarters, aligning the pencil marks (fig. 1). Trim the paper, cutting along the outside rectangle. (If you are working with brown paper, do not fold it until after you have cut the outside triangle.) With the paper still folded, make cuts from the outside corners of the paper to the corners of the smaller rectangle. Lightly grease the pan with melted butter. Open the paper and center it over the pan, press it into place, then press the corners down against the sides of the pan (fig. 3). Brush the paper with melted butter, sealing the cut edges flush to the pan.

▶ *To line a jelly roll pan with parchment or waxed paper*: Line jelly roll pans only on the bottom, unless otherwise indicated. Cut an oblong strip of paper 2 inches longer than your pan. Lightly butter the pan. Starting at the upper left corner of the pan, lay the paper on the bottom of the pan, aligning it along the far side of the pan without extending it up the side (fig. 1). Excess paper should be on your right and along the side of the pan closest to you.

   With the point of a sharp paring knife, trim the excess paper along the creases on these two sides (fig. 2), leaving a 1-inch tab extending upward and slightly higher than the pan at one of the corners (fig. 3). You will use this as a tab to help remove the baked cake from the pan when the pan is inverted.

1.

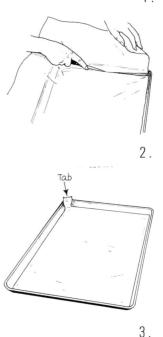

2.

3.

FILLING PANS

To get a nicely shaped cake care should be taken when filling cake pans. Pour thin batters into the pan and gently tilt so the batter flows evenly around the edges or into the corners. If a thin batter is full of air bubbles, it's okay to give the pan a firm tap on the counter to burst them. Spoon thick batters into the pan and spread them evenly, especially at the corners of the pan, with the back of a tablespoon.

   Cake pans should be filled about half to two-thirds full. If you are making a pan substitution it is essential to use a size that can be filled to this capacity. When the pan is too large, the cake overbakes, becoming dry and flat. When a pan is too small, the batter overflows, not only making a mess of the oven but causing the cake to sink in the center and underbake.

   If you have to divide a batter evenly among two or three pans, weigh them on a kitchen scale after adding batter to ensure accuracy. If you do not own a kitchen scale, check the level of the batter in each pan with toothpicks.

Ingredients,
Equipment,
Procedures
and Techniques

67

HOW TO USE A BAIN-MARIE
(HOT WATERBATH)

The French term *bain-marie*, also called a hot waterbath, is a name for an improvised piece of equipment used to buffer heat. The concept is similar to a double boiler, except that for a bain-marie, a bowl or pan is generally placed directly into a larger bowl or pan containing hot or simmering—never boiling—water.

A bain-marie is useful for keeping food warm, in warming eggs, and for melting chocolate. It can also add moisture to foods that are baked in an oven to prevent them from drying out. For years it was commonly used for such desserts as custards, soufflés, and puddings, or for savory dishes that required lengthy baking, like meat terrines and pâtés.

More currently, cooks use a bain-marie for baking cheesecakes and certain dense chocolate tortes. The batter-filled pan is placed into a second larger pan that is filled to a depth of about 1 inch with near-boiling water, depending upon the recipe. The steam released as the cake bakes creates a more moist and velvety cake.

A stainless steel pan is best for a bain-marie because the water will not discolor the pan. If you must use aluminum, add 1/2 teaspoon of baking soda, vinegar, or lemon juice per quart of water to prevent discoloration. The water temperature should remain just under boiling. If necessary, reduce the heat by adding a small amount of cold water.

To use a bain-marie for baking:

▶ Select a pan larger than your baking pan. Pans such as a shallow stainless steel open roasting pan measuring about 12" x 17½" x 2", or a disposable aluminum foil roasting pan of similar size, are ideal for most cakes. Any large shallow pan or utensil such as a 12-inch skillet or paella pan may be used as well. There should be at least 1 inch of surface area around the sides of the smaller pan to allow for adequate moisture evaporation.

▶ Place the larger pan *empty* on the oven rack, then place the batter-filled pan inside. Fill the larger pan with very hot water, using a teapot or 1-quart measuring cup and taking care not to spill water into the batter. Ease the rack into the oven.

► Check the bain-marie periodically. If the water evaporates too quickly, add additional hot water.
► Remove the hot baking pan from a waterbath wearing *heavy* rubber gloves. These are far less cumbersome than pot holders.

❧ HOW TO MARBLEIZE

Marbling is achieved by alternating layers of different flavored and colored batters or by blending in various fillings. The usual combination is chocolate and vanilla, but such combinations as vanilla and coffee also make tasty cakes. Tinting a cake batter two or three pastel shades is another pretty effect. Sugar and spice fillings or fillings made with chopped nuts, mini chocolate chips, raisins or currants, preserves, or seeds can also be added.

There are three techniques for marbleizing, each resulting in a different marbled appearance.

► Alternating layers of batter and filling. This gives the least amount of marbling.
► Running a knife through the alternated layers of batter and filling gives a moderate marbleized effect.
► Folding the filling into the batter with a knife. This gives the greatest amount of marbling.

Whichever method you choose, the object is to keep the secondary flavor or filling from sinking to the bottom of the pan. Remember that chocolate batters are heavier than vanilla batters, and textured fillings are heavier than cake batters.

To counteract sinking, place a greater amount of plain batter on the bottom of the pan than you will use for the remaining layers. If you have only a small amount of batter left to complete the top layer, don't worry about it. It will sink. It's all right to have some of the contrasting batter or filling exposed.

❧ ALL ABOUT OVENS

Ovens, like any other piece of kitchen equipment, differ not only from brand to brand but from unit to unit. Some people swear by electric and others prefer gas.

The heating element of electric ovens is exposed on the floor of the oven; the heating element in gas ovens is underneath and the heat comes up through small holes on the oven floor. Since hot air rises, the air at the top of the oven is hotter than the air in the middle, but the hottest area in both electric and gas ovens is on the bottom, because the heating elements are located there.

When purchasing an oven, look for one that has three or four racks. (The positioning of the racks varies according to the manufacturer.) This allows maximum flexibility in adjusting the rack levels. I like to position an oven rack in the lower third of the oven. With the bottom of the pan at this level, the top is just about in the middle of the oven.

For best results, center the pans on the rack. At no time should they touch the sides of the oven or each other. Allow at least an inch or more between the pans. When you are using two racks at a time, stagger the pans so that one will not be directly under the other. If you must bake a cake near the top of the oven and the surface browns too quickly, place a piece of aluminum foil loosely over the top of the cake during the last 10 minutes of baking. If you must bake a cake on the lowest rack position, double-pan the cake, that is, place an extra pan underneath the filled pan to give added insulation. Some poorly insulated ovens develop hot spots, usually in the corners in the rear of the oven. If one side of a cake over-bakes, turn the pan around during the last 10 minutes of baking.

Ovens should be preheated at least 10 to 15 minutes before baking. A good habit is to start the oven when you begin the recipe, unless the preparation time is especially lengthy. When a cake does not bake in the time specified, or if it bakes too quickly, it is a sign that the oven needs adjusting. An oven thermometer can be used to check temperature, although many are not reliable. Until the repairman pays you a visit, you may increase or decrease the oven temperature, starting with about 25°. It is wise to have your oven calibrated about once a year. Electric ovens require a serviceman, but in some parts of the country gas ovens are calibrated by your local public utility.

Convection and microwave ovens have gained enormous popularity in recent years. Convection ovens bake faster than conventional ovens because the air inside is circulated by a fan. This also makes it possible to bake more pans at a time. However, the moving air blows the batter around, making the surface uneven, and it also causes baked goods to dry out on the surface. This is a plus for pies and breads, but a drawback for delicate pastries. For convection ovens, the oven temperature should generally be reduced by 25° to compensate for the faster baking, but again this will depend on the particular unit.

I like the microwave oven for melting chocolate and butter, warming liquids, and defrosting frozen cakes. For baking purposes, it is best to use recipes that have been specially developed for this unit. Cakes that are moist and dense, like carrot or apple cakes, are usually the best choices for microwave baking. Most other types of baked goods come out tough and rubbery.

My own preference is an electric oven because it bakes evenly and emits less fumes, but excellent results are also possible with a gas oven. The important thing is that the oven is well insulated, has no hot spots, and maintains an even temperature. When you purchase an oven, you must determine your baking needs, and when you find a good one, care for it, as it's worth its weight in gold.

OVEN TEMPERATURES

Here is a temperature chart showing common oven temperatures for various tasks. As a general rule, bigger, higher cakes are baked slowly at lower temperatures, and smaller, thinner cakes are baked faster at higher temperatures. A creamed butter cake, for example, would bake in a 10-inch angel food cake pan at 325°, while cupcakes from the same batter would bake at 375°. This information is meant only as an overall guide. Many recipes will vary according to a particular type. Also, many recipes use two temperatures, starting at high for a thrust of heat, then lower for slower baking.

225° or under (very low to warm)
   For melting chocolate, warming whole eggs or egg whites, drying meringues

250° to 275° (very low)
   For baking meringue layers and cookies, crisping cookies

300° to 325° (low)
   For baking fruit cakes, chiffon cakes, cheesecakes, nut and chocolate meringue layers, and some pound and sponge cakes, and for toasting nuts, bread crumbs, and seeds

350° to 375° (moderate)
> For most cakes, cupcakes, roulades, bar and chewy cookies, rich sweet breads and pastries, some breads, custard pies, thawing wrapped frozen cakes, meringue topping

400° to 425° (hot)
> For breads, rolls, quick breads, filled pies, pie shells, crisp cookies

450° to 475° (very hot)
> Not used for most baking purposes

🌾 HIGH-ALTITUDE BAKING

At elevations of more than 3,000 feet, where the air is thinner, adjustments must be made in recipes to compensate for the decrease in atmospheric pressure.

Lower air pressure means a lower boiling point for water: at sea level, the boiling point is 212°, at 2,000 feet it is 208°, at 5,000 feet it is 203°, and at 7,500 feet it is 198°. Since water also takes longer to reach a boil, foods take longer to cook and more evaporation takes place. This is a negative for baking because when too much moisture is lost cakes become dry.

When baking under these conditions, the object is to set or bake the batter as rapidly as possible to prevent moisture evaporation, so cakes are baked at a temperature 15 to 25 degrees higher than usual.

Excessive liquid evaporation throws off the balance of the ingredients, resulting in an overconcentration of sugar. Because of this, the sugar in the recipe should be reduced. At 3,000 feet, reduce the sugar about 1 tablespoon per cup; at 5,000 feet, 2 tablespoons; and at 7,000 feet, 3 to 4 tablespoons.

In mountainous regions, the air is less humid. Flour absorbs moisture, and where the air is dry, there is less liquid for the flour to absorb. Therefore, more liquid is required. For each cup used, at 3,000 feet, increase the liquid by 1 to 2 tablespoons; at 5,000 feet, 2 to 4 tablespoons; and at 7,000 feet, 3 to 4 tablespoons.

Another problem is that cakes will rise more because the air is thinner. If cakes rise too much, the air cells burst and the cake will collapse. To correct this, it is especially important not to overbeat batters, especially those that have a lot of air whipped into them, such as sponge, chiffon, and angel food cakes. Working with colder ingredients will also help. The baking powder must also be reduced. At 3,000 feet, for each teaspoon of baking powder used, reduce the amount by 1/8 teaspoon; at 5,000 feet, reduce it by 1/8 to 1/4 teaspoon; at 7,000 feet, reduce it by 1/4 teaspoon.

At best, this information is only a guideline. Start with the minimum adjustments and work your way up until your high-altitude baking is successful.

For additional baking and cooking information, write to:

Cooperative Extension Service
U. S. Department of Agriculture
Colorado State University
Fort Collins, CO 80523

Request *High Altitude Food Preparation*, Pamphlet #41.

❧ HOW TO TELL WHEN CAKES ARE DONE

I always tell my students, "Let your nose be your guide." There is no need to panic if you forgot to set the timer. The first fragrance that comes from the oven is the signal that the cake is about two-thirds to three-quarters done. About 5 minutes later, check the cake.

I look for three signs to tell me when a cake is done. The sides of the cake begin to release from the pan, vanilla or other light-colored batters are golden brown, and the top is springy to the touch. This means that when you press your finger gently on the top of the cake, it should spring back without leaving an indentation. If all three of these requirements are not met, the cake is not ready. Immediately close the door to keep the oven hot, then retest a few minutes later.

Pound cakes should be tested with a straw twig from a whisk broom or a toothpick. Since they are quite firm-textured, they are not springy and it can be difficult to judge doneness by touch. Also, the tops of pound cakes often look slightly uncooked because beads of moisture collect, especially at the crack.

Because their pans are not greased, sponge and chiffon cakes do not release from the sides of the pan. The only way to test for doneness is to insert a twig or a toothpick into the center of the cake. If it comes out dry, the cake is done. If a few particles of cake cling, bake a few minutes longer.

Ingredients,
Equipment,
Procedures
and Techniques

73

European tortes, which are usually dense and moist, can be tested with a toothpick. It is okay for a few particles of crumb to cling to the wood.

I do not like to use a toothpick for testing tall cakes because it is too short to reach into the middle of the cake. A metal cake tester is undesirable because particles of cake will not stick to the slippery surface. Instead, I prefer to use a twig from a straw broom. I break off a 5- to 6-inch piece of straw from the top of a broom and wash it before use. It can be wiped off and reused many times.

🌿 RELEASING CAKES FROM PANS

When a cake is first removed from the oven, it is fully expanded with heat and very fragile. With the exception of a few sponge roulades, most cakes must stand for about 10 minutes to shrink slightly and stabilize before they can be safely removed from the pan. Do this while they are still warm. If a cake becomes too cool, it may stick to the pan.

Here are some general guidelines for releasing cakes from pans:

▶ If a cake sticks to the sides of the pan, run a thin, sharp knife gently around the sides to release.

▶ If a cake becomes too cold, it may stick to the bottom of the pan even when the bottom has been lined with paper. To overcome this problem, warm the bottom of the pan by either of these two methods:

1. Set the cake pan in a sink filled with a small amount of hot water and allow it to stand for 1 to 2 minutes.
2. Place the cake into a 350° oven to warm briefly.

▶ Cakes baked in fluted cake pans such as bundt or kugelhopf should stand at least 10 to 15 minutes before being removed. Very large cakes may need a little extra time, also.

▶ Cakes baked in pans that have been completely lined with waxed paper are the easiest to release. When the cake is inverted, a little tug on the waxed paper will pull it out of the pan. With the paper lining, cakes can be removed from the pan either warm or cool, and they can stand longer without frosting because they are protected from the air. This is especially helpful if you wish to bake the cake ahead.

▶ To prevent very delicate cakes from sticking to a cake rack, spray the rack first with Pam or other nonstick coating.

▶ Cool cakes with domed tops that are not to be frosted, like pound cakes or sponge cakes, bottom side down on cake racks. Otherwise, the wires leave indentations in the surface.

▶ To avoid damaging cakes with toppings, cover the top of the pan snugly with aluminum foil, then invert the cake onto a rack. The foil will hold the topping in place. Reinvert the cake onto a serving platter. Use the same procedure to remove a cheesecake or other type of cake from the bottom metal disk of a springform pan. Cover the top of the cake with foil, invert gently onto a rack, lift off the metal disk, and discard the paper lining. Invert the cake onto a serving platter.

❧ HOW TO STORE CAKES

When you store a cake made in advance, or leftover cake, you want to maintain freshness and moistness as long as possible. There are many ways to accomplish this, depending on cake type. Refrigeration, since it dries out baked goods and impairs their flavor, should be done only when absolutely necessary. The moister the cake, the greater the chance of spoilage. Frostings and fillings add moisture, making cakes more perishable. For these reasons it is best not to frost cakes with perishable frostings and fillings too much in advance.

Cheesecakes and buttercream-frosted genoise must be refrigerated, and in fact benefit from aging a day or two before serving. Other cakes that require refrigeration are those made with fillings and frostings containing eggs, cooked custards, whipped creams, and fresh fruits and berries. Store them *loosely* covered with aluminum foil to keep excess moisture from accumulating under the wrapping. Cakes with moist fillings and frostings must breathe. If they are covered too tightly, they become soggy.

Plain cakes such as pound cakes, unfrosted butter cakes, tortes, crunchy cakes, and sponge, chiffon, and angel food cakes do not require refrigeration. They can also be stored at room temperature

*Ingredients,
Equipment,
Procedures
and Techniques*

75

when frosted with eggless confectioners' sugar frostings, fondants, or sugar glazes.

Fruit cakes made with dried fruits and brandy can be kept at room temperature for a week or longer; cakes made with fresh fruit will keep for up to 3 days, depending upon the temperature of the kitchen. Refrigerate them sooner when the weather is warm, because fresh fruit cakes develop mold and deteriorate quickly. Cakes made with fresh fruit should also be covered loosely with aluminum foil to keep them from becoming soggy.

Cakes with meringue-style toppings or frostings should also not be stored airtight. Allow a small amount of air to circulate around the cake by propping a knife handle on the edge of a plate under the cake dome or storage container to keep it ajar.

I like to store unfrosted cakes in the freezer along with freezable frostings.

Decorated cakes should be stored in the refrigerator, preferably in a cake box. If you don't have one, leave the cake uncovered so as not to damage the decorations. I have stored whole decorated cakes uncovered in the refrigerator for up to 8 hours. However, once a cake has been cut, it begins to dry out quickly. To combat this, press a strip of waxed paper, plastic film, or cellophane wrap against the cut opening, secure it with a few toothpicks into the top, and then cover the cake with aluminum foil, shaped into a hood to protect the decoration. Do not make the covering too tight or too much moisture will collect, causing the frosting to sweat. Do not cover decorated cakes with plastic wrap as it easily sticks to a cake. Long refrigeration of an uncovered cake results in the frosting either drying out or changing color from circulating air.

Store cakes near the bottom of the refrigerator to keep them from picking up odors from other foods and from being accidentally jarred.

I like to store cakes that can be kept at room temperature under a glass dome, as I think glass maintains freshness well. These domes are available in the glassware or gift sections of most department stores, gift shops, and some housewares stores. Cake boxes such as those used by bakeries are ideal storage containers. These boxes are porous and allow just the right amount of air to circulate around the cake. You can purchase them at a local bakery or some kitchenware shops, especially those that carry professional equipment.

Department store gift boxes are also ideal storage containers and are especially attractive when you are presenting a cake as a gift. Or you can buy such boxes from stationery stores. Oblong and square cakes are sometimes stored directly in their baking pans. Occasionally, these pans come with plastic or metal lids, which eliminates the need for a foil or plastic wrap covering. Cakes baked in heatproof glass may also be stored in the pan, covered with aluminum foil.

A storage container for rolls and roulades can be improvised from shoe boxes. Choose two of equal size, cut an end from each, then slide the two boxes together, securing them with tape or staples. Cut along each side of one of the ends to make a flap. Place the cake on a foil-wrapped strip of heavy-duty cardboard and ease the cake into the elongated box, then secure the flap. Flatten one end of each lid and place the lids on the box with the flat edges in the middle. The opening of the box should be completely covered. Then refrigerate the cake.

You can also temporarily remove the fruit and vegetable bins of the refrigerator and store large decorated cakes there. In the winter, the garage is also a good place for storage, as is the trunk of your car.

ALL ABOUT FREEZING

The freezer is a wonderful convenience when you wish to make cakes ahead or store leftover cakes, and for quantity baking.

For optimum freezing temperature the freezer must be at zero degrees or below. Side-by-side freezers and combination refrigerator/freezers usually do not maintain a zero temperature because the freezer door is opened too often. With these units, it is probably best to freeze cakes for relatively short periods of time—up to two months or so, depending upon how often you open the freezer door. For long-term freezing, a freestanding or chest-style deep freezer is ideal. I own and prefer a unit that is not self-defrosting, as the temperature within the freezer remains constant. It's all right if small amounts of ice crystals form in the freezer, as they help to protect the food. Also, freezers keep foods better when the freezer is well stocked rather than too empty. Since cold air sinks, the coldest part of the freezer is on the bottom. If you are unsure about the temperature of your freezer, keep a freezer thermometer inside the unit and check it from time to time.

To avoid freezer burn, frozen foods must be double wrapped. I like to wrap a cake first in aluminum foil and then place it in a tightly secured plastic bag. The advantage of aluminum foil is that it molds snugly around the cake and, unlike plastic wrap, it can be placed in the oven when it's time to defrost. The problem with foil is that it tears easily.

Under perfect storage conditions, most unfrosted cakes can be frozen for up to four months if they contain butter or some form of fat. The more fat the cake contains, the better it freezes. This includes creamed butter cakes, crunchy cakes, cakes with fruits and vegetables, chiffon cakes, cheesecakes, genoise, and tortes. Cakes made with no fat, such as sponge and angel food, do not freeze as well and should be used within 6 to 8 weeks, as should spice cakes, which lose their flavor. Cakes made with soft meringues cannot be frozen at all.

Confectioners' sugar frostings and all buttercreams freeze well. Most glazes, such as ganache, can be frozen, but they must be reheated after thawing to achieve the correct pouring consistency. Whipped cream fortified with gelatin, Bavarian cream, and mousses can be frozen for a short period of time.

Preparations that do not freeze well are meringue-style toppings and boiled frostings. Custards or any fillings that are made with eggs also are not candidates for freezing. Trimmings such as chocolate shavings lose their gloss and praline or anything made with caramelized sugar sweats when thawed and ultimately melts.

HOW TO WRAP CAKES FOR THE FREEZER

To wrap unfrosted cakes: Place the cooled unwrapped cake on a cardboard disk or other nonstick surface and put it in the freezer to freeze partially. When the cake is firm enough to handle, wrap the cake in aluminum foil using a drugstore or butcher's fold. Tuck the ends under and seal with tape, then place in a tightly sealed plastic bag. Label and date the package.

To wrap frosted and/or decorated cakes: Place the cake, unwrapped, on a flat surface such as a cookie sheet and put it in the freezer. When the frosting is completely frozen, transfer to a cake box. Wrap the box with plastic wrap and then aluminum foil. Tuck the ends of the foil underneath the box and secure with tape. Label and date the box.

To wrap unfrosted cakes in disposable pans: Cakes stored in these pans do not require partial freezing. Cover the pan with the matching lid, seal the edges well, and label and date the container.

HOW TO THAW FROZEN CAKES
....

I like to thaw unfrosted cakes in the oven. Not only is it faster, but the cake will taste almost as though it was freshly made. Cake can also be thawed at room temperature or overnight in the refrigerator. No matter how the cake is thawed, I recommend reheating it briefly to freshen it.

To defrost cake in the oven, remove the plastic bag, release the freezer tape, and pull the folded ends of the foil from under the cake, but don't unwrap the cake completely. Preheat the oven to 350°. Place the foil-wrapped cake on the oven shelf. It will take from 20 to 30 minutes to thaw, depending on the thickness of the cake.

To test, press the foil to see if the cake feels soft. If you are in doubt, you can also test the cake to see if it has thawed by opening the aluminum foil slightly and inserting a straw twig or toothpick into the cake. When you see that the cake is thawed, tear the foil open at the top of the cake to allow the warm oven air to reach its surface. Continue to bake the cake for another 5 minutes to re-freshen it; the cake should be warm, not hot.

Cool the cake on a rack, then remove the foil. The cake can now be frosted and/or filled, or served as is.

A frosted cake is best thawed slowly in the refrigerator. Allow at least 12 hours before you plan to serve it. I suggest doing this either the day before you plan to use the cake, or early in the morning of the same day. If you have frozen the cake in a box, unwrap the box but leave the cake in the box to thaw. If the cake was frozen without a box, remove all the wrappings from the cake as soon as you remove it from the freezer. Place the cake on a plate and cover with an aluminum foil tent.

Obviously, the smaller the cake and/or piece, the less time it will take to thaw. You can test the cake by inserting a straw twig. If it is still partially frozen, allow the cake to stand at room temperature until it is thawed.

ALL ABOUT CUPCAKES
....

Cupcakes have a certain charm. They make wonderful party and lunchbox treats for youngsters, and they become elegant fare when served as minicupcakes at a fancy sweet buffet. Cupcakes are equally popular when made into a he-man size, like the muffins that are currently so much in vogue. I also recommend them for those who are trying to watch their waistlines; they are a great way to practice portion control.

Butter cakes make the best cupcakes. Very thick batters such as that for Carrot Pineapple Cake will work well, too. Sponge, chiffon, and angel food cake recipes are not suitable for cupcakes. Figure on a yield of 20 to 30 medium-sized cupcakes, depending upon the amount of flour and leavening in the batter. It's all right if you can't bake all the cupcakes at once. Since most creamed butter batters are leavened with double-acting baking powder, they can stand if you must bake them in batches.

If you invest in muffin tins, purchase at least two pans, each to hold 12 medium-sized muffins. Be wary of odd sizes; some of the pans are too shallow. I like to use cupcake liners as they keep the pans clean and preserve freshness in the cake. However, the pans can also be buttered or sprayed with nonstick pan coating.

Fill the pans ²/₃ full. Allow ¹/₄ cup of batter for each medium-sized cupcake. If you are making minicupcakes, each takes only about 1 tablespoon of batter. A quick calculation will tell you that at least four to six pans will make the job faster. For the giant muffin tins, estimate at least ¹/₂ cup of batter per cupcake. Use a 350° oven for both minicupcakes and giants. A slightly hotter oven, 375°, is best for medium-sized cupcakes.

Petite cupcakes will take about 12 to 14 minutes to bake, the medium-sized cupcakes about 18 to 22 minutes, and the giant cupcakes could take up to 30 minutes or more. The time will depend on the kind of batter used. Since cupcakes are not delicate, when you catch a whiff of them baking, that's the time to peek into the oven to check for doneness. If they are bouncy on the top and feel dry when pressed with a finger, they are done. If you are unsure, test a cupcake with a toothpick.

After the cupcakes are baked, you can either frost them and serve, or pop them, unfrosted, in the freezer arranged in foil containers to use at a later date.

Here is a list of recipes that make great cupcakes:

Black Chocolate Zinger (page 110)
Cornmeal Cake (page 112)
Espresso Cake (page 116)
Absolutely the Best Yellow Cake (page 120)
Gingerbread (page 125)
Sour Cream Cake (page 127)

Shaved Chocolate Cake (page 129)
Whole Wheat Honey Cake (page 132)
Sour Cream Chocolate Cake (page 134)
Lemon Velvet Squares (page 138)
Chocolate Jimmy Cake (page 142)
Applesauce Spice Cake (page 194)
Maple Walnut Cake (page 166)
Chunky Chocolate Chip Cake (page 172)
Hungarian Poppy Seed Kugelhopf (page 174)
Crisp Brazil Nut Cake (page 178)
Pignoli Lemon Cake (page 151)
Oat Bran Apple Cake* (page 198)
Banana Nut Cake (page 200)
Nutty Cranberry Orange Cake (page 209)
Rosy Rhubarb Cake (page 217)
Australian Apricot Cake (page 223)
Nutmeg Cake with Dried Red Cherries (page 229)
Brandied Chocolate Prune Cake (page 225)
Pineapple Macadamia Loaf (page 227)
Gingery Pumpkin Pecan Cake* (page 231)
Carrot Pineapple Cake* (page 232)
Zucchini Tea Loaf* (page 234)

🌰 A BAKER'S PANTRY

Keeping a well-stocked pantry enables you to put together a delicious cake on the spur of the moment. It is so frustrating to find, when you have a spare 45 minutes to whip up a cake, that you are out of an ingredient. Here are some of the basic ingredients that I feel every home baker should have on hand. They all have a reasonable shelf life, so you have only to pay attention to your inventory and you will have a cake baked in no time.

Flours: cake flour, unbleached all-purpose flour, stone-ground whole wheat, fine cornmeal, potato flour.

Sugars and sweeteners: granulated, superfine, confectioners', light and dark brown, light and dark corn syrup, dark molasses, honey, apricot preserves, red currant jelly, raspberry and strawberry preserves, orange marmalade.

*Giant muffin tins are best for these recipes.

Ingredients, Equipment, Procedures and Techniques

Leavenings and thickeners: double-acting baking powder, baking soda, active dry yeast, cream of tartar, cornstarch, unflavored gelatin.

Chocolates: imported and domestic bittersweet chocolate, semisweet chocolate, unsweetened chocolate, white chocolate, dutch-process alkaline and American nonalkaline cocoa, chocolate bits.

Extracts and liqueurs: pure vanilla, almond, orange, peppermint, maple, instant coffee, ground espresso, Grand Marnier, Cointreau, or Triple Sec, Armagnac, Kahlúa, light and dark rum, kirsch.

Spices: allspice, cardamom, ground cinnamon and cinnamon sticks, ground and whole cloves, coriander, ginger, whole nutmeg, black peppercorns.

Nuts, nut pastes, and seeds: almonds, walnuts, pignoli, pecans, hazelnuts, peanut butter, praline paste, shredded coconut, sesame, poppy. Also convenient to have on hand are specialty nuts and seeds such as Brazil and macadamia nuts, and pepitas (pumpkin seeds).

Fruits, dried and canned: dried apricots, cherries, prunes, dark and golden raisins, currants, sundried and candied pineapple, mixed chopped dried fruits, dates, figs, canned pumpkin, glacéed cherries, candied rinds, assorted canned fruits, maraschino cherries.

Fats and shortenings: solid vegetable shortening (Crisco), flavorless vegetable oil, Pam or other nonstick coating product, unsalted butter, unsalted margarine.

Decorations: nonpareils, peppermints, sprinkles, candied violets and rose petals, crystallized ginger.

Paper goods: waxed paper, plastic wrap, heavy-duty and regular aluminum foil, baking parchment, doilies, paper towels, plastic bags.

Miscellany: amaretto biscuits, graham crackers, evaporated milk, cultured buttermilk powder, toothpicks, assorted food colors.

Part Two

QUICK

and

EASY

CAKES

POUND CAKES

························ ❧ ························

I thought it might be fun to lead off my book with a traditional pound cake recipe inspired by my research into cookbooks dating from before the American Revolution. The equipment in the kitchens where those cakes were first made was a far cry from the conveniences we enjoy today. I suspect those early bakers worked to near exhaustion during the long creaming process—it was not uncommon for a pound cake batter to be beaten by hand for more than one hour. Cakes were baked over wood-burning stoves where the only temperature control was the type and amount of wood added to the fire. Since they were such an effort to bake, pound cakes were treasured and served only to the most honored guests.

The 18th-century pound cake is a recipe believed to have been brought to this country by the original English settlers. It consists of equal weights of flour, sugar, butter, and eggs. The formula for classic pound cake would be the same today.

Thorough creaming of the butter and sugar, a procedure known as "rubbing" in many early cookbooks, is critical to the success of a pound cake batter. Incorporating the eggs into the batter could be done either by mixing them in alternately with the flour or by separating the eggs and folding the beaten whites into the batter at the end.

Preparing these old-fashioned pound cakes can be tricky because they do not contain baking powder or baking soda. Nor do they contain liquid, so the batter is very thick. Lengthy beating is necessary to make the cake rise. It is this extensive beating that incorporates the right amount of air to give the cake its characteristically fine texture.

In the middle of the nineteenth century chemical leavenings such as baking powder and baking soda began to be commercially produced. As these were gradually introduced into home kitchens, a new form of pound cake came into existence. While the traditional pound cake concept remained, bakers began to add small amounts of leavening and liquid to lighten the crumb and lessen the risk factor in baking these sensitive cakes. Instead of baking them only in loaf pans, cooks made rounded shapes as well.

Pound cakes are as popular now as they were centuries ago, with one important difference—with today's modern appliances, preparing them is easy. It is from the basic pound cake formula that all American-style butter cakes made in this country evolved.

BEFORE YOU BEGIN . . .

▶ It is best to use an electric or hand mixer when making pound cakes because the thick batter requires lengthy beating to draw in as much air as possible.

▶ Pound cake batters curdle after the eggs are added. This is self-correcting when the flour is added.

▶ Separating the eggs makes a lighter pound cake and may be done as an optional procedure. Add the yolks as you would whole eggs, and fold in the beaten whites at the end.

▶ In pound cake recipes, flour is generally added at a slightly higher mixer speed than for regular batters.

▶ Since pound cake batters are very thick and require long baking, loaf pans should be lined with parchment paper where indicated. The paper prevents overbrowning and keeps the cake from drying out. If you do not have baking parchment, a brown grocery bag may be used. You could substitute waxed paper or aluminum foil in a pinch, but they are less desirable.

▶ If a cake does not dome too much on the top, you can use a fluted 8-cup round cake pan in place of a 7-cup loaf pan. Omit the baking parchment. Butter the pan well and dust with flour. Serve the fluted cake inverted instead of top side up.

▶ Pound cake recipes made with less than 1¹/₂ cups of flour may be doubled and baked in round 3-quart flat-bottomed tube pans.

▶ If a pound cake has been baked in a parchment-lined pan, removing the paper after baking is optional. If you are not planning to serve the cake at once, leaving the paper on will help to retain freshness.

▶ It is best to test pound cakes for doneness with a 5- or 6-inch piece of straw twig from a whisk broom, since it can reach to the bottom of the pan.

▶ Beads of moisture that form at the crack on top of a pound cake are common. The moisture forms from the steam that escapes from the split in the cake. Do not wait for the moisture beads to disappear as the cake can overbake and become dry. If the center of the straw comes out dry when the cake is tested with a twig, the cake is done.

▶ Pound cakes are generally served in thin slices, no more than ¹/₂ inch. Slice pound cake with a serrated knife, using a back-and-forth sawing motion.

▶ Leftover pound cakes are delicious sliced and heated in a toaster. They do not fall apart because they are tight-grained.

🌰 18TH-CENTURY POUND CAKE

This is an old-fashioned recipe taken from the classic formula that was popular during that period. The cake has a smooth, velvety texture and a rich buttery taste. The baked cake is traditionally wrapped in a brandy-soaked cheesecloth, stored in an airtight container, and tucked away in a cool place—a basement is ideal—where the wonderful flavors can mellow.

AT A GLANCE

SERVINGS: 8 to 10
PAN: 9″ × 5″ × 2³/4″ (8-cup capacity)
PAN PREP: Butter/parchment
OVEN TEMP: 325°
RACK LEVEL: Lower third
BAKING TIME: 85 to 90 minutes
METHOD: Electric mixer

2¹/2	cups sifted enriched all-purpose flour (do not use unbleached flour)
¹/2	teaspoon salt
1¹/4	cups (2¹/2 sticks) unsalted butter
1	cup plus 6 tablespoons superfine or strained sugar
6	large eggs
2	teaspoons rosewater or vanilla extract

1. Position rack in the lower third of the oven. Preheat oven to 325°. Butter an 8-cup loaf pan (9″ × 5″ × 2³/4″). Line with baking parchment (page 65).
2. Using a triple sifter, sift together the flour and salt into a medium-sized bowl. Set aside.
3. Place the eggs into the small bowl of an electric mixer. With the beaters or paddle attachment whip on medium-high speed until thickened and light in color, about 5 minutes. Set aside.
4. Cut the butter into 1-inch pieces and place in the large bowl of an electric mixer. With the beaters or paddle attachment, soften on low speed. Increase speed to medium-high. Cream until smooth and light in color, about 1¹/2 to 2 minutes.
5. Add the sugar, 1 tablespoon at a time, taking 6 to 8 minutes to blend it in well. Scrape the sides of the bowl occasionally.
6. Reduce mixer speed to medium. Slowly add half of the beaten eggs over 3 minutes. Scrape the sides of the bowl occasionally. Add the rosewater or vanilla, and beat for 30 seconds.
7. Reduce speed to medium-low. Add the dry ingredients alternately with the remaining eggs, dividing the flour into three parts and the eggs into two parts, mixing until well incorporated after each addition. Scrape the sides of the bowl as necessary. The

batter should be smooth and creamy. Increase mixer speed to medium and mix for 20 seconds longer.

8. Spoon the batter into the prepared pan, smoothing the surface with the bottom of a tablespoon. Bake in the preheated oven for 85 to 90 minutes. After 1 hour of baking, carefully make a 1/4-inch-deep slit lengthwise down the center of the cake using a sharp knife, to form an even crack. *Do not remove cake from oven or jar the pan while doing this.* Continue baking until the cake is golden brown on top and begins to come away from the sides of the pan. A twig of straw or a toothpick inserted into the center of the cake should come out dry.

9. Remove the cake from the oven. Set on a cake rack for 10 to 15 minutes. Turn pan on its side and ease the cake out. Cool the cake top side up or resting on its side. Remove the parchment just before serving and dust the top with confectioners' sugar.

STORAGE: Remove the parchment paper. Moisten a large piece of cheesecloth in a brandy of your choice and wrap tightly around the cake. Cover with plastic wrap, sealing well. Store in an airtight container, in a cool place such as a basement or porch, but not in the refrigerator or the cake will dry out. Remoisten cheesecloth once a week or as needed. This cake will keep for several weeks if properly cared for.

SERVING SUGGESTION: Pound cake is delicious toasted, especially after it has aged. Slice into 1/2-inch pieces, and place in a toaster to brown. Alternatively, brush the slices with melted butter, then sprinkle the top with a mixture of cinnamon and sugar. Bake in a 400° oven until golden brown.

🌿 MERINGUE POUND CAKE WITH WARM LEMON SAUCE

18th-century pound cake becomes an elegant dessert when slices are piled high with swirls of meringue and topped with sliced almonds. Bake to a golden brown and serve in a pool of warm lemon sauce.

▽ ....

AT A GLANCE

SERVES: 6
PAN: Jelly roll pan
PAN PREP: Ungreased
OVEN TEMP: 350°
RACK LEVEL: Lower third
BAKING TIME: 6 to 8 minutes
METHOD: Electric mixer

MERINGUE TOPPING:

- 1/4 cup superfine sugar
- 2 tablespoons strained confectioners' sugar
- 3 egg whites
  Pinch of salt
- 6 slices 18th-Century Pound Cake, cut 1/2 inch thick
- 1 tablespoon sliced almonds
- 1 recipe Warm Lemon Sauce (page 471)

1. To make the meringue topping: Combine sugars and set aside. In the large bowl of an electric mixer fitted with the beaters or a whip attachment, whip the egg whites on medium speed until frothy. Add the salt, increase speed to medium-high, and continue beating until mixture stands in firm peaks. Toward the side of the bowl gradually add sugars, 1 tablespoon at a time, taking 1 minute. Continue beating 1 minute longer. Meringue should be stiff and glossy.

2. Preheat oven to 350°.

3. Place slices of cake on a jelly roll pan. Cover each entire slice to the edge with meringue, swirling peaks higher at the center with the back of a spoon. Scatter with sliced almonds. Bake for 6 to 8 minutes or until meringue turns a light golden brown.

4. Place 1/4 to 1/3 cup warm lemon sauce on each welled dessert plate. Tilt the plate gently in a circular motion to coat the well evenly with sauce.

5. Center each cake slice on the plate and pour about 1 tablespoon sauce in a strip across top of each piece. Serve immediately, while still warm.

NOTE: Each plate can be kept in a warm oven while you prepare the next one.

🌾 OLD-FASHIONED POUND CAKE

If you fancy pound cakes, this is the recipe for you. It has all of the qualities that a great pound cake should have—flavor, texture, and appearance. And as an added bonus, this recipe lends itself to countless variations. Try adding freshly grated lemon or orange rind, or spices to your taste, or substituting fruit juice as the liquid.

This recipe is a modernized version of the 18th-century pound cake. The crumb is lighter than the traditional cake since this batter contains baking powder and a small amount of liquid. The addition of these ingredients makes the batter more stable and reduces the chance of failure.

▽
AT A GLANCE

SERVES: 8 to 10
PAN: 9″ × 5″ × 2³/₄″ loaf pan (8-cup capacity) or an 8″ or 9″ flat-bottomed tube pan (2- to 3-quart capacity)
PAN PREP: Loaf— butter/parchment; tube—butter/flour
OVEN TEMP: 325°
RACK LEVEL: Lower third
BAKING TIME: 65 to 70 minutes
METHOD: Electric mixer

2¹/₄	cups sifted cake flour
1	teaspoon baking powder
¹/₄	teaspoon salt
1	cup (2 sticks) unsalted butter
1	cup superfine or strained sugar
4	large eggs
2	teaspoons vanilla extract
¹/₄	cup milk

1. Position rack in the lower third of the oven. Preheat oven to 325°. Butter a 9″ × 5″ × 2³/₄″ loaf pan and line the pan with baking parchment (page 65). Or, butter an 8- or 9-inch flat-bottomed tube pan. Dust with all-purpose flour, then invert the pan over the kitchen sink and tap to remove excess.
2. Using a triple sifter, sift together the flour, baking powder, and salt. Set aside.
3. Cut the butter into 1-inch pieces and place in the large bowl of an electric mixer fitted with beaters or paddle attachment. Soften on low speed. Increase the speed to medium-high and cream until smooth and light in color, about 1¹/₂ to 2 minutes.
4. Add the sugar, 1 tablespoon at a time, taking 6 to 8 minutes to blend well. Scrape the sides of the bowl occasionally.
5. Add the eggs, 1 at a time at 1-minute intervals. Scrape the sides of the bowl again. Blend in the vanilla. The mixture may appear somewhat curdled but will smooth out when the flour is added.

Quick and Easy Cakes

6. Reduce the mixer speed to low. Add the dry ingredients alternating with the liquid, dividing the flour mixture into 3 parts and the liquid into 2 parts, starting and ending with the flour. Mix only until incorporated after each addition. Scrape the sides of the bowl occasionally.

7. Spoon the batter into the prepared pan and smooth the surface with the back of a tablespoon.

8. Center the pan on the rack and bake in preheated oven for 65 to 70 minutes, or until the cake is golden brown on top and begins to come away from the sides of the pan. If the top browns too quickly, place a piece of aluminum foil loosely over the surface for the last 5 to 10 minutes. The cake is done when a twig of straw or a toothpick inserted into the center comes out dry.

9. Remove the cake from the oven and place on a rack to cool for 10 to 15 minutes. Invert the cake onto the rack and remove the pan. Turn the cake top side up onto a second cake rack to cool completely. Just before serving, carefully remove the parchment paper and dust the top of the cake with confectioners' sugar.

STORAGE: Wrap well in aluminum foil or plastic wrap. Store at room temperature for up to 5 days.

VARIATIONS

SPIRITED POUND CAKE

See how the flavor of the old-fashioned pound cake changes when spirits are added to the batter, just enough to add subtle flavor. My favorite liqueur to use is B & B, although you may use almost any type that you happen to have on hand. Mace, the dried shell of the nutmeg, is also traditional.

1. Prepare the master recipe above, making the following changes: Substitute 1/4 cup good-quality liqueur or brandy such as B & B, Grand Marnier, Drambuie, Cognac, or Courvoisier for the milk. Reduce the vanilla extract to 1 teaspoon. Add 1/8 teaspoon powdered mace.

NUTTY POUND CAKE

This pound cake is studded with finely chopped nuts, and doused with hot liqueur syrup while still warm. I tested this recipe using a delicious Italian walnut liqueur known as Nocello. However, you can substitute other liqueurs such as Frangelico, amaretto, or Grand Marnier. Each spirit will give the cake its own distinctive flavor.

....

1. Add 2 teaspoons of freshly grated navel orange rind to the butter before creaming in Step 3.
2. Put 1 cup walnuts or pecans and 1/2 teaspoon ground coriander in the container of a food processor. Pulse 6 or 8 times or until nuts are chopped medium-fine. Gently fold into the finished batter. Bake as directed.
3. While the cake is baking, make a liqueur syrup: Put 2/3 cup Nocello or other liqueur, 1/4 cup water, and 2 tablespoons sugar into a small saucepan and bring to a slow boil to dissolve the sugar crystals. Simmer 2 to 3 minutes. Set aside.
4. Remove the cake from the oven and set the pan on a cake rack. After the cake has rested for 10 minutes, poke holes in it with a wooden skewer at 1-inch intervals, reaching to the bottom of the cake.
5. Reheat the liqueur syrup until just under boiling. Slowly spoon the hot syrup over the cake, allowing it to be absorbed. Cool the cake completely before removing from the pan. The cake flavor is at its best when the cake is allowed to stand for 24 hours before slicing.

STORAGE: Wrap airtight in plastic wrap or aluminum foil and store at room temperature for up to 10 days.

CHOCOLATE CHIP POUND CAKE

Place 1 cup of mini chocolate chips in the container of a food processor and process for 15 seconds to break up the chips into smaller pieces, approximately 1/8-inch. If chips are still too large, pulse until pieces reach the desired size. Do not overprocess! Gently fold the chopped chocolate into the finished batter. Proceed with the recipe.

Quick and Easy Cakes

CREAM CHEESE POUND CAKE

AT A GLANCE

SERVES: 8 to 10
PAN: 9″ flat-
bottomed tube or
fluted ring pan
(10 to 12 cup
capacity)
PAN PREP:
Butter/flour
OVEN TEMP: 325°
RACK LEVEL: Lower
third
BAKING TIME: 60 to
65 minutes
METHOD: Electric
mixer

The contrast of sweet butter with tangy cream cheese gives this pound cake its wonderful flavor and velvety texture. This is an especially rich cake, so I try to cut my slices a little thinner than usual. Admittedly, not taking a second helping is a struggle.

This recipe also works especially well as a lemon-flavored pound cake—cream cheese and lemon are a terrific flavor duo.

2	cups sifted cake flour
1½	teaspoons baking powder
¼	teaspoon salt
1	cup (2 sticks) unsalted butter
6	ounces cream cheese
½	teaspoon freshly grated lemon rind (optional)
1⅓	cups superfine or strained sugar
5	large egg yolks, lightly stirred
2	teaspoons vanilla extract
5	large egg whites
⅛	teaspoon cream of tartar

1. Preheat oven to 325°. Butter a 9-inch flat-bottomed tube pan or fluted ring pan and dust with all-purpose flour, inverting pan over the sink to tap out excess.
2. Using a triple sifter, sift together the flour, baking powder, and salt. Set aside.
3. Cut the butter and cream cheese into 1-inch pieces and place in the large bowl of an electric mixer fitted with the beaters or paddle attachment. Add the lemon rind. Soften on low speed for 2 to 3 minutes. Increase the speed to medium-high and cream until smooth and light in color, about 1½ to 2 minutes.
4. Add the sugar, 1 tablespoon at a time, taking 6 to 8 minutes to blend it in well. Scrape the sides of the bowl occasionally.
5. Add the egg yolks in three additions at 1-minute intervals, scraping the sides of the bowl as necessary. Blend in the vanilla.
6. Reduce mixer speed to low. Add the dry ingredients all at once and mix until blended. Scrape the sides of the bowl. Increase mixer speed to medium-low and mix about 30 seconds longer.

7. In a separate large bowl of an electric mixer fitted with beaters or whip attachment, beat egg whites on medium speed until frothy. Add the cream of tartar and increase the mixer speed to medium-high. Continue to beat until the whites are shiny and stand in firm peaks. *Do not overbeat.*

8. With a 2¾-inch-wide rubber spatula, fold ⅓ of the beaten whites into the batter, taking about 20 turns to lighten. Then fold in the remaining whites, taking about 40 additional turns.

9. Spoon the batter into the prepared pan and smooth the surface with the back of a tablespoon. Center the pan on the rack and bake in the preheated oven for 60 to 65 minutes, or until the cake is golden brown on the top and begins to come away from the sides of the pan. The cake is done when a twig of straw or a toothpick inserted into the center comes out dry.

10. Remove the cake from the oven and set the pan on a cake rack for 10 to 15 minutes to cool. Invert the cake onto a cake rack and remove the pan. To protect the top of the cake if you have used a flat-bottomed pan, turn the cake top side up on a second rack to cool completely. If you have baked the cake in a fluted tube pan, cool it top side down. Just before serving, dust the top lightly with confectioners' sugar.

STORAGE: Store at room temperature under a glass cover or in an airtight container for up to 7 days.

VARIATION
....

LEMON CREAM CHEESE POUND CAKE

Increase freshly grated lemon rind from ½ teaspoon to 1 tablespoon. Reduce the vanilla extract to 1 teaspoon.

🌿 RUM RAISIN POUND CAKE

This is a taste sensation flavored with yellow raisins, dark Jamaican rum, orange and lemon rinds, and cinnamon. It is essential to age this cake in a rum-soaked cheesecloth to mellow the flavors.

After two or three days the cake will be ready to serve and easy to slice. Not only is the taste of the cake worth the wait, but the ahead-of-time preparation can be a great convenience.

AT A GLANCE

SERVES: 8 to 10
PAN: 8″ or 9″ flat-bottomed tube pan (2- to 3-quart capacity)
PAN PREP: Butter/flour
OVEN TEMP: 350°
RACK LEVEL: Lower third
BAKING TIME: 45 to 50 minutes
METHOD: Electric mixer

1	cup yellow raisins
2¹/₃	cups sifted cake flour
³/₄	teaspoon baking powder
¹/₄	teaspoon salt
1	teaspoon cinnamon
1	cup (2 sticks) unsalted butter
1¹/₂	teaspoons freshly grated navel orange rind
¹/₂	teaspoon freshly grated lemon rind
1	cup superfine or strained sugar
4	large eggs
1	teaspoon vanilla extract
¹/₃	cup dark rum, preferably Jamaican

1. Preheat oven to 350°. Butter an 8- or 9-inch flat-bottomed tube pan. Dust with all-purpose flour, invert over the kitchen sink, and tap to remove excess.
2. To soften the raisins, place them in a steam basket in a medium saucepan and steam for 1 minute over boiling water. (Do not submerge the raisins or they will absorb too much water.) Spread them out over several layers of paper toweling and dry thoroughly.
3. Using a triple sifter, sift together the flour, baking powder, salt, and cinnamon. Set aside.
4. Cut the butter into 1-inch pieces and place it along with the rinds in the large bowl of an electric mixer fitted with beaters or paddle attachment. Soften on low speed. Increase speed to medium-high and cream until smooth and light in color, about 1¹/₂ to 2 minutes.

5. Add the sugar, 1 tablespoon at a time, taking 6 to 8 minutes to blend it in well. Scrape the sides of the bowl occasionally.

6. Add the eggs, 1 at a time at 1-minute intervals, scraping the sides of the bowl again. Blend in the vanilla. The mixture may look somewhat curdled, but will smooth out when the flour is added.

7. Reduce the mixer speed to low. Add the dry ingredients in three additions alternately with the rum in two additions, mixing until incorporated after each addition. Mix the batter for 15 seconds longer. Remove the bowl from the mixer and fold in the raisins with a rubber spatula.

8. Spoon the batter into the prepared pan and smooth the surface with the back of a tablespoon. Center the pan on the rack and bake in the preheated oven for 45 to 50 minutes, or until the cake is golden brown on top and begins to come away from the sides of the pan. The cake is done when a twig of straw or a toothpick inserted into the center comes out dry.

9. Remove the cake from the oven and set the pan on a cake rack for 10 to 15 minutes to cool slightly. Invert the cake onto a rack and remove the pan. Turn the cake top side up onto a second cake rack to cool at room temperature.

10. Cut a double thickness of cheesecloth to measure approximately 18 × 24 inches. Saturate in 1/4 cup dark Jamaican rum. Open the rum-soaked cheesecloth and stretch flat on an 18-inch square of heavy-duty aluminum foil. Arrange the cake in the center of the cheesecloth. Wrap the cheesecloth over the cake by lifting the ends and bringing them to the center. Then wrap tightly in the aluminum foil. Place the cake in a plastic bag and seal. Let stand at room temperature overnight.

11. The following day remove the aluminum foil and unwrap the cake. Remoisten the cheesecloth with an additional 1/4 cup rum. Rewrap the cake in the cheesecloth and foil and return to the plastic bag to age for 2 to 3 days or up to 10 days. It is not necessary to remoisten cheesecloth after the second day. The cake may be eaten plain, or served with Spiked Honey Bell Orange Sauce (page 485).

STORAGE: Wrap leftover cake in the cheesecloth. Store in plastic wrap or aluminum foil at room temperature for up to 10 days.

🦋 FRESH FRUIT POUND CAKE

Just when I thought I had completed the pound cake section of this book, one of my assistants, Dolores Cameron, brought me a freshly baked blueberry pound cake. It had a rich, buttery flavor enhanced with flecks of grated orange rind and deep purple berries. She told me she had made the recipe with many varieties of fresh fruit and wanted to know if it was good enough to put in the book. Indeed it was. Here is her very special recipe.

AT A GLANCE

SERVES: 10 to 12
PAN: 9 × 5 × 2¾-inch loaf pan (2-quart capacity)
PAN PREP: Butter/flour
OVEN TEMP: 350°
RACK LEVEL: Lower third
BAKING TIME: 60 to 65 minutes
METHOD: Electric mixer

1	cup fresh fruit such as blueberries, raspberries, pitted Bing cherries, peaches, nectarines, or orange sections, alone or in combination
2	cups sifted unbleached all-purpose flour
2	teaspoons baking powder
1	cup (2 sticks) unsalted butter
1	tablespoon freshly grated navel orange rind
1½	cups strained confectioners' sugar
4	large eggs
2	teaspoons vanilla extract
2	tablespoons orange juice

1. Wash the fruit, if necessary, and dry it well on paper toweling. Cut large pieces into ½-inch chunks to measure *only* 1 cup.
2. Preheat the oven to 350°. Butter the loaf pan well and dust with flour. Invert over the kitchen sink and give pan a tap to remove excess flour.
3. Sift together the flour and baking powder. Set aside.
4. Cut the butter into 1-inch pieces and put in the large bowl of an electric mixer fitted with the beaters or paddle attachment. Add the orange rind and soften on low speed. Increase speed to medium-high. Cream until smooth and light in color, 1½ to 2 minutes.
5. Add the sugar, ⅓ at a time, scraping sides of bowl as necessary. Then beat until well blended, approximately 2 minutes.
6. Add the eggs, 1 at a time, at 1-minute intervals, scraping the sides of the bowl occasionally. Reduce speed to low. Blend in vanilla and orange juice. The batter will look curdled.

7. Add the dry ingredients all at once, scraping the sides of the bowl again. Increase speed to medium-low and beat approximately 30 seconds longer.
8. Spread $1/3$ of the batter evenly on the bottom of baking pan. Scatter half of the fruit on top. Spread on the second third of batter and cover with the remaining fruit. Spread the remaining batter on top, smoothing the surface with the bottom of a spoon.
9. Bake for 60 to 65 minutes, or until cake is golden brown on top, and begins to come away from the sides of the pan. Test by inserting a twig of straw or a toothpick into the center. If it come out dry, the cake is finished.
10. Remove the pan from oven and set on a cake rack to cool for 10 to 15 minutes. Invert cake onto rack and remove pan, then turn cake top side up to finish cooling. When ready to serve, dust top lightly with confectioners' sugar.

STORAGE: Store at room temperature under a glass cover or in an airtight container for up to 4 days.

❧ TOASTED COCONUT POUND CAKE

Crushed, toasted coconut flakes give a slight crunch and a special flavor to this different and delicious-tasting pound cake. As it ages, the coconut develops a more pronounced taste. I like to serve the cake with a scoop of pineapple sherbet.

▽

AT A GLANCE

SERVES: 8 to 10
PAN: 9″ × 5″ × 2¾″ loaf (8-cup capacity)
PAN PREP: Butter/parchment
OVEN TEMP: 325°
RACK LEVEL: Lower third
BAKING TIME: 65 to 70 minutes
METHOD: Electric mixer

1¹/₃	cups flaked coconut
2	cups sifted cake flour
¹/₂	teaspoon baking powder
¹/₄	teaspoon salt
¹/₄	teaspoon ground nutmeg
1	cup (2 sticks) unsweetened butter
¹/₂	teaspoon freshly grated navel orange rind
⁷/₈	cup superfine or strained sugar
4	large egg yolks
1	teaspoon vanilla extract
¹/₂	teaspoon imitation coconut extract
¹/₄	cup orange juice
4	large egg whites
¹/₈	teaspoon cream of tartar

1. Position rack in the lower third of the oven and preheat to 325°. Butter a 9″ × 5″ × 2³/₄″ loaf pan and line with baking parchment (page 65).
2. Scatter the coconut in a shallow baking pan and toast in the oven for 8 to 10 minutes. Watch carefully, as the coconut around the outer edges of the pan darkens first. Stir occasionally with a fork for even browning. When all the coconut is nicely browned, remove it from the oven. The coconut will become crispy as it cools. Crumble it into smaller pieces by crushing it lightly in your hands.
3. Using a triple sifter, sift together the flour, baking powder, salt, and nutmeg. Set aside.
4. Cut the butter into 1-inch pieces and put it in the large bowl of an electric mixer fitted with beaters or paddle attachment. Add the orange rind and soften the mixture on low speed. Increase

the speed to medium-high and cream until smooth and light in color, about 1½ to 2 minutes.

5. Add the sugar, 1 tablespoon at a time, taking 4 to 6 minutes to blend it in well. Scrape the sides of the bowl occasionally.

6. Add the egg yolks, 2 at a time at 1-minute intervals, scraping the sides of the bowl as necessary. Blend in the vanilla and coconut extracts.

7. Reduce mixer speed to low. Add the dry ingredients in three additions alternately with the orange juice in two additions, mixing only until incorporated after each addition. Raise the mixer speed to medium and mix for 10 seconds longer. Remove the bowl from mixer and fold in the coconut.

8. In a separate bowl, beat the egg whites with beaters or whip attachment on medium speed until frothy. Add the cream of tartar and increase the mixer speed to medium-high. Continue to beat until whites are shiny and stand in firm peaks. *Do not overbeat.*

9. With a 2¾-inch-wide rubber spatula, fold ⅓ of the beaten whites into the batter, taking about 20 turns to lighten. Then fold in remaining whites, taking about 40 additional turns.

10. Spoon the batter into the prepared pan and smooth the surface with the back of a tablespoon. Center the pan on a rack and bake in the preheated oven for 65 to 70 minutes, or until the cake is golden brown on top and begins to come away from the sides of the pan. A twig of straw or a toothpick inserted into the center of the cake will come out dry.

11. Remove the cake from the oven and set the pan on a cake rack for 10 to 15 minutes to cool slightly. Invert the cake onto a rack and remove the pan, then turn the cake top side up onto a second cake rack to cool completely. Just before serving, carefully remove the parchment paper and dust the top with confectioners' sugar.

STORAGE: Wrap airtight in plastic wrap or aluminum foil. Store at room temperature for up to 5 days.

❧ SOUTHERN PECAN POUND CAKE

AT A GLANCE

SERVES: 10 to 12
PAN: 9″ flat-bottomed tube pan (3-quart capacity)
PAN PREP: Butter/flour
OVEN TEMP: 325°
RACK LEVEL: Lower third
BAKING TIME: 60 to 70 minutes
METHOD: Electric mixer

When I was a young girl in Memphis, Tennessee, the bakery at Goldsmith's department store made the most wonderful pecan pound cake, and my mother's weekly shopping trip always included a stop at their pastry shop to bring home a cake for my brother and me. This recipe was created from my sweet memories of childhood.

1	cup pecan halves
1	tablespoon unsifted cake flour
2¼	cups sifted cake flour
1	teaspoon baking powder
¼	teaspoon salt
1	cup (2 sticks) unsalted butter
1⅓	cups superfine or strained sugar
5	large eggs
1½	teaspoons vanilla extract
¼	cup sour cream

1. Position rack in the lower third of the oven and preheat to 325°. Butter a 9-inch flat-bottomed tube pan, dust with all-purpose flour, and invert the pan over the kitchen sink to tap out excess.
2. By hand, break the pecans into ¼-inch pieces. Scatter the pecan pieces in a shallow pan and toast in the oven for 6 to 8 minutes. Cool. Toss with 1 tablespoon unsifted cake flour. Set aside.
3. Using a triple sifter, sift together the flour, baking powder, and salt. Set aside.
4. Cut the butter into 1-inch pieces and place in the large bowl of an electric mixer fitted with beaters or paddle attachment. Soften on low speed. Increase speed to medium-high and cream until smooth and light in color, about 1½ to 2 minutes.
5. Add the sugar, 1 tablespoon at a time, taking 6 to 8 minutes to blend it in well. Scrape the sides of the bowl occasionally.
6. Add the eggs, 1 at a time at 1-minute intervals. Scrape the sides of the bowl again, then blend in vanilla. The mixture may look somewhat curdled at this point; it will smooth out once all the flour is added.
7. Reduce mixer speed to low. Blend in half of the flour. Add the

sour cream and mix about 15 seconds, then add the remaining flour. Scrape down the sides of the bowl. Increase mixer speed to medium-low and mix batter for about 20 seconds.

8. Remove the bowl from the mixer. Fold in the nuts using a rubber spatula. Spoon the batter into the prepared pan, smoothing the surface with the back of a tablespoon. For a pretty finish, sprinkle 2 to 3 tablespoons broken pecans and 1 to 2 teaspoons granulated sugar over the batter. Bake in the preheated oven for 60 to 70 minutes, or until cake is golden brown on top and begins to come away from the sides of the pan. A twig of straw or a toothpick inserted into the center will come out dry.

9. Remove the pan from the oven. Cool the cake in its pan on a cake rack for 10 to 15 minutes. Invert the pan onto the rack and remove the cake, then turn right side up to cool completely.

STORAGE: Store at room temperature under a glass cover or in an airtight container for up to 5 days.

❧ MARBLE POUND CAKE

▽
AT A GLANCE

SERVES: 8 to 10
PAN: 9″ × 5″ ×
2¾″ loaf (8-cup
capacity)
PAN PREP:
Butter/parchment
OVEN TEMP: 325°
RACK LEVEL: Lower
third
BAKING TIME: 65 to
70 minutes
METHOD: Electric
mixer

When I was a child, I cut my marble pound cake into small squares to see how the dark chocolate would weave in and out of the vanilla; then I would pop the little pieces into my mouth, sometimes choosing those that had more chocolate and sometimes those that had more vanilla. I guess I'm still a kid at heart, because when I am alone I still cut marble pound cake into little pieces. It just tastes better that way.

1	teaspoon vegetable shortening
1	ounce unsweetened chocolate
2	tablespoons light corn syrup
2	teaspoons hot water
⅛	teaspoon baking soda
1¼	cups sifted cake flour
½	teaspoon baking powder
¼	teaspoon salt
½	cup (1 stick) unsalted butter
⅔	cup superfine or strained sugar
2	eggs
1	teaspoon vanilla extract
⅓	cup milk

1. Put the shortening and the chocolate in a small heatproof bowl and set in a skillet containing ½ inch of simmering water until melted. Whisk in the corn syrup, then the hot water, 1 teaspoon at a time, stirring well. The mixture should be thick and smooth. Sprinkle on the baking soda and stir well to dissolve. Remove the bowl from the water and set aside.
2. Position a rack in the lower third of the oven and preheat to 325°. Butter an 8-cup loaf pan (9″ × 5″ × 2¾″) and line with baking parchment (page 65).
3. Sift together the flour, baking powder, and salt in a triple sifter. Set aside.
4. Cut the butter into 1-inch chunks and place in the large bowl of an electric mixer fitted with beaters or paddle attachment. Soften on low speed. Increase speed to medium-high. Cream until smooth and light in color, 1½ to 2 minutes.

5. Add the sugar, 1 tablespoon at a time, taking 4 to 5 minutes to blend it in well. Scrape the sides of the bowl occasionally.
6. Add the eggs, 1 at a time at 1-minute intervals. Scrape sides of bowl again. Blend in the vanilla.
7. Reduce mixer speed to low. Add the dry ingredients alternately with milk, dividing the flour into 3 parts and the liquid into 2 parts. Increase speed to medium. Mix for 15 seconds longer.
8. Remove 1/4 of the batter to a separate bowl and blend in the reserved chocolate mixture. Set aside.
9. Spoon 3/4 of the vanilla batter into the prepared pan. Spread the chocolate batter on top. Then dab on the remaining vanilla batter. Using a kitchen knife, cut into batter almost to bottom of pan. Gently fold about 6 times with knife to marbleize. Smooth the top of the batter with the back of a teaspoon.
10. Bake in the preheated oven for 65 to 70 minutes or until cake is golden brown on top and begins to come away from the sides of the pan. A twig of straw or a toothpick inserted into the center of the cake should come out clean.
11. Remove the cake from oven and set the pan on a rack to cool for 10 to 15 minutes. Turn pan on its side and ease cake out onto the rack, then turn top side up to finish cooling. Just before serving, remove paper and dust top lightly with confectioners' sugar.

STORAGE: Wrap in aluminum foil or plastic wrap. Store at room temperature for up to 5 days.

🌰 CHOCOLATE WALNUT POUND CAKE

AT A GLANCE

SERVES: 8 to 10
PAN: 8″ or 9″ flat-bottomed tube pan (2- to 3-quart capacity)
PAN PREP: Butter/flour
OVEN TEMP: 325°
RACK LEVEL: Lower third
BAKING TIME: 60 to 70 minutes
METHOD: Electric mixer

Walnuts are delicious in a chocolate pound cake, especially when the flavor is enhanced with Kahlúa and honey. As the cake matures the liqueur, honey, and oil from the walnuts give it a wonderful moistness that improves flavor and makes it easier to slice.

Chocolate-lovers who do not fancy nuts may simply omit them. This cake is terrific either way.

2 tablespoons instant espresso
2 tablespoons boiling water
1/2 cup strained unsweetened cocoa
1/4 cup Kahlúa liqueur
2 tablespoons honey
1 teaspoon vanilla extract
2 cups sifted unbleached all-purpose flour
1/2 teaspoon baking soda
1/2 teaspoon salt
2 cups walnuts
2/3 cup (1 1/3 sticks) unsalted butter
1 1/3 cups superfine or strained sugar
2 large eggs
2/3 cup milk

1. Position rack in the lower third of the oven and preheat to 325°. Butter an 8- or 9-inch flat-bottomed tube pan and dust with flour, inverting pan over the kitchen sink to tap out excess.
2. In a small bowl, dissolve the espresso in the boiling water. Add the cocoa, Kahlúa, honey, and vanilla and stir with a whisk until blended and smooth. Set aside.
3. Using a triple sifter, sift together the flour, baking soda, and salt. Set aside.
4. Cut the walnuts into 1/4- to 3/8-inch pieces. Set aside.
5. Cut the butter into 1-inch pieces and put them in the large bowl of an electric mixer fitted with beaters or paddle attachment. Soften on low speed, then increase speed to medium-high and cream until smooth and light in color, about 1 1/2 to 2 minutes.
6. Add the sugar, 1 tablespoon at a time, taking 6 to 8 minutes to

blend it in well. Add the eggs, 1 at a time at 1-minute intervals. Beat 1 minute longer, scraping the sides of the bowl as necessary.

7. Reduce mixer speed to medium. Stir the reserved chocolate mixture and add to the batter, mixing until well blended, about 1 minute.

8. Reduce the mixer speed to low. Add the dry ingredients in three additions alternating with the milk in two additions, mixing until incorporated after each addition. Scrape the sides of the bowl as necessary. Mix the batter for 30 seconds longer. Remove the bowl from the mixer.

9. Fold in the walnuts using a rubber spatula. Spoon the batter into the prepared pan and smooth the surface with the back of a tablespoon.

10. Center the pan on the rack and bake in the preheated oven for 60 to 70 minutes, until cake begins to come away from the sides of the pan and a twig of straw or a toothpick inserted into the center comes out dry.

11. Remove the cake from the oven and cool in the pan on a cake rack for 10 to 15 minutes. Invert the cake onto a rack and gently remove the pan. Turn the cake right side up onto a second rack to cool completely.

STORAGE: Wrap airtight in plastic wrap or aluminum foil. Store at room temperature for up to 10 days.

Plain Butter Cakes

· · · · · · · · ✦ · · · · · · · ·

Although similar in composition to pound cakes, plain butter cakes are generally lighter in texture and less rich. The batter contains proportionally less butter, and because these cakes contain substantially more leavening and liquid, their crumb is less dense.

Whenever I think of these simple homespun cakes, my thoughts turn to my children. I remember how when they were young, their little fingers would pluck out the raisins and larger nuts from their serving of cake, leaving their plates scattered with these tiny morsels that they did not like. As they grew older their tastes changed. However, many people, young and old alike, do prefer the smoothness and texture of a plain cake.

This chapter, more than any other in the book, contains easy-to-make recipes. It includes a range of great buttery cakes in such flavors as vanilla, chocolate, ginger and other spices, tangy sour cream, honey, tart lemon, and the stone-ground grains of whole wheat and cornmeal. These cakes are delicious served unfrosted, simply dusted with confectioners' sugar or covered with a very light glaze. This collection of recipes is meant to be used with imagination.

▶ Most of the recipes in this chapter use the creamed-butter method of combining ingredients. See page 41 for comprehensive information on how to prepare these batters.

▶ Adding various spices, like nutmeg, cinnamon, cardamom, and ginger, makes an interesting flavor change for butter cakes.

▶ Adding extracts can also make a nice change of pace. Try coconut, almond, maple, lemon, or orange, or coffee or espresso zest (page 58). Always use extracts sparingly. The flavor should be subtle. Excess extract will leave an aftertaste.

▶ Fruit juices, such as orange, apple, and pineapple, make a nice substitute for milk in a batter. If your recipe does not contain baking soda, reduce the baking powder by $1/2$ teaspoon and add $1/4$ teaspoon baking soda. This will neutralize the acid in the juice and prevent the cake from sinking in the middle.

▶ Grated orange, lemon, or lime rind is always a great flavor enhancer. They can be used individually, blended together, or used in addition to the fruit juice suggestions listed above.

❧ BLACK CHOCOLATE ZINGER

This is truly a cake for chocolate-lovers because of its intense dark chocolate flavor. The black pepper gives it added zing and a touch of honey provides luscious moistness. This is especially delicious served with coffee ice cream.

AT A GLANCE

SERVES: 10 to 12
PAN: 9½″ fluted ring (12-cup capacity)
PAN PREP: Butter/flour
OVEN TEMP: 350°
RACK LEVEL: Lower third
BAKING TIME: 65 to 70 minutes
METHOD: Electric mixer

¾	cup water
1	tablespoon instant coffee
6	ounces unsweetened chocolate, coarsely chopped
3	tablespoons honey
2	cups sifted unbleached all-purpose flour
1	teaspoon baking soda
¼	teaspoon salt
1½ to 2	teaspoons freshly ground black pepper
½	cup (1 stick) unsalted butter, at room temperature
¼	cup vegetable shortening
2	cups superfine or strained sugar
4	large eggs
2	teaspoons vanilla extract
½	cup ice water

1. Position rack in the lower third of the oven and preheat to 350°. Butter and flour a 9½-inch fluted ring pan.
2. Bring the ¾ cup water to a boil in a small saucepan. Immediately remove from the heat. Stir in the coffee until dissolved. Add the chocolate and honey and whisk until chocolate is melted and the mixture thickens. Set aside.
3. Using a triple sifter, sift together the flour, baking soda, salt, and black pepper. Set aside.
4. Cut the butter into 1-inch pieces and place in the large bowl of an electric mixer fitted with beaters or the paddle attachment to soften on low speed. Increase the speed to medium. Cream until softened and smooth, about 45 to 60 seconds. Add the vegetable shortening. Increase the speed to medium-high and beat 30 seconds longer.

5. Add the sugar, 1 tablespoon at a time, taking 8 to 10 minutes to blend well. Scrape the sides of the bowl occasionally.

6. Add the eggs, 1 at a time at 1-minute intervals. Reduce speed to medium. Stir the reserved chocolate mixture once or twice, then add to the batter along with the vanilla, scraping the sides of the bowl as necessary. Beat 30 seconds longer.

7. Reduce the mixer speed to low. Add the dry ingredients in three additions alternating with the ice water in two additions. Mix just until incorporated after each addition. Scrape the sides of the bowl and mix for 10 seconds longer.

8. Pour the batter into the prepared pan and smooth the surface with the back of a tablespoon. Center the pan on the rack and bake in the preheated oven for 65 to 70 minutes, or until the cake begins to come away from the sides of the pan and a twig of straw or a toothpick inserted into the center comes out dry.

9. Remove the cake from the oven and set the pan on a rack to cool for 15 to 20 minutes. Invert the cake onto a rack and remove the pan. When cool, coat top with Ganache Glaze (page 464) or dust the top lightly with confectioners' sugar.

STORAGE: Store at room temperature under a glass cover or in an airtight container for up to 5 days.

🌾 CORNMEAL CAKE

AT A GLANCE

SERVES: 6 to 8
PAN: 8″ × 8″ × 2″ square
PAN PREP: Butter/flour
OVEN TEMP: 375°
RACK LEVEL: Lower third
BAKING TIME: 30 to 35 minutes
METHOD: Electric mixer

This delightfully different cake made with cornmeal was inspired by my years of living in the South. The cornmeal imparts a slightly grainy but very pleasant texture. I strongly recommend using stone-ground cornmeal. Not only is the flavor far superior to that of the supermarket brands, it is more nutritious. Stone-ground cornmeal can be purchased at most health food stores and is usually packaged in one-pound bags. Be sure to store the unused portion in the refrigerator or freezer as it is highly perishable.

Although this cake is delicious plain, it also makes an excellent base for any fruit shortcake.

1¼	cups sifted unbleached all-purpose flour
1½	teaspoons baking powder
½	teaspoon baking soda
½	teaspoon salt
½	cup stone-ground yellow cornmeal
⅓	cup (⅔ stick) unsalted butter
⅔	cup sugar
2	large eggs, well beaten
1	teaspoon vanilla extract
⅔	cup plain low-fat yogurt

1. Position rack in the lower third of the oven and preheat to 375°. Butter an 8″ × 8″ × 2″ pan, dust it with flour, and invert the pan over the kitchen sink and tap to remove excess.
2. Using a triple sifter, sift together the flour, baking powder, baking soda, and salt into a medium-sized bowl. Add the cornmeal and stir with a whisk to combine. Set aside.
3. Cut the butter into 1-inch pieces and place in the large bowl of an electric mixer fitted with beaters or paddle attachment to soften on low speed. Increase speed to medium-high and cream until smooth and light in color, about 1 to 1½ minutes.
4. Add the sugar, 1 tablespoon at a time, taking 4 to 5 minutes to blend it in well. Scrape the sides of the bowl as necessary.
5. Slowly pour in the beaten eggs, taking 10 seconds to add. Scrape

the sides of the bowl, beat 1½ minutes longer, then blend in the vanilla.

6. Reduce mixer speed to low. Add the dry ingredients alternating with the yogurt, dividing the flour mixture into three parts and the yogurt into two parts, starting and ending with the flour. Mix only until incorporated after each addition. Scrape the sides of the bowl and mix for 10 seconds longer.

7. Spoon the batter into the prepared pan and smooth the surface with the back of a tablespoon. Center the pan on the rack and bake in the preheated oven for 30 to 35 minutes or until the cake is golden brown on top and begins to come away from the sides of the pan. A toothpick inserted into the center should come out dry.

8. Remove the cake from the oven and set the pan on a cake rack for 10 to 15 minutes to cool slightly. Invert the cake onto the rack and remove the pan. When cake is completely cool, turn top side up and place on a serving platter. Just before serving dust the top lightly with confectioners' sugar. This cake may also be used as a base for fruit shortcakes.

STORAGE: Tightly wrap the cake with aluminum foil and store at room temperature for up to 5 days.

❧ LITTLE TEA SHOP CAKE WITH CHOCOLATE PUDDING SAUCE

▽

AT A GLANCE

SERVES: 8 to 10
PAN: 9″ × 9″ × 2″ square
PAN PREP: Butter
OVEN TEMP: 350°
RACK LEVEL: Lower third
BAKING TIME: 35 to 40 minutes
METHOD: Electric mixer

When I was growing up in Memphis, eating lunch with my mother at the Little Tea Shop was a special treat. Needless to say, my favorite part was dessert. My mother and I savored the delicate squares of vanilla cake topped with warm chocolate pudding sauce. This is real comfort food, the kind of cake you eat with a spoon.

THE CAKE:

1³⁄₄	cups sifted cake flour
2	teaspoons baking powder
¹⁄₄	teaspoon salt
¹⁄₃	cups (²⁄₃ stick) unsalted butter
³⁄₄	cup superfine or strained sugar
1	large egg
1	teaspoon vanilla extract
²⁄₃	cup milk

THE CHOCOLATE PUDDING SAUCE:
Serves 6 to 8

6	tablespoons sugar
2	tablespoons unsifted all-purpose flour
¹⁄₈	teaspoon salt
2¹⁄₂	cups milk
1	ounce unsweetened chocolate, finely chopped
1	ounce semisweet chocolate, finely chopped
1¹⁄₂	teaspoons vanilla extract

1. Position rack in the lower third of the oven and preheat to 350°. Butter a 9″ × 9″ × 2″ square pan.
2. To make the cake: Using a triple sifter, sift together the cake flour, baking powder, and salt. Set aside.
3. Cut the butter into 1-inch pieces and place in the large bowl of an electric mixer fitted with beaters or the paddle attachment to soften on low speed. Increase speed to medium-high and cream until smooth and light in color, about 1 to 1¹⁄₂ minutes.
4. Add the sugar, 1 tablespoon at a time, taking about 4 to 5 min-

Great Cakes

114

utes to blend it in well. Scrape the sides of the bowl as necessary.

5. Add the egg and beat for 1 minute, scraping the sides of the bowl occasionally. Then blend in the vanilla.

6. Reduce mixer speed to low. Add the dry ingredients alternately with the milk, dividing the flour mixture into three parts and the liquid into two parts, starting and ending with the flour. Mix just until incorporated after each addition. Mix for 10 seconds longer, scraping the sides of the bowl as necessary.

7. Spoon the batter into the prepared pan and smooth the surface with the back of a tablespoon. Center the pan on the rack and bake in the preheated oven for 35 to 40 minutes, or until the cake is golden brown on top, springy to the touch, and begins to come away from the sides of the pan.

8. Remove the cake from the oven. Set on a cake rack to cool completely in the pan.

9. To make the sauce: Place the sugar, flour, and salt in a medium-sized saucepan and stir to blend, using a wire whisk. Slowly add the milk, whisking until smooth. When the dry ingredients are completely blended into the milk, add the chocolates.

10. Place the pan over medium-low heat and cook, whisking constantly, until the mixture reaches a boil and thickens, about 5 minutes. Reduce the heat to low and simmer about 5 minutes longer, stirring frequently to keep the sauce from burning. If the sauce simmers too rapidly, lift the saucepan off the heat for a few seconds occasionally to cool it down. Be sure to reach into the edges of the pan with a wooden spoon to remove any of the pudding that may stick, then whisk again to remove lumps.

11. Remove the pan from the heat and blend in the vanilla. Pour it over the cake squares while it is still warm. If you wish to prepare the sauce in advance, refrigerate it in a covered container until ready to use. Before serving, reheat the sauce in a double boiler or bain-marie, or in the microwave on a medium setting.

12. When ready to serve, cut the cake into squares as needed and place each square in a shallow bowl. Top with warm sauce and serve at once.

STORAGE: Cover the top of the pan with aluminum foil. Store at room temperature for up to 7 days.

ESPRESSO CAKE WITH HOT KAHLÚA SYRUP

AT A GLANCE

SERVES: 8 to 10
PAN: 9″ fluted ring
(10-cup capacity)
PAN PREP:
Butter/flour
OVEN TEMP: 350°
RACK LEVEL: Lower
third
BAKING TIME: 55 to
65 minutes
METHOD: Electric
mixer

Roasted espresso beans are sold whole or ground in vacuum-packed cans. For instant espresso, the beans are ground into a highly concentrated powder. Substituting regular coffee crystals for espresso powder is not a good idea; the flavor will be much weaker.

Chocolate and lemon have an affinity with espresso, as does coffee liqueur. This sophisticated cake is enhanced with all three. The batter contains a touch of cocoa and a bit of lemon rind, and the baked cake is moistened with Kahlúa liqueur. The embellishments suggested for serving are not essential—the cake and syrup are wonderful without further adornment—but they do make this a very special treat.

THE CAKE:

3	tablespoons instant espresso
1/4	cup boiling water
1/4	cup cold water
2 1/4	cups sifted cake flour
1	tablespoon unsweetened cocoa powder
1	teaspoon baking soda
1/2	teaspoon salt
1/2	cup (1 stick) unsalted butter
1/2	teaspoon freshly grated lemon rind
1 1/2	cups superfine or strained sugar
3	large eggs
1	teaspoon vanilla extract
1/2	cup sour cream

THE HOT KAHLÚA SYRUP:

2/3	cup Kahlúa or Tía María liqueur
1/3	cup water
3	tablespoons honey

1. Position rack in the lower third of the oven and preheat to 350°. Butter a 9-inch fluted ring. Dust the pan with all-purpose flour, then invert the pan over the kitchen sink and tap to remove excess.

2. To make the cake: In a small bowl, dissolve the espresso in boiling water. Stir in the cold water and set aside to cool.

3. Using a triple sifter, sift together the flour, cocoa, baking soda, and salt. Set aside.

4. Cut the butter into 1-inch pieces and put them and lemon rind in the large bowl of an electric mixer fitted with beaters or paddle attachment. Soften on low speed, then increase speed to medium-high and cream until smooth and light in color, about 1½ to 2 minutes.

5. Add the sugar, 1 tablespoon at a time, taking about 6 to 8 minutes to blend it in well. Scrape the sides of the bowl occasionally.

6. Add the eggs, 1 at a time at 1-minute intervals. Blend in the vanilla and sour cream. The mixture will look somewhat curdled at this point. This is okay.

7. Reduce mixer speed to medium-low. Add the dry ingredients alternating with the espresso, dividing the dry ingredients into three parts and the espresso into two parts, starting and ending with the flour. Mix just until incorporated after each addition. Scrape the sides of the bowl and mix for 10 seconds longer.

8. Pour the batter into the prepared pan and smooth the surface with the back of a tablespoon. Center the pan on the rack and bake in the preheated oven for 55 to 65 minutes, or until the cake begins to come away from the sides of the pan and a twig of straw or toothpick inserted into the center comes out dry.

9. Remove from the oven. Set the pan on a cake rack for 10 to 15 minutes to cool slightly.

10. To make the syrup: In a small saucepan blend the Kahlúa, water, and honey. Bring to a slow boil and simmer 2 to 3 minutes. Remove from heat. Pierce the top of the cake with a wooden skewer and slowly spoon the hot syrup over the top of the hot cake. Let stand in the pan for at least 1 hour to allow cake to absorb all the liqueur, then invert onto a rack and remove pan.

SERVING SUGGESTION: Prepare ½ recipe of Ganache Glaze (page 464). Leave the cake on the rack, and place the rack over a large shallow pan. Spoon the glaze over the top, allowing the icing to flow gently down the sides in between the ridges. All of the cake does not have to be covered with the glaze. If you like, sprinkle candied lemon slivers (page 507) on the top. Carefully arrange the cake on a serving plate.

STORAGE: Store at room temperature under a glass dome or in an airtight container for up to 7 days.

BROWNED BUTTER CAKE WITH BROWNED BUTTER GLAZE

The pleasing taste of this fine-textured cake comes from browned clarified butter, clarified butter (page 43) that is cooked slowly until the color turns a golden brown. It has a delicious nutty flavor.

AT A GLANCE

SERVES: 8 to 10
PAN: 9″ × 9″ × 2″ square
PAN PREP: Butter
OVEN TEMP: 350°
RACK LEVEL: Lower third
BAKING TIME: 35 to 40 minutes
METHOD: Electric mixer

THE CAKE:

- 2/3 cup (1 1/3 sticks) unsalted butter
- 2 cups sifted cake flour
- 1 1/2 teaspoons baking powder
- 1/4 teaspoon salt
- 3 large eggs, at room temperature
- 1 cup superfine or strained sugar
- 1/2 cup orange juice
- 1 teaspoon vanilla extract

THE BROWNED BUTTER GLAZE:

- 1 tablespoon browned butter
- 3/4 cup strained confectioners' sugar
- 1 tablespoon boiling water
- 1/4 teaspoon vanilla extract

1. To make browned butter: In a small heavy-bottomed saucepan melt the butter over low heat. Using a tablespoon, skim the white foam as it accumulates, until the butter is clear. This will take a few minutes. Continue to simmer the clear butter until it turns a rich golden brown, about 5 to 7 minutes. Take care not to burn it. Pour the butter into a clean measuring cup and set aside until tepid. Do not allow the butter to become too cold or it will re-solidify.

2. To make the cake: Position rack in the lower third of the oven and preheat to 350°. Butter a 9″ × 9″ × 2″ cake pan.

3. Using a triple sifter, sift together the flour, baking powder, and salt. Set aside.

4. Put the eggs in the large bowl of an electric mixer fitted with beaters or the whip attachment. On medium-high speed, whip the eggs until light in color and thickened, approximately 3 min-

utes. Add the sugar, 1 tablespoon at a time, taking about 3 to 4 minutes to beat it in well.

5. Reduce mixer speed to medium-low. Measure out ¼ cup of the flour mixture and set aside. Add the remaining flour mixture to the eggs in three additions, alternating with the orange juice in two additions, starting and ending with the flour. Mix just until incorporated after each addition. Scrape the sides of the bowl as necessary. Mix in the vanilla.

6. Test the browned butter for correct temperature; it should be tepid. Reserve 1 tablespoon for the glaze. Slowly pour the remaining butter into the batter, taking about 1 minute. After the melted fat has been added to the batter, quickly blend in the remaining ¼ cup of flour. Mix 15 seconds longer. It is important to work quickly after the butter has been added because the fat is heavy and has a tendency to separate from the batter and sink.

7. Immediately pour the batter into the buttered pan and smooth the surface with the back of a tablespoon. Center the pan on the rack and bake in the preheated oven for 35 to 40 minutes, or until the cake begins to come away from the sides of the pan, is golden brown, and the top is springy to the touch.

8. Remove the cake from the oven and set on a cake rack to cool for 15 minutes.

9. To make the browned butter glaze: Warm the reserved 1 tablespoon browned butter. In a small bowl, combine the butter, confectioners' sugar, boiling water, and vanilla extract and beat with a wire whisk until smooth. Pour on the warm cake and spread thinly over its surface with the back of a tablespoon. The glaze will harden as it stands. Cut the cake into pieces just before serving.

STORAGE: Cover the top of the pan with aluminum foil. Store at room temperature for up to 5 days.

❧ ABSOLUTELY THE BEST YELLOW CAKE

AT A GLANCE

SERVES: 12 to 16
PAN: 10″ angel food cake pan (4-quart capacity) (see Note)
PAN PREP: Butter or butter/flour (see Note)
OVEN TEMP: 350°
RACK LEVEL: Lower third
BAKING TIME: 65 to 70 minutes

One of the most popular yellow cakes baked in this country is undoubtedly the 1-2-3-4 cake. It derives from the original pound cake formula of one pound each of butter, sugar, eggs, and flour. With the addition of more leavening and more liquid, that formula becomes the best butter cake that I know of. The ingredients are perfectly balanced. It is the ideal birthday cake.

3	cups sifted cake flour
1	tablespoon baking powder
1/2	teaspoon salt
1	cup (2 sticks) unsalted butter
2	cups superfine or strained sugar
4	large eggs
1 1/2	teaspoons vanilla extract
1	cup milk

1. Position rack in the lower third of the oven and preheat to 350°. Butter a 10-inch angel food cake pan (see Note).
2. Using a triple sifter, sift together the flour, baking powder, and salt. Set aside.
3. Cut the butter into 1-inch pieces and put them in the large bowl of an electric mixer fitted with beaters or the paddle attachment. Soften on low speed. Increase the speed to medium-high and cream until smooth and light in color, about 1 1/2 to 2 minutes.
4. Add the sugar, 1 tablespoon at a time, taking about 8 to 10 minutes to blend it in well. Scrape the sides of the bowl occasionally.
5. Add the eggs, 1 at a time at 1-minute intervals. Scrape the sides of the bowl as necessary. Blend in the vanilla.
6. Reduce mixer speed to medium-low. Add the dry ingredients alternately with the milk, dividing the flour mixture into four parts and the liquid into three parts and starting and ending with the flour. Mix just until incorporated after each addition. Scrape the sides of the bowl and mix for 10 seconds longer.
7. Spoon the batter into the prepared pan and smooth the surface with the back of a tablespoon. Center the pan on the rack and

bake in the preheated oven for 65 to 70 minutes, or until the cake is golden brown on top and comes away from the sides of the pan. A twig of straw or a toothpick inserted into the center should come out dry.

8. Remove the cake from the oven and set the pan on a cake rack to cool to room temperature. If you are using a pan with a removable bottom, remove the pan by lifting up the center tube and running a sharp, thin-bladed knife under the cake and around the inner tube to loosen the cake. Invert the cake onto the cake rack. If your pan does not have a removable bottom, run a thin, sharp knife around the outer sides and inner tube, then invert the cake onto the rack. Place on a cake platter top side up. Just before serving, dust the top of the cake with confectioners' sugar.

STORAGE: Store at room temperature under a glass cake dome or in an airtight container for up to 5 days.

NOTE: This is a large cake. If you prefer, you can substitute three 9-inch layers for the angel food cake pan. Or the recipe can easily be cut in half and baked in any ring or flat-bottomed 2-quart pan. Another alternative would be to make the whole recipe, and bake it in 2 smaller pans, one to eat now, and one to freeze to enjoy at a later date. Remember to reduce the baking time when using smaller pans. Let your nose be the guide in judging the time. About 3 to 5 minutes after you notice a wonderful aroma coming from the oven, the cake should be just about done.

If the cake is baked in a fluted ring pan, be sure to butter and *flour* the pan. Let the baked cake cool in the pan for 10 to 15 minutes, then remove the pan while the cake is still warm. Serve bottom side up.

ZACH'S CHOCOLATE MARBLE CAKE

AT A GLANCE

SERVES: 10 to 12
PAN: 10″ bundt (12-cup capacity)
PAN PREP: Butter/flour (see Note, page 121)
OVEN TEMP: 350°
RACK LEVEL: Lower third
BAKING TIME: 55 to 65 minutes
METHOD: Electric mixer

As my children were growing up, a rousing yuh-m-m came from them whenever I made this cake. I knew it was their favorite because it vanished so fast. Now my grandson, Zach, is following in their footsteps. I can tell by how fast his little fingers put the cake into his mouth that it's his number-one choice as well.

This is a variation of Absolutely the Best Yellow Cake. As with that one, you may divide the batter and bake it in two 6-cup ring pans. Be sure to butter and flour the pans.

This wonderful cake needs nothing more than a dusting of confectioners' sugar to be perfect, but you may also give it a chocolate glaze. Whatever you choose, it is a winner.

THE CAKE:

- 1½ ounces unsweetened chocolate, coarsely chopped
- 1½ tablespoons vegetable shortening
- 2 tablespoons honey
- Scant ½ teaspoon baking soda
- 1 teaspoon espresso powder
- 2 tablespoons boiling water
- 2⅓ cups sifted cake flour
- 2 teaspoons double-acting baking powder
- ½ teaspoon salt
- ¼ teaspoon freshly ground nutmeg
- ¾ cup (1½ sticks) unsalted butter
- 1½ cups superfine or strained sugar
- 4 large eggs
- 1 teaspoon vanilla extract
- ¾ cup milk

THE GLAZE:

- ½ cup heavy cream
- 1 tablespoon light corn syrup
- 4 ounces semisweet or bittersweet chocolate, coarsely chopped
- 1 to 2 tablespoons coffee liqueur
- ½ teaspoon vanilla extract

1. Position rack in the lower third of the oven and preheat to 350°. Butter well a 10-inch bundt pan. Dust with all-purpose flour and invert over the sink, tapping out the excess.

2. To make the cake: In a small bowl, melt the chocolate and vegetable shortening over hot water or in a microwave oven, using a medium setting. Stir well to be sure the chocolate is completely melted. Blend in the honey. Sprinkle the baking soda over the top of the chocolate and blend well. Dissolve the espresso in the boiling water and add to the chocolate mixture, stirring until completely smooth. Set aside. The mixture will thicken as it stands.

3. Using a triple sifter, sift together the flour, baking powder, salt, and nutmeg. Set aside.

4. Cut the butter into 1-inch pieces and place in the large bowl of an electric mixer fitted with beaters or paddle attachment to soften on low speed. Increase the speed to medium-high and cream until smooth and light in color, about 1½ to 2 minutes.

5. Add the sugar 1 tablespoon at a time, taking about 6 to 8 minutes to blend it in well. Scrape the sides of the bowl occasionally.

6. Add the eggs, 1 at a time at 1-minute intervals. Scrape the sides of the bowl as necessary. Blend in the vanilla.

7. Reduce the mixer speed to low. Add the dry ingredients alternately with the milk, dividing the flour into three parts and the liquid into two parts, starting and ending with the flour. Mix only until incorporated after each addition. Scrape the sides of the bowl and mix for 10 seconds longer.

8. Remove 1 generous cup of batter to a separate bowl. Stir the chocolate mixture, then blend it into the cup of vanilla batter, gently folding the two together.

9. To layer the chocolate and vanilla batters: Spoon one-half of the remaining vanilla batter into the bottom of the prepared pan, smoothing the surface with the bottom of a tablespoon. Using a tablespoon, drop one-half of the chocolate batter by spoonfuls around the pan. With the bottom of the tablespoon, spread the chocolate batter, working from the middle to the sides until the vanilla batter is completely covered. Top with a second layer of vanilla, reserving about 1 cup for the last layer. Spread the batter again from the middle, then drop the remaining chocolate batter over the vanilla, spreading it to the edges. End the layering with the remaining vanilla batter, spreading

the batter over the chocolate as best you can. You should have three layers of vanilla and two layers of chocolate.

10. To marbleize, insert a table knife into the batter with the tip pointed downward and *almost* touching the bottom. Then lift the knife up and gently fold the two batters together. Repeat by inserting the knife down again, going around the pan at about 2-inch intervals for a total of 10 to 12 times. For a less marbled effect, simply run the knife around the pan three times at 1-inch intervals. Smooth the top of the batter. Center the pan on the rack and bake in the preheated oven for 55 to 65 minutes, or until the cake is golden brown on top, and begins to come away from the sides of the pan. A twig of straw or a toothpick inserted into the center should come out dry.

11. Remove the cake from the oven and set the pan on a wire rack to cool for 15 or 20 minutes. Place a wire rack over the top of the pan and invert. Let the cake stand about 30 seconds and then gently remove the pan. Allow the cake to cool completely. Glaze the cake or dust the top with confectioners' sugar.

12. To make the glaze: Place the heavy cream, light corn syrup, and coarsely chopped chocolate in a small *heavy* saucepan. Over low heat, stir constantly until the chocolate is completely melted. Do not beat. Watch for bubbles to appear on the side of the pot. The mixture should *just* come to a boil.

13. Set the saucepan in a larger pan filled with ice water. When the mixture is tepid, blend in the liqueur and vanilla. As the glaze cools, it should thicken to the consistency of thick chocolate sauce. Pour the glaze through a fine-mesh strainer to remove any air bubbles. If the glaze fails to thicken, place it in the refrigerator for 4 to 5 minutes.

14. Set the wire rack with the cake over a shallow pan to catch the dripping glaze.

15. Spoon the glaze over the cake, allowing the icing to drip gently at random down the sides, leaving parts of the cake exposed.

STORAGE: Store at room temperature under a glass cake dome or in an airtight container for up to 4 days.

🌿 GINGERBREAD

G̲ingerbread is believed to have been created in Greece around 2800 B.C., making it probably the oldest sweet cake in the world. (Despite the word "bread" in the name, gingerbread is really a cake.) During baking, the tantalizing aroma of molasses, spices, and orange liqueur really whets the appetite.

▽
AT A GLANCE

SERVES: 8 to 10
PAN: 9″ × 9″ × 2″ square
PAN PREP: Butter
OVEN TEMP: 350°
RACK LEVEL: Lower third
BAKING TIME: 40 to 45 minutes
METHOD: Electric mixer

2¹/₃	cups sifted unbleached all-purpose flour
1¹/₂	teaspoons baking soda
¹/₄	teaspoon salt
1	teaspoon ground ginger
1	teaspoon ground cinnamon
¹/₈	teaspoon ground cloves
¹/₂	cup (1 stick) unsalted butter
¹/₃	cup sugar
2	large eggs
³/₄	cup light or dark molasses, preferably unsulphured
	Juice of 1 medium navel orange plus enough milk to make ³/₄ cup liquid
2	tablespoons Grand Marnier, Cointreau, or Triple Sec
1¹/₂	teaspoons white vinegar

1. Position rack in the lower third of the oven and preheat to 350°. Butter a 9″ × 9″ × 2″ square pan.
2. Using a triple sifter, sift together the flour, baking soda, salt, and spices. Set aside.
3. Cut the butter into 1-inch pieces and place in the large bowl of an electric mixer fitted with beaters or paddle attachment to soften on low speed. Increase speed to medium-high and cream until smooth and light in color, about 1¹/₂ to 2 minutes.
4. Add the sugar, 1 tablespoon at a time, taking about 2 to 3 minutes to blend it in well. Scrape the sides of the bowl occasionally.
5. Add the eggs, 1 at a time at 1-minute intervals. Gradually pour in the molasses, and beat for about 1 minute, scraping the sides of the bowl as necessary. The mixture will look somewhat curdled at this point. This is okay. The curdled look will disappear when all the dry ingredients have been added.

6. Reduce mixer speed to low. Combine the juice/milk mixture with the liqueur and the vinegar. Add the dry ingredients alternately with the liquid ingredients, dividing the flour mixture into three parts and the liquid into two parts, starting and ending with the flour. Mix just until incorporated after each addition. Scrape the sides of the bowl occasionally. Mix 10 seconds longer. The batter will be loose.
7. Pour the batter into the prepared pan. Center the pan on the rack and bake in the preheated oven for 40 to 45 minutes, or until the cake comes away from the sides of the pan and is springy to the touch. Remove from the oven and set the pan on a cake rack to cool completely.

STORAGE: Cover the top of the pan with aluminum foil and store at room temperature for up to 7 days.

SERVING SUGGESTIONS: Serve slightly warm with liqueur-flavored Whipped Cream (page 486) or garnish with a dash of cinnamon and sugar, crystallized ginger, or crystallized orange rind. Gingerbread squares are also delicious served with Warm Lemon Sauce (page 471).

🌰 SOUR CREAM CAKE

Sour cream is one of the best flavor enhancers for butter cakes. In addition to wonderful flavor, it produces a delicate crumb, and a longer shelf life due to its high fat content and acidity. This recipe lends itself to many delicious variations.

▽

AT A GLANCE

SERVES: 10 to 12
PAN: 9½″ fluted ring pan (12-cup capácity)
PAN PREP: Butter/flour
OVEN TEMP: 350°
RACK LEVEL: Lower third
BAKING TIME: 55 to 60 minutes
METHOD: Electric mixer

2½	cups sifted cake flour
2	teaspoons baking powder
½	teaspoon baking soda
½	teaspoon salt
⅔	cup (1⅓ stick) unsalted butter
1¼	cups superfine or strained sugar
3	large eggs
1½	teaspoons vanilla extract
1⅓	cups sour cream

1. Position rack in the lower third of the oven and preheat to 350°. Butter a 9½-inch fluted ring pan. Dust the pan with all-purpose flour, then invert the pan over the kitchen sink and tap to remove excess.
2. Sift together the flour, baking powder, baking soda, and salt in a triple sifter. Set aside.
3. Cut the butter into 1-inch pieces and place in the large bowl of an electric mixer fitted with beaters or paddle attachment. Soften on low speed. Increase speed to medium-high and cream until smooth and light in color for 1½ to 2 minutes.
4. Add the sugar, 1 tablespoon at a time, over 6 to 8 minutes to blend it in well. Scrape sides of bowl occasionally.
5. Add the eggs, 1 at a time at 1-minute intervals. Scrape the sides of the bowl again. Reduce speed to medium and blend in vanilla.
6. Reduce mixer speed to low. Add the dry ingredients alternately with the sour cream, dividing the flour into four parts and sour cream into three parts, starting and ending with the flour. Scrape sides of bowl again. Mix 10 seconds longer.
7. Spoon the batter into the prepared pan, smoothing the surface with the back of a tablespoon. Bake in the preheated oven for 55

Quick and Easy Cakes

to 60 minutes, or until the cake is golden brown, springy to the touch, and begins to come away from the sides of the pan. A twig or straw or a toothpick inserted into the center will come out dry.

8. Remove the cake from the oven. Cool on a cake rack for 10 to 15 minutes, then invert onto the rack and remove pan to finish cooling. When completely cool, place onto a cake platter. Just before serving, dust top lightly with confectioners' sugar.

STORAGE: Store at room temperature under a glass cover or an airtight container. The cake will keep up to 5 days.

VARIATIONS

CINNAMON SWIRL BUNDT

$1/4$ cup sugar
4 teaspoons cinnamon

1. In a small bowl combine the sugar and cinnamon.
2. Spoon about $1/4$ of the batter into the pan. Sprinkle on $1/3$ of the sugar/cinnamon mixture. Continue alternating batter and sugar/cinnamon mixture, ending with a layer of batter. You should have four layers of batter and three of cinnamon sugar.
3. Smooth the batter with the back of a tablespoon, spreading it out from the center.
4. Using a kitchen knife, cut into batter almost to the bottom of the pan. Gently fold about 8 times, rotating pan.

COFFEE MARBLE CAKE

  1 tablespoon coffee zest (page 58)
  1 teaspoon freshly grated navel orange rind
 1/4 teaspoon cinnamon

1. Add orange rind to butter. Reduce the vanilla extract to 1 teaspoon.
2. Transfer about 1 1/2 cups of the batter and place in a medium-sized mixing bowl. Stir in the coffee zest and cinnamon, blending well.
3. Spoon about 1/4 of the batter into the pan. Using a tablespoon, drop mounds of the coffee batter on top of the vanilla, using about 1/3 of the batter. Continue alternating vanilla and coffee batters, ending with a layer of vanilla batter. You should have four layers of vanilla and three layers of coffee.
4. Using a kitchen knife, cut into batter almost to the bottom of the pan. Gently fold batters together about 8 times, rotating pan.

SERVING SUGGESTION: This cake is a special treat when served with a mound of sour cream on the side and some sliced summer peaches.

SHAVED CHOCOLATE CAKE

  1 recipe Sour Cream Cake
  2 ounces Bittersweet or German Chocolate

1. Cut chocolate into very fine shavings with a sharp knife.
2. At the end of Step 6 in master recipe, fold in the chocolate with a wide rubber spatula. Proceed with Step 7.

🌿 STREUSEL SQUARES

AT A GLANCE

SERVES: 10 to 12
PAN: 9″ × 13″ ×
2″ oblong
PAN PREP: Butter
OVEN TEMP: 350°
RACK LEVEL: Lower
third
BAKING TIME: 40 to
45 minutes
METHOD: Electric
mixer

Streusel crumbs made from a mixture of flour, sugar, cinnamon, and melted butter originated in Middle Europe and are most commonly used as a topping on yeast doughs or fruit tarts. However, they are equally delicious sprinkled on plain butter cakes.

The secret of making a good streusel is to shape the crumb mixture twice. After the first stirring with a fork the crumbs are small and delicate and will not hold their shape in baking, but if you follow the procedure in Step 2, you will get larger, firmer crumbs that will be crispy on the outside and flaky on the inside when baked.

Streusel is absolutely addicting. Don't be surprised if you see people guiltily sneaking an extra crumb or two. This is one of those cakes everyone loves to nibble at.

THE STREUSEL TOPPING:

- 1/3 cup (2/3 stick) unsalted butter
- 1 1/4 cups unsifted unbleached all-purpose flour
- 2/3 cup sugar
- 1 teaspoon ground cinnamon

THE CAKE:

- 2 1/4 cups sifted unbleached all-purpose flour
- 2 teaspoons baking powder
- 1/2 teaspoon salt
- 3/4 cup (1 1/2 sticks) unsalted butter
- 1 cup superfine or strained sugar
- 2 large eggs
- 1 large egg yolk
- 1 1/2 teaspoons vanilla extract
- 1 cup milk
- 1 large egg white

1. Position rack in the lower third of the oven and preheat to 350°. Butter a 9″ × 13″ × 2″ oblong pan.
2. To make the streusel topping: Melt the butter in a medium saucepan over a low flame. Remove from the heat and cool for about 5 minutes, but do not allow the butter to become cold. Add the flour, sugar, and cinnamon all at once and stir with a

table fork until the mixture forms small crumbs. Take a handful of the crumbs and make a fist to press the mixture into a large clump. Then separate into smaller clusters, at least two or three times the size of the original crumbs. Repeat until all of the crumbs have been reshaped. Set aside.

3. To make the cake: Using a triple sifter, sift together the flour, baking powder, and salt. Set aside.

4. Cut the butter into 1-inch pieces and place in the large bowl of an electric mixer fitted with beaters or paddle attachment to soften on low speed. Increase speed to medium-high and cream until smooth and light in color, about 1½ to 2 minutes.

5. Add the sugar, 1 tablespoon at a time, taking about 6 to 8 minutes to blend it in well. Scrape the sides of the bowl as necessary.

6. Add the eggs and additional yolk, 1 at a time at 1-minute intervals, scraping the sides of the bowl as necessary. Blend in the vanilla.

7. Reduce mixer speed to low. Add the dry ingredients alternately with the milk, dividing the flour mixture into three parts and the milk into two parts, starting and ending with the flour. Mix just until incorporated after each addition. Scrape the sides of the bowl and mix for 10 seconds longer.

8. Spoon the batter into the prepared pan and smooth the surface with the back of a tablespoon. Beat the egg white lightly with a fork. Using a pastry brush, spread about half of the beaten egg white over the top of the cake batter. Discard the remainder. (The egg white helps the streusel adhere to the top of the cake.) Sprinkle the entire surface of the batter generously with the streusel. Gently pat the crumbs into the batter with the palm of your hand; do not press hard.

9. Center the pan on the rack and bake in the preheated oven for 40 to 45 minutes, or until the cake is golden brown on top, begins to come away from the sides of the pan, and the streusel is crisp. A toothpick inserted into the center should come out dry.

10. Remove the cake from the oven and set on a cake rack to cool. When ready to serve, dust the top with confectioners' sugar and cut into squares.

STORAGE: Cover the top of the pan with aluminum foil and store at room temperature for up to 5 days.

🌿 WHOLE WHEAT HONEY CAKE

AT A GLANCE

SERVES: 8 to 10
PAN: 9″ fluted ring (10-cup capacity)
PAN PREP: Butter/flour
OVEN TEMP: 350°
RACK LEVEL: Lower third
BAKING TIME: 45 to 50 minutes
METHOD: Electric mixer

This tasty cake blends the flavors of honey, orange juice, and whole wheat flour, the latter providing a pleasant earthy flavor. Since it contains the bran and the germ of the wheat kernel, whole wheat flour has a coarser grain than white flour. If you sift it all the nutritious fiber will be removed. Instead, blend the whole wheat flour thoroughly into the white flour with a wire whisk. Cakes made with honey have a moister and slightly denser texture than those made with sugar because the honey is fluid and does not aerate with butter in the same manner as sugar. This cake is not too sweet, making it the perfect snack from breakfast to midnight!

THE CAKE:

1¼	cups sifted cake flour
1½	teaspoons baking powder
½	teaspoon baking soda
½	teaspoon salt
¼	teaspoon ground nutmeg
1	cup whole wheat flour, preferably stone-ground
½	cup (1 stick) unsalted butter
1	teaspoon freshly grated navel orange rind
1	cup honey
2	large eggs
½	cup orange juice

THE HONEY GLAZE:

2	tablespoons soft unsalted butter
1	tablespoon honey

1. Position rack in the lower third of the oven and preheat to 350°. Butter a 9-inch fluted ring pan, dust the pan with all-purpose flour, invert over the kitchen sink, and tap to remove excess.
2. To make the cake: Using a triple sifter, sift together the cake flour, baking powder, baking soda, salt, and nutmeg. Stir in the whole wheat flour, mixing thoroughly with a wire whisk. Set aside.
3. Cut the butter into 1-inch pieces and place in the large bowl of an electric mixer fitted with beaters or paddle attachment. Add

the grated orange rind and soften on low speed. Increase the speed to medium-high and cream until smooth and light in color, about 1½ to 2 minutes.

4. Gradually add the honey, taking about 1 minute to blend it in well. Continue beating for about 2 minutes longer, scraping the sides of the bowl occasionally.

5. Add the eggs, 1 at a time at 1-minute intervals, scraping the sides of the bowl as necessary.

6. Reduce mixer speed to low. Add the dry ingredients alternately with the orange juice, dividing the flour mixture into three parts and the liquid into two parts, starting and ending with the flour. Mix just until incorporated after each addition. Scrape the sides of the bowl and mix for 10 seconds longer.

7. Spoon the batter into the prepared pan and smooth the surface with the back of a tablespoon. Center the pan on the rack and bake in a preheated oven for 45 to 50 minutes, or until the cake is springy to the touch and begins to come away from the sides of the pan. A twig of straw or a toothpick inserted into the center should come out dry.

8. Remove the cake from the oven and set the pan on a cake rack to cool for 20 minutes.

9. To make the glaze: Blend the honey into the softened butter until smooth. After 20 minutes invert the cake onto the rack and carefully remove the pan. Immediately brush the hot cake with the glaze, using a soft brush, and continue to cool to room temperature. When the cake is completely cool, transfer to a cake platter.

STORAGE: Store at room temperature under a glass cake dome or in an airtight container for up to 7 days.

🌿 SOUR CREAM CHOCOLATE CAKE

SERVES: 10 to 12
PAN: 9" × 13" ×
2" oblong
PAN PREP: Butter
OVEN TEMP: 350°
RACK LEVEL: Lower
third
BAKING TIME: 40 to
45 minutes
METHOD: Electric
mixer

This is one of those "great to have on hand" cakes. Not meant for fancy dining, it makes a delicious between-meals snack. The sour cream gives it a pleasing smooth texture and a moist crumb. I like to store it in the pan and cut off squares as I need them. This cake has been a family favorite for years.

2	teaspoons freeze-dried coffee
1/4	cup boiling water
3	squares unsweetened chocolate, cut into pieces
2	cups sifted cake flour
1	teaspoon baking soda
3/4	teaspoon salt
1/2	cup (1 stick) unsalted sweet butter
1 1/3	cups superfine or strained sugar
2	large eggs
1	teaspoon vanilla extract
1 1/4	cups sour cream

1. Position rack in the lower third of the oven and preheat to 350°. Butter a 9" × 13" × 2" oblong pan.
2. Dissolve the coffee in the boiling water. Set aside. Place the chocolate in a small bowl. Set the bowl in a small skillet filled with 1/2 inch simmering water and stir the chocolate until it is completely melted and smooth. Set aside.
3. Using a triple sifter, sift together the flour, baking soda, and salt. Set aside.
4. Cut the butter into 1-inch pieces and put them in the large bowl of an electric mixer fitted with beaters or paddle attachment. Soften on low speed. Increase the speed to medium-high and cream until smooth and light in color, about 1 1/2 to 2 minutes.
5. Add the sugar, 1 tablespoon at a time, taking about 6 to 8 minutes to blend it in well. Scrape the sides of the bowl as necessary.
6. Add the eggs, 1 at a time at 2-minute intervals, scraping the sides of the bowl occasionally. Reduce speed to medium. Blend in the coffee, melted chocolate, and vanilla.

7. Reduce mixer speed to low. Add the dry ingredients alternately with the sour cream, dividing the flour mixture into four parts and the sour cream into three parts, starting and ending with the flour. Mix only until incorporated after each addition. Scrape the sides of the bowl and mix for 10 seconds longer.

8. Spoon the batter into the prepared pan and smooth the surface with the back of a tablespoon. Center the pan on the rack and bake in the preheated oven for 40 to 45 minutes, or until the cake just begins to come away from the sides of the pan and is springy to the touch.

9. Remove the cake from the oven and set the pan on a cake rack to cool completely. This is luscious with Sour Cream Chocolate Frosting (page 453), but delicious plain, too.

STORAGE: Cover the top of the pan with aluminum foil and store at room temperature for up to 5 days.

🍰 SUGARCRUST CAKE

The buttery flavor and crunchy topping make this the perfect cake to enjoy with a cup of tea.

AT A GLANCE

SERVES: 8 to 10
PAN: 9″ × 9″ × 2″ square
PAN PREP: Butter
OVEN TEMP: 350°
RACK LEVEL: Lower third
BAKING TIME: 30 to 35 minutes
METHOD: Electric mixer

THE CAKE:

2	cups sifted unbleached all-purpose flour
1½	teaspoons baking powder
½	teaspoon salt
⅔	cup (1⅓ sticks) unsalted butter
1	cup superfine or strained sugar, less 2 tablespoons
2	large eggs
1	large egg yolk
1	teaspoon vanilla extract
⅔	cup milk
1	large egg white

THE SUGARCRUST TOPPING:

¼	cup sugar
1	tablespoon unbleached all-purpose flour
¼	teaspoon vanilla extract

1. Position rack in the lower third of the oven and preheat to 350°. Butter a 9″ × 9″ × 2″ cake pan.
2. To make the cake: Using a triple sifter, sift together the flour, baking powder, and salt. Set aside.
3. Cut the butter into 1-inch pieces and place in the large bowl of an electric mixer fitted with beaters or paddle attachment to soften on low speed. Increase speed to medium-high and cream until smooth and light in color, about 1½ to 2 minutes.
4. Add the sugar, 1 tablespoon at a time, taking about 4 to 6 minutes to blend it in well. Scrape the sides of the bowl occasionally.
5. Add the eggs and the egg yolk, 1 at a time at 1-minute intervals, scraping the sides of the bowl as necessary. Blend in the vanilla.
6. Reduce mixer speed to low. Add the dry ingredients alternately with the milk, dividing the flour into three parts and the liquid

into two parts, starting and ending with the flour. Mix only until incorporated after each addition. Scrape the sides of the bowl and mix for 10 seconds longer. Spoon the batter into the prepared pan and smooth the surface with the back of a tablespoon.

7. Beat the egg white with a fork until frothy, about 20 to 30 whips. Spread about 1/2 to 2/3 of the beaten white on top of the batter, using a pastry brush. Discard the remaining white.

8. To make the sugar crust topping: Combine the sugar, flour, and vanilla in a small bowl. Using your fingertips, work together until well blended. Sprinkle the sugar mixture over the cake.

9. Center the pan on the rack and bake in the preheated oven for 30 to 35 minutes, or until the cake just begins to come away from the sides of the pan. The topping should be brown and form a glaze.

10. Remove the cake from the oven and set the pan on a cake rack to cool. When ready to serve, cut the cake into 2 1/4-inch squares.

STORAGE: Cover the top of the pan with aluminum foil and store at room temperature for up to 5 days.

❧ LEMON VELVET SQUARES

*L*emon-flavored desserts enjoy great popularity due to their tart, refreshing flavor. Often guests who shy away from sweets will succumb to pastries like these delicate, lemony, velvety squares of cake.

AT A GLANCE

SERVES: 8 to 10
PAN: 9″ × 13″ × 2″ oblong
PAN PREP: Butter
OVEN TEMP: 350°
RACK LEVEL: Lower third
BAKING TIME: 30 to 35 minutes
METHOD: Electric mixer

2¼	cups sifted cake flour
2½	teaspoons baking powder
½	teaspoon salt
½	cup (1 stick) unsalted butter
1	teaspoon freshly grated lemon rind
½	teaspoon freshly grated navel orange rind
1⅓	cups superfine or strained sugar
3	large eggs
⅓	cup water
3	tablespoons fresh lemon juice
¼	cup fresh orange juice
1	tablespoon confectioners' sugar for garnish (optional)

1. Position rack in the lower third of the oven and preheat to 350°. Butter a 9″ × 13″ × 2″ cake pan.
2. Using a triple sifter, sift together the flour, baking powder, and salt. Set aside.
3. Cut the butter into 1-inch pieces and place in the large bowl of an electric mixer fitted with beaters or paddle attachment. Add the lemon and orange rinds and soften on low speed. Increase the speed to medium-high and cream until smooth and light in color, about 1½ to 2 minutes.
4. Add the sugar 1 tablespoon at a time, taking about 6 to 8 minutes to blend it in well. Scrape the sides of the bowl occasionally.
5. Add the eggs, 1 at a time at 1-minute intervals, scraping the sides of the bowl as necessary.
6. Reduce mixer speed to low. In a small bowl, combine the water, lemon juice, and orange juice. Add the dry ingredients alternating with the liquids, dividing the flour mixture into three parts and the liquid into two parts, starting and ending with the flour. Mix just until incorporated after each addition. Do not worry if the batter appears to curdle; it should smooth out after the flour

is blended in. Scrape the sides of the bowl and mix for 10 seconds longer.

7. Spoon the batter into the prepared pan, smoothing the surface with the back of a tablespoon. Center the pan on the rack and bake in the preheated oven for 30 to 35 minutes, or until the cake is golden brown on top, springy to the touch, and begins to come away from the sides of the pan.

8. Remove the pan from the oven and set the pan on a cake rack to cool. Just before serving, place the confectioners' sugar in a fine-mesh strainer and dust the top of the cake. Cut into squares.

STORAGE: Cover the cake with aluminum foil and store at room temperature for up to 5 days if unglazed and 3 days glazed.

SERVING SUGGESTIONS: If you like a bit more pizzazz than the dusting of confectioners' sugar, coat the cake with a thin Lemon Glaze (page 463) or serve with Warm Lemon Sauce (page 471).

🐌 YOGURT SPICE CAKE

AT A GLANCE

SERVES: 8 to 10
PAN: 8″ flat-bottomed tube pan (2-quart capacity)
PAN PREP: Butter/flour
OVEN TEMP: 350°
RACK LEVEL: Lower third
BAKING TIME: 50 to 55 minutes
METHOD: Electric mixer

Although yogurt has been used in cooking for centuries, its use in baking has greatly increased in recent years as people have become more health-conscious. Plain unsweetened yogurt is most commonly used for baking and cooking. In most instances low-fat and nonfat whole milk yogurt can be used interchangeably. However, the less fat that the yogurt contains, the more gently it must be handled. Since there is little fat to act as a stabilizer, overmixing can cause low-fat yogurts to thin down.

Yogurt can often be used in place of sour cream. Both are cultured and have some similar qualities; the major difference is that the higher fat content of sour cream gives cakes a richer, smoother texture. When used in baking, both extend the shelf life of a cake and produce a velvety crumb.

- 2 cups sifted cake flour
- 1 teaspoon baking powder
- 1/2 teaspoon baking soda
- 1/2 teaspoon salt
- 2 teaspoons ground cinnamon
- 3/4 teaspoon ground nutmeg
- 1/4 teaspoon ground allspice
- 1/4 teaspoon ground mace
- 1/8 teaspoon ground cloves or to taste
- 1/2 cup (1 stick) unsalted butter
- 1/2 cup granulated sugar
- 1/2 cup light brown sugar, lightly packed
- 2 tablespoons honey
- 2 large eggs
- 1 teaspoon vanilla extract
- 1 cup plain low-fat yogurt

1. Position rack in the lower third of the oven and preheat to 350°. Butter an 8-inch flat-bottomed tube pan. Dust the pan with all-purpose flour, inverting over the kitchen sink to tap out excess.

2. Using a triple sifter, sift together the flour, baking powder, baking soda, salt, and spices. Set aside.

3. Cut the butter into 1-inch pieces and place in the large bowl of an electric mixer fitted with beaters or paddle attachment and soften on low speed. Increase the speed to medium-high and cream until smooth and light in color, about 1½ to 2 minutes.

4. Add the granulated sugar, 1 tablespoon at a time, taking about 3 to 4 minutes to blend it in well. Then add the light brown sugar, taking an additional 3 to 4 minutes. Add the honey and beat until just blended. Scrape the sides of the bowl occasionally.

5. Add the eggs, 1 at a time at 1-minute intervals, scraping the sides of the bowl as necessary. Blend in the vanilla.

6. Reduce mixer speed to low. Add the dry ingredients alternately with the yogurt, dividing the flour mixture into three parts and the yogurt into two parts, starting and ending with the flour. Mix only until incorporated after each addition. Scrape the sides of the bowl and mix for 10 seconds longer.

7. Spoon the batter into the prepared pan and smooth the surface with the back of a tablespoon. Center the pan on the rack and bake in the preheated oven for 50 to 55 minutes, or until the cake is golden brown on top and begins to come away from the sides of the pan. A toothpick inserted into the center of the cake should come out dry.

8. Remove the cake from the oven and set the pan on a cake rack to cool for 10 to 15 minutes. Invert the cake onto the rack and remove the pan. Continue to cool to room temperature. When the cake is completely cool, place it on a serving platter. Just before serving, dust the top with confectioners' sugar.

STORAGE: Store at room temperature under a glass dome or in an airtight container for up to 5 days.

🌰 CHOCOLATE JIMMY CAKE

AT A GLANCE

SERVES: 10 to 12
PAN: 10″ bundt
(12-cup capacity)
(see Note)
PAN PREP: Butter/
flour
OVEN TEMP: 350°
RACK LEVEL: Lower
third
BAKING TIME: 55 to
60 minutes
METHOD: Electric
mixer

Chocolate jimmies are the tiny dark brown sprinkles most often seen on top of ice cream cones. You'll be surprised at the delicious flavor and moist, fudgy texture they give to this cake.

2	cups sifted unbleached all-purpose flour
1/4	cup cornstarch
1 1/2	teaspoons baking powder
1/2	teaspoon baking soda
1/2	teaspoon salt
1/2	cup strained unsweetened cocoa
3/4	cup chocolate jimmies, divided
2/3	cup (1 1/3 sticks) unsalted butter
1 1/4	cups superfine or strained sugar
3	large eggs
1	teaspoon vanilla extract
3/4	cup milk
1/3	cup water
1	recipe Quick Chocolate Glaze for a large cake (page 462)

1. Position rack in the lower third of the oven and preheat to 350°. Butter a 10-inch bundt pan. Dust the pan with flour, invert over the kitchen sink, and tap to remove excess.
2. Using a triple sifter, sift together the flour, cornstarch, baking powder, baking soda, salt, and cocoa. Stir in *1/2 cup* of the chocolate jimmies. Set aside.
3. Cut the butter into 1-inch pieces and place in the large bowl of an electric mixer fitted with beaters or paddle attachment. Soften on low speed, then increase the speed to medium-high and cream until smooth and light in color, about 1 1/2 to 2 minutes.
4. Add the sugar gradually, 1 tablespoon at a time, taking about 6 to 8 minutes to blend it in well. Scrape the sides of the bowl as necessary.
5. Add the eggs, 1 at a time at 1-minute intervals, scraping the sides of the bowl occasionally. Beat for 1 minute longer. Blend in the vanilla.

6. Reduce mixer speed to medium-low. In a small bowl, combine the milk with the water. Add the dry ingredients alternately with the liquid, dividing the flour mixture into three parts and the milk mixture into two parts, starting and ending with the flour. Mix only until incorporated after each addition. Scrape the sides of the bowl and mix 10 seconds longer.

7. Spoon the batter into the prepared pan and smooth the surface with the back of a tablespoon. Center on the rack and bake in the preheated oven for 55 to 60 minutes, until the cake begins to come away from the sides of the pan. A twig of straw or a toothpick inserted into the center should come out dry.

8. Remove the pan from the oven and place on a cake rack to cool for 15 minutes. Invert the cake onto the rack and remove the pan. When the cake is almost cool, prepare the chocolate glaze, using the recipe for a large cake.

9. Place the rack over a large, shallow pan. Spoon the glaze over the top of the cake, allowing the icing to flow randomly down the sides. Sprinkle immediately with the remaining 1/4 *cup* chocolate jimmies and allow to set.

STORAGE: Store at room temperature under a glass dome or in an airtight container for 5 days.

NOTE: When prepared in two 9-inch layers, this recipe makes an extra-special party cake. Bake the layers 30 to 35 minutes, and cover thickly with swirls of Shiny Fudge Frosting (page 455).

Cakes with Crunch

Texture is what these cakes are all about. They will delight those who love to bite into sweet morsels of chunky chocolate, crackly praline, or nuts of any kind. Here are wonderful cakes made with poppy seeds, sesame and pepita seeds, pecans, Brazil nuts, almonds, walnuts, filberts, and pignolis.

Many of these recipes can be varied to suit your own tastes or when the specified ingredients are not available. Just remember that the correct balance must be achieved between the density of the batter and the weight of the filling. Too much filling makes a cake heavy, and if a filling is too heavy and the batter too thin, the filling will sink to the bottom of the pan. For detailed information on handling nuts and other crunchy ingredients in these cakes, see "Before You Begin," page 145.

Few of the cakes in this chapter need the additional embellishment of icing. The flavor of the nuts and fillings gives them all the character they need.

144

▶ Always chop or cut coarse ingredients like nuts or chocolate to the size specified in the recipe, or the cake might not rise properly.

▶ To keep nuts, dried fruit, or chocolate bits from sinking to the bottom of the pan during baking, avoid overmixing the batter. Overmixing thins the batter. Thin batters do not have the ability to keep these ingredients suspended.

▶ If you are using a KitchenAid mixer, you may mix nuts and other textured ingredients into a batter with the paddle attachment instead of folding them in by hand.

▶ If you are coating a pan with nuts or other textured ingredients like sesame seeds, butter the pan heavily so the mixture will adhere.

▶ If you are sprinkling nuts or candy over the batter, do not press them in too deeply, or they will sink as the batter bakes.

▶ If a cake has a sticky filling or a textured coating on the pan, invert the hot cake when it is done and do not remove the pan for 5 minutes. This allows the cake to shrink from the sides of the pan and prevents sticking.

▶ Cakes that have crisp baked toppings keep better if they are not dusted with confectioners' sugar. The sugar will melt and soften the topping.

HAZELNUT TORTE WITH MERINGUE TOPPING

AT A GLANCE

SERVES: 6 to 8
PAN: 9″ springform
PAN PREP: Butter/
parchment
OVEN TEMP: 350°—
cake; 275°—
meringue
RACK LEVEL: Lower
third
BAKING TIME: cake—
35 to 40 minutes;
meringue—40
minutes; plus 1
hour for oven
cooling
METHOD: Electric
mixer/food
processor

Here is my version of a lovely hazelnut torte recipe given to me by my very dear friend Valerie Michaels, of Chorley Wood, Herts, a suburb of London.

To her simple, unadorned original, I've added a meringue topping, which is baked slowly until golden brown and crusty. This gives the cake a more elegant look.

The batter does not contain flour and therefore can be sensitive to work with. Be sure to follow carefully the directions for incorporating the eggs, as the procedure is essential to the cake's success. The torte may be made with pecans or toasted almonds in place of hazelnuts, if you wish.

THE CAKE:

1/2 pound shelled hazelnuts
2 large whole eggs
4 large eggs yolks
2/3 cup superfine or strained sugar
1 teaspoon vanilla extract
4 large eggs whites
1/8 teaspoon cream of tartar

THE MERINGUE TOPPING:

2 large egg whites
  Pinch of salt
1/4 teaspoon lemon juice
8 tablespoons superfine or strained sugar
1/2 teaspoon vanilla extract
1/2 teaspoon cocoa powder for garnish

1. Position rack in the lower third of the oven and preheat to 325°. Butter a 9-inch springform and line the bottom with parchment paper.
2. Put the nuts in a shallow pan. Toast for 15 minutes, or until the skins pop. Empty the hot nuts onto a double thickness of paper toweling or a clean dish towel and rub with the towel to

remove skins (page 58). When the nuts are cool, place in the bowl of a food processor fitted with the steel blade and process until chopped very fine, about 30 seconds. Set aside. Increase the oven temperature to 350°.

3. To make the cake: Place one whole egg and the egg yolks in the small bowl of an electric mixer fitted with beaters or the whip attachment. On medium speed, beat until light in color and thickened, about 3 minutes. Gradually add the sugar, 1 tablespoon at a time, taking about 2 to 3 minutes to blend it in well. Reduce speed to medium-low. Blend in the vanilla and remove the bowl from the mixer. Transfer mixture to a large mixing bowl and set aside.

4. In a separate small bowl beat the remaining whole egg with a whisk or rotary beater until foamy. Using a 2¾-inch-wide rubber spatula, fold the nuts into the yolk/sugar mixture alternately with the beaten whole egg, dividing the nuts into three parts and the whole egg into two parts, starting and ending with the nuts. Mix only until incorporated after each addition. Scrape the sides of the bowl as necessary.

5. In a large bowl of an electric mixer fitted with beaters or the whip attachment, beat the egg whites on medium speed until frothy. Add the cream of tartar. Increase the speed to medium-high and continue to beat until the whites stand in shiny, firm peaks but are not dry (page 49).

6. Remove the bowl from the mixer. Using a 2¾-inch-wide rubber spatula, fold ⅓ of the beaten egg whites into the nut batter, taking about 20 turns to lighten (pages 52–53). Then add the remaining egg whites, taking an additional 40 turns.

7. Pour the batter into the prepared pan. Center the pan on the rack and bake in the preheated oven for 35 to 40 minutes or until the torte begins to come away from the sides of the pan, is lightly browned on top, and springs back on top when touched with a finger.

8. Remove from the oven and place the pan on a cake rack to cool completely. Although the torte rises to the top of the pan, it will shrink at least 1 inch upon cooling. Run a sharp knife around the edge of the pan, then remove the side. Invert the cake onto a cookie sheet lined with parchment paper, and carefully peel off the parchment paper from the bottom.

9. Reduce the oven temperature to 275°.

10. To make the meringue: Put the egg whites in the large bowl of

an electric mixer fitted with beaters or the whip attachment. Beat on medium speed until frothy, and add the salt and lemon juice. Increase the speed to medium-high and beat until the mixture stands in firm peaks. Add 7 *tablespoons* of the sugar, 1 tablespoon at a time, taking about 2 minutes to blend. Add vanilla. Continue beating about 1½ to 2 minutes longer until the whites are stiff and glossy. Remove bowl from the mixer. Fold in the remaining *1 tablespoon* of sugar.

11. Spread the meringue topping around the sides of the cake using an offset, or flat, metal spatula, then cover the top. Run a pastry comb or the tines of a fork in a wave pattern around the sides and top of the torte. Center the pan on the rack and bake in a 275° oven for about 40 minutes, or until the meringue is firm to the touch and slightly brown in color.

12. Turn off the oven and allow the cake to cool in the oven, with the door closed, for 1 hour to crisp the meringue. Remove from the oven, set the pan on a cake rack, and cool the cake completely. Place cocoa in a strainer and sprinkle over cake. With a spatula gently lift the cake from the parchment paper and place on a cake platter.

STORAGE: When stored airtight, meringue will sweat and become soft from condensation. In order to prevent this, store under a glass dome with a kitchen utensil wedged underneath it to keep it slightly ajar. This will allow air to circulate around the torte. The cake may also be loosely covered with aluminum foil. Store at room temperature for up to 5 days.

SERVING SUGGESTIONS: This torte is super with Chocolate Whipped Cream (page 488), garnished with a few fresh raspberries. It is also delicious with one of the Fresh Fruit Toppings (pages 482–85).

SNOW-CAPPED CHOCOLATE CREAM CAKE

In this unusual cake, coarsely cut nonpareil candies are sprinkled over the top of a chocolate whipped cream batter. As the cake bakes, the candy sinks slightly and forms a rippled surface with an attractive snow-capped effect.

Be sure to purchase a fine-quality chocolate nonpareil, such as those sold in specialty candy stores. Do not try to chop them in the processor; too many of the tiny beads will separate from the wafer, while the candy will remain almost whole. Even with a minimum of handling some beads will fall from the candies. Put aside these extra beads to sprinkle over the top of the glazed cake.

▽

AT A GLANCE

SERVES: 10 to 12
PAN: 9″ × 13″ × 2″ oblong
PAN PREP: Butter
OVEN TEMP: 350°
RACK LEVEL: Lower third
BAKING TIME: 40 to 45 minutes
METHOD: Electric mixer

1	cup (6 ounces) semisweet chocolate nonpareil candies
4	ounces semisweet chocolate, such as Lindt Excellence, Tobler Tradition, or Baker's German's Sweet, broken into pieces
1/4	cup hot water
2	teaspoons instant espresso
2	cups sifted cake flour
1 1/2	teaspoons baking powder
1/8	teaspoon baking soda
3	large eggs
1 1/4	cups superfine or strained sugar
1 1/2	teaspoons vanilla extract
1 1/4	cups heavy cream, whipped to firm peaks
1	recipe Quick Chocolate Glaze for a small cake (page 462)

1. Position rack in the lower third of the oven and preheat to 350°. Butter a 9″ × 13″ × 2″ oblong pan.
2. Cut the nonpareil candies by hand into 1/4- to 1/2-inch pieces, and set aside.
3. Put the chocolate, hot water, and espresso in a small dish. Melt in the microwave on medium power, or set the dish in a skillet containing 1/2 inch of hot water. Stir until the chocolate melts. Blend with a whisk until completely smooth. Set aside to cool.

Quick and Easy Cakes

149

4. Using a triple sifter, sift together the flour, baking powder, and baking soda. Set aside.
5. Place the eggs in the large bowl of an electric mixer fitted with beaters or whip attachment. Beat on medium-high speed until light in color and thickened, approximately 2 minutes. Add the sugar, 1 tablespoon at a time, taking about 3 to 4 minutes to blend it in well.
6. Reduce mixer speed to low. Add the vanilla. Blend in the melted chocolate, mixing just until incorporated. Scrape the sides of the bowl as necessary.
7. Add the dry ingredients alternately with the whipped cream, dividing the flour mixture into three parts and the cream into two parts, and starting and ending with the flour. Mix just until incorporated after each addition. Scrape the sides of the bowl as necessary.
8. Spoon the batter into the buttered pan and smooth the surface with the back of a tablespoon. Sprinkle the nonpareils evenly over the top, but do not press them into the batter. Place the pan in the center of the rack and bake in the preheated oven for 40 to 45 minutes, or until the cake is springy to the touch and begins to come away from the sides of the pan.
9. Remove the cake from the oven and place the pan on a cake rack to cool to room temperature. Prepare the chocolate glaze using the small cake measurements. Dip a teaspoon into the glaze and drizzle randomly over the top of the cake. Be sure to leave parts of the rippled surface of the cake exposed. Immediately sprinkle the extra nonpareil beads over the cake. Shake the pan two or three times so the beads will cling to the glaze. Cut the cake into squares just before serving.

STORAGE: Cover the top of the pan with aluminum foil and store at room temperature for up to 5 days.

🌰 PIGNOLI LEMON CAKE

....

Pignolis, pine nuts, or Indian nuts—whatever you choose to call these small, cream-colored oval nuts—are versatile and delicious. Recipes containing pignolis usually come from countries along the Mediterranean and Balkan Seas, where they adorn all sorts of baked goods in addition to providing an accent in a variety of savory dishes and salads.

This cake is pleasingly tart, with a smooth-textured crumb and a sugar-glazed surface.

....

1	cup shelled pignolis
2¼	cups sifted cake flour
1	teaspoon baking powder
½	teaspoon baking soda
¼	teaspoon salt
½	cup (1 stick) unsalted butter
1½ to 2	teaspoons freshly grated lemon rind
1⅓	cups superfine or strained sugar
2	large egg yolks
2	large whole eggs
1	tablespoon fresh lemon juice
1	teaspoon vanilla extract
1	cup unsweetened plain low-fat yogurt

1. Position rack in the lower third of the oven and preheat to 325°. Generously butter a 10-inch bundt pan. Dust heavily with granulated sugar, invert over the kitchen sink, and tap to remove excess.
2. Place the pignolis in a shallow pan and toast for 6 to 8 minutes. Watch carefully so that they don't burn. Set aside to cool. Increase oven temperature to 350°.
3. Using a triple sifter, sift together the flour, baking powder, baking soda, and salt. Set aside.
4. Cut the butter into 1-inch pieces and place in the large bowl of an electric mixer fitted with beaters or the paddle attachment, add the lemon rind, and soften on low speed. Increase to medium-high and cream until smooth and light in color, about 1½ to 2 minutes.

▽

AT A GLANCE

SERVES: 10 to 12
PAN: 10″ bundt
(12-cup capacity)
PAN PREP: Well
buttered/sugared
OVEN TEMP: 350°
RACK LEVEL: Lower
third
BAKING TIME: 50 to
55 minutes
METHOD: Electric
mixer

....

Quick and Easy Cakes

5. Add the sugar, 1 tablespoon at a time, taking about 6 to 8 minutes to blend it in well. Scrape the sides of the bowl as necessary.

6. Add the egg yolks and beat for 1 minute, scraping the sides of the bowl occasionally. Add the whole eggs at 1-minute intervals. Beat for 1 minute longer. Blend in the lemon juice and vanilla.

7. Reduce mixer speed to low. Add the dry ingredients alternately with the yogurt, dividing the flour mixture into three parts and the yogurt into two parts, starting and ending with the flour. Mix just until incorporated after each addition. Scrape the sides of the bowl as necessary, and mix for 10 seconds longer.

8. Remove the bowl from the mixer. Fold in the pignolis.

9. Spoon the cake batter into the sugar-coated pan, smoothing the surface with the back of a tablespoon. Center the pan on the rack and bake in the preheated oven for 50 to 55 minutes, or until the cake begins to come away from the sides of the pan. A twig of straw or a toothpick inserted into the center should come out dry.

10. Remove the cake from the oven. Set on a cake rack to cool for 15 to 20 minutes, then invert the cake onto the rack. Gently remove the pan and allow the cake to cool completely. When ready to serve, cut into 1-inch slices.

STORAGE: Store the cake at room temperature under a glass dome or in an airtight container for up to 5 days.

Sour Cream Coffee Cakes

Sour cream coffee cakes are like old friends. They are among the most popular types of cakes baked in home kitchens and always turn up whenever an assortment of pastries is displayed, even on the dessert carts of fine restaurants. Sour cream is a marvelous complement to most butter cake batters. When it is combined with sugar, the sweet and the sour create a perfect flavor balance.

Sour cream coffee cakes are often baked in a fluted ring pan such as a kugelhopf, Turk's head, or bundt, and filled with a combination of brown and white sugars, nuts, cinnamon, and sometimes raisins, currants, chocolate chips, thinly sliced apples, or jam. A sprinkling of powdered sugar over the top of the cake outlines the ripples as the sugar falls at random down the sides.

Other popular pans are angel food or loaf pans. Sour cream cakes that are baked in these pans often have a crisp crumb topping made from reserved filling.

In the coffee cake recipes that follow, the first is the least rich, the second is moderately rich, and the third is the richest. As the amount of butter, eggs, and sour cream that the batter contains increases in quantity, the flavor of the cake is fuller and the crumb becomes more compact and velvety.

These three sour cream batters make wonderful bases for experimenting. Try your hand at mixing and matching fillings. This is such a versatile cake medium, one can hardly miss coming up with a winning combination.

🍂 SOUR CREAM COFFEE CAKE

A wonderful coffee cake classic, this is the least rich of the sour cream coffee cake recipes in this book. Since the batter is made with a smaller ratio of butter, the cake has a lighter texture than most. The filling contains mini chocolate chips, but you may omit them if you wish.

THE FILLING:
- ⅔ cup walnuts or pecans
- ¼ cup granulated sugar
- 2 tablespoons unsweetened cocoa
- 1 teaspoon ground cinnamon
- ¼ cup mini chocolate chips

THE CAKE:
- 2 cups sifted cake flour
- 1 teaspoon baking powder
- ¼ teaspoon baking soda
- ½ teaspoon salt
- ⅓ cup (⅔ stick) unsalted butter
- 1 cup superfine or strained sugar
- 2 large eggs
- 1 teaspoon vanilla extract
- 1 cup sour cream

1. Position rack in the lower third of the oven and preheat to 350°. Butter a 8½-inch fluted ring pan and dust the pan with all-purpose flour. Invert pan over the kitchen sink and tap to remove excess flour.
2. To make the filling: Place the nuts, sugar, cocoa, and cinnamon in the bowl of a food processor fitted with the steel blade. Pulse 6 to 8 times, or until the nuts are chopped into medium-sized pieces. Transfer to a bowl, combine with the chocolate chips, and set aside.
3. To make the cake: Using a triple sifter, sift the flour, baking powder, baking soda, and salt together. Set aside.
4. Cut the butter into 1-inch pieces and put them in the large bowl

of an electric mixer fitted with beaters or paddle attachment. Soften on low speed. Increase the speed to medium-high and cream until smooth and light in color, about 1½ to 2 minutes.

5. Add the sugar, 1 tablespoon at a time, taking about 6 to 8 minutes to blend it in well. Scrape the sides of the bowl occasionally.

6. Add the eggs, 1 at a time at 1-minute intervals, scraping the sides of the bowl as necessary. Beat for 1 minute longer. Blend in the vanilla.

7. Reduce the mixer speed to low. Add the dry ingredients alternately with the sour cream, dividing the flour mixture into three parts and the sour cream into two parts, starting and ending with the flour. Mix just until incorporated after each addition. Scrape the sides of the bowl occasionally. Mix for 10 seconds longer. Remove the bowl from the mixer.

8. Spoon about ¼ of the batter into the bottom of the fluted pan. Smooth the surface with the back of a rounded tablespoon. Sprinkle ⅓ of the chocolate/nut mixture over the batter. Spoon another ¼ of the batter into the pan, spreading the batter from the center out. Except at the top layer, it is important that all of the filling be covered with batter. Repeat, alternating batter and filling, ending with a layer of batter. You should have four layers of batter and three of the chocolate/nut mixture.

9. To marbleize the batter: Using a table knife, cut into the batter almost to the bottom of the pan. Gently fold about 8 times, rotating the pan in a complete circle. Smooth the top of the cake with the bottom of a tablespoon.

10. Center the pan on the rack and bake in the preheated oven for 55 to 60 minutes, or until the cake is golden brown on top and begins to come away from the sides of the pan. A twig of straw or a toothpick inserted into the center should come out clean. Remove the cake from the oven and cool in the pan on a rack. After 15 to 20 minutes invert the cake onto the rack and carefully lift off the pan. Allow the cake to cool completely. Just before serving, dust with confectioners' sugar.

STORAGE: Store the cake at room temperature under a glass dome or in an airtight container for up to 5 days.

🍂 RICH SOUR CREAM COFFEE CAKE

This recipe is slightly richer and smoother-textured than the previous cake because it contains more butter.

When marbleizing this cake, cut through the batter with a table knife instead of folding the batter and filling together. This gives the filling a more layered effect, whereas the other method tends to blend it through the batter.

AT A GLANCE

SERVES: 10 to 12
PAN: 9″ fluted ring (10-cup capacity)
PAN PREP: Butter/flour
OVEN TEMP: 350°
RACK LEVEL: Lower third
BAKING TIME: 60 to 65 minutes
METHOD: Electric mixer/food processor

THE FILLING:

1	cup walnuts or pecans
1/4	cup granulated sugar
1/4	cup light brown sugar, lightly packed
2	teaspoons ground cinnamon
1/2	cup plumped currants (page 63)

THE CAKE:

2 1/4	cups sifted cake flour
2	teaspoons baking powder
1/4	teaspoon baking soda
1/2	teaspoon salt
2/3	cup (1 1/3 sticks) unsalted butter
1	cup superfine or strained sugar
2	large eggs
1	teaspoon vanilla extract
1	cup sour cream

1. Position rack in the lower third of the oven and preheat to 350°. Butter a 9-inch fluted ring pan. Dust the pan with all-purpose flour, then invert pan over the kitchen sink and tap to remove excess.
2. To make the filling: Place the walnuts, sugars, and cinnamon in the bowl of a food processor fitted with the steel blade. Pulse 6 to 8 times or until nuts are medium chopped. Transfer to a bowl and stir in the currants. Set aside.
3. To make the cake: Sift together the flour, baking powder, baking soda, and salt in a triple sifter. Set aside.
4. Cut the butter into 1-inch pieces and place in the large bowl of

an electric mixer fitted with beaters or the paddle attachment to soften on low speed. Increase the speed to medium-high and cream until smooth and light in color, about 1½ to 2 minutes.

5. Add the sugar, 1 tablespoon at a time, taking about 6 to 8 minutes to blend it in well. Scrape the sides of the bowl occasionally.

6. Add the eggs, 1 at a time at 1-minute intervals, scraping the sides of the bowl as necessary. Beat for about 1 minute longer. Blend in the vanilla.

7. Reduce mixer speed to low. Add the dry ingredients alternately with the sour cream, dividing the flour mixture into three parts and the sour cream into two parts, starting and ending with the flour. Mix just until incorporated after each addition. Scrape the sides of the bowl as necessary and mix for 10 seconds longer.

8. Spoon about ¼ of the batter into the bottom of the prepared pan, smoothing the surface with the back of a tablespoon. Sprinkle ⅓ of the nut/currant mixture over the batter. Spoon another ¼ of the batter into the pan, spreading it from the center out. Except at the top layer, it is important that all of the filling be covered with batter. Repeat, alternating batter and filling, ending with a layer of the batter. You should have four layers of batter and three of the nut/currant filling.

9. To marbleize the batter: Insert the tip of a table knife straight down into the batter, going almost to the bottom of the pan. Holding the knife upright, gently run the blade around the pan twice at 1-inch intervals. Smooth the top of the cake with the bottom of a tablespoon.

10. Center the pan on the rack and bake in the preheated oven for 60 to 65 minutes, or until the cake is golden brown on top and begins to come away from the sides of the pan. A twig of straw or a toothpick inserted into the center of the cake should come out clean.

11. Remove the cake from the oven and place on a rack to set for 15 to 20 minutes, then invert the cake onto the rack and gently remove the pan. Allow the cake to cool completely. If desired, dust the top of the cake with confectioners' sugar just before serving.

STORAGE: Store at room temperature under a glass domed cover or in an airtight container for up to 5 days.

DOUBLE-RICH SOUR CREAM COFFEE CAKE

AT A GLANCE

SERVES: 10 to 12
PAN: 10″ bundt
(12-cup capacity)
PAN PREP: Well
buttered/floured
OVEN TEMP: 350°
RACK LEVEL: Lower
third
BAKING TIME: 60 to
65 minutes
METHOD: Electric
mixer/food
processor

Lots of butter and sour cream give this coffee cake its decadently rich flavor and extra-velvety texture. Its dense nut filling moistened with apricot preserves is layered in rather than marbleized. Use a fine-quality preserve as it will contain more of the fruit pulp and is less watery. The filling becomes chewier as it bakes.

A filling made with jam needs a thick batter such as this. If the batter is too thin, the filling will sink to the bottom of the pan and stick. Be sure to grease the pan well.

THE FILLING:

1¼	cups walnuts or pecans
⅓	cup light brown sugar, lightly packed
1	teaspoon ground cinnamon
½	cup apricot preserves

THE CAKE:

2½	cups sifted cake flour
1	teaspoon baking powder
1	teaspoon baking soda
½	teaspoon salt
1	cup (2 sticks) unsalted butter
1⅓	cups superfine or strained sugar
3	large eggs
1½	teaspoons vanilla extract
1⅓	cups sour cream

1. Position rack in the lower third of the oven and preheat to 350°. Generously butter a 10-inch bundt pan. Dust the pan with all-purpose flour, then invert over the kitchen sink and tap to remove excess.

2. To make the filling: Place the nuts, brown sugar, cinnamon, and preserves in the bowl of a food processor fitted with the steel blade. Pulse 6 to 8 times or until the nuts are chopped medium and the ingredients are combined into a sticky mass. Do not overprocess. Remove from the bowl and set aside.

3. To make the cake: Sift together the flour, baking powder, baking soda, and salt in a triple sifter. Set aside.

4. Cut the butter into 1-inch pieces, place in the large bowl of an electric mixer fitted with beaters or paddle attachment, and soften on low speed. Increase the speed to medium-high and cream until smooth and light in color, about 1½ to 2 minutes.

5. Add the sugar, 1 tablespoon at a time, taking about 6 to 8 minutes to blend it in well. Scrape the sides of the bowl occasionally.

6. Add the eggs, 1 at a time at 1-minute intervals, scraping the sides of the bowl as necessary. Beat for about 1 minute longer. Blend in the vanilla.

7. Reduce the mixer speed to low. Add the dry ingredients alternately with the sour cream, dividing the flour mixture into three parts and the sour cream into two parts, starting and ending with the flour. Mix only until incorporated after each addition. Scrape the sides of the bowl occasionally and mix for 10 seconds longer.

8. Spoon about ½ of the batter into the bottom of the bundt pan, smoothing the surface with the back of a tablespoon. Using your fingertips, distribute ⅓ of the filling evenly over the batter as best you can. Do not try to spread it with a spoon. Spoon ½ of the remaining batter into the pan, then cover with the remaining filling. Cover with the remaining batter, spreading evenly over the filling from the center out. It is important that the last layer of filling be completely covered with batter. *Do not run a knife through this batter.*

9. Center the pan on the rack and bake in the preheated oven for 60 to 65 minutes, or until the cake is golden brown on top and begins to come away from the sides of the pan. A twig of straw or a toothpick inserted into the center should come out clean.

10. Remove the cake from the oven and cool the cake in the pan on a rack. After 10 to 15 minutes, invert the cake onto the rack and gently remove the pan. Allow the cake to cool completely. Just before serving, dust the top with confectioners' sugar.

STORAGE: Store the cake at room temperature under a glass dome or in an airtight container for up to 5 days.

OATMEAL CAKE WITH CRUNCHY BROILED TOPPING

AT A GLANCE

SERVES: 10 to 12
PAN: 9″ × 13″ × 2″ oblong
PAN PREP: Butter
OVEN TEMP: 350°
RACK LEVEL: Lower third
BAKING TIME: 40 to 45 minutes
METHOD: Electric mixer

Cooked oatmeal added to this batter makes a tasty and wonderfully moist coffee cake. The baked cake receives a delightful nut, brown sugar, and coconut topping, which is caramelized briefly under the broiler. It's the perfect complement to the slightly nutty flavor of the oatmeal.

1¼	cups boiling water
1	cup instant oatmeal
1½	cups sifted unbleached all-purpose flour
1	teaspoon baking soda
1	teaspoon salt
1	teaspoon ground cinnamon
½	teaspoon ground nutmeg
½	cup (1 stick) unsalted butter
½	teaspoon freshly grated lemon rind
¾	cup granulated sugar
¾	cup light brown sugar, lightly packed
2	large eggs
1	teaspoon vanilla extract
1	recipe Broiled Topping (page 480)

1. In a medium saucepan, bring the water to a boil. Add the oatmeal. Return to a boil and cook for 1 minute. Set aside.
2. Position rack in the lower third of the oven and preheat to 350°. Butter a 9″ × 13″ × 2″ oblong cake pan.
3. Sift flour, baking soda, salt, and spices together in a triple sifter. Set aside.
4. Cut the butter into 1-inch pieces and place in the large bowl of an electric mixer fitted with beaters or the paddle attachment. Add the lemon rind. Soften on low speed, then increase speed to medium-high and cream until smooth and light in color, about 1½ to 2 minutes.
5. Add the granulated sugar, 1 tablespoon at a time, taking 3 to 4

utes to blend it in well. Add the light brown sugar over an additional 3 to 4 minutes. Scrape sides of bowl as necessary.

6. Add the eggs, 1 at a time at 1-minute intervals, scraping sides of the bowl. Blend in the cooled oatmeal and the vanilla.

7. Reduce mixer speed to medium-low. Add the dry ingredients all at once, and mix for 30 seconds longer, scraping the bowl as necessary.

8. Spoon the batter into the prepared pan and smooth the surface with the back of a tablespoon.

9. Bake in the preheated oven for 40 to 45 minutes or until the cake is springy to the touch and begins to come away from the side of the pan. Remove cake from oven and let stand 10 minutes.

10. Prepare broiled topping. Spoon warm topping over the cake, spreading it gently with the back of a tablespoon as best you can. Take care not to tear cake.

11. Set oven temperature to broil and return cake to oven. Broil for 45 to 60 seconds, or until the topping bubbles and turns golden brown. *Watch carefully to avoid burning.*

12. Remove the cake from the oven and set on a cake rack to cool. When ready to serve, cut cake into squares.

STORAGE: Cover the cake lightly with aluminum foil and store at room temperature for up to 5 days.

❧ PRALINE CRUNCH CAKE

P raline, a candy made by caramelizing pecans with sugar, is traditional to New Orleans Creole cuisine. In this recipe, the candy is crushed and stirred into the buttery brown sugar batter along with additional chopped pecans. The batter is then marbleized with a crunchy pecan filling. This is a pecan lover's dream.

AT A GLANCE

SERVES: 8 to 10
PAN: 8½″ fluted
ring (8-cup capacity)
PAN PREP:
Butter/flour
OVEN TEMP: 350°
RACK LEVEL: Lower
third
BAKING TIME: 45 to
50 minutes
METHOD: Electric
mixer/food
processor

THE NUT FILLING:

1	cup pecans
¼	cup granulated sugar
¼	cup light brown sugar
2	teaspoons ground cinnamon

THE CAKE:

2	cups sifted cake flour
1	teaspoon baking soda
¼	teaspoon salt
½	cup (1 stick) unsalted butter
1	cup light brown sugar, lightly packed
2	large eggs
1	teaspoon vanilla extract
¾	cup buttermilk
½	cup crushed praline (page 498)
½	cup pecans, chopped medium-fine

1. Position rack in the lower third of the oven and preheat to 350°. Butter an 8½-inch fluted ring pan and dust with all-purpose flour. Invert the pan over the kitchen sink and tap to remove excess flour.
2. To make the filling: Place nuts, sugars, and cinnamon in the container of a food processor fitted with a steel blade. Pulse 6 to 8 times or until the nuts are medium chopped. Transfer to a small bowl and set aside.
3. To make the cake: Sift flour, baking soda, and salt together in a triple sifter. Set aside.
4. Cut the butter into 1-inch pieces and put them in the large bowl of an electric mixer fitted with beaters or paddle attachment.

Soften on low speed, then increase to medium-high and cream until smooth and light in color, about 1½ to 2 minutes.

5. Add brown sugar, 1 tablespoon at a time, taking 6 to 8 minutes to blend it in well. Scrape sides of bowl occasionally.

6. Add the eggs, 1 at a time at 1-minute intervals, scraping sides of bowl as necessary. Beat for 1 minute longer. Blend in vanilla.

7. Reduce mixer speed to low. Add the flour mixture alternately with buttermilk, dividing the dry ingredients into three parts and liquid into two parts, starting and ending with the flour. Scrape sides of bowl and mix for 10 seconds longer. Remove the bowl from mixer. Fold in the crushed praline and chopped pecans.

8. Spoon about ⅓ of the batter into the bottom of the prepared pan. Sprinkle with ½ of the chopped nut filling. Repeat, alternating batter and filling, ending with a layer of batter. You should have three layers of batter and two layers of nut filling.

9. To marbleize the batter: Using a table knife, cut into the batter almost to the bottom of the pan. Rotating the pan, gently fold about 8 times.

10. Bake in the preheated oven for 45 to 50 minutes, or until the cake begins to leave sides of pan. A twig of straw or a toothpick inserted into center will come out dry.

11. Remove the cake from oven and place the pan on a cake rack to cool for 10 to 15 minutes. Invert onto the rack and gently remove the pan. Allow the cake to cool completely. Just before serving, dust the top of the cake with confectioners' sugar, if you wish. When ready to serve cut into 1-inch slices.

STORAGE: Cover with a glass cake dome and store at room temperature for up to 4 days.

✤ HOLIDAY HONEY CAKE

AT A GLANCE

SERVES: 8 to 10
PAN: 8″ flat-bottomed tube pan (2-quart capacity)
PAN PREP: Butter/flour
OVEN TEMP: 350°
RACK LEVEL: Lower third
BAKING TIME: 50 to 55 minutes
METHOD: Hand

This moist, aromatic cake is richly flavored with spices, orange rind, and a hint of Cognac. You may substitute any nut you choose for the almonds.

While honey cake is traditionally enjoyed in Jewish homes during the holiday of Rosh Hashanah, it is also popular in many countries that border the Mediterranean Sea. It is especially pleasing when accompanied by fresh autumn fruits.

1	tablespoon freeze-dried coffee
2/3	cup boiling water
3/4	cup honey
2	tablespoons Grand Marnier, Cointreau, or Triple Sec
1	tablespoon dark molasses
2	cups sifted cake flour
1 1/4	teaspoons baking powder
1/2	teaspoon baking soda
1/4	teaspoon salt
1/2	cup sugar
3/4	teaspoon ground cinnamon
1/4	teaspoon powdered cloves
1/4	teaspoon ground nutmeg
2	large egg yolks
2	tablespoons vegetable oil
1	teaspoon freshly grated navel orange rind
2	large egg whites
1/8	teaspoon cream of tartar
3/4	cup lightly toasted sliced almonds (page 58)

1. Position rack in the lower third of the oven and preheat to 350°. Butter an 8-inch flat-bottomed tube pan and dust with all-purpose flour. Invert it over the kitchen sink to tap out excess flour.
2. Place the coffee in a small bowl. Add the boiling water and stir until dissolved. In another small bowl, combine the honey, Grand Marnier, and molasses. Add the hot coffee, stir well, and set aside.

3. Sift together the flour, baking powder, baking soda, salt, sugar, and spices into a large mixing bowl.

4. Make a well in the center of the flour and add egg yolks, oil, orange rind, and coffee/honey mixture. Blend with a wire whisk until batter is very smooth.

5. In a small bowl beat egg whites with a rotary beater or hand-held mixer until frothy. Add cream of tartar and continue beating until whites form firm, moist peaks. Fold 1/4 of the whites into the batter, taking about 10 turns. Crush the toasted almonds with your hand (see Note) into smaller pieces and sprinkle over batter while folding in remaining whites, taking about 40 turns to incorporate.

6. Pour the batter into the prepared pan. Bake for 50 to 55 minutes, until the cake begins to leave sides of pan and a twig of straw or a toothpick inserted into the center comes out dry. If the cake is browning too fast, cover it loosely with aluminum foil for the last 10 minutes of baking.

7. Remove the cake from the oven and set the pan on a cake rack to cool and set for 10 to 15 minutes. Invert cake onto a rack and remove pan. Continue to cool to room temperature. This cake is best if allowed to mature at least 24 hours before slicing. When ready to serve, cut into 1/2-inch slices with a serrated knife, using a back-and-forth sawing motion.

STORAGE: Wrap in plastic wrap or aluminum foil. Store at room temperature for up to 5 days or refrigerate for up to 10 days.

NOTE: Sliced almonds can be easily crushed with your hand. If substituting slivered almonds or other nuts, chop them to medium size.

✿ MAPLE WALNUT CAKE

*D*uring the early years of my marriage, I lived in Burlington, Vermont, and learned to appreciate the beauty of Vermont's sugar maple trees. In the early spring, when the snow still chills the ground, the sap from the trees begins to run. Among the workers it is traditional to celebrate the end of the tapping season at "sugar-in-snow" parties, where the intensely sweet hot syrup is poured over clean white snow to form a candylike maple ice enjoyed by children and adults alike.

Maple sap is processed into several grades of syrup. Fancy Grade, which is light amber in color with a delicate flavor, is considered prime, but many native Vermonters prefer the stronger-flavored Grade A. If you have the opportunity, try this thick sweet syrup. I, too, think it has more character.

Although I recommend that you make this with pure Vermont maple syrup, you may substitute any store brand of genuine (not imitation) maple syrup. I think you'll find the combination of walnuts and maple syrup intriguing. This cake does not just appeal to adults. As with the maple ice, children will love it too.

················

2/3	cup sour cream
2/3	cup maple syrup
1/4	teaspoon baking soda
2 1/2	cups sifted cake flour
2	teaspoons baking powder
1/2	teaspoon salt
3/4	cup (1 1/2 sticks) unsalted butter
1/2	cup granulated sugar
2/3	cup light brown sugar, lightly packed
3	large eggs
1 1/2	teaspoons vanilla extract
1/2	teaspoon imitation maple extract
1 1/2	cups walnuts, chopped medium-fine

1. Position a rack in the lower third of the oven and preheat to 350°. Butter a 10-inch bundt pan, dust the pan with all-purpose flour, and invert it over the kitchen sink to tap out excess.

2. In a small bowl whisk together the sour cream, maple syrup, and baking soda. Set aside.

3. Using a triple sifter, sift together the flour, baking powder, and salt. Set aside.

4. Cut the butter into 1-inch pieces and place it in the large bowl of an electric mixer fitted with beaters or paddle attachment to soften on low speed. Increase to medium-high and cream until smooth and light in color, about 1½ to 2 minutes.

5. Add the granulated sugar, 1 tablespoon at a time, taking about 3 to 4 minutes to blend it in well. Then add the light brown sugar, 1 tablespoon at a time, taking an additional 3 to 4 minutes. Scrape the sides of the bowl as necessary.

6. Add the eggs, 1 at a time at 1-minute intervals, scraping the sides of the bowl. Blend in the vanilla and maple extracts.

7. Reduce mixer speed to low. Add the dry ingredients, alternating with the sour cream mixture, dividing the flour mixture into three parts and the sour cream into two parts, starting and ending with the flour. Mix just until incorporated after each addition. Scrape the sides of the bowl as necessary, and mix for 10 seconds longer.

8. Remove the bowl from the mixer and fold in the walnuts with a rubber spatula. Spoon the batter into the prepared pan, smoothing the surface with the back of a tablespoon. Center the pan on the rack and bake in the preheated oven for 55 to 60 minutes, or until the cake begins to come away from the sides of the pan and a twig of straw or a toothpick inserted into the center comes out dry.

9. Remove the cake from the oven. Set it on a cake rack to cool for 15 to 20 minutes. Invert the cake onto the rack and gently lift the pan off the cake. While the cake is still slightly warm, frost with Vanilla Glaze (page 461), flavored with ½ teaspoon imitation maple extract using the large-cake measurements. Or, simply dust the top of the cake with confectioners' sugar just before serving.

STORAGE: Store the cake at room temperature under a glass dome or in an airtight container for up to 5 days.

🌰 SESAME ALMOND SWIRL

A crumb mixture of sesame seeds, almonds, and Amaretti biscuits dusted onto a fluted cake pan bakes into a crunchy topping. The same crumb mixture is sprinkled throughout the tasty amaretto liqueur–flavored batter. Second helpings will be hard to resist.

AT A GLANCE

SERVES: 10 to 12
PAN: 9″ fluted ring
(10-cup capacity)
PAN PREP:
Generously
buttered/nut
crumbs
OVEN TEMP: 350°
RACK LEVEL: Lower
third
BAKING TIME: 60 to
65 minutes
METHOD: Electric
mixer/food
processor

THE FILLING:

1/2	cup sesame seeds
2/3	cup sliced almonds
6	Amaretti biscuits, broken, about 1/4 cup
1/4	cup sugar

THE CAKE:

2 1/3	cups sifted cake flour
1 1/2	teaspoons baking powder
1/4	teaspoon baking soda
1/2	teaspoon salt
2/3	cup (1 1/3 sticks) unsalted butter
1 1/4	cups superfine or strained sugar
3	large eggs
1	teaspoon vanilla extract
1/2	teaspoon almond extract
1	cup sour cream
1/4	cup amaretto liqueur

1. Position a rack in the lower third of the oven and preheat to 325°.
2. To make the filling: Place the sesame seeds in a shallow pan and bake for 4 to 5 minutes, or until lightly brown. Transfer to a small bowl and set aside. Toast almonds for 6 to 8 minutes, or until lightly brown.
3. Put the toasted almonds, broken Amaretti biscuits, and sugar in the container of a food processor fitted with the steel blade. Pulse until finely chopped. Transfer to a bowl and stir in the sesame seeds.
4. Increase the oven temperature to 350°. Using about 2 table-spoons of very soft butter, heavily grease a 9-inch fluted ring pan. Sprinkle 1/4 cup of the nut/crumb filling evenly over the pan, setting the remainder aside. Refrigerate the pan while preparing the batter.

5. To make the cake: Using a triple sifter, sift together the flour, baking powder, baking soda, and salt. Set aside.

6. Cut the butter into 1-inch pieces and place in the large bowl of an electric mixer fitted with beaters or paddle attachment. Soften on low speed. Increase to medium-high and cream until smooth and light in color, about 1½ to 2 minutes.

7. Add the sugar, 1 tablespoon at a time, taking about 6 to 8 minutes to blend it in well. Scrape the sides of the bowl as necessary.

8. Add the eggs, 1 at a time at 1-minute intervals, scraping the sides of the bowl as needed. Blend in the vanilla and almond extracts.

9. Reduce mixer speed to low. Combine the sour cream and the amaretto liqueur. Add the dry ingredients alternating with the sour cream, dividing the flour mixture into three parts and the sour cream into two parts, starting and ending with the flour. Mix just until incorporated after each addition. Scrape the sides of the bowl as necessary.

10. Remove the bowl from the mixer. Spoon about ¼ of the batter into the pan, then sprinkle ⅓ of the remaining nut/crumb filling evenly over the batter. Repeat, alternating batter and nut/crumb mixture, ending with a layer of the batter. You should have four layers of batter and three layers of nut/crumb filling. Smooth the surface with the back of a tablespoon, spreading from the center out.

11. To marbleize the batter: Using a table knife, cut into the batter almost to the bottom of the pan. Gently fold about 8 times, rotating the pan with each turn.

12. Center the pan on the rack and bake in the preheated oven for 60 to 65 minutes, or until the cake is golden brown on top and begins to come away from the sides of the pan. A twig of straw or a toothpick inserted into the center of the cake should come out dry.

13. Remove from the oven and place the pan on a cake rack to cool for 10 minutes. Invert the pan onto the cake rack and let stand in the pan for 5 minutes longer, then carefully remove the pan and finish cooling.

STORAGE: Store at room temperature under a glass dome or in an airtight container for up to 5 days.

🌿 SPANISH MERINGUE CAKE

AT A GLANCE

SERVES: 10 to 12

PAN: 9″ × 13″ × 2″ oblong

PAN PREP: Butter

OVEN TEMP: 325°

RACK LEVEL: Lower third

BAKING TIME: 40 to 45 minutes

METHOD: Electric mixer.

In 1975 I judged a baking contest for Steinbach's Department Store in Asbury Park, New Jersey. One of the more unusual recipes was entered by Robert McNamara of Atlantic City. The cake was made with a lightly spiced brown sugar base that was topped with chopped walnuts, then covered with a brown sugar meringue. When baked, the meringue turned into a delicate, chewy caramel-flavored topping.

According to Mr. McNamara, the recipe originally belonged to his mother. Here is my version of Mother McNamara's delicious cake.

THE CAKE:

1	cup buttermilk
1/2	teaspoon baking soda
2 1/4	cups sifted cake flour
1	teaspoon baking powder
1/2	teaspoon ground cinnamon
1/4	teaspoon ground nutmeg
1/2	cup (1 stick) unsalted butter
1 1/4	cups light brown sugar, lightly packed
1	large egg
3	large egg yolks
1	teaspoon vanilla extract
1	cup walnuts, chopped medium

THE SPANISH MERINGUE TOPPING:

3	large egg whites
1/8	teaspoon cream of tartar
3/4	cup light brown sugar, lightly packed
1/2	teaspoon ground cinnamon
1/4	teaspoon ground nutmeg

1. Position rack in the lower third of the oven and preheat to 325°. Butter a 9″ × 13″ × 2″ oblong pan.

2. To make the cake: In a small bowl combine the buttermilk and the baking soda. Set aside.

3. Using a triple sifter, sift together the flour, baking powder, and spices. Set aside.

4. Cut the butter into 1-inch pieces and place in the large bowl of an electric mixer fitted with beaters or paddle attachment. Soften on low speed, then increase to medium-high and cream until smooth and light in color, about 1½ to 2 minutes.

5. Add the brown sugar, 1 tablespoon at a time, taking about 6 to 8 minutes to blend it in well. Scrape the sides of the bowl as necessary.

6. Add the whole egg and beat 1 minute, then add the egg yolks, 1 at a time at 30-second intervals, scraping the sides of the bowl occasionally. Beat 1 minute longer. Blend in the vanilla.

7. Reduce mixer speed to low. Add the dry ingredients alternately with the buttermilk, dividing the flour mixture into three parts and the buttermilk into two parts, starting and ending with the flour. Mix just until incorporated after each addition. Scrape the sides of the bowl as necessary. Mix for 10 seconds longer.

8. Spoon the batter into the pan, smoothing the surface with the back of a tablespoon. Sprinkle the walnuts over the top. Set aside.

9. To make the topping: In the clean, dry, large bowl of an electric mixer fitted with beaters or whip attachment, beat the egg whites on medium speed until frothy. Add the cream of tartar. Increase the speed to medium-high and beat until the whites form firm peaks but are not dry. Reduce mixer speed to medium. Add the brown sugar, 2 tablespoons at a time, beating just until blended. Then add the spices and mix briefly; do not overmix the meringue.

10. With the back of a tablespoon, spread the meringue evenly over the batter in the pan.

11. Center the pan on the rack and bake in the preheated oven for 40 to 45 minutes or until the cake begins to come away from the sides of the pan and a twig of straw or a toothpick inserted into the center comes out dry.

12. Remove the cake from the oven. Set on a cake rack to cool. When ready to serve, cut into squares in the pan.

STORAGE: Cover loosely with a strip of waxed paper; do not seal the edges. Meringue-topped cakes easily become soggy if air does not circulate around them. Store in the pan at room temperature for up to 3 days.

🍫 CHUNKY CHOCOLATE CHIP CAKE

Full of semisweet chocolate bits and coarsely chopped walnuts, this soft-textured cake is especially delicious when served with ice cream.

AT A GLANCE

SERVES: 10 to 12
PAN: 9″ × 13″ × 2″ oblong
PAN PREP: Butter
OVEN TEMP: 350°
RACK LEVEL: Lower third
BAKING TIME: 35 to 40 minutes
METHOD: Electric mixer

3	ounces unsweetened chocolate, coarsely chopped
¾	cup plus 2 tablespoons boiling water
2	cups sifted cake flour
1	teaspoon baking soda
½	teaspoon salt
⅔	cup (1⅓ sticks) unsalted butter
1¼	cups superfine or strained sugar
2	large eggs
1	teaspoon vanilla extract
One	6-ounce package semisweet chocolate chips
1	cup walnuts, coarsely chopped

1. Position rack in the lower third of the oven and preheat to 350°. Butter a 9″ × 13″ × 2″ oblong pan.
2. Put the chocolate in a small bowl and add the boiling water. Let stand 5 minutes to soften the chocolate, then stir with a whisk until the chocolate is completely melted and the mixture is smooth. Set aside.
3. Using a triple sifter, sift together the flour, baking soda, and salt. Set aside.
4. Cut the butter into 1-inch pieces and place in the large bowl of an electric mixer fitted with beaters or paddle attachment to soften on low speed. Increase to medium-high and cream until smooth and light in color, about 1½ to 2 minutes.
5. Gradually add the sugar, 1 tablespoon at a time, taking about 6 to 8 minutes to blend it in well. Scrape the sides of the bowl as necessary.
6. Add the eggs, 1 at a time at 1-minute intervals. Beat 1 minute longer. Scrape the sides of the bowl again. Blend in the vanilla.
7. Reduce the mixer speed to low. Stir the chocolate mixture. Add the dry ingredients alternating with the chocolate, dividing the flour mixture into four parts and the chocolate into three parts, starting and ending with the flour. Mix just until incorporated

after each addition. Scrape the sides of the bowl as necessary, and mix for 10 seconds longer.

8. Remove the bowl from the mixer. With a rubber spatula, fold in the chocolate chips and walnuts. Spoon the batter into the prepared pan, smoothing the surface with the back of a tablespoon. Center the pan on the rack and bake in a preheated oven for 35 to 40 minutes, or until the cake begins to come away from the sides of the pan and a twig or straw or a toothpick inserted into the center comes out dry.

9. Remove the cake from the oven and set the pan on a cake rack to cool. Just before serving, dust the top with confectioners' sugar or frost with Quick Chocolate Glaze (page 462), made with the measurements for a large cake. Since the cake is stored in the pan, the first piece may be difficult to remove because the chocolate and nuts may cause it to crumble. The trick to removing it easily is to cut the first piece with a wet knife, using a gentle sawing motion. Lift the square of cake with a small metal spatula pressed flat against the bottom of the pan. The remaining pieces will lift out easily.

STORAGE: Cover the cake with aluminum foil and store in the pan at room temperature for up to 5 days.

HUNGARIAN POPPY SEED KUGELHOPF

Poppy seeds, which come from the white poppy, have been used for centuries in cooking. The tiny seeds can be used whole, as they are here, or ground to a meal for pastry fillings.

In this recipe, poppy seeds are blended into an orange-flavored batter made with egg whites. Allow time to soak the seeds in scalded milk before starting the cake.

AT A GLANCE

SERVES: 10 to 12
PAN: 9″ fluted ring (10-cup capacity)
PAN PREP: Butter/ flour
OVEN TEMP: 350°
RACK LEVEL: Lower third
BAKING TIME: 55 to 60 minutes
METHOD: Electric mixer

1	cup milk
1/2	cup poppy seeds
2	cups sifted unbleached all-purpose flour
2	teaspoons baking powder
1/2	teaspoon salt
1/2	cup (1 stick) unsalted butter
1	teaspoon freshly grated navel orange rind
1 1/4	cups superfine or strained sugar
1	teaspoon vanilla extract
1/2	teaspoon orange extract
4	egg whites
1/4	teaspoon cream tartar

1. Scald the milk in a small saucepan. Remove from the heat, add the poppy seeds, and cover. Let stand 1 hour.
2. Position rack in the lower third of the oven and preheat to 350°. Butter a 9-inch fluted ring. Dust the pan with flour, invert over the kitchen sink, and tap out the excess.
3. Using a triple sifter, sift together the flour, baking powder, and salt. Set aside.
4. Cut the butter into 1-inch pieces and place in the large bowl of an electric mixer fitted with beaters or paddle attachment; soften on low speed. Add the orange rind. Increase speed to medium-high and cream until smooth and light in color, about 1 1/2 to 2 minutes.
5. Add the sugar, 1 tablespoon at a time, taking about 6 to 8 minutes to blend it in well. Scrape the sides of the bowl as necessary. Blend in the vanilla and orange extracts.

6. Reduce mixer speed to low. Add the dry ingredients alternately with the cooled poppy seed/milk mixture, dividing the flour mixture into three parts and the poppy seed/milk mixture into two parts, starting and ending with the flour. Mix only until incorporated after each addition. Scrape the sides of the bowl as necessary. Remove the bowl from the mixer and set aside.

7. Place the egg whites in a separate bowl of the electric mixer fitted with beaters or whip attachment. Beat on medium speed until frothy. Add the cream of tartar. Increase speed to medium-high and continue beating until peaks are firm, but not dry. With a 2¾-inch-wide rubber spatula, fold ⅓ of the beaten egg whites into the batter, taking about 20 turns to lighten. Then fold in the remaining whites, taking about 40 additional turns.

8. Gently spoon the cake batter into the prepared pan, smoothing the surface with the back of a tablespoon. Center the pan on the rack and bake in the preheated oven for 55 to 60 minutes, or until the cake is golden brown on top and begins to come away from the sides of the pan. A twig of straw or a toothpick inserted into the center should come out dry.

9. Remove the cake from the oven and set the pan on a cake rack to cool for 10 to 15 minutes. Then invert the cake onto the rack. Carefully remove the pan and cool the cake completely. Just before serving, dust the top with confectioners' sugar.

STORAGE: Cover the cake with a glass dome or store in an airtight container for up to 5 days.

🍫 CHOCOLATE MACAROON CAKE

AT A GLANCE

SERVES: 10 to 12
PAN: 10″ bundt
(12-cup capacity)
PAN PREP: Butter/
flour
OVEN TEMP: 350°
RACK LEVEL: Lower
third
BAKING TIME: 65 to
70 minutes
METHOD: Electric
mixer/food
processor

A mixture of meringue, coconut, and toasted pecans swirled through the batter gives this chocolate cake a chewy texture that makes it an excellent choice for cake à la mode. It calls for really top-quality vanilla ice cream.

Take care not to reach too deeply into the pan when marbleizing this cake. It is important that a layer of batter remain on the bottom to keep the thick filling from sinking all the way through to the pan and sticking. Refer to marbleizing (page 69) for more detailed instructions.

THE MERINGUE FILLING:

One	3½-ounce can flaked coconut
¾	cup pecans
2	large egg whites
½	cup superfine sugar
½	teaspoon vanilla extract
¼	teaspoon almond extract

THE CAKE:

2¼	cups sifted cake flour
1	teaspoon baking powder
¼	teaspoon baking soda
½	teaspoon salt
⅔	cup (1⅓ sticks) unsalted butter
1	cup superfine or strained sugar
3	large eggs
1½	ounces unsweetened chocolate, melted
1	teaspoon vanilla extract
One	16-ounce can Hershey's chocolate syrup

1. Position rack in the lower third of the oven and preheat to 325°. Heavily butter a 10-inch bundt pan. Dust with all-purpose flour, invert pan over the kitchen sink, and tap out the excess.
2. To make the filling: Place the pecans in a shallow pan and toast in the oven for 6 to 8 minutes, or until lightly toasted.
3. Put the coconut and pecans in the container of a food processor

fitted with a steel blade. Pulse 6 to 8 times or until the pecans are chopped medium. Set aside.

4. Put the egg whites in the small bowl of an electric mixer fitted with beaters or whisk attachment. Beat on medium-low speed until frothy. Increase speed to medium-high, and beat to firm peaks. Add the sugar, 1 tablespoon at a time, taking about 45 to 60 seconds. Add the extracts, and beat 1 minute longer to form a stiff meringue. Remove from the mixer and fold in the coconut/pecan mixture. Set aside. Increase oven temperature to 350°.

5. To make the cake: Using a triple sifter, sift together the flour, baking powder, baking soda, and salt. Set aside.

6. Cut the butter into 1-inch pieces and place in the large bowl of an electric mixer fitted with beaters or paddle attachment. Soften on low speed. Increase to medium-high and cream until smooth and light in color, about 1½ to 2 minutes.

7. Add the sugar, 1 tablespoon at a time, taking about 6 to 8 minutes to blend it in well. Scrape the sides of the bowl.

8. Add the eggs, 1 at a time at 1-minute intervals, scraping the sides of the bowl as necessary. Blend in the melted unsweetened chocolate and vanilla and scrape the sides of the bowl again.

9. Reduce mixer speed to low. Add the dry ingredients alternating with the chocolate syrup, dividing the flour mixture into three parts and the syrup into two parts, starting and ending with the flour. Mix just until incorporated after each addition. Scrape the sides of the bowl as necessary.

10. Remove the bowl from the mixer. Spoon ¼ of the batter into the bottom of the prepared pan. Run the back of a tablespoon around the batter to form a well. Spoon ⅓ of the meringue filling into the well (fig. 1). Repeat, alternating the batter and filling, ending with a layer of batter (fig. 2). You should have four layers of batter and three layers of filling. Smooth the surface with the bottom of a tablespoon, spreading from the center out.

11. To marbleize the batter: Using a table knife, cut into the batter, but do not go completely to the bottom of the pan. Gently fold about 8 times, rotating the pan (fig. 3).

12. Center the pan on the rack and bake in the preheated oven for 65 to 70 minutes or until the cake begins to come away from the sides of the pan and the top is springy to the touch. A twig of straw or a toothpick inserted into the center should come out dry.

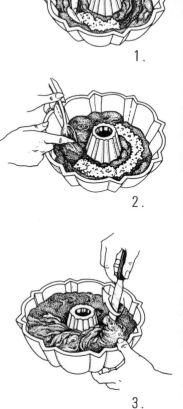

1.

2.

3.

13. Remove the cake from the oven and set the pan on a cake rack to cool for 20 to 30 minutes. Invert the pan onto the rack and carefully remove it. While cake is still slightly warm, frost with Quick Chocolate Glaze (page 462) made with the large cake measurements. Or simply dust the top with confectioners' sugar just before serving.

STORAGE: Store the cake at room temperature under a glass dome or in an airtight container for up to 5 days.

CRISP BRAZIL NUT CAKE

Often called the king of nuts, the Brazil nut has a most appealing taste and texture. Shelled Brazil nuts are difficult to find in supermarkets, but you can usually purchase them in a specialty store. The texture of these sweet, crunchy nuts reminds me of water chestnuts. A dash of nutmeg adds just the right touch to give this cake its fabulous flavor.

AT A GLANCE

SERVES: 10 to 12
PAN: 10″ bundt
(12-cup capacity)
PAN PREP: Butter/
flour
OVEN TEMP: 350°
RACK LEVEL: Lower
third
BAKING TIME: 45 to
50 minutes
METHOD: Electric
mixer/food
processor

1	cup shelled whole Brazil nuts
2	tablespoons poppy seeds
2¼	cups sifted cake flour
1	teaspoon baking soda
¼	teaspoon ground nutmeg
⅔	cup (1⅓ sticks) unsalted butter
1¼	cups superfine or strained sugar
4	large egg yolks
1½	teaspoons vanilla extract
1	cup plain low-fat yogurt
4	large egg whites
⅛	teaspoon salt

1. Position rack in the lower third of the oven and preheat to 350°. Butter a 10-inch bundt pan and dust with all-purpose flour. Invert the pan over the kitchen sink to tap out the excess.
2. Put the nuts and poppy seeds in the container of a food pro-

cessor fitted with the steel blade. Pulse 6 to 8 times, or until the nuts are chopped medium. Set aside.

3. Using a triple sifter, sift together the flour, baking soda, and nutmeg. Set aside.

4. Cut the butter into 1-inch pieces and place in the large bowl of an electric mixer fitted with beaters or paddle attachment; soften on low speed. Increase to medium-high and cream until smooth and light in color, about 1½ to 2 minutes.

5. Add the sugar, 1 tablespoon at a time, taking about 6 to 8 minutes to blend it in well. Scrape the sides of the bowl as necessary.

6. Add the egg yolks, 2 at a time at 1-minute intervals, scraping the sides of the bowl occasionally. Beat for 1 minute longer, then blend in the vanilla.

7. Reduce mixer speed to low. Add the dry ingredients alternately with the yogurt, dividing the flour mixture into three parts and the yogurt into two parts, starting and ending with the flour. Mix just until incorporated after each addition. Scrape the sides of the bowl as necessary, and mix for 10 seconds longer.

8. Remove the bowl from the mixer and fold in the nut mixture with a rubber spatula.

9. Place the egg whites in a clean, dry bowl of the electric mixer fitted with beaters or whip attachment. Beat on medium speed until frothy. Add the salt. Increase the speed to medium-high and continue to whip the egg whites until firm but not dry.

10. With a 2¾-inch-wide rubber spatula, fold ¼ of the beaten egg whites into the batter, taking about 20 turns to lighten. Then fold in the remaining whites, taking an additional 40 turns.

11. Spoon the cake batter into the prepared pan, smoothing the surface with the back of a tablespoon. Center the pan on the rack and bake in the preheated oven for 45 to 50 minutes, or until the cake begins to come away from the sides of the pan. A twig of straw or a toothpick inserted into the center should come out dry.

12. Remove the cake from the oven and set the pan on a cake rack to cool for 10 to 15 minutes. Invert the cake onto the rack, gently remove the pan, and allow the cake to cool completely. When ready to serve, dust the top with confectioners' sugar.

STORAGE: Store at room temperature under a glass dome or in an airtight container for up to 5 days.

THREE-NUT TORTE WITH VANILLA GLAZE

This European-style cake is densely packed with walnuts, filberts, and Brazil nuts and sweetened with dark corn syrup. The combination of nuts may be varied to suit your taste.

AT A GLANCE

SERVES: 10 to 12
PAN: 9″ springform
PAN PREP: Butter/ parchment
OVEN TEMP: 350°
RACK LEVEL: Lower third
BAKING TIME: 45 to 50 minutes
METHOD: Electric mixer/food processor

THE CAKE:

1	cup walnuts
2/3	cup Brazil nuts
2/3	cup toasted filberts (page 58)
1¼	cups sifted unbleached all-purpose flour
1	teaspoon baking powder
¼	teaspoon baking soda
½	teaspoon salt
¼	teaspoon ground nutmeg
4	large eggs
¾	cup sugar
⅓	cup dark corn syrup
1½	teaspoons vanilla extract
½	cup (1 stick) unsalted butter, melted and cooled

THE VANILLA GLAZE:

1½	cups strained confectioners' sugar
6	tablespoons boiling water
1½	teaspoons light corn syrup
¾	teaspoon vanilla extract
12	walnut halves for garnish

1. Position rack in the lower third of the oven and preheat to 350°. Butter a 9-inch springform pan. With a pencil trace a parchment paper circle, using the bottom of the springform as a guide. Cut the circle and press into the bottom of the pan.
2. Place the nuts in the bowl of a food processor fitted with the steel blade. Process 8 to 10 seconds or just until the nuts are coarsely chopped. Set aside.
3. To make the cake: Using a triple sifter, sift together the flour, baking powder, baking soda, salt, and nutmeg. Set aside.
4. Put the eggs in the large bowl of an electric mixer. Using the beaters or whip attachment, beat on medium-high speed until the

eggs are light in color and thickened, approximately 5 minutes.

5. Add the sugar, 1 tablespoon at a time, taking about 4 to 5 minutes to blend it in well. Pour in the dark corn syrup in a steady stream, scraping the sides of the bowl as necessary, and beat for 30 seconds longer. Reduce speed to medium. Blend in the vanilla. Pour in the melted butter in a steady stream, taking about 30 seconds, and beat 2 minutes longer.

6. Reduce speed to medium-low. Add the dry ingredients all at once. Scrape the sides of the bowl and mix for 20 seconds longer.

7. Remove the bowl from the mixer, fold in all the chopped nuts. Pour the batter into the prepared pan. Set the pan on a 12-inch square of aluminum foil, bringing the edges of the foil up to form a drip pan.

8. Center the pan on the rack and bake in the preheated oven 45 to 50 minutes, or until the cake begins to come away from the sides of the pan and is golden brown, and the top is springy to the touch. (Cakes made with dark corn syrup tend to brown too quickly. If this happens, place a square of aluminum foil over the top during the last 10 minutes of baking.)

9. Remove the cake from the oven and set on a rack to cool for 15 minutes. Run a thin knife around the sides of the cake, then remove the side of the springform pan. Invert the cake onto the rack, lift off the bottom of the pan, and carefully peel off the parchment. Turn the cake top side up. While the cake is still warm, prepare the glaze.

10. To make the vanilla glaze: Put the confectioners' sugar in a medium mixing bowl. Add the boiling water, corn syrup, and vanilla and blend with a wire whisk until smooth. Brush glaze thinly on the sides and top of the warm cake, reserving about ³/₄ of the glaze.

11. Add the walnut halves to the remaining glaze, turning the nuts with a fork until coated. (If the glaze is too thick, thin with a few drops of hot water.) Lift the nuts individually out of the glaze and position in a circle 1 inch from the edge of the cake, spacing them evenly. The cake should stand uncovered until the glaze hardens and is firm to the touch, about ¹/₂ hour.

STORAGE: Store the cake at room temperature under a glass dome or in an airtight container for up to 5 days.

❧ CHEWY CHOCOLATE NUT CAKE

AT A GLANCE

▽

SERVES: 8 to 10
PAN: 9″ springform
PAN PREP: Butter/
parchment/butter
OVEN TEMP: 350°
RACK LEVEL: Lower
third
BAKING TIME: 55 to
60 minutes
METHOD: Electric
mixer/food
processor

A candylike mixture goes on the bottom of a springform pan, followed by a delicious golden batter, then another layer of sweet nut concoction, and finally more batter. When baked, the center remains crunchy while the bottom forms a chewy, gooey syrup that hardens as it cools. There is no need to make a frosting. It makes itself while the cake is baking!

THE TOPPING:

1 1/2	cups pecan or walnut pieces
1/2	cup strained unsweetened cocoa
1/3	cup light brown sugar, lightly packed
1/3	cup granulated sugar
2	tablespoons light corn syrup
1/4	cup (1/2 stick) unsalted butter, melted and cooled

THE CAKE:

2 1/4	cups sifted cake flour
2	teaspoons baking powder
1/2	teaspoon salt
2/3	cups (1 1/3 sticks) unsalted butter
1	cup superfine or strained sugar
3	large eggs
1	teaspoon vanilla extract
3/4	cup milk

1. Position rack in the lower third of the oven and preheat to 350°. Butter a 9-inch springform pan. With a pencil trace a parchment paper circle, using the bottom of the pan as a guide. Cut the circle and press into the bottom of the pan. Butter the parchment well.

2. To make the topping: Place all the ingredients in the bowl of a food processor fitted with the steel blade. Pulse 4 to 5 times or until the mixture forms medium-large pieces. Do not overprocess. Sprinkle 1/2 of the chocolate/nut mixture into the bottom of the springform pan, evenly distributing the pieces as best you can. Reserve the remaining mixture to spread on the batter.

3. To make the cake: Using a triple sifter, sift together the flour, baking powder, and salt. Set aside.

4. Cut the butter into 1-inch pieces and place in the large bowl of an electric mixer fitted with beaters or paddle attachment. Soften on low speed, then increase speed to medium-high and cream until smooth and light in color, approximately $1\frac{1}{2}$ to 2 minutes.

5. Add the sugar, 1 tablespoon at a time, taking about 6 to 8 minutes to blend it in well. Scrape the sides of the bowl occasionally.

6. Add the eggs, 1 at a time at 1-minute intervals, scraping the sides of the bowl as necessary. Blend in the vanilla.

7. Reduce mixer speed to low. Add the dry ingredients alternately with the milk, dividing the flour mixture into three parts and the milk into two parts, starting and ending with the flour. Mix just until incorporated after each addition. Scrape the sides of the bowl occasionally.

8. Spoon $\frac{2}{3}$ of the batter into the prepared pan, smoothing the surface with the back of a tablespoon. Break remaining chocolate/nut mixture into small clumps and sprinkle over the batter. Spoon the remaining batter on top, spreading from the center out to cover the topping completely.

9. Put the pan in the center of the rack and bake in the preheated oven 55 to 60 minutes, or until the cake comes away from the sides of the pan and the top is springy to the touch.

10. Remove from the oven and set the pan on a cake rack for 10 minutes to cool slightly. Run a thin knife around the sides of the pan to loosen the cake. Remove the outer ring of the springform and invert the cake onto the rack. Carefully remove the bottom disk of the pan, leaving the parchment pressed against the topping.

11. Using a pastry brush, brush the top of the parchment lightly with *very* hot water. Let stand 10 seconds, then gently peel off the paper. If the topping sticks, repeat the procedure. When the cake is cool, transfer to a cake platter or plate bottom side up.

STORAGE: Store at room temperature under a glass cake dome or in an airtight container for up to 5 days.

❧ GLAZED ALMOND BUTTER CAKE

AT A GLANCE

SERVES: 8 to 10
PAN: 9″ springform
PAN PREP: Butter
OVEN TEMP: 350°
RACK LEVEL: Lower third
BAKING TIME: 30 to 35 minutes
METHOD: Electric mixer

I discovered this delicious cake one cold afternoon many years ago at a bakery in Denmark, where it is often served as an alternative to Danish pastry. I have since encountered it many times in homes of Danish friends. It has a lovely buttery taste and an attractive topping of caramelized almonds. It is a delightful treat.

THE CAKE:

1¼	cups sifted cake flour
1	teaspoon baking powder
¼	teaspoon salt
3	large eggs
¾	cup sugar
½	cup (1 stick) unsalted butter, melted and cooled
1	teaspoon vanilla extract
3	tablespoons heavy cream

THE ALMOND BUTTER GLAZE:

3	tablespoons unsalted butter
¼	cup light brown sugar
⅔	cup sliced (not slivered) almonds
1	tablespoon heavy cream
1	tablespoon all-purpose flour

1. Position rack in the lower third of the oven and preheat to 350°. Butter a 9-inch springform pan.
2. To make the cake: Using a triple sifter, sift together the flour, baking powder, and salt. Set aside.
3. Put the eggs in the large bowl of an electric mixer. Using the beaters or whip attachment, beat on medium-high speed until light in color and thickened, approximately 5 minutes. Add the sugar, 1 tablespoon at a time, taking about 4 to 5 minutes to blend it in well.
4. Reduce mixer speed to medium-low. Add the vanilla. Measure out ¼ cup of the dry ingredients and set aside. Add ½ of the remaining flour mixture to the egg mixture, then pour in the heavy cream and *quickly* add the remaining flour except for

the reserved 1/4 cup. Scrape the sides of the bowl occasionally.

5. Slowly pour the melted butter into the batter, taking about 1 minute. Add the reserved 1/4 cup flour mixture and mix 15 seconds longer.

6. Immediately spoon the batter into the buttered pan, smoothing the surface with the back of a tablespoon. Center the pan on the rack and bake in the preheated oven for 25 minutes.

7. While the cake is baking, measure out the ingredients for the glaze but *do not assemble*. This topping will become too thick to spread if it stands.

8. To make the glaze: Five minutes before the cake is finished, melt the butter in a heavy 10-inch skillet on low heat. Add the remaining ingredients in the order listed and stir just to blend.

9. At the end of 25 minutes, remove the cake from the oven and *immediately* pour on the glaze. Spread it gently with the back of a tablespoon, taking care not to tear the cake. Return the cake to the oven for another 8 to 10 minutes. The glaze should bubble and then turn a golden brown.

10. Remove the pan from the oven and set on a cake rack to cool completely. Run a long, thin knife around the pan to loosen the cake, and remove the rim. Then run the knife underneath the bottom of the cake to remove from the metal disk. Using two large metal spatulas, lift the cake onto a serving platter.

STORAGE: Store the cake at room temperature under a glass cake dome or in an airtight container for up to 5 days.

🌸 GREEK HONEY NUT CAKE

AT A GLANCE

SERVES: 8 to 10
PAN: 9″ × 9″ × 2″
square
PAN PREP: Butter
OVEN TEMP: 350°
RACK LEVEL: Lower
third
BAKING TIME: 25 to
30 minutes
METHOD: Electric
mixer/food
processor

Rummaging through my recipe files one day, I came across an old, worn piece of paper containing nothing more than a list of ingredients. My guess was that it was from my mother's collection and that it was a recipe for a wonderful Greek honey cake known as karidpeta.

My update reduces the sweetness and substitutes vegetable oil for butter. The result is a lovely, warm, cinnamon-flavored cake laden with finely chopped walnuts and topped with hot honey syrup. It has real melt-in-your-mouth flavor.

THE CAKE:

2	cups walnuts
1	cup sifted unbleached all-purpose flour
1	teaspoon baking powder
1/2	teaspoon baking soda
1/2	teaspoon salt
1	teaspoon cinnamon
3	large eggs
1/2	cup light brown sugar, lightly packed
1	tablespoon dark molasses
1	teaspoon vanilla extract
1	teaspoon freshly grated navel orange rind
1/2	cup safflower oil
1/4	cup orange juice

THE HOT HONEY SYRUP:

2/3	cup water
1/4	cup sugar
One	1/4-inch-thick slice lemon
1/4	cup honey

1. Position rack in the lower third of the oven and preheat to 350°. Butter a 9″ × 9″ × 2″ square pan.
2. To make the cake: Place the nuts, flour, baking powder, baking soda, salt, and cinnamon in the bowl of processor fitted with a steel blade. Process until the nuts are ground very fine. Set aside.

3. Put the eggs in a large bowl of an electric mixer fitted with beaters or whip attachment. Beat on medium-high speed until light in color and thickened, about 3 minutes. Add the brown sugar in about 2 minutes, then beat in the molasses, vanilla, and orange rind.
4. Slowly pour in the oil, taking about 30 seconds. Beat 30 seconds longer.
5. Reduce mixer speed to medium-low. Add ½ of the nut/flour mixture. Pour in the orange juice, and quickly add the remaining nut/flour mixture, scraping the sides of the bowl as necessary.
6. Pour the batter into the prepared pan. Center the pan on the rack and bake in the preheated oven for 25 to 30 minutes, or until the cake leaves the sides of the pan and is springy to the touch.
7. Remove the cake from the oven and set the pan on a cake rack to cool slightly.
8. To make the syrup: Place the water, sugar, and lemon slice in a small saucepan, bring to a slow boil, and simmer for 5 minutes. Stir in the honey and cook on a low flame for 2 minutes longer. Remove the lemon slice. After the cake has stood for 15 minutes, cut into 2¼-inch squares and, leaving the cake in the pan, spoon the hot syrup over the cake. Let stand 2 hours or until syrup is absorbed.

STORAGE: Cover the pan with aluminum foil. Stored at room temperature, this cake will keep up to 2 days. For longer storage, refrigerate up to 1 week.

🌺 CANDIED PEPITA SEED CAKE

SERVES: 10 to 12
PAN: 9″ × 13″ ×
2″ oblong
PAN PREP: Butter
OVEN TEMP: 350°
RACK LEVEL: Lower
third
BAKING TIME: 25 to
30 minutes
METHOD: Electric
mixer

When I am in a health food or specialty nut store, I frequently buy a snack called Trail Mix. It contains all sorts of interesting seeds, nuts, raisins, and oddly shaped sesame crackers. But my favorites in this concoction are the pepitas, the oblong, olive-colored pumpkin seeds frequently used in Mexican cuisine.

Fortunately, pepita seeds are sold in bulk and are easily obtained. I thought it would be fun to make a cake using these attractive, tender seeds. Since they are rather soft, I candied them. They add a mild nutty flavor and a delicate crumb to this moist, lightly spiced cake. The finished cake is very unusual, very pretty, and very delicious, bound to be a conversation piece whenever you serve it.

THE CANDIED SEEDS:

1 cup pepita seeds, preferably unsalted
2 tablespoons sugar

THE CAKE:

1¾ cups sifted unbleached all-purpose flour
1 teaspoon baking powder
1 teaspoon baking soda
½ teaspoon salt
1 teaspoon ground cinnamon
½ teaspoon ground coriander
¼ teaspoon ground nutmeg
3 large eggs
⅓ cup granulated sugar
½ cup light brown sugar, lightly packed
⅓ cup cooked mashed yams (about 4 ounces raw)
1 teaspoon vanilla extract
½ teaspoon grated navel orange rind
½ cup olive oil
½ cup orange juice

1 recipe Vanilla Glaze (page 461), using measurements for large cake

1. Position the rack in the lower third of the oven and preheat to 350°. Butter a 9″ × 13″ × 2″ oblong pan and set aside. Butter a 15-inch sheet of wax paper; set aside.

2. To candy the pepita seeds: Put the seeds and the sugar in a heavy 10-inch skillet. Cook over low heat, stirring occasionally until the sugar turns a light brown and glazes the seeds, about 3 to 5 minutes. Spread the seeds on the buttered waxed paper as best you can. They will harden as they cool. Break the clusters apart, separating the nuts with your fingers. Set aside.

3. To make the cake: Using a triple sifter, sift together the flour, baking powder, baking soda, salt, and spices. Set aside.

4. Place the eggs in the large bowl of an electric mixer fitted with the beaters or whip attachment. On medium-high speed, beat until light in color and thickened, about 5 minutes. Add the sugars, starting with the granulated sugar, 1 tablespoon at a time, taking about 5 minutes to blend well. Add the mashed yams and beat for 2 minutes longer.

5. Reduce mixer speed to medium. Add the vanilla extract and orange rind, then pour in the olive oil in a steady stream, taking about 30 seconds. Beat 1 minute longer. *Work quickly from this point because the oil is heavier than the batter and has a tendency to separate from the batter and sink.*

6. Reduce mixer speed to medium-low. Add the dry ingredients alternating with the orange juice, dividing the flour mixture into three parts and the liquid into two parts, starting and ending with the flour. Mix just until incorporated after each addition. Scrape the sides of the bowl occasionally.

7. Remove the bowl from the mixer and fold in ½ of the candied pepitas. Reserve the rest for garnish.

8. Pour the batter into the buttered pan. Center the pan on the rack and bake in the preheated oven for 25 to 30 minutes, or until the cake leaves the sides of the pan and is springy to the touch.

9. Remove the cake from the oven and set the pan on a cake rack to cool for 15 minutes. Prepare the vanilla glaze.

10. While the cake is still warm, spread the icing thinly over the top with the back of a tablespoon. Immediately sprinkle on the remaining candied pepita seeds. Cut into squares just before serving.

STORAGE: Cover the top of the pan with aluminum foil. Store at room temperature for up to 5 days.

CAKES FROM THE GARDEN

..........✿..........

akes made with luscious fruits and vegetables have all the qualities that I love—natural flavor, texture, and moistness.
  Spices such as cinnamon, nutmeg, cloves, and ginger complement all varieties of fruits. Chocolate and nuts are also a natural
match.

We start with very simple butter-type cakes in which many fresh
seasonal fruits (and even tomatoes) can play a starring role. Dried
fruits have not been overlooked either. Lovers of dates, apricots,
prunes, and raisins will revel in the cakes combining one or another
of these treats with nuts, chocolate, and spices.

There are several recipes for dear old favorites like the upside-
down cake, as well as for the always popular vegetable-based carrot,
zucchini, and pumpkin cakes.

These wonderful cakes are even better when served warm with
contrasting cool toppings of whipped cream, ice cream, yogurt, or
sour cream.

BEFORE YOU BEGIN . . .
....

When purchasing fruits for cake look for fruit that is of fine quality,
perfectly ripe, and ready to eat. It is always advisable to use seasonal

produce at its flavor peak. Also keep in mind that the juices exuded from fresh fruit cannot be controlled in cakes as they can in pies and other fruit cookery. For example, the juiciness of apples in a pie can be modified by the amount of thickening agent used, whereas a cake recipe is structured and cannot be altered.

These tips will help you make glorious cakes from the garden:

▶ Fruits such as purple *Italian plums* and *grapes* do not require peeling. If you wish to peel thin-skinned fruits such as peaches and nectarines, blanch them first in boiling water to cover. Let stand for 1 minute. Pour off the water, give a quick cold water rinse, and dry with paper toweling. Insert the tip of a sharp knife under the skin and gently lift off the peel.

▶ Wash *berries* and *cherries* by placing them in a bowl of cold water. Drain and refill with water three times to free dirt and sand. Empty berries into a colander, then into a shallow pan lined with layers of paper toweling. Rotate pan back and forth to release more water from berries. Gently pat dry with additional toweling. Cultivated berries do not need washing.

▶ Always dry fruits and/or vegetables as much as possible between double thicknesses of paper towels before using them in baking. If the fruit is too wet or has absorbed too much liquid, the cake will be soggy.

▶ *Apples* are easier to peel if you cut them into quarters. Remove the core and peel, cutting as close to the peel as possible.

▶ Do not substitute frozen fruits for fresh. Frozen fruit is presweetened and too watery.

▶ Most cakes made with fresh fruit can be stored at room temperature for no longer than 2 days. Refrigerate them after this time to avoid spoilage. If your kitchen is very warm, refrigerate them the day they are made.

▶ Slice cakes made with coarsely cut fruits with a serrated knife that has been moistened with warm water. Use a sawing or back-and-forth motion to avoid tearing the cake.

▶ Cakes made with dried fruit always slice better after standing. Both the texture of the cake and the fruit itself become more compact, as is also the case with a classic dark fruit cake.

SWEET MAYS' GREEN MOUNTAIN APPLE CAKE

AT A GLANCE

SERVES: 6 to 8
PAN: 8″ × 8″ × 2″ square
PAN PREP: Butter
OVEN TEMP: 350°
RACK LEVEL: Lower third
BAKING TIME: 35 to 40 minutes
METHOD: Electric mixer/food processor

This recipe was created by the mother of May Sutter, my friend of many years. May's mother, also named May, lives in the rural Green Mountains of Vermont. Daughter May, a marvelous cook and baker in her own right, refined her mother's "dump and pour" recipe into this moist, delicious apple cake. I named this cake after them both.

2	medium-large cooking apples (about 1 pound), such as Northern Spy, McIntosh, Rome, or Empire
1¼	cups sifted unbleached all-purpose flour
1	teaspoon baking soda
¼	teaspoon salt
1	teaspoon ground cinnamon
¼	teaspoon ground nutmeg
¼	cup (½ stick) unsalted butter
½	cup sugar
1	large egg
1	teaspoon vanilla extract
½	cup plumped raisins (see page 63)
½	cup walnuts, chopped medium-fine

1. Position rack in the lower third of the oven and preheat to 350°. Butter an 8″ × 8″ × 2″ square cake pan.
2. Quarter, core, and peel apples. Divide each apple into eighths and place in container of a food processor fitted with the steel blade. Pulse 4 to 5 times, or until pieces are about ¼ inch in size. Be careful not to overprocess, or the pieces will be too small. You should have about 2 cups of chopped apple. Set aside.
3. Sift together the flour, baking soda, salt, and spices in a triple sifter.
4. Cut the butter into 1-inch pieces and place in the small bowl of an electric mixer fitted with the beaters or paddle attachment. On low speed, soften. Increase speed to medium-high, and cream until smooth and light in color, about 1 minute.
5. Add the sugar, 1 tablespoon at a time, taking 2 to 3 minutes to blend it in well. Scrape sides of bowl occasionally.

6. Add the egg, and beat for 1 minute, scraping the sides of bowl as necessary. Blend in the vanilla.

7. Reduce mixer speed to low. Add the apples and mix for about 10 seconds. Then blend in the dry ingredients, half at a time. Mix 10 seconds longer.

8. Remove the bowl from the mixer. Fold in the raisins and nuts. Spoon the batter into the prepared pan and smooth the surface. Center the pan on the rack and bake in the preheated oven for 35 to 40 minutes, or until cake is springy to the touch and begins to come away from the sides of the pan.

9. Remove from the oven and set the pan on a cake rack to cool. Just before serving, dust top with confectioners' sugar. Cut the cake into squares in the pan.

STORAGE: Cover the pan loosely with aluminum foil. Store at room temperature for up to 2 days or refrigerate for up to 5 days.

APPLESAUCE SPICE CAKE

This moist cake contains both applesauce and tart freshly grated green apple. Chopped toasted pecans add texture and flavor. The combination is unbeatable, especially accompanied by a mug of mulled apple cider.

AT A GLANCE

SERVES: 8 to 10
PAN: 9″ fluted tube pan (10-cup capacity)
PAN PREP: Butter/flour
OVEN TEMP: 350°
RACK LEVEL: Lower third
BAKING TIME: 55 to 60 minutes
METHOD: Electric mixer

2 1/4	cups sifted unbleached all-purpose flour
1	teaspoon baking soda
1/2	teaspoon salt
1 1/2	teaspoons ground cinnamon
1	teaspoon ground allspice
1	teaspoon ground nutmeg
3/4	cup pecans, lightly toasted and chopped medium-fine
1/3	cup (2/3 stick) butter
1	teaspoon grated lemon rind
1/3	cup vegetable shortening
3/4	cup granulated sugar
2/3	cup light brown sugar, lightly packed
2	large eggs
1	medium-sized tart greening or Granny Smith apple, peeled and chopped medium-small (about 2/3 cup)
1	teaspoon vanilla extract
1	cup sweetened bottled applesauce

1. Position rack in the lower third of the oven and preheat to 350°. Butter a 9-inch fluted tube pan, dust it lightly with flour, and invert over the kitchen sink to tap out excess flour.
2. Sift together flour, baking soda, salt, and spices in a triple sifter. Stir in chopped pecans. Set aside.
3. Cut the butter into 1-inch pieces and place in large bowl of an electric mixer fitted with the beaters or paddle attachment. Soften on low speed. Add the lemon rind. Increase speed to medium-high and cream until smooth, about 1 minute. Add the vegetable shortening and mix for 1 minute longer.
4. Add the granulated sugar, 1 tablespoon at a time, taking 3 to 4 minutes to blend it in well. Add the light brown sugar over an

Great Cakes
194

additional 3 to 4 minutes. Scrape the sides of the bowl occasionally.

5. Add the eggs, 1 at a time at 1-minute intervals. Reduce speed to medium-low. Add the fresh apple and the vanilla.

6. Reduce mixer speed to low. Add the flour/nut mixture alternately in three additions with the applesauce in two additions, starting and ending with the flour. Beat just until incorporated after each addition. Scrape the sides of the bowl occasionally.

7. Spoon the batter into the prepared pan and smooth the top. Center the pan on the rack and bake in the preheated oven for 55 to 60 minutes or until the cake begins to leave the sides of the pan and a twig of straw or a toothpick inserted into the center comes out dry.

8. Remove from oven. Place the pan on a cake rack to set for 10 to 15 minutes, then invert the cake onto the rack and remove pan. While the cake is still warm, you may want to pour Brown Sugar Glaze (page 464) over the top, letting it drip naturally down the sides. Garnish the top with chopped pecans, if you wish.

STORAGE: Store at room temperature under a glass cover or in an airtight container for up to 2 days. For longer storage, wrap the unglazed cake in plastic wrap and refrigerate for up to 10 days.

🐌 APPLE STREUSEL CREAM SQUARES

M̄ake this whenever you need a quick treat for family or friends. It's simple to make and luscious.

▽
AT A GLANCE

SERVES: 6 to 8
PAN: 9″ × 9″ × 2″
PAN PREP: Butter
OVEN TEMP: 375°
RACK LEVEL: Lower third
BAKING TIME: 1 hour, 20 minutes
METHOD: Food processor

THE CAKE:

- 1½ pounds tart apples (4 to 5 medium), such as Granny Smith or greening
- 2⅓ cups unsifted unbleached all-purpose flour
- 1 teaspoon baking powder
- ¾ cup sugar, divided
- 1 teaspoon ground cinnamon
- ⅔ cup (1⅓ sticks) unsalted butter, melted and cooled
- 1 cup sour cream
- 1 large egg yolk
- ½ teaspoon vanilla extract

THE STREUSEL TOPPING:

- ¾ cup reserved crumbs
- ¼ cup chopped walnuts
- 1 teaspoon sugar
- ¼ teaspoon cinnamon

1. Position rack in the lower third of the oven and preheat to 375°. Butter a 9″ × 9″ × 2″ square cake pan.
2. To make the cake: Quarter, core, and peel apples. Fit a food processor with the medium slicing disk. Pack the apples into the feeder tube and slice, using medium pressure on the pusher. Remove from the bowl and set aside.
3. Clean the processor bowl, fit with the steel blade, and add flour, baking powder, ½ *cup* sugar, and cinnamon. Pulse 2 or 3 times to blend. Pour in the butter and pulse 3 or 4 times or just until medium crumbs are formed. Be careful not to overprocess.
4. Reserve ¾ cup of the crumbs for streusel topping. Press the remaining crumbs into the prepared pan with the palm of your hand to form a cookielike dough.
5. Arrange apples evenly over surface of the dough. In a small bowl

combine the sour cream, *1/4 cup* sugar, egg yolk, and vanilla, mixing until smooth. Spread evenly over the apples.

6. To make the streusel topping: Distribute the reserved crumbs and the walnuts evenly over the top of the sour cream mixture. In a small bowl, combine the sugar and cinnamon and sprinkle over the streusel. Center the pan on the rack and bake for 1 hour and 20 minutes, until the top is golden brown and the fruit begins to bubble around the sides.

7. Remove from the oven and set on a cake rack to cool. When ready to serve, cut into squares.

STORAGE: Cover loosely with waxed paper and store at room temperature for 4 to 6 hours or refrigerate for up to 5 days. Rewarm the cake before serving.

🍂 OAT BRAN APPLE CAKE

AT A GLANCE

SERVES: 10 to 12
PAN: 9″ × 13″ × 2″ oblong
PAN PREP: Butter
OVEN TEMP: 375°
RACK LEVEL: Lower third
BAKING TIME: 35 to 40 minutes
METHOD: Electric mixer/food processor

This tasty cake is made with thinly sliced apples, nuts, honey, and yogurt, and is topped with a crunchy mixture of oat bran flakes, nuts, honey, and cinnamon. Although most supermarkets stock these products in the cereal section, I prefer to purchase my oat bran and oat bran flakes at a health food store. This cake is not rich, and makes a delicious offering with a cup of tea or coffee.

Oat bran does not always perform well in baking; it often produces a heavy, bland product. I have found that the trick to making a lighter, moister cake is to soften the oat bran first in boiling water. The already softened bran does not absorb as much liquid from the batter.

THE TOPPING:

- 1 cup walnuts
- 1 cup oat bran flakes
- 2 tablespoons light brown sugar
- 2 tablespoons honey
- 1/4 teaspoon cinnamon

THE CAKE:

- 1 cup oat bran cereal
- 1 teaspoon cinnamon
- 1 cup boiling water
- 2 tablespoons honey
- 1 cup plain low-fat yogurt
- 1 1/4 teaspoons baking soda
- 1 large Granny Smith apple
- 3 large eggs
- 1/2 cup light brown sugar, lightly packed
- 1 teaspoon vanilla
- 1/3 cup safflower oil
- 1 1/2 cups stone-ground whole wheat flour
- 1/2 teaspoon salt

1. Position a rack in the lower third of the oven and preheat to 375°. Butter a 9″ × 13″ × 2″ oblong pan.
2. To make the topping: Place walnuts in the bowl of a food pro-

cessor fitted with the steel blade. Pulse 5 or 6 times to chop coarsely. Remove 1/2 cup nuts and set aside for the batter.

3. To the remaining nuts in the processor, add oat bran flakes, light brown sugar, honey, and cinnamon. Pulse 3 or 4 times, or until the mixture is blended and the oat bran flakes are coarsely broken. Empty the contents of the processor into a medium-sized bowl and set aside.

4. To make the cake: Place the oat bran cereal and cinnamon in a medium-sized bowl. Add the boiling water and honey and stir until the mixture is smooth. Set aside to cool.

5. Measure the yogurt in a 2-cup measuring cup. Stir in the baking soda and set aside. The mixture will rise and foam in the cup.

6. Quarter, core, and peel the apple. Cut into 1-inch pieces, coarsely chop in the food processor, and set aside.

7. In the large bowl of an electric mixer fitted with beaters or whip attachment, beat the eggs on medium-high speed until thick and light in color, about 3 minutes. Gradually add the light brown sugar, 1 tablespoon at a time, over 3 to 4 minutes. Blend in the vanilla, then slowly pour in the oil in a steady stream over 30 seconds. Spoon in the cooled oatbran mixture and continue to beat for 1 minute longer.

8. Reduce the mixer speed to low and all at once add the whole wheat flour, salt, yogurt, reserved 1/2 cup nuts, and chopped apple. Mix only until blended. Pour the batter into the prepared pan, and sprinkle the topping mixture evenly across the top.

9. Bake in the center of the preheated oven for 35 to 40 minutes. About halfway through baking, check the cake. If the top is browning too fast, lay a strip of aluminum foil loosely across the surface to protect it from overbrowning. The cake is done when the sides begin to come away from the pan and the top is springy to the touch.

STORAGE: Store in the pan at room temperature loosely covered with aluminum foil for up to 2 days, or refrigerate for up to 5 days.

🌰 BANANA NUT CAKE

△
AT A GLANCE

SERVES: 10 to 12
PAN: 9″ × 13″ ×
2″ oblong
PAN PREP: Butter
OVEN TEMP: 350°
RACK LEVEL: Lower
third
BAKING TIME: 40 to
45 minutes
METHOD: Electric
mixer/food
processor

*My earliest recollection of homemade cake was my grandmother's
banana cake. I was no more than three years old when I sat perched
on her kitchen table and watched her open the oven door, carefully
sliding out what seemed to my child's eyes like an enormous flat pan
filled with a cake that had the most wonderful aroma. It wasn't until
I was much older that it occurred to me that it was not the pan that
was so big but that I was so small. I still have my grandmother's hand-
written recipe with her scrawled measurements and notes, which I am
sure she knew by heart. Here is my version of her delicious cake.*

1	cup puréed banana (about 3 small bananas)
1/2	cup sour cream
2 1/4	cups sifted cake flour
1	teaspoon baking soda
1	teaspoon salt
1/4	teaspoon ground nutmeg
1	cup walnuts or pecans, chopped medium-size
1/2	cup (1 stick) unsalted butter
1	cup granulated sugar
1/2	cup light brown sugar, lightly packed
2	large eggs
1	teaspoon vanilla extract

1. Position rack in the lower third of the oven and preheat to 350°.
   Butter a 9″ × 13″ × 2″ oblong pan.
2. Break the bananas into 1-inch pieces and place them in the container of a food processor. Pulse a few times until the bananas
   are puréed but not watery. Alternatively, press them through a
   strainer with medium-large holes. Stir the purée into the sour
   cream.
3. Sift together the flour, baking soda, salt, and nutmeg in a triple
   sifter. Stir in the chopped nuts and set aside.
4. Cut the butter into 1-inch pieces and put them in the large bowl
   of an electric mixer fitted with beaters or paddle attachment.
   Soften on low speed. Increase speed to medium-high and cream
   until smooth and light in color, about 1 1/2 to 2 minutes.

5. Add the sugars, starting with granulated sugar, 1 tablespoon at a time, taking 6 to 8 minutes to blend both in well. Scrape the sides of bowl occasionally.
6. Add the eggs, 1 at a time at 1-minute intervals, scraping sides of the bowl as necessary. Blend in the vanilla.
7. Reduce mixer speed to low. Add the flour/nut mixture alternately with sour cream/banana mixture, dividing the dry ingredients into three parts and the banana mixture into two parts, starting and ending with the flour. Scrape the sides of the bowl and mix for 10 seconds longer.
8. Spoon the batter into the prepared pan and smooth the surface with the back of a tablespoon. Bake in the preheated oven for 40 to 45 minutes, until cake is golden brown on top, springy to the touch, and comes away from the sides of the pan.
9. Remove from the oven and set the pan on a cake rack to cool. Just before serving, dust top with confectioners' sugar. When ready to serve, cut into squares in the pan.

STORAGE: Cover the pan loosely with aluminum foil and store at room temperature for up to 5 days.

🌾 BING CHERRY KUCHEN

AT A GLANCE

SERVES: 8 to 10

PAN: 9″ springform

PAN PREP: Butter/
parchment/butter

OVEN TEMP: 350°

RACK LEVEL: Lower
third

BAKING TIME: 60 to
65 minutes

METHOD: Electric
mixer/food
processor

When purchasing cherries, select those that are firm and deep red in color. Removing the pits is a breeze if you own a cherry pitter; it's practically a must. The rings of cherries in this scrumptious kuchen will sink into the cake a bit as it bakes.

THE CRUMB MIXTURE:

1/2	cup unsifted unbleached all-purpose flour
1/8	teaspoon baking powder
2	tablespoons light brown sugar
1/2	cup pecans
3	tablespoons melted unsalted butter

THE CAKE:

1	pound Bing cherries
1	cup sifted unbleached all-purpose flour
1	teaspoon baking powder
1/4	teaspoon salt
1/2	cup (1 stick) unsalted butter
2/3	cup sugar
3	eggs
1/2	teaspoon vanilla extract

1. Generously butter a 9-inch springform pan, line with parchment paper, and generously butter the paper.
2. To make the crumb mixture: Place the flour, baking powder, sugar, and nuts in a food processor fitted with the steel blade. Pulse 6 to 8 times, or until the nuts are finely chopped. Add the butter. Pulse 2 to 3 times or until mixture forms pea-size crumbs. Do not overprocess.
3. Sprinkle 1/3 of the crumbs evenly on the bottom of the pan. Reserve the remaining 2/3 for the topping. Press crumbs down lightly in the pan to form a bottom crust. Set aside.
4. Position a rack in the lower third of the oven and preheat to 350°.
5. To make the cake: Wash the cherries and dry well on paper toweling. Remove the pits with a cherry pitter. Set aside.

6. Sift together flour, baking powder, and salt in a triple sifter. Set aside.

7. Cut the butter into 1-inch pieces and put in the large bowl of an electric mixer fitted with beaters or paddle attachment to soften on low speed. Increase speed to medium-high and cream until smooth and light in color, about $1\frac{1}{2}$ to 2 minutes.

8. Add the sugar 1 tablespoon at a time, taking 3 to 4 minutes to blend it in well. Scrape sides of bowl occasionally.

9. Add eggs, 1 at a time at 1-minute intervals, scraping the sides of the bowl as necessary. Blend in the vanilla.

10. Reduce mixer speed to low. Add the flour mixture in 3 additions, beating just until incorporated after each addition. Mix for about 15 seconds longer. Carefully spread the batter over the crumb layer in the pan and arrange the cherries in rings on top. Use about 20 cherries on the outer circle, working inward to 15, 10, and then 3 in the center. Sprinkle the reserved crumbs on top of the cherries.

11. Center the pan on the oven rack and bake in the preheated oven for 60 to 65 minutes, or until the cake begins to come away from the sides of pan and the top is golden brown. Remove from the oven and set on a cake rack to cool. Cover the pan with a piece of aluminum foil, pressing it snugly against the sides to hold in the topping. Invert the cake onto the rack. Lift off the pan and carefully peel off the parchment paper. Turn cake right side up onto a serving platter. To serve, slice into wedges and accompany with a scoop of vanilla ice cream, Chantilly Whipped Cream (page 489), or Yogurt Topping (page 479).

STORAGE: Cover the cake loosely with aluminum foil. Store at room temperature for 1 to 2 days or refrigerate for up to 5 days. Reheat in a 350° oven before serving.

BLUEBERRY CRUMB SQUARES

AT A GLANCE

SERVES: 8 to 10
PAN: 7½″ × 11½″
× 2″ ovenproof
glass dish
PAN PREP: Butter
OVEN TEMP: 375°
RACK LEVEL: Lower
third
BAKING TIME: 30 to
35 minutes
METHOD: Hand

Think of a truly American berry, and it is apt to be the blueberry. When cooked these delicate deep purple berries give up a rich, reddish-blue liquid with a flavor all its own. I do not bother with fresh berries for this cake. Since the tiny Maine canned variety works quite well, I can enjoy my kuchen year round.

This quick dough should be made the old-fashioned way, by hand, with a wooden spoon. Take care not to overmix. I hope you enjoy this delicious recipe; it is a favorite with my husband and has been in my collection for more years than I care to admit.

THE BLUEBERRY FILLING:

Two	15-ounce cans of blueberries, well drained
2	tablespoons cornstarch
¼	cup sugar
1	teaspoon freshly squeezed lemon juice

THE CAKE:

2	cups plus 3 tablespoons sifted unbleached all-purpose flour
2	teaspoons baking powder
½	teaspoon salt
¾	cup unsalted butter, at room temperature
⅔	cup plus 1 tablespoon sugar
2	large eggs
½	teaspoon vanilla extract
¼	teaspoon ground cinnamon

1. Position rack in lower third of the oven and preheat oven to 375°. Butter a 7½″ × 11½″ × 2″ Pyrex dish.
2. To make the blueberry filling: Thoroughly drain the blueberries, reserving ¾ cup of the syrup. Combine the cornstarch and sugar thoroughly in a medium-sized saucepan. Gradually blend in the syrup. Bring to a slow boil, stirring constantly until thickened, smooth, and clear. Remove from heat. Gently fold in the berries and the lemon juice. Set aside to cool.

3. To make the cake: Sift together 2 *cups* of the flour, the baking powder, and salt using a triple sifter. Set aside.

4. Put the butter in a large mixing bowl. Using a wooden spoon, cream until smooth. Gradually add ⅔ *cup* of the sugar, mixing until well blended. Blend in the eggs, 1 at a time, mixing well. Add the vanilla extract. Stir in the dry ingredients in three additions, mixing just until incorporated after each addition. At the end you should have a soft dough.

5. Reserve 2 tablespoons of the dough for a crumb topping. Spread a little more than half the remaining dough into the buttered baking dish. To do this easily, lightly flour your hand and pat the dough to form a smooth and somewhat even surface. Cover with the blueberry filling.

6. Place *1 tablespoon* flour in a small dish. Make balls the size of walnuts from remaining half of dough. Roll each ball in the flour and flatten in your hand to a thickness of ⅛ inch. Arrange the dough disks over the blueberries, starting at the edges of the baking dish, and working toward the center. Continue until filling is mostly covered. (There will be some bare spots.)

7. To make the topping: In a small bowl, combine the reserved 2 tablespoons dough, the remaining *2 tablespoons* flour, *1 tablespoon* sugar, and the cinnamon. Work with a pastry blender until coarse crumbs are formed. Sprinkle the topping over dough. Bake in the preheated oven 30 to 35 minutes, until top and bottom crusts are golden brown.

8. Remove from oven. Set the pan on a cake rack to cool. Before serving, dust with confectioners' sugar and cut into pieces.

STORAGE: Cover the pan loosely with aluminum foil and store at room temperature for up to 2 days. For longer storage refrigerate, but heat briefly before serving. The cake will keep for 5 days.

🌾 GOLDEN PEACH CAKE

▽ ··

AT A GLANCE

SERVES: 8 to 10

PAN: 9″ springform

PAN PREP: Butter

OVEN TEMP: 350°

RACK LEVEL: Lower third

BAKING TIME: 55 to 60 minutes

METHOD: Electric mixer/food processor

·····················

Peaches are my favorite summer fruit. It is impossible for me to pass a bin of fragrant, ripe peaches without stopping. I always pick up one or two to get a closer whiff, then I gently press the brilliant red, orange, and gold skin to see if they are ready for baking.

THE TOPPING:

1/4	cup walnuts
1	teaspoon sugar
1/4	teaspoon ground cinnamon

THE CAKE:

3	medium peaches
1	teaspoon freshly squeezed lemon juice
1 3/4	cups sifted cake flour
2	teaspoons baking powder
1/2	teaspoon salt
1/2	cup (1 stick) unsalted butter
1/2	teaspoon grated lemon rind
3/4	cup plus 2 tablespoons sugar
4	large egg yolks or 2 large eggs
1	teaspoon vanilla extract
1/3	cup milk

1. Position rack in the lower third of the oven and preheat to 350°. Butter a 9-inch springform pan.
2. To make the topping: Place the nuts, sugar, and cinnamon in container of a food processor fitted with the steel blade. Pulse until the nuts are chopped medium-sized. Set aside.
3. To make the cake: Wipe the peaches with a damp paper towel. Peel only if you wish. Cut the peaches into 1-inch chunks, to make about 2 cups. Sprinkle the peaches with lemon juice. Set aside.
4. Sift together flour, baking powder, and salt in a triple sifter. Set aside.
5. Cut the butter into 1-inch pieces and place in the large bowl of an electric mixer fitted with beaters or paddle attachment.

Soften on low speed, then add the lemon rind. Increase speed to medium-high and cream until smooth and light in color, about 1½ to 2 minutes.

6. Add the sugar, 1 tablespoon at a time, taking 6 to 8 minutes to blend it in well. Scrape the sides of the bowl occasionally. Add the yolks, 1 at a time at 30-second intervals. Beat for 2 minutes longer, scraping sides of bowl as necessary. Blend in the vanilla.

7. Reduce mixer speed to low. Add the flour mixture alternately with the milk, dividing the dry ingredients into three parts and the liquid into two parts, starting and ending with the flour. Beat just until incorporated after each addition. Scrape the sides of the bowl and mix for 10 more seconds.

8. Spread ⅔ of the batter in the prepared pan. Arrange the peaches over the top in a single layer. Drop remaining batter by table-spoons evenly around the pan. Working from the center out-ward, gently spread the batter over the fruit with the back of the tablespoon as best you can. It is not necessary to cover the peaches completely. Do not press too hard or fruit will cling to spoon.

9. Sprinkle the topping evenly over the batter. Center the pan on the rack and bake in the preheated oven for 55 to 60 minutes, until the cake begins to come away from sides of pan and is golden brown on top.

10. Remove from oven and set the pan on a cake rack to cool. When ready to serve, remove the side of the pan. If you wish to re-move the metal bottom from the cake before serving, use a parchment lining (see Bing Cherry Kuchen, page 202).

STORAGE: Cover the cake loosely with aluminum foil and store at room temperature for the first day after baking. For longer storage refrigerate up to 4 additional days. Reheat before serving in a 350° oven for about 10 minutes, until slightly warm.

SERVING SUGGESTION: Serve this delectable cake cut into wedges, either plain or with peach ice cream or Yogurt Topping (page 479).

(variations follow)

VARIATIONS

NECTARINE CAKE

Substitute nectarines for the peaches, preparing them as in Step 3.

BLUEBERRY CAKE

Substitute 1¼ cups fresh blueberries for peaches. Prepare as follows: Wash and dry thoroughly on paper towels. Sprinkle berries with 2 teaspoons all-purpose flour. Omit the lemon juice.

GREEN GRAPE CAKE

Substitute 1¼ cups seedless Thompson grapes for peaches. Prepare as follows: Spread the grapes in a single layer on a flat pan lined with paper toweling. Wipe the grapes with damp paper toweling, shaking the pan occasionally to move the grapes. Omit the lemon juice.

PURPLE PLUM CAKE

Substitute ¾ pound purple plums for peaches. Prepare as follows: Wipe with damp paper toweling, slice in half and remove pits. Cut plums into ½-inch pieces. Proceed with master recipe.

🍂 NUTTY CRANBERRY ORANGE CAKE

....

ranberries received their name from the early settlers of Massachusetts. According to an article written by Steven Raichlen for the New York Times *on November 23, 1988, "these wild cone-shaped blossoms of the low vines, a relative of the honeysuckle, reminded these settlers of the beak of a crane, and over the years, craneberry was shortened to cranberry."*

Although traditionally used as a condiment, cranberries are now showing up on the dessert table, where they lend themselves to a variety of tasty treats such as this delightful coffee cake, wonderful to have on hand for impromptu holiday gatherings. It's especially pleasing to those who do not like their cakes too sweet.

Fresh cranberries are in season during the late autumn months; however, they freeze well for use all year round. Use them straight from the freezer. They become too watery when thawed.

....

▽ ....
AT A GLANCE

SERVES: 10 to 12
PAN: 9 1/2 " fluted tube pan (12-cup capacity)
PAN PREP: Butter/flour
OVEN TEMP: 350°
RACK LEVEL: Lower third
BAKING TIME: 60 to 65 minutes
METHOD: Electric mixer/food processor

....

1	small navel orange, unpeeled
1	cup walnuts
2	cups fresh cranberries, washed and dried
2 1/4	cups sifted cake flour
2	teaspoons baking powder
1/2	teaspoon salt
2/3	cup (1 1/3 sticks) unsalted butter
1 1/3	cups superfine or strained sugar
3	large eggs
2	tablespoons Grand Marnier, Cointreau, or Triple Sec
1	teaspoon vanilla extract
1/3	cup milk
1	recipe Vanilla Glaze (page 461), using measurements for large cake

1. Place the orange in a small saucepan. Fill the pan halfway with water, cover, and bring to a boil. Reduce heat and simmer 30 to 35 minutes. Drain. Rinse the orange with cold water to stop the cooking. Set aside to cool.
2. Position rack in the lower third of the oven and preheat to 350°. Butter and dust with all-purpose flour a 9 1/2-inch fluted tube pan. Invert over the sink and tap to remove excess flour.

Quick and Easy Cakes

3. In the container of a food processor fitted with the steel blade, chop nuts until medium fine. Transfer to a small bowl and set aside.

4. Slice off the stem end of the orange. Cut the orange into quarters and place in the processor. Pulse 3 to 4 times, then add the cranberries and pulse until mixture is coarsely chopped. Transfer to another small bowl.

5. Sift together flour, baking powder, and salt, using a triple sifter. Set aside.

6. Cut the butter into 1-inch pieces and put them in the large bowl of an electric mixer fitted with beaters or paddle attachment; soften on low speed. Increase speed to medium-high and cream until smooth and light in color, about $1\frac{1}{2}$ to 2 minutes.

7. Add sugar, 1 tablespoon at a time, taking 6 to 8 minutes to blend it in well. Scrape the sides of the bowl occasionally.

8. Add eggs, 1 at a time at 1-minute intervals, scraping the sides of bowl as necessary. Blend in the liqueur and vanilla.

9. Reduce mixer speed to low. Add the flour mixture alternately with the milk, dividing the dry ingredients into three parts and the liquid into two parts, starting and ending with the flour. Mix just until incorporated after each addition. Scrape the sides of the bowl and mix for 10 seconds longer.

10. Remove the bowl from the machine. With a $2\frac{3}{4}$-inch-wide rubber spatula, gently fold in the nuts and fruits. Spoon the batter into the pan, smoothing the surface with the back of a tablespoon. Bake in the preheated oven for 60 to 65 minutes, until cake is golden brown on top and begins to come away from the sides of the pan. A twig of straw or a toothpick inserted into center of the cake should come out dry.

11. Remove from oven. Set the pan on a cake rack to cool for 10 to 15 minutes, then invert the cake onto the rack and carefully lift off the pan. Allow the cake to cool to room temperature.

12. To glaze the cake: Dribble the glaze over the cake from the tip of a teaspoon, allowing it to drip randomly down the sides. It is not necessary for the icing to cover the cake completely. To slice the cake easily, dip a sharp knife in warm water and cut straight down in a single motion.

STORAGE: Store the cake at room temperature under a glass cover or in an airtight container for up to 1 week.

🌾 CRANBERRY OATMEAL SQUARES

These are the ideal choice for a holiday buffet table. They also make a wonderful ending to an elegant brunch, as well as to most fall and early winter casual dinner parties.

THE TOPPING:

¼	cup (½ stick) butter
1	tablespoon honey
⅓	cup light brown sugar, firmly packed
½	cup quick-cooking oatmeal
¾	cup unsifted, unbleached all-purpose flour
½	teaspoon cinnamon

THE CAKE:

2	cups cranberries, washed and thoroughly dried
1⅓	cups sifted unbleached all-purpose flour
2	teaspoons baking powder
¼	teaspoon baking soda
½	teaspoon salt
1	teaspoon ground nutmeg
1	cup unsifted whole wheat flour
½	cup (1 stick) unsalted butter
1	teaspoon freshly grated navel orange rind
¼	cup honey
⅔	cup sugar
2	large eggs
1	teaspoon vanilla extract
¾	cup milk
½	cup currant jelly

▽ AT A GLANCE

SERVES: 10 to 12
PAN: 10½" × 15½" × 1" jelly roll
PAN PREP: Butter
OVEN TEMP: 350°
RACK LEVEL: Lower third
BAKING TIME: 30 to 35 minutes
METHOD: Electric mixer/food processor

1. To make the topping: In a small saucepan, combine the butter and the honey. Cook over *low* heat until the butter is melted. Let cool for 5 minutes. Add the remaining ingredients and stir with a fork until crumbs form. Set aside.
2. To make the cake: Place the cranberries in the container of a food processor fitted with the steel blade. Pulse 6 to 8 times, until pieces are chopped medium-small. Set aside.

Quick and Easy Cakes

211

3. Position a rack in the lower third of the oven and preheat to 350°. Butter a 10½″ × 15½″ × 1″ jelly roll pan.

4. Sift together the flour, baking powder, baking soda, salt, and nutmeg in a triple sifter. Using a wire whisk, blend in the whole wheat flour. Set aside.

5. Cut the butter into 1-inch pieces and place in the large bowl of an electric mixer fitted with beaters or paddle attachment. Soften on low speed, add the grated orange rind, and increase speed to medium-high. Cream until smooth and light in color, about 1½ to 2 minutes.

6. Add the honey and mix for 1 minute. Add the sugar, 1 tablespoon at a time, taking 3 to 4 minutes to blend it in well. Scrape the sides of bowl occasionally.

7. Add the eggs, 1 at a time at 1-minute intervals, scraping the sides of the bowl as necessary. Beat for 1 minute longer. Blend in the vanilla. Batter will appear to separate; this is okay.

8. Reduce mixer speed to low. Add the flour mixture alternately with the milk, dividing the dry ingredients into three parts and the liquid into two parts, starting and ending with the flour. Mix just until incorporated after each addition. Scrape sides and mix for 10 seconds longer.

9. Spoon the batter into the prepared pan, smoothing the surface with the back of a tablespoon. Cover the batter with chopped cranberries, then with the crumb topping, pressing it *lightly* into the batter. Center the pan on the rack and bake in the preheated oven for 30 to 35 minutes, or until the cake begins to leave sides of pan and the top is springy to the touch.

10. Remove from oven and set the pan on a cake rack to cool while you prepare the glaze.

11. To make the currant glaze: Heat the jelly in a small saucepan until warm and smooth. Gently brush over the hot cake, lightly coating the entire surface. Let the cake cool completely before serving.

STORAGE: Cover the pan with aluminum foil. Store at room temperature for up to 5 days.

🐚 CRANBERRY CHEESE KUCHEN

Tangy cranberries and a sweetened cream cheese topping over a cakelike cookie dough make a combination that's hard to beat. The topping is a cinch to make, but it is crucial that the cream cheese be very soft to blend smoothly with the other ingredients. This cake must be stored in the refrigerator, but I highly recommend warming it before serving. It is heavenly!

▽

AT A GLANCE

SERVES: 8 to 10
PAN: 9″ springform
PAN PREP: Butter/flour
OVEN TEMP: 350°
RACK LEVEL: Lower third
BAKING TIME: 60 to 65 minutes
METHOD: Food processor/hand

THE BOTTOM LAYER:

One   1-pound can whole cranberry sauce
1⅓   cups unsifted unbleached all-purpose flour (see Note)
1   teaspoon baking powder
½   cup sugar
¼   teaspoon salt
½   cup (1 stick) unsalted butter, practically frozen
1   large egg
1   large egg yolk
1   teaspoon vanilla extract
½   teaspoon freshly grated navel orange rind

THE CREAM CHEESE TOPPING:

Two   3-ounce packages cream cheese, at room temperature
½   cup sour cream
½   cup sugar
1   large egg
1   teaspoon vanilla extract
1   teaspoon fresh lemon juice
1   tablespoon Grand Marnier, Cointreau, or Triple Sec
½   teaspoon freshly grated navel orange rind
¼   teaspoon freshly grated lemon rind

1. Position a rack in the lower third of the oven and preheat to 350°. Butter and flour a 9-inch springform pan, then invert the pan over the kitchen sink and tap to remove excess flour.
2. To make the bottom layer: Discard the excess juice that accumulates at the top of the can of cranberries. Empty the cran-

Quick and Easy Cakes

213

berry sauce into a measuring cup. Fruit and juice should measure about 1⅓ cups. Set aside.

3. Put the flour, baking powder, sugar, and salt in container of a food processor fitted with the steel blade. Pulse 2 or 3 times to blend. Cut the butter into ½-inch pieces and add. Pulse 10 or 12 times, or until fine crumbs are formed.

4. In a small bowl, combine the whole egg, egg yolk, vanilla, and orange rind. Add to the crumbs and pulse 6 to 8 times, just until the mixture forms a dough. Remove the dough and shape it into a flat 5-inch disk with floured hands.

5. Center the dough in the prepared pan. Reflour your hands. Press the dough down with your palm to spread it into the pan, working from the center out. As you reach the side of the pan, make a ¾-inch rim around the edge, using the side of your forefinger.

6. Spread cranberry sauce evenly across top of dough to edge of rim.

7. To make the topping: Place all the topping ingredients in container of a food processor fitted with the steel blade and process until completely smooth. Scrape down the sides of container as needed.

8. Slowly pour topping over cranberries, being careful not to extend beyond edge of dough.

9. Set pan on a 12-inch square of aluminum foil, molding the edges of the foil around the pan. Bake in the preheated oven 60 to 65 minutes, or until the crust is brown and begins to leave the sides of the pan. The topping will remain creamy colored and should not darken.

10. Remove from the oven and set on a cake rack to cool completely. Just before serving, run a thin knife around the edge of pan and carefully remove the rim.

STORAGE: Cover loosely with aluminum foil. Store at room temperature for up to 6 hours or refrigerate for up to 5 days.

NOTE: If you are making the cake by hand, increase flour measurement to 1½ cups *sifted*.

🌰 ITALIAN PURPLE PLUM CAKE

*D*eep *purple, oval plums, often called Italian plums, work particularly well in baking because they are not too juicy. Look for them in August and September when they make their seasonal appearance.*

This cake is especially quick to make because the fruit does not require peeling and the batter is made in the food processor. Circles of plums glazed with a touch of sugar decorate the surface. As they bake, the skins of the plums run, giving the fruit a magnificent hot pink hue.

▽

AT A GLANCE

SERVES: 6 to 8
PAN: 9″ springform
PAN PREP: Butter
OVEN TEMP: 375°
RACK LEVEL: Lower third
BAKING TIME: 55 to 60 minutes
METHOD: Food processor/hand

1 1/2	cups unsifted, unbleached all-purpose flour (see Note)
2/3	cup plus 3 tablespoons sugar
2	teaspoons baking powder
1/2	teaspoon salt
1/2	cup (1 stick) unsalted butter, partially frozen
2	large egg yolks
1/4	cup milk
1	teaspoon vanilla extract
7	medium-sized Italian plums (about 1 pound)

1. Position rack in lower third of the oven and preheat to 375°. Butter a 9-inch springform pan and put it in the refrigerator until ready to use.
2. Place the flour, 2/3 *cup* of sugar, baking powder, and salt in the container of a food processor fitted with the steel blade. Pulse 2 or 3 times to blend. Cut the butter into 1/4-inch pieces and add. Pulse 10 to 12 times or until fine crumbs are formed.
3. In a small bowl, blend the egg yolks, milk, and vanilla together with a a fork. Add to the processor. Pulse 6 to 8 times or just until a soft dough is formed.
4. Turn the dough into the prepared pan. With floured hands, press the dough down with your palms to spread it into the pan, working from the center out. Then press the dough against the side of the pan, forcing it upward to form a 1/2-inch edge.
5. Wipe the plums well with damp paper toweling. Slice the plums in half lengthwise, remove the pits, and cut in half again. Arrange the plums, flesh side up, in circles starting from the outer rim.

Quick and Easy Cakes

You should have three circles. Sprinkle tops of plums with the remaining 3 *tablespoons* sugar.

6. Bake in the preheated oven for 55 to 60 minutes, or until the sides of the cake begin to release from the pan and the top surface is golden brown. Remove from oven and set the pan on a cake rack to cool. Just before serving, remove the outside rim of pan. To serve, cut the cake into wedges.

STORAGE: Cover loosely with aluminum foil. Store at room temperature for up to 2 days, or refrigerate for up to 5 days. Reheat before serving.

SERVING SUGGESTION: Though this cake is fabulous unadorned, it is especially delicious served with Yogurt Topping (page 479).

NOTE: If you are making this by hand, increase flour measurement to 1²/₃ cups sifted.

🍃 ROSY RHUBARB CAKE

This wonderful recipe comes from my friend Virginia McKinley, a fine baker with a treasury of homespun recipes. Her rhubarb cake recipe intrigued me, since rhubarb is more commonly used for pies and pastries.

Rhubarb can be considered a fruit or a vegetable. Actually, it is the stalk of an aromatic plant. Although the top leaves are poisonous, the stems are used in cooking, for making aperitifs, and for medicinal purposes. Rhubarb is very nutritious, but it is also extremely tart and must be cooked with more sugar than is necessary for most fruits.

THE FRUIT:

    1   pound fresh rhubarb
   1/2 cup sugar

THE CAKE:

    1   cup sifted unbleached all-purpose flour
    1   teaspoon baking soda
   1/4 teaspoon salt
    1   teaspoon ground cinnamon
    1   cup whole wheat flour, preferably stone-ground
   1/2 cup (1 stick) unsalted butter
    1   cup sugar
    2   large eggs
    1   teaspoon vanilla extract
    1   cup plain low-fat yogurt

1. To prepare the fruit: Wash and dry the rhubarb. Cut off the ends, making sure no trace of the poisonous leaves remains. Scrape the strings from the rhubarb with a sharp knife or a vegetable peeler, pulling any remaining loose strings with your fingertips. Cut the rhubarb stalks into 1/4- to 1/2-inch slices (you should have about 2 cups) and put in a medium-sized glass or stainless steel bowl. (Do not use aluminum.) Sprinkle with the sugar and let stand while you prepare the batter. The rhubarb will soften and release some juice. Do not prepare the fruit more than 1/2 hour in advance or the sugar will extract too much liquid from the rhubarb.

▽

AT A GLANCE

SERVES: 8 to 10
PAN: 9″ × 13″ × 2″ ovenproof glass dish
PAN PREP: Butter
OVEN TEMP: 325°
RACK LEVEL: Lower third
BAKING TIME: 40 to 45 minutes
METHOD: Electric mixer

2. Position a rack in the lower third of the oven and preheat to 325°. Butter a 9″ × 13″ × 2″ glass baking dish.

3. To make the cake: Sift together the flour, baking soda, salt, and cinnamon, using a triple sifter. Stir in the whole wheat flour, blending it in thoroughly. Set aside.

4. Cut the butter into 1-inch pieces and place in the large bowl of an electric mixer fitted with beaters or paddle attachment. Soften on low speed, then increase speed to medium-high. Cream until smooth and light in color, about 1½ to 2 minutes.

5. Add the sugar, 1 tablespoon at a time, taking 6 to 8 minutes to blend it in well. Scrape the sides of bowl occasionally. Add the eggs, 1 at a time at 1-minute intervals, scraping the sides of the bowl as necessary. Blend in the vanilla.

6. Reduce mixer speed to low. Add the flour mixture alternately with the yogurt, dividing the flour into three parts and the yogurt into two parts, starting and ending with the flour. Mix only until incorporated after each addition. Scrape the sides of the bowl as necessary. Remove the bowl from mixer.

7. Fold the rhubarb and its juices into the batter.

8. Spoon the batter into the prepared baking dish, smoothing the surface with the back of a tablespoon. Bake in the preheated oven for 40 to 45 minutes, until cake begins to come away from sides of dish, is springy to the touch, and is browned on the bottom.

9. Remove from oven and set the pan on a cake rack to cool completely. When ready to serve, cut into squares and top with whipped cream.

OPTIONAL: Combine ⅔ cup of lightly toasted broken pecans with 1 tablespoon flour and fold into the batter with the rhubarb.

STORAGE: Cover the baking dish top loosely with aluminum foil. Store at room temperature for up to 5 days.

🌰 SUGARSWEET TOMATO NUT TORTE

*C*ommonly mistaken for a vegetable, the tomato is really a fruit. It can be used in sweet as well as savory foods.

Here, sweet, plump, ripe summer tomatoes are combined with generous amounts of chopped nuts, brown sugar, and spices. While the tomato flavor is subtle, it is the nucleus that brings the various tastes together. The fruit also creates a soft, moist texture that helps preserve the torte's freshness. This is a cake to enjoy from July to September, when tomatoes are in season.

▽

AT A GLANCE

SERVES: 8 to 10
PAN: 9″ springform
PAN PREP: Butter/
parchment
OVEN TEMP: 325°
RACK LEVEL: Lower
third
BAKING TIME: 55 to
60 minutes
METHOD: Electric
mixer/food
processor

3/4	pound very ripe tomatoes
1	tablespoon cider vinegar
1 1/2	cups walnuts
1/3	cup (2/3 stick) unsalted butter
1/2	cup unbleached all-purpose flour, unsifted
1	cup sifted unbleached all-purpose flour
1	teaspoon baking soda
1/2	teaspoon salt
1	teaspoon ground cinnamon
1/2	teaspoon ground nutmeg
4	large eggs
1 1/4	cups dark brown sugar, lightly packed
2	teaspoons freshly grated navel orange rind
1	teaspoon vanilla extract

1. Cut an X in the skin on the bottom of each tomato. Remove the cores, place the tomatoes in a bowl, and add boiling water to cover. Allow to stand for 1 minute, then rinse in cold water and peel off the skins. Cut each tomato in half across the core and squeeze gently to remove seeds and juice. Purée the pulp in a food processor. You should have about 1 cup of purée. Stir in the vinegar and set aside.
2. Position a rack in the lower third of the oven and preheat to 325°. Butter a 9-inch springform pan and line the bottom with parchment paper.
3. Put walnuts and 1/2 cup unsifted flour in the container of the processor fitted with the steel blade and pulse 8 to 10 times, until

Quick and Easy Cakes

219

nuts are chopped to medium size. Transfer to a bowl and set aside.

4. In a small pan, melt the butter over low heat. Set aside to cool to tepid. Sift together the 1 cup sifted flour, baking soda, salt, and spices in a triple sifter. Set aside.

5. Place the eggs in the large bowl of an electric mixer fitted with beaters or whip attachment. Beat on medium-high speed until thickened and light in color, about 1½ to 2 minutes. Gradually add the brown sugar over 2 to 3 minutes and beat for 3 minutes longer. The mixture will be very thick.

6. Reduce mixer speed to medium-low. Blend in the orange rind and vanilla. Add the flour mixture alternately with the tomato purée, dividing the dry ingredients into three parts and the purée into two parts, starting and ending with the flour. Scrape sides of bowl as needed. The batter will be very loose.

7. Quickly pour in the butter, then add the nuts, beating just until blended.

8. *Immediately* pour the batter into the prepared pan. Center the pan on the rack and bake in the preheated oven 55 to 60 minutes, until cake is golden brown, springy to the touch, and the sides begin to come away from the pan. A twig of straw or a toothpick inserted into the center should come out dry.

9. Remove from oven and set the pan on a cake rack to cool completely. Release the outer rim of pan, invert the cake onto the rack, and peel off the parchment paper. Place top side up on a serving platter. Just before serving, dust the top with confectioners' sugar. If you like, split the cake into two layers with a long thin knife, then fill and frost with Whipped Cream (page 486) made with 1½ cups heavy sweet cream. Garnish with chopped walnuts.

STORAGE: Cover the top of the cake loosely with aluminum foil and store at room temperature. (Refrigerate if you have used whipped cream.) This cake will keep up to 5 days.

❧ DATE NUT CAKE

My mother-in-law was a cook and baker with a limited repertoire, but whatever she made was done with a deft hand and a large dose of pride.

She could not eat rich desserts, so most of her recipes were simple. For her date nut cake she folded the cut dates and pecans into a spongelike batter. The result was a cake lighter and less sweet than most fruit-nut combinations. In her home it was always served with a glass of tea.

▽
AT A GLANCE

SERVES: 8 to 10
PAN: 9″ × 13″ × 2″ oblong
PAN PREP: Butter/flour
OVEN TEMP: 350°
RACK LEVEL: Lower third
BAKING TIME: 25 to 30 minutes
METHOD: Electric mixer

One 8-ounce package pitted dates
1 large egg
3 large egg yolks
3/4 cup plus 2 tablespoons superfine or strained sugar
1 teaspoon vanilla
1 cup coarsely chopped pecans
3/4 cup sifted unbleached all-purpose flour
3 large egg whites

1. Position a rack in the lower third of the oven and preheat to 350°. Butter and flour a 9″ × 13″ × 2″ pan. Invert over the kitchen sink and tap to remove excess flour.
2. Cut the dates into 1/4-inch pieces. You should have 1 cup. Set aside.
3. Put the whole egg and the egg yolks in the small bowl of an electric mixer fitted with the beaters or whip attachment. Beat on medium speed until thick and light in color, about 1 1/2 to 2 minutes. Add *3/4 cup* sugar, 1 tablespoon at a time, taking 4 to 5 minutes to blend it in well. Scrape the sides of the bowl occasionally. Blend in the vanilla. Remove bowl from mixer.
4. In a medium-size bowl, combine the dates, nuts, and flour. Toss until pieces are well coated with the flour. Using a rubber spatula, fold into the yolk mixture. Set aside.
5. In the large bowl of the mixer, with clean beaters, whip the whites on medium speed until frothy. Increase the speed to medium-high and beat until soft peaks form. Gradually add *2 tablespoons* sugar and beat 15 seconds longer. Remove bowl from mixer.

Quick and Easy Cakes

221

6. Using a 2³/₄-inch-wide rubber spatula, fold ¹/₃ of the whites into the yolk mixture, taking about 20 turns to lighten. Add the remaining whites and gently fold the mixture together, taking about 40 additional turns. Spoon the batter into pan, smoothing surface with the back of a tablespoon. Bake in the preheated oven 25 to 30 minutes, until cake is golden brown on top, springy to the touch, and begins to come away from the sides of the pan.
7. Remove from oven and set the pan on a cake rack to cool. Just before serving, dust the top lightly with confectioners' sugar and cut into squares.

STORAGE: Store at room temperature covered tightly with aluminum foil for up to 4 days.

VARIATION

CHOCOLATE CHIP DATE NUT CAKE

Add one 6-ounce package (1 cup) minisize semisweet chocolate chips to the flour mixture in Step 4. Proceed with master recipe.

🐌 AUSTRALIAN APRICOT CAKE

....

ustralian apricots are huge dried apricots that have been candied. I love their moist plump exterior and contrasting sweet and tangy flavor. Do not confuse them with the ordinary dried variety, which have not been candied and are much chewier. Australian apricots are difficult to find in supermarkets, but gourmet food shops of department stores, candy stores, and specialty fruit stores generally stock them.

Candied fruits can be difficult to chop with a knife. It is easier to snip the fruit into small pieces with scissors. This cake slices better after it's mellowed for a couple of days—if you can wait that long!

....

▽ ....

AT A GLANCE

SERVES: 10 to 12
PAN: 9¹/₂″ fluted ring (12-cup capacity)
PAN PREP: Butter/flour
OVEN TEMP: 350°
RACK LEVEL: Lower third
BAKING TIME: 60 to 65 minutes
METHOD: Electric mixer/food processor

....

1	small navel orange (about 5 ounces), unpeeled
8 to 9	ounces candied Australian apricots, cut into ¹/₈- to ¹/₄-inch pieces (about 1¹/₂ cups)
1	cup walnuts, chopped medium-fine
2¹/₄	cups sifted cake flour
2	teaspoons baking powder
¹/₂	teaspoon salt
²/₃	cups (1¹/₃ sticks) unsalted butter
1¹/₄	cups superfine or strained sugar
3	large eggs
¹/₃	cup milk
3	tablespoons Grand Marnier, Cointreau, or Triple Sec
1	teaspoon vanilla extract

1. Place the orange in a small pan and add water to cover. Cover the pan, bring to a boil, reduce heat, and simmer 30 to 35 minutes, until tender. Drain. Rinse the orange under cold water to stop the cooking. Set aside for 10 to 15 minutes.

2. Slice off the stem end of the orange. Cut it into quarters, place in food processor fitted with the steel blade, and pulse 6 to 8 times or until pieces are medium-small. Measure out ¹/₂ cup pulp and set aside. Discard the remaining pulp.

3. Position rack in the lower third of the oven and preheat to 350°. Butter and dust with all-purpose flour a 9¹/₂-inch fluted ring pan.

Quick and Easy Cakes

223

Invert the pan over the kitchen sink and tap to remove excess flour.

4. Sift together the flour, baking powder, and salt, using a triple sifter. Set aside.

5. Cut the butter into 1-inch pieces and put in the large bowl of an electric mixer fitted with beaters or paddle attachment to soften on low speed. Increase speed to medium-high. Cream until smooth and light in color, about 1½ to 2 minutes.

6. Add the sugar, 1 tablespoon at a time, taking 6 to 8 minutes to blend it in well. Scrape the sides of the bowl occasionally.

7. Add the eggs, 1 at a time at 1-minute intervals, scraping the sides of the bowl as necessary.

8. Reduce mixer speed to low. In a *small* bowl, combine the orange pulp, milk, liqueur, and vanilla. Add the dry ingredients alternately with the orange/milk mixture, dividing the flour into three parts and the liquid into two parts, starting and ending with the flour. Mix just until incorporated after each addition. Scrape the sides of the bowl and mix for 10 seconds longer.

9. Remove the bowl from the machine. Using a rubber spatula, gently fold in the apricots and nuts just to incorporate. Spoon the batter into the prepared pan, smoothing the surface with the back of a tablespoon.

10. Bake in the preheated oven 60 to 65 minutes, until cake is golden brown on top and begins to come away from the sides of the pan. A twig of straw or a toothpick inserted into the center of the cake will come out dry.

11. Remove from oven and set the pan on cake rack to cool for 15 to 20 minutes, then invert the cake onto the rack and gently lift off the pan. Turn the cake top side up and allow to cool completely. Just before serving, dust the top lightly with confectioners' sugar. To slice, dip a serrated knife in warm water and cut, using a sawing motion. Moisten the knife frequently to avoid tearing cake.

STORAGE: Store at room temperature under a glass cover or in an airtight container, or wrapped in plastic wrap, for up to 1 week.

🌰 BRANDIED CHOCOLATE PRUNE CAKE

....

The flavors of chocolate and prunes complement each other with great finesse. The prunes also add moistness.

....

▽............................

AT A GLANCE

SERVES: 10 to 12
PAN: 9″ × 13″ ×
2″ oblong
PAN PREP: Butter
OVEN TEMP: 350°
RACK LEVEL: Lower
third
BAKING TIME: 35 to
40 minutes
METHOD: Electric
mixer

....

1	cup pitted prunes, packed (about 8 ounces)
1¼	cups water, divided
½	cup brandy, such as Armagnac, Grand Marnier, or Cointreau, divided
1½	teaspoons instant freeze-dried coffee
2	ounces unsweetened chocolate, coarsely chopped
2	cups sifted cake flour
1	teaspoon baking powder
½	teaspoon salt
⅔	cup (1⅓ sticks) unsalted butter
¾	cup plus 1 teaspoon granulated sugar
¾	cup light brown sugar, lightly packed
2	large eggs
3	tablespoons finely chopped almonds

1. Put the prunes in a small heavy 1-quart saucepan. Add *¾ cup* of the water. Bring to a boil, cover, and simmer 20 to 25 minutes, or until prunes are very soft and water is almost completely evaporated. If the prunes are not tender and the water cooks out, add a bit more liquid. Remove from heat. Stir with a fork until you get a smooth purée. Stir in *¼ cup* brandy.

2. Bring *½ cup* water to a boil in a small saucepan. Remove from the heat and add the coffee. When the coffee is dissolved, add the chocolate and stir until melted and smooth. Blend into the prune mixture and set aside.

3. Position rack in the lower third of the oven and preheat to 350°. Butter a 9″ × 13″ × 2″ pan.

4. Sift together the flour, baking powder, and salt, using a triple sifter. Set aside.

5. Cut the butter into 1-inch pieces and place in the large bowl of an electric mixer fitted with beaters or paddle attachment. Soften on low speed, increase speed to medium-high, and cream until smooth, about 1½ to 2 minutes.

Quick and Easy Cakes

225

6. Add *3/4 cup* granulated sugar, 1 tablespoon at a time, taking 3 to 4 minutes to blend it in well. Add light brown sugar over an additional 3 to 4 minutes. Scrape the sides of the bowl occasionally.
7. Add the eggs, 1 at a time at 1-minute intervals. Reduce speed to low.
8. Add the flour mixture alternately with the prune mixture, dividing the dry ingredients into three parts and the prune mixture into two parts, starting and ending with the flour. Mix just until incorporated after each addition. Scrape the sides of the bowl as necessary.
9. Spoon the batter into the prepared pan. Combine almonds with *1 teaspoon* sugar and sprinkle over the top of the batter. Bake in the preheated oven 35 to 40 minutes, until cake begins to leave sides of pan and the top is springy to the touch.
10. Remove from oven. While the cake is still hot, drizzle remaining *1/4 cup* brandy over the top, then set the pan on a cake rack to cool. If you wish, make 1 small recipe Quick Chocolate Glaze (page 462). Place in small pastry bag fitted with #2 round tube. Starting from a corner of the pan, run diagonal lines across top of the cake, then reverse and run the lines in the opposite direction to form a webbed design.

STORAGE: Cover the cake with aluminum foil and store at room temperature for up to 5 days.

PRECEEDING PAGE:
Raspberry Ribbons

*Filbert Gateau with
Praline Buttercream*

Candied Pepita Seed Cake

OPPOSITE, TOP:
Bing Cherry Kuchen
OPPOSITE, BOTTOM:
*Flourless Chocolate
Roulade with
Whipped Apricot Soufflé*

Meringue Pound Cake with Warm Lemon Sauce

Graham Cracker Cake

Zach's Chocolate Marble Cake

Black Chocolate Zinger

OPPOSITE, TOP:
*Fresh Fruit
Pound Cake*
OPPOSITE, BOTTOM:
*Black Bottom Mint
Cheesecake*
OVERLEAF:
*Hungarian
Magyar
Torte*

Sesame Almond Swirl

Swiss Chocolate Silk

🌺 PINEAPPLE MACADAMIA LOAF

Pineapple and macadamia nuts are two fabulous flavors of the tropics. They are absolutely wonderful together in this scrumptious pound-style cake.

Sun-dried pineapple has a thin, sugary, slightly brittle surface. It is available in specialty nut shops or health food stores. Unsalted macadamias can usually be bought there too.

I like to bake this cake in two loaves, one to eat right away, and one to keep on hand in the freezer. If you don't have two pans the same size, use disposable aluminum foil loaf pans. To bake, place the pans on a cookie sheet for added insulation.

▽
AT A GLANCE

SERVES: 6 to 8 per loaf
PANS: Two 8″ × 4″ × 2¼″ loaf pans (5-cup capacity)
PAN PREP: Butter/flour
OVEN TEMP: 350°
RACK LEVEL: Lower third
BAKING TIME: 55 to 65 minutes
METHOD: Electric mixer

³⁄₄	cup sun-dried pineapple
¹⁄₄	cup dark Jamaican rum
³⁄₄	cup coarsely cut macadamia nuts, preferably unsalted, cut by hand
2¹⁄₄	cups sifted cake flour
1	teaspoon baking powder
¹⁄₂	teaspoon baking soda
³⁄₄	cup (1¹⁄₂ sticks) unsalted butter
1¹⁄₃	cups superfine or strained sugar
3	large eggs
1	teaspoon vanilla extract
²⁄₃	cup sour cream

1. Position a rack in the lower third of the oven and preheat to 350°. Butter and dust with all-purpose flour two 8″ × 4″ × 2¼″ loaf pans. Invert over the kitchen sink and tap to remove excess flour.
2. Cut the pineapple into ¼-inch pieces. Drop them into a small bowl and add the rum. Set aside to marinate while you prepare the batter.
3. If you are using salted nuts, remove the salt by rubbing the nuts between a few layers of paper toweling. Set aside.
4. Sift together the flour, baking powder, and baking soda, using a triple sifter. Set aside.
5. Cut the butter into 1-inch pieces and place in the large bowl of

Quick and Easy Cakes

227

an electric mixer fitted with beaters or paddle attachment. Soften on low speed, then increase speed to medium-high. Cream until smooth and light in color, about $1\frac{1}{2}$ to 2 minutes.

6. Add the sugar, 1 tablespoon at a time, taking 6 to 8 minutes to blend it in well. Scrape the sides of the bowl occasionally.

7. Add the eggs, 1 at a time at 1-minute intervals, scraping the sides of the bowl as necessary. Add the vanilla. Mix 10 seconds longer.

8. Reduce mixer speed to low. Add the flour mixture alternately with the sour cream, dividing the dry ingredients into three parts and the sour cream into two parts, starting and ending with the flour. Mix only until incorporated after each addition. Scrape the sides of the bowl and mix for 10 seconds longer.

9. Remove bowl from the mixer. Using a rubber spatula, fold in the pineapple and nuts, reserving 2 tablespoons of nuts for the topping.

10. Spoon the batter into the prepared pans, smoothing surface with the back of a tablespoon. Sprinkle reserved nuts on top. Bake in the preheated oven 55 to 65 minutes, until cakes are golden brown on top and begin to leave sides of pans. A twig of straw or a toothpick inserted into the center should come out dry.

11. Remove from oven. Set the pans on a cake rack to cool and set for 10 to 15 minutes, then turn the pans on their sides and ease out the cakes. Turn the cakes top side up and continue cooling. To serve, cut into $\frac{1}{2}$-inch slices with a serrated knife, using a back-and-forth sawing motion.

STORAGE: Wrap the cakes in plastic wrap or aluminum foil and store at room temperature for up to 1 week. Or freeze (page 77) one or both loaves.

🐚 NUTMEG CAKE WITH DRIED RED CHERRIES

This recipe was given to me by Judith Moore, one of my former students at the Cookingstudio in Short Hills, New Jersey. The cake has a rich nutmeg flavor—I think you'll be surprised at just how pleasant an intense nutmeg taste can be. Judith made her cake with dark raisins, but I have substituted dried red cherries. The full-bodied flavor of the slightly tart cherries provides a nice balance to the aromatic nutmeg.

Dried cherries can be purchased at most specialty food stores. They can be used interchangeably with raisins, although they are larger in size. When used in cakes, they should be snipped in half with a pair of scissors, otherwise they may sink to the bottom of the batter.

▽ AT A GLANCE

SERVES: 8 to 10
PAN: 9″ fluted ring (10-cup capacity)
PAN PREP: Butter/flour
OVEN TEMP: 350°
RACK LEVEL: Lower third
BAKING TIME: 60 to 65 minutes
METHOD: Electric mixer

1	cup dried sour cherries or raisins
2	cups plus 2 teaspoons sifted unbleached all-purpose flour
2	teaspoons baking powder
³/₄	teaspoon salt
2	teaspoons ground nutmeg
²/₃	cup (1¹/₃ sticks) sweet butter
1¹/₃	cups superfine or strained sugar
2	large eggs
1¹/₂	teaspoons vanilla extract
1	cup milk

1. Plump the cherries (page 63) and cut them in half with scissors. Set aside.
2. Position a rack in the lower third of the oven and preheat to 350°. Butter and flour a 9-inch fluted ring pan. Invert over the kitchen sink and tap to remove excess flour.
3. Sift together *2 cups* flour, baking powder, salt, and nutmeg, using a triple sifter. Set aside.
4. Cut the butter into 1-inch pieces and place in the large bowl of an electric mixer fitted with beaters or paddle attachment. Soften on low speed. Increase speed to medium-high and cream until smooth and light in color, about 1¹/₂ to 2 minutes.

Quick and Easy Cakes

5. Add the sugar, 1 tablespoon at a time, taking 6 to 8 minutes to blend it in well. Scrape the sides of the bowl occasionally.
6. Add the eggs, 1 at a time at 1-minute intervals, scraping the sides of the bowl as necessary. Blend in the vanilla.
7. Reduce mixer speed to low. Add the flour mixture alternately with the milk, dividing the dry ingredients into three parts and the liquid into two parts, starting and ending with the flour. Mix only until incorporated after each addition. Mix 10 seconds longer.
8. Remove the bowl from the mixer. Add *2 teaspoons* flour to the dried cherries and toss to coat well. Using a rubber spatula, fold into the batter in three additions. Spoon the batter into the prepared pan, smoothing the surface with the back of a tablespoon. Bake in the preheated oven 60 to 65 minutes, until cake is springy to the touch and begins to come away from the sides of the pan. A twig of straw or toothpick inserted into the center should come out dry.
9. Remove from oven and set the pan on a cake rack to cool and set for 10 to 15 minutes. Invert onto the rack, gently remove the pan, and let cool completely. Dust the top with confectioners' sugar just before serving.

STORAGE: Store at room temperature under a glass dome or in an airtight container for up to 5 days.

❧ GINGERY PUMPKIN PECAN CAKE

A trio of very popular cakes that share similar characteristics are pumpkin, carrot, and zucchini, moist cakes made with a generous amount of vegetable oil and a blend of spices, nuts, and raisins.

This is a spiffy version of a pumpkin cake, dressed up with a colorful array of yellow and dark raisins and bits of glacéed cherries. A touch of crystallized ginger gives the cake a subtle, pungent flavor.

▽
AT A GLANCE

SERVES: 12 to 16
PAN: 10″ angel food cake pan (4-quart capacity) or two 9″ × 5″ × 2¾″ loaf pans (2-quart capacity)
PAN PREP: Butter
OVEN TEMP: 350°
RACK LEVEL: Lower third
BAKING TIME: 65 to 70 minutes
METHOD: Electric mixer

3	cups sifted unbleached all-purpose flour
2	teaspoons baking powder
2	teaspoons baking soda
1	teaspoon salt
2	teaspoons ground cinnamon
1	teaspoon ground nutmeg
5	large eggs
1	cup granulated sugar
1	cup light brown sugar, lightly packed
One	1-pound can (2 cups) puréed pumpkin (do not use pumpkin pie mix)
1¼	cups unflavored vegetable oil
1½	cups pecans chopped medium, 2 tablespoons reserved for top
1	cup mixed light and dark plumped raisins (page 63)
2	tablespoons minced crystallized ginger
½	cup quartered red glacéed cherries, optional

1. Position rack in the lower third of the oven and preheat to 350°. Butter a 10-inch angel food cake pan.
2. Sift together the flour, baking powder, baking soda, salt, and spices, using a triple sifter. Set aside.
3. Put the eggs in the large bowl of an electric mixer. Using the beaters or whip attachment, beat on medium-high speed for 2 minutes.
4. Add the granulated sugar, 1 tablespoon at a time, taking 3 to 4 minutes to blend it in well. Then add the light brown sugar over an additional 3 to 4 minutes, beating until mixture is light in color and thickened. Add the pumpkin purée and beat for 1 min-

Quick and Easy Cakes

231

ute. Slowly pour in the oil in a steady stream, and beat 1 minute longer.

5. Reduce mixer speed to medium-low. Blend in the dry ingredients all at once, mixing just until incorporated. Remove the bowl from the mixer. Using a 2¾-inch-wide rubber spatula, fold in all but 2 tablespoons of the nuts, then the raisins, ginger, and optional cherries.

6. Pour the batter into the prepared pan. Sprinkle top with the reserved 2 tablespoons of nuts. Bake in the preheated oven for 65 to 70 minutes, until cake begins to leave sides of pan and a twig of straw or a toothpick inserted into the center of the cake comes out dry.

7. Remove from the oven and set the pan on a cake rack to cool completely. To remove the cake, run a thin, sharp knife around the sides and center tube. Lift up center tube and run a thin, sharp knife under the cake. Invert the cake onto the rack. Turn top side up and cool completely.

STORAGE: Store at room temperature under a glass dome, in an airtight container, or in plastic wrap or aluminum foil for up to 5 days. For longer storage, refrigerate up to 10 days.

❧ CARROT PINEAPPLE CAKE

....

Carrot cake has become one of the most popular cakes in this country. Once considered humble, it can now be found on the dessert menus of fine restaurants or even as the base of a beautifully decorated wedding cake.

Many flavors complement carrots. For this recipe, I have added crushed pineapple, cinnamon, and nutmeg. Ginger, allspice, or powdered clove make nice additions too.

Carrot cakes are traditionally served with a thick cream cheese frosting. This idea may trace its origins to the fact that date nut bread, similar to carrot cake, is often served with cream cheese.

....

³/₄	pound carrots, scraped
2	cups sifted unbleached all-purpose flour
2	teaspoons baking soda
¹/₂	teaspoon salt
2	teaspoons ground cinnamon
¹/₂	teaspoon ground nutmeg
4	large eggs
1¹/₂	cups superfine sugar
1	teaspoon vanilla extract
1	teaspoon freshly grated navel orange rind
1	cup safflower oil or other unflavored vegetable oil
One	8¹/₄-ounce can crushed pineapple, well-drained
1¹/₄	cups walnuts, chopped medium-fine
¹/₂	cup yellow raisins, plumped (page 63)

▽ ....

AT A GLANCE

SERVES: 10 to 12
PAN: 9″ × 13″ ×
2″ oblong
PAN PREP: Butter
OVEN TEMP: 350°
RACK LEVEL: Lower
third
BAKING TIME: 45 to
50 minutes
METHOD: Electric
mixer/food
processor

....

1. Cut the carrots into 1-inch chunks. Shred in a food processor fitted with the medium shredder blade, using light pressure on pusher for a finer shred. You should have 3 cups. Set aside.
2. Position rack in lower third of the oven and preheat to 350°. Butter a 9″ × 13″ × 2″ pan.
3. Sift together flour, baking soda, salt, and spices, using a triple sifter. Set aside.
4. Place the eggs in the large bowl of an electric mixer. Beat on medium-high speed with beaters or whip attachment for 2 minutes, or until light in color and thickened. Add the sugar, 1 tablespoon at a time, taking 5 to 6 minutes to blend it in well. Scrape the sides of the bowl occasionally. Add the vanilla and orange rind.
5. Slowly pour in the oil in a steady stream. Beat 1 minute.
6. Reduce mixer speed to medium-low. Add the flour mixture all at once, blending for 10 to 15 seconds just until incorporated.
7. Remove the bowl from the mixer. Using a 2³/₄-inch-wide spatula, fold in carrots, pineapple, walnuts, and raisins. Pour the batter into the prepared pan, smoothing the surface with the back of a tablespoon.
8. Center the pan on the rack and bake in the preheated oven for 45 to 50 minutes, until cake begins to leave the sides of the pan and a toothpick inserted into center comes out dry.

(recipe continues)

*Quick and
Easy Cakes*

9. Remove from the oven and set the pan on a cake rack to cool completely. Ice with Cream Cheese Frosting (page 450), if desired.

STORAGE: Cover the pan loosely with aluminum foil and store at room temperature for the first day. Refrigerate for longer storage, but serve at room temperature. This cake will keep up to 7 days.

🐚 ZUCCHINI TEA LOAF

Zucchini cake is often too moist for my taste, due to the high water content of the vegetable, but this problem is easily overcome by extracting the water before blending the zucchini into the batter. The result is a wonderfully moist but lighter cake filled with coarsely chopped nuts and chewy raisins, and flavored with cinnamon.

Zucchini loaves stay fresh for a long time and therefore make wonderful gifts. I like to bake them in minisize foil loaf pans, wrap them in clear cellophane, and tie them with a pretty ribbon.

△

AT A GLANCE

SERVES: 6 to 8, per loaf
PAN: 2 medium loaf pans, 8″ × 4″ × 2¼″ (5-cup capacity each), or 4 miniloaf pans (2¼-cup capacity each)
PAN PREP: Butter/flour
OVEN TEMP: 350°
RACK LEVEL: Lower third
BAKING TIME: 60 to 70 minutes or 40 to 50 minutes for miniloaf pans
METHOD: Electric mixer/food processor

Great Cakes
234

3	medium zucchini (about 1¼ pounds)
1¼	teaspoons salt
2¼	cups sifted unbleached all-purpose flour
2	teaspoons baking soda
1	tablespoon ground cinnamon
¼	teaspoon ground nutmeg
3	large eggs
1⅓	cups sugar
1	cup safflower oil or other unflavored vegetable oil
2	teaspoons vanilla extract
1¼	cups walnuts, coarsely chopped
1	cup plumped golden raisins (page 63)

1. Scrub the zucchini well with a vegetable brush; trim the ends but do not peel. Cut into 1-inch chunks. Shred in a food processor fitted with the medium shredder blade, using medium pres-

sure on pusher. You should have 4 cups. Transfer to a 3-quart bowl. Sprinkle with *1 teaspoon* of the salt, working it through with your hands to distribute it evenly. Place an 8-inch plate directly on top of zucchini and weigh down with a heavy object, such as a large can of juice. Let stand for about 20 minutes.

2. Position rack in the lower third of the oven and preheat to 350°. Butter and flour two 8″ × 4″ × 2¼″ loaf pans or 4 mini-pans. Invert over the kitchen sink and tap to remove excess flour.

3. Remove 2 tablespoons flour and set aside. Sift together the remaining flour, baking soda, ¼ *teaspoon* salt, and spices, using a triple sifter. Set aside.

4. Place the eggs in the large bowl of an electric mixer fitted with the beaters or whip attachment. Beat on medium-high speed for 3 minutes.

5. Add sugar, 1 tablespoon at a time, taking 4 to 5 minutes to blend it in well. Beat 2 minutes longer, until mixture is thickened and light in color. Pour in the oil in a steady stream. Beat 1 minute longer.

6. Meanwhile, empty the zucchini into a colander and drain off the water. Take handfuls of zucchini and squeeze firmly to remove additional liquid. Reduce mixer speed to medium-low and blend in the vanilla and zucchini.

7. Add the dry ingredients all at once, mixing just until incorporated. Remove the bowl from the mixer. In a small bowl combine the reserved *2 tablespoons of flour*, nuts, and raisins and toss to coat. Using a 2¾-inch-wide rubber spatula, fold nut/raisin mixture into the batter. Pour the batter into the prepared pans.

8. Bake in the preheated oven 60 to 70 minutes for medium loaf pans or 40 to 50 minutes for miniloaf pans, until cake begins to leave sides of pan and a twig of straw or a toothpick inserted into the center comes out dry.

9. Remove from oven and set the pan on a cake rack to cool. Turn pans on their sides and ease out cakes. Turn the cakes top side up and finish cooling. To serve, cut into ½-inch slices with a serrated knife, using a back-and-forth sawing motion.

STORAGE: Wrap in plastic film or aluminum foil. Store at room temperature for up to 5 days or refrigerate for up to 10 days.

🍂 DARK FRUIT CAKE

AT A GLANCE

SERVES: 12 to 14 per loaf
PANS: Two 9" × 5" × 2¾" loaf pans (8-cup capacity)
PAN PREP: Melted butter/brown paper/melted butter
OVEN TEMP: 300°
RACK LEVEL: Lower third
BAKING TIME: 1½ hours
METHOD: Electric mixer/hand

This recipe is a perennial favorite with my students. The chunky fruits absorb the flavorful moisteners, becoming soft and chewy. This recipe can easily be doubled or, if you prefer, halved in four miniloaves. Make it weeks in advance so the flavor can mature. Then all you need do is devise pretty wrappings (cellophane is ideal) and you have sensational gifts to offer at holiday time.

Since making fruit cakes is a long, involved process, this is a nice time to recruit the children or other family members to help. It will put everyone in a festive holiday mood. On the day before you plan to bake the cake, the pans can be lined, the dry ingredients combined, and the fruit and nut preparation done. The easiest way to cut the fruit is by snipping the pieces with a pair of scissors. Don't try to chop it or the pieces will stick together. Chop the nuts coarsely by hand so they will be visible when you slice the cake.

To keep them from drying out during the long baking time, fruit cakes should be baked in moist heat. Place a large pan of water on the bottom shelf of the oven. An open roasting pan measuring about 10" × 14" × 2" is ideal; however, any pan will do as long as it is shallow enough to fit on the rack directly below the cake.

1½	cups golden raisins
1	cup pitted dates, cut into ¼-inch pieces
1	cup dried apricots, cut into ¼-inch pieces
1	cup candied pineapple, cut into ¼-inch pieces
2	tablespoons each candied lemon rind and orange rind (optional, see Note)
½	cup red and green glacéed cherries, cut into ¼-inch pieces
½	cup currants
1	cup thick preserves (damson plum and apricot/pineapple mixed)
½	cup dark Jamaican rum, plus additional for brushing and for soaking cheesecloth
⅓	cup canned apricot nectar
2¼	cups sifted, unbleached all-purpose flour
1	teaspoon baking soda

       ³/₄   teaspoon salt
      1¹/₂   teaspoons ground cinnamon
       ¹/₄   teaspoon ground allspice
       ¹/₄   teaspoon ground nutmeg
       ¹/₄   teaspoon mace
        1   cup (2 sticks) unsalted butter
        4   large eggs
        1   cup dark brown sugar, lightly packed
        2   teaspoons vanilla extract
        1   cup coarsely hand-chopped pecans
        1   cup coarsely hand-chopped almonds, lightly toasted
        2   tablespoons light corn syrup
        2   teaspoons hot water
             Almond halves and glacéed cherries for garnish
             (optional)

1. Combine the fruit, preserves, rum, and apricot nectar in a large
   glass or stainless steel bowl. Cover tightly with plastic wrap or
   aluminum foil and macerate at room temperature about 24
   hours.
2. Place a large pan on the lowest shelf of oven and fill with about
   1 inch of hot water. Position second rack on the next level up.
   Preheat the oven to 300°. Butter, line with brown paper, and
   re-butter two 9″ × 5″ × 2³/₄″ loaf pans (page 66).
3. Sift together the flour, baking soda, salt, and spices, using a
   triple sifter. Set aside.
4. Cut the butter into 1-inch pieces and place in the large bowl of
   an electric mixer fitted with beaters or paddle attachment.
   Soften on low speed. Increase speed to medium-high and cream
   until smooth and light in color, about 1¹/₂ to 2 minutes.
5. Reduce mixer speed to low. Gradually add flour mixture over
   30 seconds, blending until a stiff batter forms.
6. In the small bowl of an electric mixer, beat the eggs on medium
   speed for 2 minutes, until thick and light in color. Add the brown
   sugar, 1 tablespoon at a time, taking 3 to 4 minutes to blend it
   in well. The mixture should be very thick. Blend in the vanilla.
   Remove the bowl from the mixer.
7. With a large wooden spoon, stir the egg mixture gradually into
   the flour batter, blending until smooth. Stir in the hand-chopped
   nuts and the macerated fruits.
8. Spoon the batter into prepared pans, smoothing surface with

back of a tablespoon. Tap pan firmly to remove air pockets. Bake in the preheated oven for 1½ hours.

9. Measure the corn syrup into a small bowl and mix with the hot water. Five minutes before the end of the baking time, brush the top of each cake with the syrup. If you wish, remove the cake from the oven and gently press halved almonds and glacéed cherries onto surface as a garnish. Cover with another thin layer of syrup glaze and bake 5 minutes longer to set.

10. Cakes are done when they begin to come away from the sides of the pan and a twig of straw or a toothpick inserted into the center comes out clean. Remove from oven, set the pans on cake racks, and let stand ½ hour. Turn the cakes onto their sides and ease them out of the pans, carefully peel off paper, and turn cakes top side up to finish cooling.

11. When cakes are completely cool, brush tops and sides with additional rum. Wrap cakes in large pieces of rum-soaked cheesecloth. You'll need about ¼ to ⅓ cup rum for each cake, depending on the size of the piece of cheesecloth. Double-wrap in heavy aluminum foil, sealing well. Allow cakes to mature for at least 2 weeks before serving.

STORAGE: Store the wrapped cakes in a cool dry place. (A basement is ideal.) Remoisten with rum after 2 days and again after 2 weeks. Check again for moistness after 1 month, but remoistening will probably no longer be necessary if cakes were well wrapped. They will keep up to 6 months. In warmer weather, store them in the refrigerator. Serve at room temperature.

NOTE: If you use the candied lemon and orange rinds, reduce the amount of pineapple to ¾ cup.

🦋 LIGHT FRUIT CAKE

or those who do not like robust-flavored fruit cakes, here is one that is more delicate and subtle.

This buttery cake is made without leavening and is densely packed with an eye-catching combination of golden raisins, candied pineapple, glacéed red and green cherries, and nuts. Since the batter does not contain preserves, the texture of the cake is not as moist. As with the dark fruit cake, this recipe works well made in large batches that can be divided into miniloaves for holiday gift-giving.

2	cups golden raisins
1	cup diced candied pineapple, cut in 1/4-inch pieces
1/4	cup red glacéed cherries, cut in 1/4-inch pieces
1/4	cup green glacéed cherries, cut in 1/4-inch pieces
2	tablespoons candied orange rind
2	tablespoons candied lemon rind
1	cup coarsely hand-chopped walnuts
1/2	cup coarsely hand-chopped blanched almonds
2 1/4	cups sifted unbleached all-purpose flour
1/2	teaspoon salt
1	cup (2 sticks) unsalted butter
1/2	teaspoon freshly grated navel orange rind
1/2	teaspoon freshly grated lemon rind
1	cup light brown sugar, lightly packed
6	large egg yolks
1/4	cup maple syrup
1/4	cup brandy, Grand Marnier, Cointreau, or Triple Sec, plus additional for brushing on finished cakes and for soaking cheesecloth
1 1/2	teaspoons vanilla extract
6	large egg whites
1	teaspoon cream of tartar
	Pinch of salt
2	tablespoons granulated sugar
2	tablespoons light corn syrup
2	teaspoons hot water
	Almond halves and glacéed cherries for garnish (optional)

▽

AT A GLANCE

SERVES: 8 to 10 per loaf
PAN: Two 8" × 4" × 2 1/4" loaf pans (5-cup capacity)
PAN PREP: Melted butter/brown paper/ melted butter
OVEN TEMP: 300°
RACK LEVEL: Lower third
BAKING TIME: 1 1/2 hours
METHOD: Electric mixer/food processor

Quick and Easy Cakes

239

1. Combine the fruit, candied rinds, and nuts in a bowl.

2. Position rack in the lower third of the oven and preheat to 300°. Butter, line with brown paper, and re-butter two 8" × 4" × 2¼" loaf pans (page 66).

3. Sift together the flour and salt, using a triple sifter. Remove ¼ cup and add to the fruits and nuts, tossing to coat the pieces well. Set the dry ingredients and the fruit mixture aside.

4. Cut the butter into 1-inch pieces and place in the large bowl of an electric mixer fitted with beaters or paddle attachment. Add the grated orange and lemon rinds and soften on low speed. Increase speed to medium-high. Cream until smooth and light in color, about 1½ to 2 minutes.

5. Add the brown sugar, 1 tablespoon at a time, taking 3 to 4 minutes to blend it in well. Scrape the sides of the bowl occasionally.

6. Add the egg yolks, 2 at a time at 1-minute intervals, scraping the sides of bowl as necessary. Beat 1 minute longer.

7. Reduce mixer speed to low. In a small bowl combine the maple syrup, brandy, and vanilla. Add the flour mixture alternately with the syrup/brandy mixture, dividing the dry ingredients into three parts, the liquid into two parts, and starting and ending with the flour. Mix for 10 seconds longer. Remove the bowl from mixer and set aside.

8. In a large clean bowl of the electric mixer fitted with clean beaters or whip attachment, beat the egg whites on medium-high speed until frothy. Add the cream of tartar and salt. Increase the speed to medium-high and beat until soft peaks form. Add the granulated sugar, 1 tablespoon at a time, and beat until mixture stands in firm peaks, about 15 to 20 seconds.

9. Remove the bowl from the machine. Fold ⅓ whites and ½ fruit/nut mixture into batter, taking about 20 turns. Fold in remaining whites and fruit/nut mixture, taking an additional 40 turns to combine.

10. Spoon the batter into the prepared pans, smoothing the surface with back of a tablespoon. Tap the pans firmly to remove air pockets. Bake in the preheated oven for 1½ hours.

11. Five minutes before the end of the baking time, brush top of each cake with light corn syrup thinned with hot water. If you wish, gently press halved almonds and glacéed cherries onto surface of cakes as a garnish. Cover with another thin layer of glaze and bake 5 minutes longer to set.

12. Cakes are done when they are golden brown on top and begin to come away from the sides of the pan. A twig of straw or a toothpick inserted into the center should come out dry. Place the pans on cake racks and let stand ½ hour. Turn cakes onto their sides and ease out of pans. Carefully peel off paper. Turn cakes top side up and finish cooling.

13. When they are completely cool, brush top and sides of each cake with additional brandy. Wrap cakes in a large piece of brandy-soaked cheesecloth, then in heavy aluminum foil, sealing well. Allow the cakes to mature in a cool place for at least 6 weeks before serving.

STORAGE: Store wrapped cakes in a cool dry place. (A basement is ideal if you have one.) Otherwise, refrigerate. Remoisten cloth with brandy after 2 days and periodically thereafter. The cakes will keep up to 6 months.

Upside-Down Cakes

In Europe, where visual presentation is a paramount consideration in pastry-making, inverted cakes have always been popular. An American counterpart might be the upside-down cake. Fruits and nuts are arranged on the bottom of the pan in a geometric pattern in a syrup of butter and sugar. After baking, the cake is quickly inverted and served.

Upside-down cakes contain a generous amount of leavening, which makes them light, perfect for soaking up the delicious caramelized juices from the topping. These cakes are best served slightly warm within 2 or 3 hours of baking. Cakes that stand too long after inverting become soggy. If you wish to keep the cake for a later use, do not invert it immediately. Instead, let it cool in the pan; the fruit and juices will stick, but this can be remedied. Return the cake to a 350° oven for 10 to 15 minutes or heat the pan on a very low stove burner. After the bottom of the pan is well warmed, invert the cake and let it stand 5 minutes before removing the pan.

It is traditional to bake these cakes in cast-iron skillets, but sometimes acid in the fruit may react with the iron, transferring its taste and black color to the cake. Using a stainless steel skillet will eliminate this problem. If your skillet does not have an ovenproof handle, cut a strip of heavy-duty aluminum foil and wrap it 3 or 4 times tightly around the handle to protect it from burning. You may also use an aluminum baking pan, if the cake is not kept long in the pan. However, prolonged contact with the aluminum can cause the fruit acids to react with the metal.

🌰 PINEAPPLE UPSIDE-DOWN CAKE

This is the most traditional of all the inverted cake varieties. If you prefer a less sweet topping, reduce the sugar and butter.

THE TOPPING:

3 to 4	tablespoons unsalted butter
1/3 to 1/2	cup dark brown sugar, lightly packed
9	pineapple rings, well drained on paper toweling (reserve 1/2 cup juice)
9	maraschino or canned Bing cherries, pitted
	Pecan halves

THE CAKE:

1 1/2	cups sifted cake flour
2 1/2	teaspoons baking powder
1/4	teaspoon salt
1/3	cup (2/3 stick) sweet butter
1/2	cup sugar
2	large eggs
1	teaspoon vanilla extract
1/2	cup reserved pineapple juice

1. To make the topping: Put the butter in an ungreased 9″ × 9″ × 2″ square cake pan and heat over a very low flame just to melt the butter. Remove from heat, and tilt the pan to coat the bottom completely with the melted butter. Sprinkle the brown sugar over the butter and press it evenly across surface. Arrange the pineapple slices, 3 to a row, making 3 rows. Place a cherry in the center of each ring. Neatly fill in the empty spaces around the cherries with pecan halves, rounded side down. Set aside.
2. Position rack in the lower third of the oven and preheat to 350°.
3. To make the cake: Sift together the flour, baking powder, and salt, using a triple sifter. Set aside.
4. Cut the butter into 1-inch pieces and place in the large bowl of an electric mixer fitted with beaters or the paddle attachment to

▽ AT A GLANCE

SERVES: 9
PAN: 9″ × 9″ × 2″ square
OVEN TEMP: 350°
RACK LEVEL: Lower third
BAKING TIME: 30 to 35 minutes
METHOD: Electric mixer

Quick and Easy Cakes

243

soften on low speed. Increase speed to medium and cream until smooth and light in color, about 1 to 1½ minutes.

5. Add the sugar, 1 tablespoon at a time, taking 3 to 4 minutes to blend it in well. Scrape the sides of the bowl occasionally.

6. Add the eggs, 1 at a time at 1-minute intervals, scraping the sides of bowl as necessary. Blend in the vanilla.

7. Reduce mixer speed to low. Add the flour mixture alternately with the pineapple juice, dividing the dry ingredients into three parts and the liquid into two parts, starting and ending with the flour. Mix just until incorporated after each addition. Scrape the sides of the bowl and mix for 10 seconds longer.

8. Spoon the batter into prepared pan, spreading from the sides to the center. Smooth the top surface with the back of a tablespoon.

9. Bake in the preheated oven 30 to 35 minutes, until the edges of the cake are brown and the juices around the sides of the pan begin to bubble. Remove from oven and place on a cake rack. Let the cake cool in the pan for 5 to 10 minutes. Then run a thin knife around the edge of the pan to loosen the sides. Invert the pan onto a serving platter. *Let stand 5 minutes before removing pan*. Carefully lift pan. If any fruit clings to the pan, remove and arrange on top of the cake. When ready to serve, slice into squares and accompany with a dollop of whipped cream or Yogurt Topping (page 479). This cake is best served slightly warm.

STORAGE: Cover the cake loosely with aluminum foil. Store at room temperature for up to 1 day.

APRICOT-GINGER
UPSIDE-DOWN CAKE

This upside-down cake was the favorite of my team of cake testers. They loved the touch of molasses that enhances the ginger and apricot flavors.

▽
AT A GLANCE

SERVES: 6 to 8
PAN: 8″ square or 9″ round
OVEN TEMP: 350°
RACK LEVEL: Lower third
BAKING TIME: 35 to 40 minutes
METHOD: Electric mixer

THE TOPPING:

3	tablespoons unsalted butter
1/4 to 1/3	cup light brown sugar, lightly packed
One	17-ounce can apricot halves, well drained on paper toweling
1	whole almond per apricot half

THE CAKE:

1/2	cup hot water
2	tablespoons dark molasses
1 1/4	cups sifted unbleached all-purpose flour
2	teaspoons baking powder
1/4	teaspoon baking soda
1/4	teaspoon salt
1/2	teaspoon powdered ginger
1/4	teaspoon ground cinnamon
1/4	cup (1/2 stick) unsalted butter
1/3	cup sugar
1	large egg
1/2	teaspoon vanilla extract

1. To make the topping: Place the butter in an 8-inch square or 9-inch round cake pan and heat over a very low flame just until melted. Remove from the heat and tilt the pan to distribute the melted butter. Sprinkle brown sugar over butter. Press the brown sugar evenly across the surface of the pan with your fingers. Fit one almond into the cavity of each apricot and arrange fruit in the pan, nut side down, using 4 apricots across and 4 rows down if you are using a square pan. If your pan is round, arrange in concentric circles. Set aside.

Quick and Easy Cakes

2. Position a rack in the lower third of the oven and preheat to 350°.
3. To make the cake: In a small bowl, combine the hot water with the molasses, stirring until blended. Set aside to cool.
4. Using a triple sifter, sift together the flour, baking powder, baking soda, salt, and spices. Set aside.
5. Cut the butter into 1-inch pieces and place in the large bowl of an electric mixer fitted with beaters or paddle attachment. Soften on low speed, then increase speed to medium and cream until smooth and light in color, about 1 to 1½ minutes.
6. Add the sugar, 1 tablespoon at a time, taking 2 to 3 minutes to blend it in well. Scrape the sides of the bowl occasionally.
7. Add the egg and beat for 1 minute, scraping the sides of bowl as necessary. Blend in the vanilla.
8. Reduce mixer speed to low. Add the flour mixture alternately with the molasses mixture, dividing the dry ingredients into three parts and the molasses mixture into two parts, starting and ending with the flour. Mix just until incorporated after each addition. Scrape the sides and mix for 10 seconds longer.
9. Spoon the batter into the prepared pan, spreading from the sides to the center. Smooth the top with the back of a tablespoon.
10. Center the pan on the rack and bake in the preheated oven 35 to 40 minutes, until edges have browned and the top of the cake is springy to the touch. Remove from oven and place on a cake rack. Let the cake cool in the pan for 5 to 10 minutes. Run a thin knife around edge of pan to loosen the sides and invert the pan onto a serving platter. *Allow to stand 5 minutes before removing pan*, to release the fruit and syrup. Carefully lift off the pan. If any fruit clings to the pan, remove and arrange on top of the cake. To serve, cut into squares or wedges. Cake is best served slightly warm.

STORAGE: Cover loosely with aluminum foil. Store at room temperature for up to 1 day.

🌰 APPLE WALNUT UPSIDE-DOWN CAKE

Slices of Golden Delicious apples sautéed in butter, walnuts, and brown sugar form the base of a delightful topping accented with a dash of dark Jamaican rum.

<table>
<tr><td>▽</td></tr>
</table>

AT A GLANCE

SERVES: 8 to 10
PAN: 10″ skillet with ovenproof handle
OVEN TEMP: 375°
RACK LEVEL: Lower third
BAKING TIME: 30 to 35 minutes
METHOD: Electric mixer

THE TOPPING:

1½	pounds (about 3 large) Golden Delicious apples
¼	cup (½ stick) unsalted butter
⅓	cup light brown sugar, lightly packed
¼	teaspoon freshly grated lemon rind
½	teaspoon ground cinnamon
1	tablespoon dark Jamaican rum
⅓	cup coarsely chopped walnuts

THE CAKE:

1⅔	cups sifted cake flour
2	teaspoons baking powder
½	teaspoon salt
⅓	cup (⅔ stick) unsalted butter
¼	teaspoon freshly grated lemon rind
½	cup sugar
2	large eggs
1	teaspoon vanilla extract
½	cup apple juice

1. To make the topping: Core and peel the apples and cut each into eighths. In a 10-inch skillet with an ovenproof handle, melt the butter over low heat. Blend in the brown sugar, lemon rind, and cinnamon. Add the apples and stir to coat with the syrup. Spread the fruit in a single layer. Cover the pan, and simmer 3 to 5 minutes, or until apples are tender. Remove the lid, raise heat to medium-high, and cook for 1½ to 2 minutes to thicken the syrup. Remove from the heat. Arrange the apples in a circle, leaving a few for the center. Sprinkle them with the rum and nuts. Set aside while you prepare the cake.
2. Position rack in the lower third of the oven and preheat to 375°.

Quick and Easy Cakes

3. To make the cake: Sift together the flour, baking powder, and salt, using a triple sifter. Set aside.

4. Cut the butter into 1-inch pieces and place in the large bowl of an electric mixer fitted with beaters or paddle attachment to soften on low speed. Add the lemon rind. Increase speed to medium. Cream until smooth and light in color, about 1 to 1½ minutes.

5. Add the sugar, 1 tablespoon at a time, taking 3 to 4 minutes to blend it in well. Scrape the sides of the bowl occasionally.

6. Add the eggs, 1 at a time at 1-minute intervals, scraping the sides of the bowl as necessary. Blend in the vanilla.

7. Reduce mixer speed to low. Add the flour mixture alternately with the apple juice, dividing the dry ingredients into three parts and the liquid into two parts, starting and ending with the flour. Mix just until incorporated after each addition. Scrape the sides of the bowl and mix for 10 seconds longer.

8. Spoon the batter into the prepared skillet, spreading from the sides to the center. Smooth the top with the back of a tablespoon.

9. Center the skillet on the rack and bake in the preheated oven 30 to 35 minutes, until edges are brown. Remove from oven and set on a cake rack to cool for 5 to 10 minutes. Run a thin knife around edge of skillet to loosen the sides. Invert the pan onto a serving platter. *Let stand 5 minutes before removing pan*, to release the fruit and syrup. Carefully remove skillet. If any fruit remains in skillet, remove and arrange on top of cake. When ready to serve, slice into wedges and accompany with a dollop of whipped cream or Yogurt Topping (page 479). This cake is best served slightly warm.

STORAGE: Cover the cake loosely with aluminum foil. Store at room temperature for up to 1 day.

CHOCOLATE PEAR UPSIDE-DOWN CAKE

Chocolate and pears are a heavenly combination. The honey glaze gives the top of this delectable cake an attractive sheen.

△ AT A GLANCE

SERVES: 8 to 10
PAN: 10″ skillet with ovenproof handle
OVEN TEMP: 350°
RACK LEVEL: Lower third
BAKING TIME: 50 to 55 minutes
METHOD: Electric mixer

THE TOPPING:

¼	cup (½ stick) unsalted butter
¼	cup sugar
2	tablespoons honey
One	29-ounce can pear halves, well drained on paper toweling
1	walnut half for each pear

THE CAKE:

1¼	cups sifted cake flour
1	teaspoon baking powder
½	teaspoon salt
⅓	cup (⅔ stick) unsalted butter
¾	cup sugar
2	large eggs
2	squares unsweetened chocolate, melted
1	teaspoon vanilla extract
⅔	cup milk

1. To make the topping: In a 10-inch skillet with an ovenproof handle, melt the butter over a very low flame. Stir in the sugar and honey and cook just until sugar melts. Remove from heat. Set aside. Fit one walnut half into each pear cavity. With the narrow ends toward center, arrange the pears in a circle in the skillet, cavity side down. Fill the space in the center with one pear half. Set aside.
2. Position rack in the lower third of the oven and preheat to 350°.
3. To make the cake: Sift together the flour, baking powder, and salt, using a triple sifter. Set aside.
4. Cut the butter into 1-inch pieces and place in the large bowl of an electric mixer fitted with beaters or paddle attachment. Soften

Quick and Easy Cakes

on low speed, then increase speed to medium and cream until smooth and light in color, about 1 to 1½ minutes.

5. Add the sugar, 1 tablespoon at a time, taking 3 to 4 minutes to blend it in well. Scrape the sides of the bowl occasionally.

6. Add the eggs, 1 at a time at 1-minute intervals, scraping the sides of the bowl again. Blend in the melted chocolate and the vanilla.

7. Reduce mixer speed to low. Add the flour mixture alternately with the milk, dividing the flour into three parts and the liquid into two parts, starting and ending with the flour. Mix just until incorporated after each addition. Scrape the sides of the bowl and mix for 10 seconds longer.

8. Spoon the batter into the prepared skillet, spreading from the sides toward the center. Smooth the surface with the back of a tablespoon.

9. Center the skillet on the rack and bake in the preheated oven for 50 to 55 minutes, until the top of the cake feels springy to the touch. Remove from oven and place on a cake rack. Let cool in the pan for 5 to 10 minutes. Run a thin knife around the edge of the skillet to loosen the sides, and invert onto a serving platter. *Let stand 5 minutes before removing pan.* If any fruit remains in skillet, remove and arrange on top of cake. When ready to serve, slice into wedges and accompany with a dollop of whipped cream or Yogurt Topping (page 479). This cake is best when served slightly warm.

STORAGE: Cover the cake loosely with aluminum foil. Store at room temperature for up to 1 day.

WHOLE WHEAT PEACH
UPSIDE-DOWN CAKE

....

Whole wheat flour gives this cake its delicious flavor. Canned cling peaches work best for the topping because of their firmness.

....

▽.........................

AT A GLANCE

SERVES: 9
PAN: 10″ skillet with ovenproof handle
OVEN TEMP: 350°
RACK LEVEL: Lower third
BAKING TIME: 40 to 45 minutes
METHOD: Electric mixer

....

THE TOPPING:

3 to 4	tablespoons unsalted butter
1/4 to 1/3	cup dark brown sugar, lightly packed
One	29-ounce can cling peach halves
One	maraschino cherry half or canned pitted Bing cherry for each peach

THE CAKE:

2/3	cup sifted unbleached all-purpose flour
2 1/2	teaspoons baking powder
1/2	teaspoon salt
1/4	teaspoon ground nutmeg
2/3	cup whole wheat flour
1/3	cup (2/3 stick) unsalted butter
1/3	cup granulated sugar
1/3	cup light brown sugar, lightly packed
2	large eggs
1	teaspoon vanilla extract
1/3	cup orange juice
1/3	cup peach syrup

1. To make the topping: In a 10-inch skillet with an ovenproof handle, melt the butter over a very low flame. Stir in the sugar and heat just until the sugar melts, about 10 seconds. Remove from the heat.
2. Drain the peaches, reserving 1/3 cup of the syrup for the batter. Place peaches on paper toweling to absorb moisture.
3. Put a cherry half in each peach cavity and invert peaches into skillet, forming a circle with 1 peach half in the center. Set aside.
4. Position a rack in the lower third of the oven and preheat to 350°.

*Quick and
Easy Cakes*

251

5. To make the cake: Sift together the all-purpose flour, baking powder, salt, and nutmeg, using a triple sifter. Stir in the whole wheat flour, blending well. Set aside.
6. Cut the butter into 1-inch pieces and place in the large bowl of an electric mixer fitted with beaters or paddle attachment to soften on low speed. Increase speed to medium. Cream until smooth and light in color, about 1 to 1½ minutes.
7. Add the granulated sugar, 1 tablespoon at a time, taking 2 to 3 minutes to blend it in well. Add the brown sugar over an additional 1 to 2 minutes. Scrape the sides of the bowl occasionally.
8. Add the eggs, 1 at a time at 1-minute intervals, scraping the sides of bowl as necessary. Blend in the vanilla.
9. Reduce mixer speed to low. In a small bowl, combine the orange juice and the peach syrup. Add the flour mixture alternately with the fruit liquids, dividing the dry ingredients into three parts and the liquid into two parts, starting and ending with the flour. Mix just until incorporated after each addition. Scrape the sides of the bowl and mix for 10 seconds longer.
10. Spoon the batter into the fruit-lined skillet, spreading from the sides to the center. Smooth the surface with the back of a tablespoon.
11. Center the skillet on the rack and bake 40 to 45 minutes, until the edges of the cake are brown. Remove from oven. Place the skillet on a cake rack to cool for 5 to 10 minutes. Run a thin knife around edge of the skillet to loosen sides and invert the pan onto a serving platter. *Let stand 5 minutes before removing pan*, to release fruit and syrup. Carefully remove skillet. If any fruit remains in the pan, remove and arrange on top of cake. When ready to serve, slice into wedges and accompany with a dollop of whipped cream or Yogurt Topping (page 479). This cake is best served slightly warm.

STORAGE: Cover the cake loosely with aluminum foil. Store at room temperature for 1 day.

SPONGE CAKES

Sponge cakes are light and airy cakes containing more eggs and less flour than butter cakes. Made without solid fat, they are delicate and delicious, and can be served plain or used as the base for more elaborate cakes. Because they contain no solid fat, they can be refrigerated without hardening. Sponge batters are sometimes leavened chemically with baking powder, but the principal leavening is the air whipped into the eggs. Long and proper beating is crucial to achieving a successful sponge.

Most frequently the eggs are separated and the yolks beaten with all or part of the sugar. Then the flavoring and dry ingredients are added. The whites, which sometimes also contain sugar, are whipped to expand to as much as eight times their original volume. Proper folding of the whites into the dense yolk batter is also critical to the success of sponges. It must be done quickly and with as few folding strokes as possible to avoid loss of air. At the same time, care must be taken not to overbeat the whites. Beating egg whites too long can break the suspension of the air cells, causing the mixture to deflate.

This chapter offers a wonderful selection of basic sponge cakes. Once you master the techniques, you can experiment with creative ideas for embellishments.

► Sponge cakes are generally baked in ungreased tube pans. The batter must cling to an ungreased surface in order to maintain its volume. The tube or funnel in the middle of the pan creates an opening through which hot air can circulate so that the heat penetrates to the middle of the cake.

► Since the pan is ungreased, tall sponge cakes should be baked in pans with removable bottoms to make releasing the cake easier. If yours does not have one, line the bottom of the pan with parchment (page 66).

► If your electric mixer has two bowls of different sizes, choose the smaller one for beating the egg yolks. The narrower base pushes more egg mass into the beaters. If you are using a standard mixer, it is best not to exceed medium speed or the small bowl will turn too rapidly. On a KitchenAid mixer the bowl remains stationary, so higher speeds can be used.

► When transferring the batter to a separate bowl for folding, choose one with sloped sides and a wide rim. A 4-quart size is ideal for most batters. It is easier to handle the rubber spatula when the top of the bowl is wider than the bottom.

► Use a 2-3/4-inch wide rubber spatula for folding. Since this spatula is much larger than the standard kitchen size, folding can be accomplished with fewer turns, reducing air loss.

► Nuts added to sponge cake batters must be very finely chopped and not oily. If you are chopping the nuts in a food processor, add 1 additional tablespoon of flour for each 1/2 cup of nuts. The flour helps absorb the nut oils.

► Finely grated chocolate can also be added to sponge batters. Use the technique described on page 496.

► Unless instructed otherwise, invert a sponge cake as soon as it comes out of the oven. If your pan has metal feet or a center tube that is higher than the rim, simply invert the pan onto a countertop. Otherwise, invert the cake onto a cake rack sprayed with a nonstick coating. Suspending sponge cakes upside down helps to keep them from shrinking and therefore maintains the volume.

✿ ORANGE SPONGE CAKE

Every baker's repertoire should contain a special cake that can stand on its own merits or be modified into other delectable creations. This is such a recipe, an airy cake, refreshing and moist, tinged with a lovely orange flavor. It is satisfying whether eaten plain or fancied up into a party presentation.

▽
AT A GLANCE

SERVES: 14 to 16
PAN: 10″ angel food with a removable bottom (4-quart capacity)
PAN PREP: Ungreased
OVEN TEMP: 325°
RACK LEVEL: Lower third
BAKING TIME: 40 to 45 minutes
METHOD: Electric mixer

7	large egg yolks
1	large whole egg
⅔	cup plus ½ cup superfine or strained sugar
1	teaspoon freshly grated navel orange rind
1	teaspoon freshly grated lemon rind
¼	cup fresh navel orange juice
1	cup plus 2 tablespoons sifted cake flour
7	large egg whites
¼	teaspoon salt
1	teaspoon cream of tartar

1. Preheat oven to 325° and position rack in lower third. Have ready a 10-inch angel food pan.
2. Place the yolks and the whole egg in the small bowl of an electric mixer fitted with beaters or the whip attachment. Whip on medium speed for about 2 minutes. Add ⅔ *cup* sugar, 1 tablespoon at a time, taking about 5 to 6 minutes to blend it in well. Scrape sides of bowl occasionally. The mixture will be thick and light yellow in color.
3. Reduce mixer speed to medium-low. Add the grated rinds and orange juice and beat about 1 minute longer.
4. Reduce mixer speed to low. Add the flour and mix just until incorporated. Remove the bowl from the mixer and transfer yolk mixture to a large mixing bowl. Set aside.
5. Wash and dry the beaters. In the large bowl of the mixer, whip whites at medium speed until frothy. Add the salt and cream of tartar. Increase speed to medium high and beat just until the whites form soft peaks. Gradually add ½ *cup* sugar, over 15 sec-

Quick and Easy Cakes

onds, and continue beating for 30 seconds longer to form a glossy soft meringue. Remove bowl from the machine.

6. With a 2³/₄-inch-wide rubber spatula, fold ¹/₄ of the meringue into the yolk mixture, taking about 20 turns. Add the remaining meringue, using about 50 turns to incorporate the two together.

7. Gently spoon the batter into the pan, smoothing the top with the back of a tablespoon. Insert a knife into the batter and circle the pan twice to remove any air pockets. Smooth the surface again. Bake in the preheated oven for 40 to 45 minutes, or until the cake is golden brown on top and springy to the touch.

8. Remove the cake from the oven and *immediately* invert onto a cake rack. Let the cake cool completely in the pan.

9. To remove the pan, turn the cake upright and carefully run a sharp, thin-bladed knife in 2 or 3 strokes around the side of pan to loosen the cake. Then run it around the center tube. Lift the cake by the center tube and remove the outer rim. Run knife under cake in 2 or 3 strokes, then invert onto a cake rack and remove the tube. Place on a cake platter, top or bottom side up.

STORAGE: Store at room temperature under a glass dome or covered with aluminum foil for up to 1 week.

NOTE: This cake is the foundation for the Majestic Mandarin Cake (page 342). Since this is a very large cake, you may also prepare half the recipe and filling to make a mandarin orange roulade. For information on roulades, see pages 264–80. Use a 10¹/₂″ × 15¹/₂″ × 1″ jelly roll pan.

🪶 STARMOUNT SPONGE CAKE

I have a special fondness for the city of Greensboro, North Carolina, because just after I was married my parents moved there. On my frequent visits I was often entertained by a number of extraordinary cooks, many of whom lived in the Starmount section of that city. The sumptuous foods and pastries that I sampled there have been a source of inspiration to me throughout my culinary career. This cake is named in remembrance of the gracious hospitality of those cooks and in respect for their talents.

Starmount Sponge Cake, as high as the pan, is feather-light and has a lovely lemon flavor. It comes from my friend Shirley Lynch of Greensboro. No doubt you will agree that her cake is a grand one.

▽

AT A GLANCE

SERVES: 14 to 16
PAN: 10″ angel food with removable bottom (4-quart capacity)
PAN PREP: Ungreased
OVEN TEMP: 325°
RACK LEVEL: Lower third
BAKING TIME: 45 to 50 minutes
METHOD: Electric mixer

1²/₃	cups sifted cake flour
1	teaspoon baking powder
¹/₈	teaspoon salt
5	large egg yolks
1	large whole egg
1¹/₂	cups superfine or strained sugar, divided
2	teaspoons freshly grated lemon rind
2	tablespoons fresh lemon juice
¹/₄	cup plus 1 teaspoon water
5	large egg whites
¹/₂	teaspoon cream of tartar

1. Position rack in the lower third of the oven and preheat to 325°. Have ready a 10-inch angel food pan.
2. Sift together the flour, baking powder, and salt in a triple sifter. Set aside.
3. Place the egg yolks and the whole egg in the small bowl of an electric mixer fitted with beaters or the whip attachment. Whip on medium speed for about 2 minutes. Add *1¹/₄ cups* sugar, 1 tablespoon at a time, taking about 5 to 6 minutes to blend it in well. Scrape the sides of the bowl occasionally. The mixture will thicken and turn light yellow in color.
4. Reduce mixer speed to medium-low. Add the lemon rind and juice. Beat 1 minute longer.

Quick and Easy Cakes

5. Reduce mixer speed to low. Gradually add the dry ingredients alternately with ¼ *cup* of the water, dividing the flour into three parts and the liquid into two parts and starting and ending with the flour. Mix just until incorporated after each addition. Transfer the yolk mixture to a large mixing bowl.

6. Wash and dry the beaters. In the large bowl of the mixer, beat the egg whites and the remaining 1 *teaspoon* of water on medium speed until frothy. Add the cream of tartar. Increase the speed to medium-high and beat until the whites form soft peaks. Gradually add the remaining ¼ *cup* sugar, taking about 15 seconds, and continue beating for 30 seconds longer to form a glossy, soft meringue. Remove the bowl from the machine.

7. With a 2¾-inch-wide rubber spatula, fold ¼ of the meringue into the yolk mixture, taking about 20 turns to lighten. Then fold in the remaining meringue, taking about 50 additional turns.

8. Gently spoon the batter into the pan, smoothing the top with the back of a tablespoon. Insert a knife into the batter and circle the pan twice to remove any air pockets. Smooth the surface again. Bake in the preheated oven 45 to 50 minutes, or until the cake is golden brown on the top and springy to the touch.

9. Remove the cake from the oven and immediately invert the pan onto a cake rack. Let the cake cool completely in the pan. To remove the pan, turn the cake upright and carefully run a sharp, thin-bladed knife 2 or 3 times around the pan to loosen the sides. Then run the knife 2 or 3 times around the center tube. Lift the cake by the center tube and remove the outer rim. Run the knife under cake in 2 or 3 strokes and invert onto a cake rack to remove the tube. Place on a cake platter, top or bottom side up.

STORAGE: Store at room temperature under a glass dome or covered with aluminum foil for up to 1 week.

🌾 SWEET CREAM SPONGE CAKE

This is an ideal cake for a fresh fruit shortcake, or try it with a scoop of your favorite ice cream. The cream in the batter gives it a firm texture that can stand up to moist toppings.

1	cup sifted cake flour
1	teaspoon baking powder
1/4	teaspoon salt
4	large eggs
3/4	cup superfine or strained sugar
1 1/2	teaspoons vanilla extract
1/3	cup heavy cream, well chilled

1. Position rack in the lower third of the oven and preheat to 350°. Have ready an 8-inch tube pan.
2. Sift together the flour, baking powder, and salt in a triple sifter. Set aside.
3. Place the eggs in the large bowl of an electric mixer. With beater or whip attachment, beat on medium-high speed for about 4 to 5 minutes. Add the sugar, 1 tablespoon at a time, taking about 5 to 6 minutes to blend it in well. Scrape the sides of the bowl occasionally. The mixture will thicken and turn light yellow in color. Reduce mixer speed to low. Add the vanilla extract.
4. While the eggs and sugar are beating, pour the cream into a small chilled bowl. Using a rotary beater or hand-held electric mixer, whip until it forms soft peaks. Add the dry ingredients to the egg mixture alternating with the cream, dividing the flour into three parts and the cream into two parts and starting and ending with the flour.
5. Gently spoon the batter into the pan. Place the pan on a 12-inch square of aluminum foil. Bring up the edges of the foil, folding it around the sides of the pan to catch batter that might leak. Bake in the preheated oven for 40 to 45 minutes, or until cake is golden brown on top and springy to the touch.
6. Remove the pan from the oven and invert onto a cake rack. Let the cake cool completely in the pan. To remove the pan, turn the cake upright and carefully run a sharp, thin-bladed knife 2 or

▽

AT A GLANCE

SERVES: 6 to 8
PAN: 8″ flat-bottomed tube pan with a removable bottom (2-quart capacity)
PAN PREP: Ungreased
OVEN TEMP: 350°
RACK LEVEL: Lower third
BAKING TIME: 40 to 45 minutes
METHOD: Electric mixer

Quick and Easy Cakes

3 times around the pan to loosen the sides, then run the knife 2 or 3 times around the center tube. Lift cake by the center tube and remove the outer rim. Run the knife under the cake in 2 or 3 strokes and invert to remove the tube. Place on a cake platter, top or bottom side up.

STORAGE: Store at room temperature under a glass dome or covered with aluminum foil for up to 3 days.

BLACK 'N' RED BERRY SHORTCAKE

Top each slice of cake with a fresh fruit combination of black and red raspberries. The berries become extra special if you macerate them first. Sprinkle each 1/2 cup of mixed berries used with 1 teaspoon of superfine or strained sugar and 1 tablespoon of Chartreuse or other liqueur. Allow the berries to stand for about 1/2 hour or until a little juice accumulates.

Place a slice of cake on a dessert plate and pour berries and juice over the top. Mound with whipped cream and garnish with a mint leaf. This is an easy-to-make and heavenly summer dessert.

TOASTED ALMOND SPONGE

The flavor of toasted chopped almonds permeates this easy-to-make sponge cake and the finely chopped nuts blended through the batter create a pretty flecked effect in the finished cake.

1 1/4	cups toasted sliced almonds (page 58)
1/3	cup unbleached all-purpose flour
1	tablespoon cornstarch
1/2	teaspoon baking powder
2	large egg yolks
1	large whole egg
3/4	cup superfine or strained sugar

    1   teaspoon vanilla extract
    5   large egg whites
  ¹/₈ teaspoon salt

1. Position rack in the lower third of the oven and preheat to 350°. Have ready an 8-inch tube pan.
2. Put the toasted almonds, flour, cornstarch, and baking powder in the container of a food processor fitted with the steel blade. Pulse 8 to 10 times, then process for 15 seconds or until the nuts are very fine and powdery. Set aside.
3. Place the yolks and the whole egg in the large bowl of an electric mixer fitted with beaters or whip attachment. Beat on medium-high speed for about 3 minutes. Add the sugar, 1 tablespoon at a time, taking about 4 to 5 minutes to blend it in well. Scrape the sides of the bowl occasionally. The mixture will thicken and turn light yellow in color.
4. Reduce mixer speed to low and add the vanilla. Add the nut flour and mix until just blended. Transfer mixture to a large mixing bowl.
5. Wash and dry the beaters and bowl. Return both to the mixer, and whip the egg whites on medium speed until frothy. Add the salt. Increase the speed to medium-high and continue beating until the whites form firm, moist peaks. Do not overbeat.
6. With a 2³/₄-inch-wide rubber spatula, fold ¹/₄ of the whites into the yolks, using about 20 turns. Add the remaining whites, using about 40 turns to incorporate the two together.
7. Gently pour the batter into the pan. Bake in the preheated oven 40 to 45 minutes, or until the cake is golden brown on top and springy to the touch.
8. Remove the cake from the oven and immediately invert the pan onto a cake rack. Let the cake cool completely in the pan. To remove the pan, turn the cake upright and run a sharp, thin-bladed knife in 2 or 3 strokes around the pan to loosen the sides. Then run the knife 2 or 3 times around center tube. Holding the center tube, lift the cake to remove it from the outer rim. To loosen the bottom of the cake, run the knife under the cake in 2 or 3 strokes and invert to remove the tube section. Transfer to a cake platter, top or bottom side up.

STORAGE: Store at room temperature under a glass dome or covered with aluminum foil for up to 1 week.

▽ ....

AT A GLANCE

SERVES: 6 to 8
PAN: 8″ flat-bottomed tube pan with a removable bottom (2-quart capacity)
PAN PREP: Ungreased
OVEN TEMP: 350°
RACK LEVEL: Lower third
BAKING TIME: 40 to 45 minutes
METHOD: Electric mixer/food processor

....

Quick and Easy Cakes

🌿 HOT MILK SPONGE CAKE

AT A GLANCE

SERVES: 6 to 8
PAN: 9″ round layer
pan
PAN PREP: Well
greased/parchment
OVEN TEMP: 350°
RACK LEVEL: Lower
third
BAKING TIME: 30 to
35 minutes
METHOD: Electric
mixer

The hot milk gives this thin layer sponge cake a somewhat denser crumb that makes it ideal for shortcakes or cake à la mode. It is also the perfect foundation for two American classics, Boston Cream Pie (page 337) and Washington Pie (see page 263).

This cake can be made in under 15 minutes, but be sure to follow the directions carefully. To ensure proper volume, the hot milk must be beaten rapidly into the batter, and the flour added immediately. When correctly made, the cake should rise to the top of the pan.

½	cup milk
1	tablespoon unsalted butter
1	cup sifted cake flour
1	teaspoon baking powder
½	teaspoon salt
2	large eggs
¾	cup superfine or strained sugar
1	teaspoon vanilla extract

1. Position rack in the lower third of the oven and preheat to 350°. Butter a 9-inch round layer pan and line with a parchment circle.
2. In a small saucepan, heat the milk and butter to almost boiling. Set aside.
3. Sift together the flour, baking powder, and salt in a triple sifter. Set aside.
4. Beat the eggs on medium-high speed in an electric mixer fitted with beaters or a whip attachment for about 2 minutes. Gradually add the sugar, 1 tablespoon at a time, taking about 4 to 5 minutes to blend it in well. Scrape the sides of the bowl occasionally. The mixture will thicken and turn light yellow in color.
5. Reduce mixer speed to medium. Add the vanilla, then pour in the hot milk *in a steady stream*, taking about 10 seconds. Immediately add the dry ingredients all at once, and beat just until blended, scraping the sides of the bowl as necessary. Increase mixer speed to medium-high and beat 10 seconds. The batter will be very thin. Remove the bowl from the mixer and quickly pour the batter into the prepared pan. Bake 30 to 35 minutes, or until

the cake begins to come away from the sides of pan and is golden brown and springy to the touch.

6. Set on a cake rack to cool for about 10 minutes. Run a thin knife around the sides of the pan to loosen. Invert pan onto the rack sprayed with nonstick coating and peel off the parchment paper. Invert again to finish cooling right side up.

STORAGE: Store the plain sponge layer under a glass dome or covered with aluminum foil at room temperature for up to 3 days. For longer storage, freeze.

WASHINGTON PIE

Divide the sponge layer into 3 thin rounds (page 500). Spread each layer with raspberry jam and dust the top generously with confectioners' sugar. For those who have difficulty handling jelly rolls, this is a nice alternative.

Rolls and Roulades

I think of these as "fun" cakes. They are generally light and festive and their lovely pinwheel design always makes a dramatic presentation. Rolls and roulades are generally sponge cakes that are baked in shallow pans so they can be rolled without cracking, usually while the cake is hot and most pliable. Some very moist sponge cakes can be rolled after the sponge sheet has cooled.

Do not let rolls and roulades intimidate you. Their method is very easy to master, and since the baking time of the cake is short, they can be put together in no time. They are ideal when you want a quick dessert for company.

BEFORE YOU BEGIN . . .

▶ Since rolls and roulades are generally sponge cakes, you may find it helpful to read "Before You Begin" in the sponge cake section (pages 253–54).

▶ For these cakes, grease sheet or jelly roll pans on the bottom only unless the recipe tells you to grease the sides. As with other sponge cakes, the batter must cling to an ungreased surface in order to maintain its volume. Sometimes the parchment lining must also be greased, despite the fact that baking parchment has been specially treated. Be sure to leave a paper lip extending from the pan (page 67).

▶ Sponge sheets usually have to be inverted as soon as they are removed from the oven. Keep a wide expanse of counter surface open so you can turn out the cake immediately onto parchment, a dry linen towel, or waxed paper, all lightly dusted with confectioners' sugar. (Some recipes specify sprinkling a small amount of granulated sugar over the parchment. Specific recipes indicate the preferred method.)

▶ If the parchment lining sticks to the cake as you are trying to remove it, brush the paper with warm water, allow to stand 2 minutes, then peel off the paper.

▶ If the edges of the baked sponge sheet are too dry, the cake may be difficult to roll. If this happens, trim 1/4 inch from the sides of the cake with a sharp knife.

▶ Sponge sheets are usually rolled twice, once to set the shape and again to enclose the filling.

▶ You can roll a sponge sheet from either the long or the short side. I prefer to roll the longer side, since this requires fewer turns and minimizes the possibility of the cake splitting. The cake will also yield more servings.

▶ When rolling a roulade, remember that the first turn is very important. The edge of the cake should actually be curled under rather than simply folded, in order to achieve an attractive swirl.

▶ To easily roll the cake and filling together, grasp the parchment or towel together with two hands and lift upward. The higher you lift, the more the cake will turn. Continue rolling the cake until the far side of the cake is on the bottom. See page 275, To Assemble, Step 2.

▶ If you cooled the roll on parchment paper dusted with confectioners' sugar, refresh the top with another small dusting of confectioners' sugar.

▶ Finding the right size and shape platter for serving roulades is often a problem. One of the nicest ways to present these cakes is on a fine wooden breadboard.

▶ To ease the roulade onto a serving platter or board, center a cake plate or wooden board on the far side of the roulade. Make the final turn of the roulade and gently remove the parchment, towel, or waxed paper. Be sure the seam is underneath. Using two wide spatulas or your hands, carefully lift up the cake and center it on the platter.

▶ To get the nicest slices, let the roulade stand 3 to 4 hours to thoroughly set before cutting.

❦ LEMON ROULADE

▽

AT A GLANCE

SERVES: 10 to 12
PAN: 11″ × 17″ ×
1″ jelly roll
PAN PREP: Butter/
parchment (bottom
only)
OVEN TEMP: 375°
RACK LEVEL: Lower
third
BAKING TIME: 12 to
14 minutes
METHOD: Electric
mixer

This golden yellow sponge cake filled with a tart lemon filling is especially appealing to those who do not like their desserts too sweet. If you wish, orange rind and juice can be substituted for lemon. One-third cup finely crushed toasted coconut added to the batter is also a nice touch.

5	large egg yolks
½	cup plus 2 tablespoons superfine or strained sugar
½	teaspoon vanilla extract
½	teaspoon freshly grated lemon rind
1	tablespoon fresh lemon juice
5	large egg whites
	Pinch of salt
⅔	cup sifted cake flour
2	tablespoons strained cornstarch
¼	teaspoon baking powder
1	recipe Clear Lemon Filling (page 440)

1. Position rack in the lower third of the oven and preheat to 375°. Butter an 11″ × 17″ × 1″ jelly roll pan and line the bottom of the pan with baking parchment. Lightly butter the parchment.
2. Sift together the flour, corn starch, and baking powder. Set aside.
3. Put the egg yolks in the small bowl of an electric mixer fitted with beaters or the whip attachment. Beat on medium speed for 3 to 4 minutes or until thick and light in color. Add *½ cup* sugar, 1 tablespoon at a time, taking about 3 to 4 minutes to blend it in well. Reduce speed to medium-low and beat in the vanilla, lemon rind, and lemon juice. Remove the bowl from the mixer and set aside.
4. Wash and dry the beaters. In the large bowl of the mixer, whip egg whites on medium speed until frothy. Add the salt and increase speed to medium-high. Beat until the whites form soft peaks. Add the remaining *2 tablespoons* sugar, taking about 15 seconds, and continue beating 15 seconds longer.
5. Pour the yolk mixture into the whites and beat for 2 minutes longer.

6. Remove the bowl from the mixer. Slowly sift the dry ingredients over the egg mixture, folding them in with a 2¾-inch-wide rubber spatula.
7. Pour the batter into the prepared pan. Gently smooth the top with the back of a tablespoon, being sure to spread evenly at corners. Tap the pan gently on the counter to even out the batter. Bake in the preheated oven 12 to 14 minutes, until top feels set and is springy to the touch. While the cake is baking, cut a 20-inch piece of parchment for inverting the cake. Put it on a flat workspace and dust heavily with 3 tablespoons confectioners' sugar passed through a fine strainer.
8. Remove the cake from the oven and *immediately* invert the cake onto the parchment. Protecting your hands with pot holders, remove the pan and gently peel off the layer of paper that lined the pan. Roll the cake and sugar-dusted paper together tightly, starting on the long side closest to you. Place seam side down to cool.
9. Prepare the lemon filling.

TO ASSEMBLE THE CAKE:
1. Carefully unroll the cake, but not completely flat. The edge closest to you should remain curled. Spoon the filling under the curled edge first, then evenly over the rest of the cake, leaving a 1-inch border on the far side.
2. Tuck the curled edge under and roll the cake up gently. Place seam side down on a wooden breadboard or oblong platter and cover loosely with aluminum foil. Refrigerate until 1 hour before serving time. Just before serving, dust the top lightly with confectioners' sugar.

STORAGE: Store leftover roulade in the refrigerator, loosely covered with aluminum foil, for up to 3 days.

✿ FLOURLESS CHOCOLATE ROULADE WITH WHIPPED APRICOT SOUFFLÉ

Intense with the flavor of dark chocolate and a hint of orange, this is a wonderful vehicle for the luscious filling. Its pale peach color against the black chocolate cake is truly handsome as well.

THE CAKE:

- 6 large egg yolks
- 2/3 cup plus 1/4 cup superfine or strained sugar
- 1 teaspoon vanilla extract
- 1 teaspoon freshly grated navel orange rind
- 2 tablespoons fresh orange juice
- 1/2 cup strained dutch-process cocoa
- 6 large egg whites
- 1 tablespoon water
- 1/4 teaspoon cream of tartar

THE WHIPPED APRICOT SOUFFLÉ:

- 3 ounces (2/3 cup) dried apricots
- 1 cup plus 1 tablespoon water
- 3/4 cup confectioners' sugar
- 1/2 teaspoon unflavored gelatin
- 1 cup heavy cream, well chilled
- 1 tablespoon Grand Marnier

1. Position rack in the lower third of the oven and preheat to 350°. Butter the jelly roll pan and line the bottom with baking parchment. Lightly butter the parchment.
2. To make the cake: Place the yolks in the small bowl of an electric mixer fitted with beaters or the whip attachment. Beat on medium speed until they are thickened and light yellow in color, about 2 minutes. Add 2/3 *cup* sugar, 1 tablespoon at a time, taking about 2 to 3 minutes to blend it in well.
3. Reduce mixer speed to medium-low. Blend in the vanilla, orange rind, and orange juice, and mix for 15 seconds. Reduce speed to low, add the cocoa, and blend until just incorporated.

Remove from the mixer and transfer to a larger mixing bowl. Set aside.

4. Wash and dry the beaters. In the large bowl of the mixer, whip the egg whites and water at medium speed until frothy. Add the cream of tartar, increase the speed to medium-high, and continue beating until the whites form soft peaks. Add 1/4 *cup* sugar, 1 tablespoon at a time, taking about 30 seconds. Whip for 15 seconds longer. Do not overbeat. Remove the bowl from the mixer.

5. With a 2³/₄-inch-wide rubber spatula, fold 1/4 of the beaten egg whites into the yolk mixture, taking about 20 turns to lighten. Then fold in the remaining whites, taking an additional 30 to 40 turns. Pour batter into the prepared pan and gently smooth the top with the back of a spoon, spreading it evenly into the corners. Tap the pan gently on the counter to even out the batter. Bake in the preheated oven for 20 to 25 minutes, until the top feels set and is springy to the touch.

6. While the cake is baking, prepare a 20-inch piece of baking parchment. Place on a flat workspace and sprinkle lightly with 1/2 teaspoon granulated sugar.

7. Remove the cake from the oven and immediately invert onto the parchment. Protecting your hands with pot holders, remove the pan and gently peel off the paper pan liner. Tightly roll together the cake and the sugared parchment paper away from you, starting on a long side. Place the cake seam side down on a cake rack to cool while you prepare the filling.

8. To make the whipped apricot soufflé: Put the apricots and *1 cup* of water in a small heavy saucepan, cover, and bring to a boil. Simmer 20 to 25 minutes or until the apricots are very soft and all but 1 to 2 tablespoons of the water has been absorbed.

9. Remove from the heat and add 1/2 *cup* confectioners' sugar. Whip with a fork until the apricots are very smooth. You should have approximately 1/2 cup of purée.

10. Put *1 tablespoon* cold water in a small heatproof glass dish and sprinkle the gelatin over the top. Let stand for 5 minutes without stirring. Place the dish in a skillet filled with 1/2 inch of boiling water. Then stir the mixture until the gelatin is dissolved and the mixture is clear. Stir it into the apricot purée. Set aside to cool to tepid.

11. Beat the cream in a small chilled bowl of an electric mixer. As

it begins to thicken, add ¼ *cup* confectioners' sugar gradually. Beat until soft peaks form. Remove from the mixer and fold in the tepid purée and Grand Marnier by hand.

TO ASSEMBLE THE CAKE:
1. Carefully unroll the cake, but not completely flat; the edge closest to you should remain curled. Spoon the filling under the curled edge first, then spread it over the rest of the cake evenly with a metal spatula, leaving a 1-inch border on far side.
2. To roll the cake, tuck the curled edge under and continue rolling. Place seam side down on a wooden breadboard or oblong platter. Cover loosely with foil and refrigerate until ½ hour before serving. Dust the top with confectioners' sugar just before serving.

STORAGE: Store leftover roulade in the refrigerator loosely covered with aluminum foil for up to 3 days.

❧ COFFEE CREAM LOG

....

This coffee-flavored sponge sheet is filled and covered with a wonderful amaretto-flavored whipped cream enhanced with crunchy chopped almonds. Be sure to toast the almonds, as toasting gives these somewhat bland nuts a far superior flavor.

....

THE CAKE:
- 1 tablespoon instant freeze-dried coffee
- 1 tablespoon boiling water
- ⅔ cup sifted cake flour
- ¾ teaspoon baking powder
- 4 large egg yolks
- ⅔ cup superfine or strained sugar, divided
- ¾ teaspoon vanilla extract
- 4 large egg whites
- ⅛ teaspoon salt

THE ALMOND CREAM FILLING:

- 1½ tablespoons cold water
- ¾ teaspoon unflavored gelatin
- 1½ cups heavy cream, chilled
- 3 tablespoons confectioners' sugar
- 2 tablespoons amaretto liqueur
- 1 teaspoon vanilla extract
- ⅓ cup finely chopped toasted almonds (page 58)
- ½ cup toasted almond slivers, for garnish

1. Preheat oven to 350° and position the rack in the lower third of the oven. Butter a 10½″ × 15½″ × 1″ jelly roll pan, line the bottom with baking parchment, and lightly butter the parchment.
2. To make the cake: Dissolve the coffee in the boiling water. Set aside.
3. Sift together the flour and baking powder in a triple sifter. Set aside.
4. Put the egg yolks in the small bowl of an electric mixer fitted with beaters or a whip attachment and beat on medium speed until thick and light in color, about 2 minutes. Add ⅓ cup sugar, 1 tablespoon at a time, taking about 2 to 3 minutes to blend it in well. Reduce speed to low and blend in the coffee and vanilla. Add the flour all at once and mix just until blended. Remove the bowl from the mixer and transfer the batter to a large mixing bowl. Set aside.
5. Wash and dry the beaters. In the large bowl of the mixer, whip the egg whites until frothy. Add the salt and beat until the whites form soft peaks. Add ⅓ cup sugar, 1 tablespoon at a time, taking 45 seconds. Beat 30 seconds longer. Remove bowl from the mixer.
6. With a 2¾-inch-wide rubber spatula, fold ¼ of the whites into the yolks, taking about 20 turns to lighten. Quickly fold the remaining whites into the batter, taking about 40 additional turns.
7. Pour the batter into the prepared pan. Gently smooth the top with the back of a spoon, spreading it evenly into the corners. Tap the pan gently on the counter to even out the sides. Bake in the preheated oven 14 to 16 minutes, until cake begins to come away from the sides of the pan and is springy to the touch.
8. While the cake is baking, generously sprinkle confectioners' sugar through a strainer on a linen kitchen towel or a 20-inch sheet of parchment.

▽
AT A GLANCE

SERVES: 8 to 10
PAN: 10½″ × 15½″ × 1″ jelly roll
PAN PREP: Butter/ parchment (bottom only)
OVEN TEMP: 350°
RACK LEVEL: Lower third
BAKING TIME: 14 to 16 minutes
METHOD: Electric mixer

Quick and Easy Cakes

271

9. Remove the cake from the oven and immediately invert onto the towel or paper. Using a pot holder to protect your hands, remove the pan and gently peel off the paper. Roll the cake and towel together tightly, starting on the long side closest to you. Place seam side down on a rack to cool.

10. To make the filling: Place the large mixer bowl and beaters in the refrigerator to chill.

11. Pour the cold water into a small heatproof custard cup. Sprinkle the gelatin over the water and let stand 5 minutes without stirring. Gelatin will swell and turn opaque.

12. Set the custard cup in a skillet filled with 1/2 inch of boiling water. Stir until the gelatin is clear and completely dissolved. Remove the custard cup from the skillet and cool to tepid.

13. Place the cream in the chilled bowl, and with chilled beaters whip the cream on medium speed. When it begins to thicken, add the confectioners' sugar, immediately pour in the gelatin, then the amaretto and vanilla. Beat until the cream forms soft peaks. After the gelatin and liqueur are added to the cream, the mixture will thicken quickly. Do not overbeat or the filling will become grainy. Remove the bowl from the mixer. Finish whipping the cream by hand until thick, using a wire balloon whisk.

14. Remove 1/3 of the cream for frosting the roll. Fold the chopped almonds into the remaining cream for the filling.

TO ASSEMBLE THE CAKE:

1. Carefully unroll the cake, but not completely flat. The edge closest to you should remain curled. Spread the filling across the length, pushing the cream evenly under the curled edge first. Leave a 1 1/2-inch border on the far side.

2. To roll, tuck the curled edge of the cake under and continue rolling. Place seam side down on a wooden breadboard or oblong platter. Spread the reserved cream over the top, and garnish with slivered almonds. Refrigerate uncovered until 1/2 hour before serving.

STORAGE: Cover leftover cake loosely with aluminum foil and refrigerate for up to 3 days.

🌰 FRENCH JELLY ROLL

....

This is made with a classic French sponge batter, biscuit au beurre. It is not as moist as a typical sponge, but a thick jam filling tenderizes the cake. The superb flavor of the biscuit comes from the small amount of clarified butter in the batter.

You may fill this with any buttercream frosting or fruit-flavored whipped cream instead of jam. If you do, be sure to moisten the cake with a sugar syrup (page 467) or it will be too dry.

....

3	large eggs
1	large egg yolk
1/2	cup sugar
1/2	teaspoon vanilla extract
1/2	cup unsifted all-purpose flour
1/4	teaspoon baking powder
2	tablespoons warm (100 to 110°) clarified butter (page 43)
1/2	cup seedless raspberry preserves, or any other jam or jelly of your choice

▽ ....

AT A GLANCE

SERVES: 8 to 10
PAN: 10½″ × 15½″ × 1″ jelly roll pan
PAN PREP: Butter/ parchment (bottom only)
OVEN TEMP: 350°
RACK LEVEL: Lower third
BAKING TIME: 14 to 16 minutes
METHOD: Electric mixer

....

1. Position a rack in the lower third of the oven and preheat to 350°. Butter the bottom of a 10½″ × 15½″ × 1″ jelly roll pan and line with parchment. Lightly butter the parchment.
2. Select a saucepan that will hold the large bowl of an electric mixer without the bowl touching the 2 inches of water in the pan. Heat until water simmers but does not boil rapidly.
3. Place the eggs and the additional egg yolk in the large bowl of an electric mixer. Using a wire whisk, stir in the sugar and vanilla, just to blend. Mix briefly; do not beat. Set the bowl over the hot water. Slowly and continuously stir with the whisk until the sugar is completely dissolved and the mixture feels quite warm. Test by rubbing a small amount of the warm egg mixture between your fingers. You should not feel the grain of the sugar crystals.
4. Remove the pan from the heat and dry the bottom of the bowl. With the beaters or whip attachment, beat the mixture on medium-high speed about 6 minutes, until thick and light in color. Remove the bowl from the mixer.

Quick and Easy Cakes

273

5. Place the flour and baking powder in a triple sifter and sift into the egg mixture, folding in with a 2¾-inch-wide rubber spatula. Pour in the clarified butter in a steady stream, folding it in quickly. Immediately transfer the batter into the prepared pan. Smooth with the back of a tablespoon, spreading it evenly into the corners. Tap the pan gently on the counter to even out the batter. Bake in the preheated oven 14 to 16 minutes, until cake begins to come away from sides of pan and top is lightly brown.
6. While the cake is baking, generously sprinkle a linen kitchen towel or 20-inch sheet of parchment with confectioners' sugar passed through a fine strainer.
7. Remove the pan from the oven and allow to stand 1 minute. Run a thin knife around the edge to release. Invert onto the prepared towel or parchment. Protecting your hands with pot holders, gently lift off the pan. Brush lining paper with warm water, let stand for 2 minutes, then peel off the paper. Trim ¼ inch off the sides of the sponge sheet with a sharp knife to remove dry or uneven edges. Tightly roll together the cake and towel away from you, starting on a long side. Place seam side down on a cake rack to cool.

TO ASSEMBLE THE CAKE:
1. Carefully unroll the cake, but do not unroll completely flat. The edge closest to you should remain curled.
2. Spread the sponge sheet with preserves, leaving a ½-inch border on the side farthest away from you.
3. To roll the cake, tuck the curled edge under and roll tightly. Place seam side down on a wooden breadboard or oblong platter. Cover loosely with aluminum foil and let stand at room temperature for up to 6 hours. Just before serving, dust the top with confectioners' sugar. Accompany with a selection of fruit sorbets and garnish with mint leaves, if desired.

STORAGE: Store leftover cake in the refrigerator, loosely covered with aluminum foil, for up to 3 days.

❧ VERY BERRY ROULADE

his is made with a French sponge *base and filled with a succulent blend of raspberries, strawberries, fresh raspberry purée, and a small amount of whipped cream. The filling is less rich than other cream-based versions and makes a colorful roulade vibrant with red and pink.*

2¼ cups fresh raspberries, divided
¼ cup sugar
1 teaspoon unflavored gelatin
½ cup heavy cream, whipped to soft peak stage
1 cup sliced strawberries, rinsed and dried
½ teaspoon vanilla extract
1 French Jelly Roll (page 273), prepared through Step 7

1. Rinse the raspberries and drain thoroughly on paper toweling. Place ½ *cup* raspberries, sugar, and gelatin in a small saucepan. Heat over a low flame, stirring constantly with a fork, until berries release their juices. Simmer over very low heat 3 to 4 minutes, until gelatin is dissolved and the mixture is somewhat syrupy. Stir occasionally to prevent burning.
2. Remove from the heat. Place the pan in a bowl of ice and chill until the purée is cold and thickened. Fold in the whipped cream, remaining 1¾ *cups* raspberries, strawberries, and vanilla.

TO ASSEMBLE THE CAKE:
1. Carefully unroll the cake onto a sugared towel, but not completely flat. The edge closest to you should remain curled. Spoon the filling under the curled edge first. Then spread it evenly over the rest of the cake as best you can, leaving a ½-inch border on far side.
2. To roll the cake, tuck the curled edge under and, using the towel to guide you, lift the towel and continue rolling. Place the roulade seam side down on a wooden breadboard or oblong platter. Cover loosely with aluminum foil and refrigerate. Just before serving, refresh the top with confectioners' sugar if necessary.

STORAGE: Refrigerate leftover cake for up to 3 days.

Quick and Easy Cakes

❧ NUT SOUFFLÉ ROLL

Finely chopped nuts are used in place of flour in this flavorful, moist sponge layer filled and covered with chocolate whipped cream.

▽
AT A GLANCE

SERVES: 8 to 10
PAN: 10½" × 15½" × 1" jelly roll pan
PAN PREP: Butter/ parchment (bottom only)
OVEN TEMP: 350°
RACK LEVEL: Lower third
BAKING TIME: 18 to 20 minutes
METHOD: Electric mixer/food processor

1	cup walnuts or pecans
⅓	cup plus 2 tablespoons superfine or strained sugar
5	large egg yolks
1	large whole egg
1	teaspoon vanilla extract
5	large egg whites
	Pinch salt
1	large recipe Chocolate Whipped Cream (page 488), made with 2 cups heavy cream

1. Position a rack in the lower third of the oven and preheat to 350°. Butter a 10½" × 15½" × 1" jelly roll pan and line the bottom of the pan with baking parchment. Lightly butter the parchment.

2. Place the nuts and 2 *tablespoons* of the sugar in the bowl of a food processor fitted with a steel blade. Process for 20 to 30 seconds, or until the nuts are ground very fine. Set aside.

3. Place the yolks and the whole egg in the small bowl of an electric mixer fitted with beaters or a whip attachment. Beat for 3 minutes on medium speed, until thick and light in color. Add ⅓ *cup* sugar, 1 tablespoon at a time, taking about 2 to 3 minutes to blend it in well.

4. Reduce mixer speed to low. Blend in the vanilla, then add the nut mixture. Remove the bowl from the mixer and set aside.

5. In a separate large bowl, with clean beaters, whip the whites at medium speed until frothy. Add the salt and continue beating until the whites form firm peaks. Remove the bowl from the mixer.

6. Using a 2¾-inch-wide rubber spatula, fold ¼ of the whites into the nut mixture, taking about 20 turns to lighten. Fold the remaining nut mixture into the whites, taking an additional 30 turns. Gently spoon the batter into the prepared pan and smooth the top with the back of a tablespoon, spreading it evenly into

the corners. Tap the pan gently on the counter to even out the batter. In the preheated oven, bake 18 to 20 minutes, until top feels set and is springy to the touch.

7. While the cake is baking, cut a 20-inch piece of parchment, set it on a flat workspace, and sprinkle lightly with 1/2 teaspoon granulated sugar.

8. Remove the cake from the oven and *immediately* invert the cake onto the parchment. Protecting your hands with pot holders, remove the pan and gently peel off the lining paper. Tightly roll together the cake with the sugar-coated paper away from you, starting on the long side closest to you. Place seam side down on a cake rack to cool.

9. While the cake is cooling, prepare the whipped cream.

TO ASSEMBLE THE CAKE:

1. Carefully unroll the cake, but not completely flat. The edge closest to you should remain curled. Spoon about 2/3 of the cream under the curled edge first, then spread the filling evenly over the rest of the cake, leaving a 1-inch border on the far side.

2. To roll the cake, tuck the curled edge under and continue rolling. Place seam side down on a wooden breadboard or oblong platter.

3. Place a strip of waxed paper along each side of cake. Using a metal spatula, spread the remaining chocolate whipped cream over the cake, smoothing the surface. To make a decorative design, press gently with the bottom of a teaspoon to create a line of small swirls. Continue this pattern, following the arch of the cake, until fully decorated. Sprinkle the top with 2 tablespoons finely chopped nuts if you like. Refrigerate, uncovered, until ready to serve.

STORAGE: Store leftover cake in the refrigerator, loosely covered with aluminum foil, for up to 3 days.

CHOCOLATE PECAN ROULADE WITH MOCHA WHIPPED CREAM

AT A GLANCE

SERVES: 8 to 10
PAN: 10½″ × 15½″ × 1″ jelly roll pan
PAN PREP: Butter/ parchment (bottom only)
OVEN TEMP: 375°
RACK LEVEL: Lower third
BAKING TIME: 12 to 14 minutes
METHOD: Electric mixer/food processor

During my catering career, this roulade was one of the most requested pastry desserts I made. Note that the cream mixture for the filling must be chilled in advance (Step 9). It is a good idea to do this before you embark on the cake preparation.

THE CAKE:

3	tablespoons unsweetened dutch-process cocoa
¼	cup pecan halves (about 1 ounce), lightly toasted
2	tablespoons all-purpose flour
6	large egg yolks
¾	cup superfine or strained sugar
1½	teaspoons vanilla extract
6	large egg whites
⅛	teaspoon cream of tartar
⅛	teaspoon salt

THE MOCHA WHIPPED CREAM:

1	teaspoon coffee zest (page 58)
⅓	cup strained confectioners' sugar
2	tablespoons strained, unsweetened dutch-process cocoa
2	cups heavy cream, well chilled
2	tablespoons cold water
1	teaspoon unflavored gelatin
2	tablespoons Kahlúa or Tía María liqueur
¼	cup coarsely chopped pecans, lightly toasted, for garnish
	Shaved semisweet chocolate (page 496), for garnish

1. Position rack in the lower third of the oven and preheat to 350°. Butter the bottom of a 10½″ × 15½″ × 1″ jelly roll pan and line with parchment. Lightly butter the parchment.
2. To make the cake: Place the cocoa, nuts, and flour in the container of a food processor fitted with the steel blade. Pulse 8 to

10 times, then process 10 to 15 seconds. Scrape the corners of the bowl to release accumulated crumbs and process 5 seconds longer, or until the nuts are ground very fine and powdery. Set aside.

3. Place the egg yolks in the small bowl of an electric mixer fitted with beaters or whip attachment. Beat on medium speed for 2 minutes, or until thick and light in color. Add sugar, 1 tablespoon at a time, taking about 3 to 4 minutes to blend it in well. Reduce speed to low, and blend in the vanilla, then the nut mixture, mixing just until blended. Do not overmix. Transfer the batter to a large mixing bowl and set aside.

4. In a large separate bowl, with clean beaters, whip the egg whites until frothy. Add the cream of tartar and salt and beat until whites form firm moist peaks. Remove the bowl from the mixer. With a 2³/₄-inch-wide rubber spatula, fold ¹/₄ of the whites into the batter, taking about 20 turns to lighten. Quickly fold in the remaining whites, taking about 40 additional turns.

5. Pour the batter into the pan. Gently smooth the top with the back of a tablespoon, spreading it evenly into the corners. Tap the pan gently on the counter to even out the batter. Bake 12 to 14 minutes in the preheated oven, or until the top has risen and the cake feels soft to the touch. This sponge cake is very delicate and will not feel springy. Take care not to overbake.

6. While the cake is baking, get ready: a fine strainer and ¹/₃ cup confectioners' sugar, a sheet of waxed paper at least 18 inches long, and a dampened kitchen towel.

7. Remove the cake from the oven and place on a rack. *Immediately* sprinkle the top generously with the confectioners' sugar. Run a thin sharp knife around the edge of the pan to loosen the sides. Cover the cake with the waxed paper, then the dampened towel, and invert onto the countertop.

8. After 20 minutes, carefully lift off the pan. Gently peel off the bottom layer of paper. Cool flat for 20 to 30 minutes.*

9. To prepare the mocha whipped cream: In a large bowl of an electric mixer, stir the coffee zest, confectioners' sugar, and cocoa into the cream. (The ingredients will not blend together thoroughly.) Chill in the refrigerator for 30 to 40 minutes.

*Do not leave the damp towel underneath the cake longer than 1 hour before rolling or the cake will become too moist. This cake should remain flat until ready to fill.

10. Pour the cold water into a small heatproof custard cup. Sprinkle the gelatin over the water and let stand 5 minutes without stirring. Gelatin will swell and turn opaque.

11. Set the custard cup in a skillet filled with ½-inch of simmering water. Stir until the gelatin is clear and completely dissolved. Remove the custard cup from the skillet and cool to tepid.

12. With the chilled beaters, whip the chilled cream mixture on medium speed. As it begins to thicken, pour in the gelatin, then the liqueur. After the gelatin and liqueur are added the mixture will thicken quickly; do not overbeat or the filling will become grainy. When the cream begins to form soft peaks, remove from the mixer. Continue the beating by hand, using a wire balloon whisk, until the cream forms firm peaks.

TO ASSEMBLE THE CAKE:

1. Trim ¼-inch off the sides of the sponge sheet with a sharp knife to remove dry or uneven edges. Spread ⅔ of mocha whipped cream across the length of the cake, leaving approximately 1½ inches bare on the far side. Gently slide the towel out (leaving the waxed paper) from under the cake if you haven't already done so.

2. Holding the edges of the waxed paper closest to you, begin turning the sponge sheet over. Press along the edge to curl the cake slightly downward. Continue to roll until the end is almost reached. Center a cake plate or wooden board on the far side of the roulade. Make the final turn of the roulade and gently remove the waxed paper. Be sure the seam of the cake is underneath. Using two wide spatulas or your hands, carefully lift up the cake and center it on the platter.

3. Using a metal spatula, spread the roulade with the remaining filling. Make lines down the length of the roulade with a pastry comb or the tines of a fork. If desired, place a small amount of the filling into an 8-inch pastry bag fitted with a #34 star tube and pipe several rosettes randomly over the cake (pages 516–17). Sprinkle with the pecans and shaved chocolate. Refrigerate for 3 to 4 hours to set. Let the cake stand at room temperature ½ hour before serving.

STORAGE: Store leftover cake in the refrigerator, loosely covered with aluminum foil. This cake will keep up to 3 days.

CHIFFON CAKES

. . . . 🌿 . . . .

Chiffon cakes are light-textured and similar in composition and appearance to sponge cakes. The difference is that chiffon cakes are made with vegetable oil, while most sponge cakes contain no oil. The addition of oil to a sponge-type batter results in a moister, more delicate cake that also will not harden in the refrigerator as most butter cakes do.

The standard method of making chiffon cake calls for sifting all the dry ingredients including the sugar into a large bowl and making a "well" to receive the egg yolks, oil, liquid, and flavorings. These ingredients are beaten together until well blended, then stiffly beaten egg whites are folded in. However, since oil is heavy, it can be difficult to whip to optimum lightness. So I prefer to whip the egg yolks and most of the sugar together, then rapidly beat in the oil and flavorings. Whipping the oil into the beaten eggs and sugar helps to keep it suspended and thus better aerates the batter. I add the flour and liquids, and fold in the meringue last. I usually achieve a higher volume and lighter crumb using this technique.

BEFORE YOU BEGIN . . .

▶ All of the rules for sponge cakes apply to chiffon cakes, so you will find it helpful to reread pages 253–54.
▶ Chiffon cakes require more leavening than other foam-style cakes because they are made with oil and so need an additional boost to help the rising.
▶ Vegetable oils, also known as liquid emulsifiers, cannot be whipped, and therefore cannot hold in air. When they are added to whipped eggs, the volume of the batter decreases. Therefore it is important always to add the oil

in a steady stream for the time period specified in the recipe. Do this on a high mixer speed to keep the oil suspended throughout the batter.

▶ Chiffon batters are quite thin, so dry ingredients are sometimes added at a higher mixer speed than is used for a regular cake batter. They are also looser in consistency due to the presence of oil.

▶ Chop nuts or chocolate fine so they will not sink or weigh down the thin batter.

▶ You can easily change the flavor of a chiffon cake by adding spices or zests, or substituting liquids such as coffee or juice for water.

🌾 ROYAL CHIFFON

An especially light chiffon cake with a hint of almond. For interesting flavor variations, try adding coffee zest or espresso zest (page 58), finely chopped nuts, or perhaps combinations of spices.

▽ ....

AT A GLANCE

SERVES: 14 to 16
PAN: 10″ angel food with a removable bottom (4-quart capacity)
PAN PREP: Ungreased
OVEN TEMP: 325°
RACK LEVEL: Lower third
BAKING TIME: 60 to 70 minutes
METHOD: Electric mixer

....

Great Cakes

282

2¼	cups sifted cake flour
1	tablespoon baking powder
½	teaspoon salt
5	large egg yolks
1	large egg
1⅓	cups superfine or strained sugar, divided
½	cup safflower oil
2	teaspoons vanilla extract
1	teaspoon almond extract
¾	cup water
6	large egg whites
¼	teaspoon cream of tartar

1. Position a rack in the lower third of the oven and preheat to 325°. Have ready a 10-inch angel food pan.
2. Sift together the flour, baking powder, and salt, using a triple sifter. Set aside.
3. Place the egg yolks and the whole egg in the large bowl of an

electric mixer fitted with the beaters or whip attachment. Beat on medium-high speed for 3 minutes. Add *1 cup* sugar, 1 table-spoon at a time, taking 4 to 5 minutes to blend it in well. The mixture will be thick and light yellow in color.

4. Pour in the oil in a steady stream over 15 seconds. Add the extracts and whip 1 minute longer. Reduce speed to medium-low.

5. Add the dry ingredients alternately with the water, dividing the flour into three parts and the water into two parts, starting and ending with the flour. Scrape the sides of the bowl and beat for 10 seconds longer. Set aside.

6. Wash and dry the beaters. In the large bowl of the mixer whip the whites on medium speed until frothy. Add the cream of tartar and increase speed to medium-high. When the whites form soft peaks, add ⅓ cup sugar, 1 tablespoon at a time, over 30 seconds to form a glossy soft meringue. Whip 1 minute longer.

7. Remove the bowl from the mixer. Using a 2¾-inch-wide rubber spatula, fold ¼ of the yolk mixture into the whites, taking about 15 turns to lighten. Then reverse and fold the whites into the yolk mixture, taking an additional 40 to 50 turns.

8. Gently spoon or pour batter into the pan. Center the pan on the rack and bake in the preheated oven for 60 to 70 minutes, or until cake is golden brown on top and springy to the touch.

9. Remove from the oven and *immediately* invert the pan onto a cake rack. Let the cake cool completely in pan. To remove, run a sharp, thin-bladed knife in 2 or 3 strokes around the side of the pan to loosen the cake, then run it around center tube. Holding the center tube, lift the cake and remove it from the outer rim. Run the knife under cake in 2 or 3 strokes, invert the cake onto a rack, and remove the tube section. Transfer to a cake platter top or bottom side up.

STORAGE: Store at room temperature under a glass dome or covered with aluminum foil for up to 5 days.

VARIATION
. . . .

CINNAMON CHIFFON CAKE

Add 2 teaspoons cinnamon and ¼ teaspoon powdered cloves to dry ingredients. Reduce vanilla to 1 teaspoon. Substitute one 5½-ounce can apple juice for the water.

🌾 GOLDEN CITRUS CHIFFON CAKE

AT A GLANCE

SERVES: 14 to 16
PAN: 10″ angel food with a removable bottom (4-quart capacity)
PAN PREP: Ungreased
OVEN TEMP: 325°
RACK LEVEL: Lower third
BAKING TIME: 60 to 65 minutes
METHOD: Electric mixer

The refreshing flavors of orange and lemon are wonderful in combination and add a nice accent to this delicate chiffon cake. Watch how quickly it disappears when you serve it.

2¼	cups sifted cake flour
1	tablespoon baking powder
½	teaspoon salt
5	large egg yolks
1	large egg
1⅓	cups superfine or strained sugar, divided
½	cup safflower oil
2	teaspoons grated navel orange rind
½	teaspoon grated lemon rind
⅔	cup orange juice
4	teaspoons fresh lemon juice
6	large egg whites
¼	teaspoon cream of tartar

1. Position a rack in the lower third of the oven and preheat to 325°. Have ready a 10-inch angel food pan.
2. Sift together the flour, baking powder, and salt using a triple sifter, and set aside.
3. Put the egg yolks and whole egg in the large bowl of an electric mixer fitted with the beaters or whip attachment. Beat on medium-high speed for 3 minutes. Add *1 cup* sugar, 1 tablespoon at a time, taking 4 to 5 minutes to blend it in well. The mixture will be thick and light yellow in color.
4. Pour in the oil in a steady stream over 15 seconds. Add the orange and lemon rinds and whip 1 minute longer. Reduce the speed to medium-low.
5. Combine the orange and lemon juices. Add to the yolk mixture alternately with the dry ingredients, dividing the dry ingredients into three parts and the juices into two parts, starting and ending with the flour. Scrape the sides of the bowl and beat for 10 seconds longer. Set aside.
6. Wash and dry the beaters. In the large bowl of the mixer, whip

the whites on medium speed until frothy. Add the cream of tartar, increase speed to medium-high, and whip until the whites form soft peaks. Add $1/3$ *cup* sugar, 1 tablespoon at a time, over 30 seconds to form a glossy soft meringue. Whip 1 minute longer.

7. Remove the bowl from the mixer. Using a $2^3/4$-inch-wide rubber spatula, fold $1/4$ of the yolk mixture into the whites, taking about 15 turns to lighten, then fold the whites into the yolk mixture, taking an additional 40 to 50 turns.

8. Gently spoon or pour batter into the pan. Center the pan on the rack and bake in the preheated oven for 60 to 65 minutes, until the cake is golden brown on top and is springy to the touch.

9. Remove from the oven and *immediately* invert the pan onto a cake rack. Let the cake cool completely in the pan. To remove, run a thin, sharp-bladed knife in 2 to 3 sweeps around the sides of the pan to loosen the cake, then run it around the center tube. Holding the center tube, lift the cake and remove it from the outer rim. Run the knife under the cake in 2 or 3 strokes, invert the cake onto a rack, and remove the tube section. Transfer to a cake platter, top or bottom side up.

STORAGE: Store at room temperature under a glass dome or covered with aluminum foil for up to 5 days.

🌿 CRANBERRY CHIFFON CAKE

Puréed cranberry sauce and finely chopped walnuts give this chiffon cake its delicious flavor. The cranberries add moistness and give the cake a subtle fruity tang. Although you might expect them to turn the cake pink, it has only a slight blush hue.

AT A GLANCE

SERVES: 6 to 8 (See Note)
PAN: 8″ flat-bottomed tube pan with removable bottom (2-quart capacity)
PAN PREP: Ungreased
OVEN TEMP: 325°
RACK LEVEL: Lower third
BAKING TIME: 45 to 50 minutes
METHOD: Electric mixer/food processor

³/₄	cup whole cranberry sauce
¹/₄	cup orange juice
1¹/₃	cups sifted cake flour
1¹/₂	teaspoons baking powder
¹/₄	teaspoon salt
2	large egg yolks
1	large egg
²/₃	cup plus ¹/₄ cup superfine or strained sugar
¹/₄	cup safflower oil
1	teaspoon grated navel orange rind
1	teaspoon vanilla extract
¹/₃	cup walnuts, finely chopped
3	large egg whites

1. Position a rack in the lower third of the oven and preheat to 325°. Have 8-inch flat-bottomed tube pan at hand.
2. Drain the excess liquid from the top of the cranberries and discard. Place cranberry sauce in a food processor fitted with the steel blade and pulse 6 to 8 times or until berries are chopped medium-fine. Add the orange juice, pulse 2 or 3 times, and set aside.
3. Sift together the flour, baking powder, and salt using a triple sifter. Set aside.
4. Place the egg yolks and the whole egg in the large bowl of an electric mixer fitted with the beaters or whip attachment. Whip on medium-high speed for 3 minutes. Add ²/₃ *cup* sugar, 1 tablespoon at a time, taking 3 to 4 minutes to blend it in well, beating until the mixture is thick and light yellow in color.
5. Pour in the oil in a steady stream over 15 seconds. Add the orange rind and vanilla extract and whip 1 minute longer. Reduce speed to medium-low. Blend in the walnuts.

6. Add the dry ingredients alternately with cranberry mixture, dividing the flour into three parts and the cranberries into two parts, starting and ending with the flour. Scrape sides of bowl and beat for 10 seconds longer. Set aside.

7. Wash and dry the beaters. In a separate bowl of the mixer, whip the whites on medium speed until they form soft peaks. Increase the speed to medium-high. Add 1/4 *cup* sugar, 1 tablespoon at a time over 30 seconds to form a glossy soft meringue. Whip 1 minute longer.

8. Remove the bowl from machine. With a 2³/₄-inch-wide spatula, fold 1/4 of the batter into the whites, taking 15 turns to lighten. Then fold the whites into the batter, taking an additional 40 to 50 turns.

9. Gently spoon or pour the batter into the pan. Bake in the preheated oven for 45 to 50 minutes, or until cake is golden brown on top and springy to the touch.

10. Remove from oven and *immediately* invert the pan onto a cake rack. Let the cake cool completely in pan. To remove pan, run a sharp, thin-bladed knife 2 to 3 strokes around the side of the pan to loosen, then run it around the center tube. Holding the center tube, lift the cake. Run the knife under the cake in 2 or 3 sweeps, invert onto a cake rack, and remove the tube section. Transfer to a serving platter, top or bottom side up.

STORAGE: Store at room temperature under a glass dome or covered with aluminum foil for up to 5 days.

NOTE: If you wish to make a larger cake, double the recipe and bake in a 10-inch angel food cake pan. Increase the baking time by 15 to 20 minutes.

🐚 PINEAPPLE CHIFFON CAKE

flecks of crushed pineapple make a moist and delicious cake. Lots of grated lemon rind complements the pineapple. This is a light, refreshing cake to enjoy at any time of year.

▽ AT A GLANCE

SERVES: 12 to 14
PAN: 10″ angel food with a removable bottom (4-quart capacity)
PAN PREP: Ungreased
OVEN TEMP: 325°
RACK LEVEL: Lower third
BAKING TIME: 50 to 55 minutes
METHOD: Electric mixer/food processor

2¼	cups sifted cake flour
1	tablespoon baking powder
½	teaspoon salt
One	8¼-ounce can unsweetened crushed pineapple, undrained
2	tablespoons orange juice
5	large egg yolks
1	large egg
1⅓	cups superfine or strained sugar, divided
½	cup safflower oil
2	teaspoons freshly grated lemon rind
6	large egg whites
¼	teaspoon cream of tartar

1. Position a rack in the lower third of the oven and preheat to 325°. Have a 10-inch angel food pan ready.
2. Sift together the flour, baking powder, and salt using a triple sifter, and set aside.
3. Place the undrained crushed pineapple and orange juice in a food processor bowl fitted with the steel blade. Pulse 4 to 5 times to break up the large pieces of pineapple. Do not chop too fine. Set aside.
4. Put the egg yolks and whole egg in the large bowl of an electric mixer fitted with the beaters or whip attachment. Beat on medium-high speed for 3 minutes. Add *1 cup* of sugar, 1 tablespoon at a time, taking 4 to 5 minutes to blend it in well. The mixture will be thick and light yellow in color.
5. Pour in the oil in a steady stream over 15 seconds. Add the lemon rind and whip for 1 minute longer. Reduce speed to medium-low.
6. Add the dry ingredients alternately with the pineapple mixture, dividing the flour into three parts and the pineapple into two

parts, starting and ending with the flour. Scrape the sides of the bowl and beat for 10 seconds longer. Set aside.

7. Wash and dry the beaters. In the large bowl of the mixer, whip the whites until frothy on medium-low speed. Add the cream of tartar. Increase the mixer speed to medium-high. When the whites form soft peaks, add 1/3 *cup* sugar, 1 tablespoon at a time, over 30 seconds to form a glossy soft meringue. Whip 1 minute longer.

8. Remove the bowl from the mixer. Using a 2³/₄-inch-wide rubber spatula, fold 1/4 of the yolk mixture into the whites, taking about 15 turns to lighten. Then fold the whites into the yolk mixture, taking an additional 40 to 50 turns.

9. Gently spoon or pour batter into the pan. Center the pan on the rack and bake in the preheated oven for 50 to 55 minutes, or until cake is golden brown on top and springy to the touch.

10. Remove from the oven and invert the pan immediately onto a cake rack. Let the cake cool completely in the pan. To remove, run a sharp, thin-bladed knife in 2 or 3 sweeps around the side of the pan to loosen the cake, then run it around the center tube. Holding the center tube, lift the cake and remove it from the outer rim. Run the knife under the cake in 2 or 3 strokes, invert onto a cake rack, and remove the tube section. Place the cake on a serving platter, top or bottom side up.

STORAGE: Store at room temperature under a glass dome or covered with aluminum foil for up to 7 days.

🏵 ORANGE BENNE SQUARES

AT A GLANCE

SERVES: 8 to 10
PAN: 9″ × 9″ × 2″ square
PAN PREP: Butter
OVEN TEMP: 350°
RACK LEVEL: Lower third
BAKING TIME: 35 to 40 minutes
METHOD: Electric mixer

The marvelous flavor of this cake is enhanced with lightly toasted sesame seeds, cardamom, and coriander. For this chiffon cake batter, the eggs are not separated. These squares are lovely to serve for afternoon tea.

THE CAKE:

 ½ cup sesame seeds
 1½ cups sifted cake flour
 1½ teaspoons baking powder
 ½ teaspoon ground cardamom
 ½ teaspoon ground coriander
 ½ teaspoon salt
 3 large eggs
 1 cup superfine or strained sugar
 ⅓ cup safflower oil
 1 teaspoon vanilla extract
 1 teaspoon freshly grated navel orange rind
 ½ cup orange juice

THE GLAZE:

 ⅔ cup strained confectioners' sugar
 1 tablespoon boiling water
 ½ teaspoon corn syrup
 ¼ teaspoon vanilla extract

1. Preheat oven to 325°.
2. Place seeds in a shallow baking pan and toast in preheated oven for 4 to 6 minutes, or until lightly brown. Watch carefully so that they do not burn. Set aside.
3. Position a rack in the lower third of the oven and increase temperature to 350°. Butter a 9″ × 9″ × 2″ square cake pan.
4. To make the cake: Sift together the flour, baking powder, spices, and salt using a triple sifter. Stir in toasted sesame seeds, reserving 1 tablespoon for garnish. Set aside.
5. Place the eggs in large bowl of an electric mixer fitted with the

beaters or whip attachment. Beat on medium-high speed for 3 minutes, or until thickened and light in color.

6. Add the sugar, 1 tablespoon at a time, taking 5 to 6 minutes to blend it in well. Scrape the sides of the bowl occasionally.

7. Slowly pour in the oil in a steady stream, taking about 15 seconds. Beat for 1 minute longer. Add the vanilla and orange rind.

8. Reduce mixer speed to medium-low. Add the flour mixture alternately with the orange juice, dividing the flour into three parts and the juice into two parts, starting and ending with the flour.

9. Pour the batter into the prepared pan. Bake in the preheated oven 35 to 40 minutes, or until cake leaves the sides of the pan and is springy to the touch.

10. Remove from oven. Set the cake on a cake rack to cool for 10 minutes. While the cake is cooling, prepare the glaze.

11. To make the glaze: Whisk the water into the sugar, then blend in the corn syrup and vanilla. The glaze should be pourable; if necessary add drops of hot water until you reach the correct consistency.

12. Spread the glaze over the warm cake with the back of a tablespoon and immediately sprinkle with the 1 tablespoon reserved sesame seed. This must be done before glaze hardens or the seeds will not adhere to the glaze.

STORAGE: Cover top of pan with aluminum foil and store at room temperature for up to 1 week.

❧ FUDGY CHIFFON RING

AT A GLANCE

SERVES: 14 to 16
PAN: 10″ angel food
with a removable
bottom (4-quart
capacity)
PAN PREP: Ungreased
OVEN TEMP: 325°
RACK LEVEL: Lower
third
BAKING TIME: 55 to
60 minutes
METHOD: Electric
mixer

....

This dark chocolate cake receives its rich color from nonalkaline cocoa, generally a domestic cocoa such as Hershey's. It has a more robust flavor than European-style dutch-process cocoas, and produces a slightly darker cake. If you wish to substitute a dutch-process alkaline cocoa like Droste, omit the baking soda. (For more information see page 22.)

For this recipe, I use the traditional chiffon cake method of beating the egg yolks, oil, and flavoring into the dry ingredients all at once in order to achieve a denser fudgy texture. This is wonderful with a scoop of vanilla ice cream or warm Chocolate Pudding Sauce (page 114).

2	teaspoons instant espresso
2/3	cup boiling water
1/2	cup nonalkaline cocoa, such as Hershey's
1²/3	cups sifted cake flour
2	teaspoons baking powder
1/4	teaspoon baking soda
1/2	teaspoon salt
1¹/3	cups superfine or strained sugar
5	large egg yolks, at room temperature
1/3	cup safflower oil
1¹/2	teaspoons vanilla extract
6	large egg whites, at room temperature
1/4	teaspoon cream of tartar

1. Position a rack in the lower third of the oven and preheat to 325°. Have ready a 10-inch angel food pan.
2. In a small bowl, dissolve the espresso in the water. Add to the cocoa, stirring until very smooth. Set aside to cool.
3. Using a triple sifter, sift together the flour, baking powder, baking soda, salt, and sugar into the large bowl of an electric mixer fitted with the beaters or whip attachment. Add the cocoa mixture, egg yolks, oil, and vanilla and beat on medium speed for 3 minutes, until smooth and creamy. Scrape the sides of the bowl occasionally. Set aside.
4. Wash and dry the beaters. In a separate large bowl of the electric mixer, whip the whites on medium speed until frothy. Add the

cream of tartar. Increase the speed to medium-high. Beat until whites form firm, shiny peaks, but are not dry.

5. Remove the bowl from the machine. With a 2³/₄-inch-wide rubber spatula fold ¹/₄ of the batter into the whites, taking 20 turns to lighten. Then fold the whites back into the batter, taking an additional 40 turns.

6. Spoon or pour the batter into the pan. Bake in the preheated oven for 55 to 60 minutes, or until the cake is springy to the touch. Remove from the oven and immediately invert the pan onto a cake rack. Let the cake cool completely in the pan. To remove the pan, run a sharp, thin-bladed knife in 2 or 3 strokes around the sides of the pan to loosen, then run the knife around center tube. Holding the cake by the center tube, run the knife under cake in 2 or 3 sweeps to loosen the bottom, invert onto a cake rack, and remove tube section. Transfer to a serving platter top or bottom side up.

STORAGE: Store at room temperature under a glass dome or covered with aluminum foil for up to 5 days.

Angel Food Cakes

A ngel food cakes are believed to have originated with the Pennsylvania Dutch sometime during the mid-nineteenth century. They are made primarily with egg whites, sugar, flour, and flavorings. They are totally fat-free when unadorned, perfect for those on a low-cholesterol and low-fat diet.

Angel food cakes are pure white in color, and slightly moist. Without solid fat, oil, or egg yolk to tenderize the crumb, they have a denser texture than sponge or chiffon cakes.

An angel food cake made from scratch has a pleasantly sweet taste, totally unlike that of the packaged cake mixes, which I think taste acrid. Many people who claim they dislike angel food cakes have a complete change of heart once they taste one made with pure ingredients.

Few recipes for angel food cakes exist because the base recipe is very sensitive and leaves little margin for ingredient variation other than a change of flavorings or the addition of spices. Nonetheless these cakes lend themselves to many marvelous recipe spin-offs.

294   This chapter contains two base recipes upon which to expand.

Sweet Angel is modeled after the classic formula, which calls for superfine sugar. Powdered Sugar Angel Food Cake uses confectioners' sugar, which contains a small amount of cornstarch. Although the batter is not usually made with leavening, I like to add a bit of baking powder for stability.

You can achieve variety with the imaginative use of fillings. Because the texture of angel food cake is dense it is easy to carve out and fill the center. Two wonderful recipes for these tunnel cakes are included here.

Wonderful accompaniments to angel food cake are Strawberry Topping (page 482) or Spiked Honey Bell Orange Topping (page 485). (This citrus fruit topping is the perfect choice for those who wish to tone down the sweetness of the cake.) These cakes are also scrumptious garnished with flavored whipped cream; for those who are on cholesterol-reduced diets, frozen yogurt is a nice alternative, which could also be used as a filling for tunnel cake.

Traditionally, angel food cakes were not cut with a knife, but were torn apart with two forks. However, today's serrated or saw-edged cake knives do the job quite well. When cutting filled or plain angel cakes, cut with this type of knife, using a gentle back-and-forth motion.

Another ideal utensil for cutting unfilled angel food and other foam-style cakes is a serving piece known as a cake breaker. It is usually made of silver and has a handle with many prongs extending from the top. The server is inserted into the cake and the slices are torn off rather than cut.

No matter how you remove the slices, do so gingerly and without pressing down. You will not want to spoil the beautiful texture of these prized ethereal cakes.

BEFORE YOU BEGIN . . .

▶ Refer to the first, second, and eighth entries in the "Before You Begin" section on sponge cakes (page 254). This information also applies to angel food cakes.
▶ Use only freshly separated egg whites for angel food cakes. Thawed frozen egg whites are not acceptable; they are too watery. Separate egg whites when you remove them from the refrigerator. Let them stand at room temperature about 20 minutes before using.

▶ Use superfine sugar in angel food cakes. Regular granulated or table sugar is too coarse. If lumpy, strain before measuring.

▶ When combining superfine sugar and flour, or superfine sugar and other dry ingredients such as confectioners' sugar, strain them through a fine-mesh strainer— preferably 4 times—to combine thoroughly.

▶ Do not overbeat the egg whites before adding the sugar or the cake will flop.

▶ Take care when you add the sugar to the whipped whites. Follow the instructions carefully. Proper adding of sugar is critical to the cakes' success.

▶ Angel food cake batter will not hold. After the flour/sugar mixture has been added to the meringue, spoon it immediately into the pan. Pass a knife through the batter to remove air pockets and be sure to smooth the surface of the batter again with the back of a spoon. Since the batter is quite thick, the top of the cake will be very uneven if this is not done.

▶ Overbaking can cause angel food cakes to deflate even before you've removed them from the oven. As little as a minute or two can make the difference, so watch the baking time carefully.

▶ Since these cakes do not contain a solid fat such as butter, they can be refrigerated without hardening or becoming dry and are ideal to use with fillings and frostings that require refrigeration.

▶ When carving out a tunnel for a filled angel food cake, save the chunks of cake. They can be cut into smaller pieces and added to gelatins or puddings.

❧ SWEET ANGEL CAKE

*like to serve this after a heavy dinner. It is light and fluffy and won-
derfully refreshing with freshly cut fruit.*

*Take care when incorporating the flour/sugar mixture into the me-
ringue, as the weight of these ingredients can cause the meringue to
deflate. I get the best results using a wire whisk instead of a rubber
spatula for folding. Never use an electric mixer.*

1	cup sifted cake flour
1½	cups superfine sugar, divided
½	teaspoon baking powder
1½	cups egg whites (about 12), defeathered (page 47), at room temperature
1	tablespoon warm water
1½	teaspoons cream of tartar
¼	teaspoon salt
1½	teaspoons vanilla extract
½	teaspoon almond extract

1. Position a rack in the lower third of the oven and preheat to
   375°. Have ready a 10-inch ungreased angel food pan.
2. On a 12-inch square of waxed paper, sift together the cake flour,
   1/2 cup of the superfine sugar, and the baking powder, 4 times,
   using a triple sifter. Set aside.
3. Place the egg whites and warm water in the large bowl of an
   electric mixer fitted with the beaters or whip attachment. Beat
   on medium speed until frothy. Add the cream of tartar, salt, and
   extracts. Increase the speed to medium-high and continue beating until the whites form soft peaks. To ensure that you catch
   the whites at just the right point, watch for a design similar to
   the ripples on the back of a seashell.
4. Immediately begin to sprinkle in the remaining *1 cup* of superfine
   sugar, 2 tablespoons at a time, taking about 2 minutes to blend
   it in well, sprinkling it toward the side of the bowl. Scrape the
   sides of the bowl occasionally. Beat 30 seconds longer, until you
   have a very stiff meringue. Do not overbeat.
5. Transfer the meringue to a very large slope-sided mixing bowl.
   (Do not use a straight-sided bowl.) Put the flour/sugar mixture

▽

AT A GLANCE

SERVES: 12 to 14
PAN: 10″ angel food
with a removable
bottom (4-quart
capacity)
PAN PREP: Ungreased
OVEN TEMP: 375°
RACK LEVEL: Lower
third
BAKING TIME: 30 to
35 minutes
METHOD: Electric
mixer

into the sifter or a strainer set on a 12-inch square of waxed paper. Gradually shake the flour/sugar mixture in 5 or 6 additions over the meringue, gently folding with a large wire whisk. Fold just as you would if you were using a rubber spatula (page 53). The dry ingredients do not have to disappear completely after each addition. Folding will take about 60 to 70 turns. Take care not to overmix, and never stir the batter. It will deflate if you do.

6. Using a 2¾-inch-wide rubber spatula, carefully push the batter into the prepared pan. Press the batter gently with a tablespoon to smooth. Lower a table knife into the batter with the blade reaching almost to the bottom of the pan. Circle the pan twice to remove air pockets, then smooth the surface with the back of a spoon.

7. Bake in the preheated oven 30 to 35 minutes, until the cake is golden brown on top and springy to the touch. *Do not overbake or the cake will deflate.* Remove the cake from the oven and *immediately* invert onto a cake rack. Let cool completely in the pan.

8. To remove the pan, insert a sharp thin-bladed knife about ½ inch down the side of the pan and sweep around the pan in 2 or 3 strokes. Do the same around the center tube. Tilt the pan on its side, and rotate, giving it several firm taps against the countertop until the cake releases. Lift the cake from the outer rim. With the blade of the knife slanted slightly downward, run the knife under the cake while turning the center tube. Invert onto a cake rack and remove the tube section. Transfer the cake to a serving platter.

STORAGE: Store at room temperature under a glass dome or covered with aluminum foil for up to 5 days.

🌱 POWDERED SUGAR
ANGEL FOOD CAKE

Confectioners' sugar gives this angel food cake a smoother, more velvety texture than Sweet Angel. The cake will not rise as high, but its finer texture makes it an ideal choice for tunnel cakes.

▽
AT A GLANCE

SERVES: 12 to 14
PAN: 10″ angel food with a removable bottom (4-quart capacity)
PAN PREP: Ungreased
OVEN TEMP: 375°
RACK LEVEL: Lower third
BAKING TIME: 30 to 35 minutes
METHOD: Electric mixer

1	cup strained cake flour
1	cup strained confectioners' sugar, divided
½	teaspoon baking powder
1	cup strained superfine sugar
1½	cups large egg whites (about 12) defeathered (page 47), at room temperature
1	tablespoon warm water
1½	teaspoons cream of tartar
½	teaspoon salt
1½	teaspoons vanilla extract
½	teaspoon almond extract

1. Position a rack in the lower third of the oven and preheat to 375°. Have ready a 10-inch ungreased angel food pan.
2. On a 12-inch square of waxed paper, strain together the cake flour, ½ *cup* of the confectioners' sugar, and the baking powder 4 times, using a fine-mesh strainer. Do not use a triple sifter; the confectioners' sugar will clog it. Set aside.
3. On another 12-inch square of waxed paper, strain together the superfine sugar and the remaining ½ *cup* confectioners' sugar 4 times. Set aside.
4. Place the egg whites and warm water in the large bowl of an electric mixer fitted with beaters or whip attachment. Beat on medium speed until frothy. Add the cream of tartar, salt, and extracts. Increase the speed to medium-high and continue beating until the whites form soft peaks. To ensure that you catch the whites at just the right point, watch for a design similar to the ripples on the back of a seashell.
5. Immediately begin to add the superfine/confectioners' sugar mixture, 1 tablespoon at a time, sprinkling it in toward the side of the bowl. Take 3 to 4 minutes to blend it in well, scraping the

Quick and Easy Cakes

sides of the bowl occasionally. Beat 30 seconds longer until you have a very stiff meringue. Do not overbeat.

6. Transfer the meringue to a very large, slope-sided mixing bowl. (Do not use a straight-sided bowl.) Put the flour/sugar mixture into a strainer set on a 12-inch square of waxed paper. Gradually shake the cake flour/sugar mixture in 5 or 6 additions over the meringue, gently folding with a large balloon whisk. Fold just as you would if you were using a rubber spatula (page 53). The dry ingredients do not have to disappear completely after each addition. This will take a total of about 60 to 70 turns. Take care not to overmix, and never stir the batter. It will deflate if you do.

7. Using a 2³/₄-inch-wide rubber spatula, carefully push the batter into the pan. Press the batter gently with the back of a tablespoon to smooth. Lower a table knife into the batter, reaching almost to the bottom of the pan. Circle the pan twice to remove air pockets, then smooth the surface with the back of a spoon.

8. Bake in the preheated oven for 30 to 35 minutes, or until cake is golden brown on top and springy to the touch. Do not overbake or the cake will deflate. Remove the cake from the oven and invert *immediately* onto a cake rack. Let the cake cool completely in the pan.

9. To remove the pan, insert a sharp thin-bladed knife about ¹/₂ inch down the sides of the pan and sweep around the pan in 2 to 3 strokes. Do the same around the inner tube. Tilt the pan on its side and rotate, giving it several firm taps against the countertop until the cake releases. Lift the cake from the outer rim and with the blade of the knife slanted slightly downward, run the knife under the cake while turning the center tube. Invert onto a cake rack and remove the tube section. Transfer to a serving platter.

STORAGE: Store at room temperature under a glass dome or covered with aluminum foil for up to 5 days.

🌿 PEPPERMINT CLOUD

....

A confetti of crushed peppermint candies is mingled throughout this billowy batter. The punch of the peppermint adds a refreshing lift and turns the cake into a pretty peppermint cloud.

....

THE CAKE:
- ½ teaspoon pure mint extract
- 2 tablespoons crushed peppermint candies (see Note)
- 1 recipe Sweet Angel Cake (page 297), modified as follows:

1. Substitute mint extract for almond in Step 3.
2. Sprinkle in crushed peppermint at Step 5, when sifting dry ingredients over meringue.

THE PINK PEPPERMINT GLAZE:
- 1¼ cups strained confectioners' sugar
- 1½ teaspoons light corn syrup
- 5 teaspoons boiling water
- ½ teaspoon pure peppermint extract
  Red food coloring
- 2 teaspoons crushed peppermint candies (optional)

1. Make the adapted cake and allow baked cake to cool completely.
2. In a small mixing bowl, combine the confectioners' sugar, corn syrup, water, and peppermint extract. Whisk until smooth and pourable.
3. Dip the tip of a toothpick into the bottle of food coloring. Dip the toothpick into the frosting, then stir to blend. This will give the frosting a lovely subtle pink hue; one drop of food coloring is far too much. Repeat 2 to 3 times until you achieve the desired color.
4. Spoon the glaze over the top of the cake, allowing it to drip randomly down the sides. If frosting becomes too thick, add a few drops of water. If desired, immediately sprinkle the crushed peppermint over the top, before the glaze hardens.

STORAGE: Store at room temperature under a glass dome or covered with aluminum foil for up to 1 day with candy on top or 3 days without candy.

NOTE: To crush peppermint candy, put candies in a plastic bag and twist top of bag, allowing room for candy to spread. Set the bag on your work surface. Hit with the bottom of a small pot or a hammer until candy is broken into pieces.

❧ CHOCOLATE MARBLE ANGEL FOOD CAKE

Chocolate-lovers on low-cholesterol, low-fat diets can relish this lovely cake made with cocoa powder and whipped egg whites.
For this cake you divide the meringue and fold the dry ingredients into each portion separately. Although this method is more time-consuming, it gives the chocolate a lighter texture when baked.

AT A GLANCE

SERVES: 12 to 14
PAN: 10″ angel food with a removable bottom (4-quart capacity)
PAN PREP: Ungreased
OVEN TEMP: 375°
RACK LEVEL: Lower third
BAKING TIME: 30 to 35 minutes
METHOD: Electric mixer

THE CHOCOLATE BATTER:
  2 tablespoons strained cake flour
  2 tablespoons strained dutch-process cocoa
  2 tablespoons strained confectioners' sugar

THE WHITE BATTER:
  3/4 cup cake flour
  1 cup strained confectioners' sugar, divided
  3/4 cup strained superfine sugar
  1 1/2 cups egg whites (about 12), defeathered (page 47), at room temperature
  1 tablespoon warm water
  1 teaspoon cream of tartar
  1/2 teaspoon salt
  2 teaspoons vanilla extract

1. Position rack in the lower third of the oven and preheat to 375°. Have ready a 10-inch angel food pan.

2. For the chocolate batter: In a small bowl, strain together cake flour, cocoa, and confectioners' sugar 4 times. Set aside.

3. For the white batter: Strain the cake flour and *1/2 cup* confectioners' sugar 4 times. Set aside.

4. In another bowl, strain the superfine sugar and the remaining *1/2 cup* confectioners' sugar together 4 times. Set aside for the meringue.

5. Put the egg whites and warm water in the large bowl of an electric mixer fitted with beaters or whip attachment. Beat on medium speed until frothy. Add the cream of tartar, salt, and vanilla. Increase the speed to medium-high and continue beating until the whites form soft peaks. Watch for a design similar to the ripples on the back of a seashell.

6. Sprinkling in toward the sides of the bowl, add the superfine/confectioners' sugar mixture, 1 tablespoon at a time, taking 3 to 4 minutes to blend it in well. Scrape the sides of the bowl occasionally. Beat 30 seconds longer until the mixture forms a stiff meringue. Do not overbeat.

7. Empty the meringue into a very large slope-sided mixing bowl. (Do not use a straight-sided bowl.) Remove 1/4 of the meringue and place it in a separate large bowl. Put the cocoa mixture in a fine strainer and tap into this meringue in three additions, folding gently with a 2 3/4-inch-wide spatula. Set the chocolate batter aside.

8. Gradually sprinkle the flour/confectioners' sugar mixture over the remaining plain meringue, gently folding with a large balloon whisk. Fold just as you would if you were using a rubber spatula (page 53). This will take about 60 to 70 turns. Do not stir or overmix.

9. To marbleize the batter: Spoon the chocolate batter into the plain batter, 1/3 at a time, folding the two together in 2 or 3 turns after each addition. *Do not overmix or marbleizing will be lost.*

10. Carefully push batter into the ungreased pan using the spatula. Press it gently with the back of a tablespoon to smooth. Insert a knife into the batter and circle the pan twice to remove air pockets. Smooth the top with the back of a spoon.

11. Center the pan on the rack and bake in a preheated oven for

Quick and Easy Cakes

303

30 to 35 minutes, or until the cake is golden brown and springy to the touch. *Do not overbake or the cake will begin to deflate.* Remove the pan from the oven and invert immediately onto a cake rack. Let the cake cool completely in the pan.

12. To remove the pan, insert a sharp thin-bladed knife about 1/2 inch down the sides of the pan and sweep around the pan in 2 or 3 strokes. Do the same around the inner tube. Tilt the pan on its side, rotate, and give a few firm taps until the cake releases. Holding the cake by the center tube, invert onto a cake rack and remove the tube section. Transfer to a serving platter. The cake may be served top or bottom side up.

STORAGE: Store at room temperature under a glass dome or covered with aluminum foil for up to 5 days.

Tunnel Angel Food Cakes

ngel food cakes are frequently carved through the center and filled with fruit gelatins, mousses, or flavored whipped creams. Since angel food cakes freeze well, ice creams or sorbets may also be used. After the cavity is filled, the cake is reassembled and chilled until ready to serve.

❧ SWEETMEAT ANGEL CAKE

....

As its name indicates, this cake harbors lots of treats in its luscious filling.

....

1	Powdered Sugar Angel Food Cake (page 299), baked and cooled
¹/₃	cup dried apricots, cut into ¹/₂-inch pieces
1	cup plus 2 tablespoons water
²/₃	cup pitted dates, cut into ¹/₂-inch pieces
3	tablespoons amaretto liqueur
1	teaspoon plain unflavored gelatin
2¹/₂	cups heavy cream, well chilled
¹/₃	cup strained confectioners' sugar
1¹/₂	teaspoons vanilla extract
¹/₂	cup coarsely chopped walnuts
2	tablespoons red glacé cherries, cut into ¹/₄-inch pieces
1	ounce semisweet chocolate, coarsely chopped

*Quick and
Easy Cakes*

1. Place apricots and *1 cup* of water into a small saucepan. Bring to a boil, reduce heat, and simmer 8 to 10 minutes, or just until tender. Add the dates, return to the boil, and simmer 1 minute longer. Transfer to a bowl, add the amaretto, cover, and let stand about 20 minutes while you prepare the whipped cream.

2. Sprinkle the gelatin over the remaining *2 tablespoons* of water in a small heatproof glass bowl and let stand 5 minutes. Place the bowl in a small skillet filled with ½ inch of boiling water. Stir until the gelatin is clear and completely dissolved. Remove from the skillet and allow to cool to tepid.

3. Put the cream in a large chilled bowl of an electric mixer fitted with beaters or the whip attachment. Whip on medium speed until the cream begins to thicken, then pour in the gelatin and add the sugar and vanilla. Continue beating until the cream forms soft peaks.

4. Remove the bowl from the mixer. Reserve about 2 cups of whipped cream for frosting. Fold the cooked fruit mixture into the remaining cream, along with the walnuts, cherries, and chocolate. You should have about 4 cups of filling.

TO ASSEMBLE THE CAKE:

1. Place the cake bottom side up on a cake plate. Using a serrated knife, gently cut a ¾-inch layer off of the top and set aside on a square of wax paper. You are now ready to make the tunnel.

2. To judge the depth of the cut for the tunnel, hold the knife upright along the outside of the cake with the point ¾ inch from the bottom. Position your thumb on the knife level with the top of the cake. Holding that position, insert the knife ¾ inch in from the side of the cake, going only as far down as your thumb. Using a gentle up-and-down motion, cut a circle around the outer edge of the cake to form a wall. Repeat around the inner circle to form a second ¾-inch wall.

3. Cut wedges from the center portion approximately every 2 inches. Pull out the wedges and set aside for another use. Be sure the bottom of the well is fairly smooth.

4. Fill the tunnel with the fruit/cream mixture. If the cavity is not completely filled, use some of the reserved whipped cream. Place the top layer over the filling and press gently to adhere.

5. Whisk the reserved whipped cream several times to thicken. Then

use it to cover the sides and top of the cake generously. Garnish the cake with semisweet chocolate shavings (page 496) if desired.

STORAGE: Store in the refrigerator loosely covered with aluminum foil. This cake will keep up to 3 days.

❦ COOL LIME ANGEL CAKE

....

This holds a refreshing lime mousse that makes it a perfect dessert for a hot summer day. A bowl of fresh berries is a colorful and tasty accompaniment.

....

1	Powdered Sugar Angel Food Cake (page 299), baked and cooled
1¼	cups sugar, divided
1	envelope unflavored gelatin
⅛	teaspoon salt
1	cup water
½	cup milk
2	large egg yolks, slightly beaten
1	teaspoon grated lime rind
½	cup fresh lime juice
1	cup heavy cream
4	large egg whites
2 or 3	drops green food coloring (optional)

1. In a small heavy saucepan, combine ¾ *cup* of the sugar, the gelatin, and salt. Stir in the water and milk and heat just until mixture reaches a boil. Remove from heat.
2. Put the yolks in a small bowl and stir in a small amount of the sugar mixture to temper. Then add the yolk mixture to saucepan, stirring well. Cook over low heat just until the mixture *almost* reaches a boil, about 6 minutes. Remove from heat and stir in the lime juice and rind.

Quick and Easy Cakes

307

3. Transfer to a medium-large bowl and chill until thickened, stirring occasionally to keep smooth. It should be the consistency of soft gelatin.

4. Using a small chilled mixer bowl with chilled beaters, whip the cream until soft peaks form. Set aside.

5. In the large bowl of an electric mixer fitted with beaters or whip attachment, beat the egg whites on medium speed until frothy. Increase the speed to medium-high and add the remaining $1/2$ *cup* sugar, 1 tablespoon at a time over 30 seconds, then whip an additional 20 seconds to form a very soft meringue about the same consistency as the whipped cream. (Adding the sugar at the frothy stage rather than the soft peak stage prevents the whites from becoming too firm.)

6. Remove the lime mixture from the refrigerator. Using a $2^3/4$-inch-wide rubber spatula, quickly fold in a large spoonful of meringue, about $1/4$ cup of whipped cream, and the green food coloring if you're using it. Then fold the remaining meringue and whipped cream into the lightened lime mixture. Be careful not to overmix. Refrigerate until mixture begins to thicken but is not firm.

7. Fill cavity of angel cake using the assembling procedure for Sweetmeat Angel Cake (page 305). If you like, prepare a recipe of Whipped Cream (page 486), using the proportions for a small cake and reducing the vanilla to $1/2$ teaspoon. Fold in any remaining lime filling, and frost the sides and top of the cake. Garnish with fresh mint leaves.

STORAGE: Store in the refrigerator lightly covered with aluminum foil for up to 3 days.

Part Three

SPECIAL OCCASION CAKES

GREAT AMERICAN PARTY CAKES

American party cakes bring to mind tall, luscious cakes layered with mounds of frosting. These are the cakes that we grew up with, the kind that we savor at birthday and anniversary parties or that adorn a special-occasion buffet table. Unlike the staid elegance of European tortes and gateaux, our cakes are feather-light and look as if they have been lovingly produced at home, not in a fancy pastry shop.

Most of our cakes derive from English pound cakes. In colonial days, these batters were blended with fruits, nuts, jams, and liqueurs. The resulting "fruit cakes," decoratively frosted, were the typical party cakes of that era.

American cakes became softer and less formal in appearance with the advent of the leavening pearl ash—potassium carbonate—

311

and then baking powder in the 1850s. While the cakes were still frosted, the decorations became more natural. Through leavening, a new style of cake was created. Over many decades, other regions of the United States had strong influences over American-style cakes. Wonderful creations were born in the kitchens of the Pennsylvania Dutch and the grand bakers of the South.

Many of the recipes in this chapter are adaptations or extended versions of those found in other chapters of this book. Although most are easy to prepare, they will take longer to complete because they are frosted.

These are all party cakes that never go out of style. They are guaranteed to find a welcome audience each and every time they are served.

BEFORE YOU BEGIN . . .

▶ Lining layer cake pans with buttered waxed paper is optional. However, lined pans make cakes easier to remove, and the area covered by the paper is less dry (page 66.)

▶ Layer cakes may be baked in pans of various sizes. If you prefer a high cake, substitute three 8-inch pans for two 9-inch pans. For thinner layers, recipes specifying two 9-inch layers can also be baked in three 9-inch pans. Adjust the baking time 5 to 10 minutes, either more or less, depending on the substitutions made. Another easy method of increasing layers is to cut each layer in half horizontally. Remember to increase the amount of frosting or filling accordingly.

▶ Since cakes made with thin layers will contain more filling or frosting, always choose your filling and frosting with overall sweetness and consistency in mind. As a rule, cooked custard-style fillings are more desirable between layers than sugary icings. The more layers a cake has, the thinner the filling and/or icing that should be applied to each layer.

▶ If you do not wish to make layer cakes, easier versions can be made by changing the baking pans. Many of the recipes in this chapter can be baked in fluted pans like bundt or kugelhopf or in 9″ × 13″ × 2″ oblong pans.

Cakes baked in fluted pans need only be finished with a dusting of confectioners' sugar or a thin glaze. When frosting the top and sides of a 9″ × 13″ × 2″ cake, use the same amount of frosting called for in the recipe. If you are covering only the top, reduce the recipe by half.

▶ The frostings that accompany the cakes in this chapter are only suggestions. See Fillings, Frostings, Glazes, and Syrups (page 435) for more ideas. Mix and match, as the spirit moves you.

▶ Since butter cakes contain solid fat that resolidifies under refrigeration, they are not generally refrigerated. However, when they contain either a custard filling or a whipped cream topping, refrigeration becomes necessary. Cakes in this chapter that require refrigeration are Coconut Layer Cake, Raspberry Ribbons, Devil's Food Cake, Graham Cracker Cake, and Hazelnut Blitz Torte. Plan to serve these the day they are made. If you have leftover cake, refrigerate it, but let it stand at room temperature for a minimum of 30 to 60 minutes before serving, depending on weather conditions and each particular type of cake.

▶ To avoid refrigerating butter cakes completely, you can prepare the cake, filling, and frosting in advance and refrigerate only the filling and frosting. Assemble the cake a few hours before serving. (With the exception of 7-Minute Frosting and Unfortified Whipped Cream, all other coverings can be made ahead.) If a made-ahead cake with long shelf life is what you are looking for, select a butter-style batter with a coating or filling that does not require refrigeration.

❧ COCONUT LAYER CAKE

AT A GLANCE

SERVES: 10 to 12
PAN: Two 9″ layers
PAN PREP:
Butter/waxed
paper/butter
OVEN TEMP: 350°
RACK LEVEL: Lower
third
BAKING TIME: 25 to
30 minutes for
layers
METHOD: Electric
mixer/food
processor

Finely chopped unsweetened coconut is steeped in milk and then puréed to give this golden butter cake a scrumptious coconut flavor. Place a single bright red strawberry rose to the side of the cake for an eye-catching finish.

³/₄	cup milk
¹/₂	cup shredded coconut, fresh (page 61) desiccated (see Note), or canned flakes
2¹/₃	cups sifted cake flour
2	teaspoons baking powder
¹/₂	teaspoon salt
²/₃	cup (1¹/₃ sticks) unsalted butter
1¹/₃	cups superfine or strained sugar
3	large eggs
1	teaspoon vanilla extract
1	recipe Quick Buttercream Frosting (page 447)
1¹/₃	cups shredded coconut, fresh, desiccated, or canned flakes

1. To prepare the coconut: In a small saucepan, scald the milk. Add the coconut, cover, and let steep for 30 minutes. Pour milk and coconut into the container of a food processor fitted with the steel blade and pulse 8 to 10 times or until coconut is finely chopped. Transfer to a measuring cup and set aside.
2. Position a rack in the lower third of the oven and preheat to 350°. Butter two 9″ round layers, line bottom and sides with waxed paper (page 66), and lightly butter the waxed paper.
3. Sift together the flour, baking powder, and salt in a triple sifter. Set aside.
4. Cut the butter into 1-inch pieces and put them in the large bowl of an electric mixer fitted with the beaters or paddle attachment. Soften on low speed. Increase the speed to medium-high. Cream until smooth and light in color, about 1¹/₂ to 2 minutes.
5. Add the sugar, 1 tablespoon at a time, taking 6 to 8 minutes to blend it in well. Scrape the sides of the bowl occasionally.

6. Add the eggs, 1 at a time at 1-minute intervals, scraping the sides of the bowl as necessary. Blend in the vanilla.

7. Reduce mixer speed to low. Add the flour mixture in three additions alternately with coconut/milk mixture in two additions, starting and ending with the flour. Mix only until incorporated after each addition. Scrape the sides of the bowl and mix for 10 seconds longer.

8. Spoon the batter into the prepared pans, smoothing the surfaces with the back of a tablespoon. Bake in the preheated oven 25 to 30 minutes, or until cake begins to come away from the sides of the pan, is golden brown on top, and is springy to the touch.

9. Remove from the oven. Set the pans on cake racks to cool for 10 minutes. Invert pans onto racks sprayed with nonstick coating and remove pan and paper. Frost when cake is completely cool.

TO ASSEMBLE THE CAKE:

1. Place one layer on a plate top side down. Cut four 4-inch strips of waxed paper and slide the strips under the edges of the layer to keep the plate clean. Spread the layer with icing, leaving a 1/2-inch unfrosted border around the edges. Put the second layer top side up on the first. Using a long metal spatula, spread a thin layer of frosting around sides of cake.

2. Cover top of cake with icing, swirling it with the rounded bottom of a tablespoon. Recoat sides of cake with the remaining frosting.

3. Generously sprinkle the top and the sides of the cake with coconut, pressing it gently into frosting. Some of the coconut will fall onto the waxed paper. Carefully remove the paper and sprinkle the excess coconut over top of cake.

4. Garnish with a strawberry rose (page 506).

STORAGE: The cake may be kept in a cool place under a glass dome if you plan to eat it shortly after it is made. For longer storage, cover loosely with an aluminum foil tent and refrigerate. Allow to stand at room temperature 2 to 3 hours before serving. The cake will keep up to 5 days.

NOTE: Desiccated coconut is unsweetened and can be purchased in health food stores. You may substitute regular sweetened canned coconut if you wish. To substitute the sweetened canned variety for fresh, add the canned coconut to the scalded milk. Then drain off the sugary milk and discard. Scald fresh milk, using the same measurement. Add the coconut and proceed with the recipe.

BROWNIE TORTE WITH FRESH FIGS

AT A GLANCE

SERVES: 10 to 12

PAN: 10″ springform

PAN PREP: Well buttered/parchment/butter/bread crumbs

OVEN TEMP: 325°

RACK LEVEL: Lower third

BAKING TIME: 60 to 70 minutes

METHOD: Electric mixer

At the top of my list of favorite sweets are brownies. Thoughts of dense, fudgy squares of chocolate cake or bar cookies flash through my mind. However, if the brownie batter is baked in a round pan and treated as a cake, the result is very similar to a European torte.

This torte is a moist, chewy cake accented with chopped walnuts. When garnished with whipped cream rosettes decorated with wedges of pink-fleshed fresh fig, the torte becomes an elegant dessert. Black-skinned figs are the prettiest to use, since this fruit is not peeled. If figs are not available, substitute halved large strawberries.

1 to 2	tablespoons unflavored dried bread crumbs
1	cup (2 sticks) unsalted butter
2½	cups superfine or strained sugar
6	large egg yolks
6	ounces unsweetened chocolate, melted
2	teaspoons vanilla extract
¾	cup sifted unbleached all-purpose flour
1	cup finely chopped walnuts
6	large egg whites
¼	teaspoon salt
¼	cup broken walnuts
½	small recipe Whipped Cream (page 486)
3	fresh figs, quartered, or 6 large unhulled strawberries, cut into halves

1. Position a rack in the lower third of the oven and preheat to 325°.
2. Butter a 10-inch springform pan, and line it with baking parchment (page 66). Butter the parchment lining. Dust the pan with the bread crumbs. Invert the pan over the kitchen sink and shake out excess crumbs.
3. Cut the butter into 1-inch pieces and place in the large bowl of an electric mixer fitted with beaters or paddle attachment. Soften on low speed, then increase the speed to medium-high. Cream until smooth and light in color, about 1½ to 2 minutes.

4. Add the sugar, 1 tablespoon at a time, taking 6 to 8 minutes to blend it in well. Scrape the sides of the bowl occasionally.

5. Add the egg yolks, 2 at a time at 1-minute intervals, scraping the sides of the bowl as necessary. Reduce mixer speed to medium. Blend in the melted chocolate, then the vanilla. Scrape the sides of the bowl again.

6. Reduce mixer speed to low. Add the flour and finely chopped nuts all at once, mixing just until blended. Transfer the batter to a large mixing bowl for folding.

7. Wash and dry the beaters. Put the egg whites in a separate large bowl. Using the beaters or whip attachment, beat the whites on medium speed until frothy. Add salt, and increase the speed to medium-high. Beat until whites stand in soft peaks.

8. Fold ¼ of the whites into the batter, taking about 20 turns. Then fold in the remaining whites, taking about 40 additional turns.

9. Pour the batter into the prepared pan, smoothing the surface with the back of a tablespoon. Sprinkle the broken walnuts over the top of the batter, distributing the greatest amount toward the center and graduating out toward the sides. Bake in the preheated oven for 60 to 70 minutes, or until cake begins to release from the sides of the pan. The top may crack slightly in the middle. A small amount of torte should cling to a toothpick inserted in the center of the cake. If the toothpick feels wet, bake a few minutes longer, but be careful not to overbake.

10. Place the torte on a cake rack to cool for 30 minutes, then loosen the sides of the pan and continue to cool completely. Remove the rim of the springform pan. Cover the top of the torte with a piece of aluminum foil, and invert onto a second rack. Carefully remove bottom of pan and peel off the parchment paper. Reinvert on a cake plate. Remove the foil.

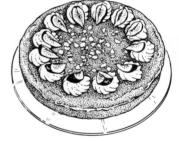

TO GARNISH: Garnish the cake just before serving, as follows: Fit a 14-inch pastry bag with a #4 large star tube. Fill it ⅓ full with whipped cream and evenly pipe 12 rosettes slightly apart around outer edge of torte, simulating hours on the face of a clock. Arrange a wedge of fig or a strawberry half, flesh side up, in the center of each rosette with points facing inward. This can be done 3 to 4 hours ahead of time. Refrigerate uncovered. Allow to stand 1 hour at room temperature before serving.

STORAGE: Store the ungarnished cake at room temperature under a glass dome, in an airtight container, or covered with aluminum foil until ready to serve, for up to 3 days. Cover leftover cake loosely with aluminum foil and refrigerate for up to 2 days.

🍃 RASPBERRY RIBBONS

Think pink! Here is an absolutely irresistable combination of raspberry cream and a lightly almond flavored angel food cake. It's also especially pretty, fancy enough for guests and surprisingly easy to decorate.

1   Sweet Angel (page 297) or Powdered Sugar Angel Food Cake (page 299), baked and cooled

THE RASPBERRY CREAM:
Two   10-ounce boxes frozen raspberries with syrup, thawed and drained
3   tablespoons cold water
2   teaspoons unflavored gelatin
1½   cups heavy cream, chilled
½   cup strained confectioners' sugar
1 to 2   tablespoons kirsch

1   pint (1½ cups) fresh raspberries

1. To make the raspberry cream: Purée the frozen raspberries in a blender. Strain through a fine-mesh strainer to remove the seeds. You should have about ¾ cup of purée.
2. Put the water in a small heatproof dish and sprinkle on the gelatin. Let stand 5 minutes, then set the dish in a small skillet filled with ½ inch boiling water. Stir until the gelatin is dissolved and completely clear. Allow to cool slightly, then stir into the raspberry purée.

3. Put the cream in a small chilled bowl of an electric mixer. Whip on medium speed. As it thickens, gradually add the sugar. Continue beating until very thick. Remove the bowl from the mixer. With a 2³/₄-inch-wide rubber spatula fold in the raspberry purée and kirsch. If the raspberry cream is too thin, chill for about 1 hour, or until firm enough to spread. At this point, filling can be spread, but *do not mix* or it will thin out.

TO ASSEMBLE THE CAKE:
1. With the bottom side up, divide the cake into 3 layers (page 500). Reserve ¹/₂ of the raspberry cream for outer frosting and decorating the cake.
2. Place the widest layer on a serving plate cut side up. Cover with a little more than ¹/₂ of the remaining raspberry cream. Position the middle layer over the first, wide side down, and cover with the rest of the cream. Arrange the top layer cut side down over the middle layer. Frost the sides and top of the cake with the reserved raspberry cream, setting aside about ¹/₃ for decoration. Arrange the fresh raspberries at random over the top of the cake, pressing them gently into the cream.
3. Fit a 14-inch pastry bag with a #114 large leaf tube. Fill the bag with the rest of the raspberry cream. Holding the bag at a 90° angle, with the tip almost touching the top of the cake, make 1- to 2-inch-long ribbons of cream, partially covering the raspberries. Turn the bag to the left or to the right as you lift it to make an attractive end to each ribbon. Allow some of the ribbons to fall about ¹/₂ inch over the side of the cake. If desired, trim the plate with fresh lemon leaves or other nonpoisonous greenery. Refrigerate 3 to 4 hours. Remove from the refrigerator ¹/₂ hour before serving.

STORAGE: Cover leftover cake loosely with an aluminum foil tent and refrigerate for up to 3 days.

DEVIL'S FOOD CAKE WITH SHINY FUDGE FROSTING

Devil's food cake is an American classic impossible to resist if you are a chocophile. This triple-layered version is dramatically high and absolutely mouthwatering.

Special thanks to my students for their patience during the developing of this recipe. It was continuously adjusted throughout many baking sessions until it met my requirements for a great devil's food cake.

AT A GLANCE

SERVES: 10 to 12
PANS: Three 9″ layers (see Note)
PAN PREP: Butter/waxed paper/butter
OVEN TEMP: 350°
RACK LEVELS: Lower and upper thirds
BAKING: 25 to 30 minutes
METHOD: Electric mixer

¾	cup strained unsweetened cocoa such as Hershey's (do not use dutch-process cocoa)
½	cup hot water
¾	cup cold water
2¾	cups sifted cake flour
1	teaspoon baking soda
¼	teaspoon salt
¾	cup (1½ sticks) unsalted butter
1	cup superfine sugar
1	cup light brown sugar, lightly packed
3	large eggs
1	teaspoon vanilla extract

Chocolate Custard Filling (page 444)
Shiny Fudge Frosting (page 455)

1. Position racks in the lower and upper third of the oven and pre-heat to 350°. Butter three 9-inch round layer pans. Line the bottom and sides with wax paper (page 66) and lightly butter the waxed paper.
2. Put the cocoa in a small bowl. Slowly add the hot water, stirring until smooth, then blend in the cold water. Set aside.
3. Sift together the flour, baking soda, and salt, using a triple sifter. Set aside.
4. Place the butter, cut into 1-inch pieces, in the large bowl of an electric mixer fitted with beaters or paddle attachment to soften on low speed. Increase mixer speed to medium-high and cream butter until smooth and light in color, about 1½ to 2 minutes.

5. Add the white sugar, 1 tablespoon at a time, taking 3 to 4 minutes to blend it in well. Then add the brown sugar, 1 tablespoon at a time over an additional 3 to 4 minutes. Scrape the sides of the bowl occasionally.

6. Add the eggs, 1 at a time at 1-minute intervals, scraping the sides of the bowl as necessary. Blend in the vanilla.

7. Reduce mixer speed to low. Add the flour mixture alternately with the cocoa liquid, dividing the flour into three parts, the liquid into two parts, starting and ending with the flour. Mix only until incorporated after each addition. Scrape sides of bowl. Mix 10 seconds longer.

8. Spoon the batter into the prepared pans, smoothing the surface with the back of a tablespoon. Place two pans on the lower shelf of the oven and center the third pan on the upper shelf. Bake in the preheated oven 25 to 30 minutes, or until cake begins to come away from the sides of the pan and the top is springy to the touch. While the cake is baking, prepare the filling.

9. Remove pans from oven. Set onto cake racks for 10 minutes to cool slightly, then invert onto the racks sprayed with nonstick coating and remove pans. Carefully peel off paper. Allow to cool completely before assembling.

TO ASSEMBLE THE CAKE:

1. Place first layer top side down on serving plate. Slide 4 strips of waxed paper between the plate and the bottom of the cake and cover the cake with 1/2 of the custard, leaving a 1/2-inch border around edge.

2. Place the second layer top side down and spread with the remaining 1/2 of the chocolate custard filling. Arrange the third layer over the second, top side up, and align the 3 layers so the sides of the cake are straight. Place the filled cake in the refrigerator to set while you prepare the frosting.

3. When ready to glaze cake, hold the container 10 inches above the cake and pour on enough glaze to cover the top. Using a 10-inch metal spatula, spread it across, allowing excess to drip down the sides. *Do this only once, as glaze sets quickly.* The icing should be fluid enough to drip, but not too runny. Holding the spatula vertically, run it around sides of cake to smooth the icing.

4. For an attractive melted tallow effect, drop spoonfuls of the remaining frosting down the sides of the cake, beginning at the top

edge (fig. 1). Drizzle 2 to 3 tablespoons randomly over the top of the cake (fig. 2).

5. When the icing is completely set, carefully remove the waxed paper from the plate. Allow the cake to stand uncovered until frosting is very firm.

STORAGE: This cake may be kept in a cool place under a glass dome if you plan to eat it shortly after it is made. For longer storage, cover loosely with an aluminum foil tent and refrigerate. Allow to stand at room temperature 2 to 3 hours before serving. The cake will keep up to 5 days.

NOTE: You may bake this in two 9-inch layer pans, then divide the baked layers into four disks. The filling will be spread a little more thinly than with 3 layers, and the cake may take an additional 5 minutes of baking time.

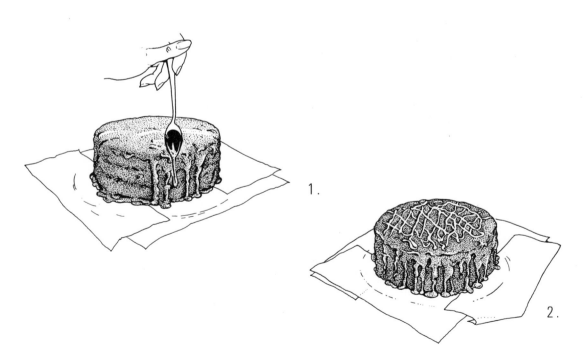

1.

2.

GEORGIA PEANUT CAKE

Peanut butter and crunchy chopped peanuts make a cake packed with peanut flavor. The bourbon-flavored creamy peanut icing is an outstanding complement. The layers are extremely delicate, so handle with care when assembling.

Use unsalted plain peanuts, not the dry-roasted variety. Dry-roasted nuts are very hard and do not exude as much of the flavorful nut oil when chopped. Don't chop the nuts in the food processor; it extracts too much oil and in short order you will have peanut butter. Use a hand chopper or place the peanuts in a plastic bag, secure tightly, and break into fine pieces with a heavy saucepan.

Peanut butter, no longer just an old standby on the pantry shelf, has become the idol of fan clubs. Whether you are a member or not, this cake is bound to please all who taste it.

▽

AT A GLANCE

SERVES: 10 to 12
PANS: Two 9″ layers
PAN PREP: Butter/
waxed paper/butter
OVEN TEMP: 350°
RACK LEVEL: Lower
third
BAKING TIME: 30 to
35 minutes
METHOD: Electric
mixer

2¼ cups sifted cake flour
2 teaspoons baking powder
½ teaspoon salt
½ cup (1 stick) unsalted butter
⅓ cup smooth peanut butter
½ cup granulated sugar
1 cup light brown sugar, lightly packed
2 large eggs
½ cup sour cream
1 teaspoon vanilla extract
⅔ cup milk
⅔ cup unsalted peanuts, chopped medium-fine, plus additional for garnish

1 recipe Creamy Peanut Bourbon Frosting (page 452)

1. Position rack in the lower third of the oven and preheat to 350°. Butter two 9-inch round layer pans, line bottom and sides with waxed paper (page 66), and lightly butter the waxed paper.
2. Sift together the flour, baking powder, and salt, using a triple sifter. Set aside.

Special Occasion Cakes

323

3. Cut the butter into 1-inch pieces and place in the large bowl of an electric mixer fitted with beaters or paddle attachment to soften on low speed. Increase speed to medium-high. Cream until smooth and light in color, about 1 minute. Add the peanut butter and cream for 30 seconds longer.

4. Add the granulated sugar, 1 tablespoon at a time, taking 3 to 4 minutes to blend it in well. Add the brown sugar over an additional 3 to 4 minutes. Scrape the sides of the bowl occasionally.

5. Add the eggs, 1 at a time at 1-minute intervals, scraping the sides of the bowl as necessary. Blend in the sour cream and vanilla.

6. Reduce mixer speed to low. Add the flour mixture alternately with the milk, dividing the flour into three parts, the milk into two parts, and starting and ending with the flour. Scrape the sides of the bowl and mix for 10 seconds longer. Blend in the nuts; *do not overmix.*

7. Spoon the batter into the prepared pans, smoothing the surface with the back of a tablespoon. Bake in the preheated oven for 30 to 35 minutes, or until cake begins to come away from the sides of the pan and is springy to the touch.

8. Remove from oven. Set the pans on cake racks for 10 minutes to cool slightly, then invert onto the racks sprayed with nonstick coating and lift off the pans. Carefully remove the waxed paper and continue to cool completely.

9. Prepare the frosting.

TO ASSEMBLE THE CAKE:

1. Place one layer on a serving plate top side down. Spread with icing, leaving a 1/2-inch unfrosted border around the edge. Set the second layer top side up on the first. Spread a thin layer of frosting around sides of cake using a long metal spatula. Thin the remaining frosting with additional milk or cream to reach a soft, creamy consistency.

2. Cover the top of the cake with icing, swirling it with the bottom of a tablespoon. To create a swirled design on the sides, recoat sides of cake with remaining frosting. Sprinkle chopped peanuts over the top. If you wish, you can swirl a touch of smooth peanut butter on the back of a teaspoon over the surface of cake for an interesting two-toned effect.

Great Cakes

324

STORAGE: Store at room temperature under a glass cake cover or in an airtight container for up to 5 days.

🌰 GRAHAM CRACKER CAKE

....

Most families have a favorite cake that is always served on special occasions. For my father's family, it was this wonderful cake. It seems unusual now, but this was actually a very popular cake during the thirties and forties.

Graham crackers ground almost to a powder are used in place of flour, and give the cake a dense texture and a marvelous nutty flavor. This cake is at its best when eaten soon after assembling.

Here is my rendition of a most unique and fabulous party cake. It is simple to make, pretty to look at, and marvelous to eat.

....

THE CAKE:

25	double graham crackers, broken (if using preground graham cracker crumbs, measure 3 1/3 cups)
1/2	cup shredded desiccated coconut*
2 1/2	teaspoons baking powder
1/2	cup (1 stick) unsalted butter
1	cup superfine or strained sugar
4	large egg yolks
1	teaspoon vanilla extract
1	cup milk
4	large egg whites
1/8	teaspoon cream of tartar

THE MOCHA WHIPPED CREAM FILLING:

2 1/2	cups heavy cream, well chilled
1	teaspoon coffee zest (page 58)
1/3	cup strained confectioners' sugar
3	tablespoons strained, unsweetened cocoa
2	tablespoons Kahlúa or Tía María
1/2	teaspoon unsweetened cocoa, for garnish

1. Position a rack in the lower third of the oven and preheat to 350°. Butter two 9-inch layer pans, and line the bottoms with parchment paper circles. Rebutter parchment paper.

*Desiccated coconut is unsweetened. Purchase it in health food stores. Regular sweetened, canned coconut may be substituted if desired.

AT A GLANCE

SERVES: 10 to 12
PANS: Two 9″ layers
PAN PREP: Butter/ parchment/butter
OVEN TEMP: 350°
RACK LEVEL: Lower third
BAKING TIME: 25 to 30 minutes
METHOD: Electric mixer/food processor

2. To make the cake: Place broken graham crackers and coconut into the container of a food processor fitted with the steel blade. Process until the graham cracker crumbs and coconut are ground very fine. Add the baking powder and pulse 6 to 8 times to blend. Set aside.

3. Cut the butter into 1-inch pieces and put them in the large bowl of an electric mixer fitted with beaters or paddle attachment. Soften on low speed. Increase speed to medium-high, and cream the butter until smooth and light in color, about 1½ to 2 minutes.

4. Add the sugar, 1 tablespoon at a time, taking 6 to 8 minutes to blend it in well. Scrape the sides of the bowl occasionally.

5. Add the egg yolks, 2 at a time at 1-minute intervals, scraping the sides of the bowl as necessary. Beat 1 minute longer. Blend in the vanilla.

6. Reduce mixer speed to low. Add the crumb mixture alternately with the milk, dividing the crumbs into three parts and the liquid into two parts, and starting and ending with the crumbs. Scrape the sides of the bowl and mix for 10 seconds longer. Transfer to a large bowl and set aside.

7. Wash and dry the beaters. Put the egg whites in a separate bowl, and beat them on medium speed with beaters or whip attachment until frothy. Add the cream of tartar and increase the speed to medium-high. Beat until the whites form firm, moist peaks. With a 2¾-inch-wide rubber spatula, fold in ¼ of the whites to lighten the batter, taking about 20 turns. Fold in the remaining whites, taking about 20 additional turns.

8. Spoon the batter into the prepared pans, smoothing the surface with the back of a tablespoon. Bake in the preheated oven 25 to 30 minutes, or until cake begins to come away from the sides of the pan and is springy to the touch.

9. Remove cake from oven. Set the pans onto cake racks for 10 minutes to cool slightly, then invert onto racks sprayed with nonstick coating. Lift off the pans and carefully peel off the parchment. When the cake is completely cool, fill and frost.

10. To make the filling: Pour the cream into a well-chilled mixing bowl. Beat in an electric mixer fitted with chilled beaters or whip attachment. Stir in the confectioners' sugar and cocoa and beat on medium speed until the cream begins to thicken. Add the coffee zest and liqueur. Continue whipping until cream

reaches the soft peak stage, and remove from the mixer. Finish beating by hand using a wire whisk, whipping until cream is quite thick but not grainy. Refrigerate.

TO ASSEMBLE THE CAKE:

1. Split each layer into halves (page 500). Set the first layer on a serving plate, top side down. Fit a 14-inch pastry bag with a large #5 plain tube, and fill it 1/3 full with mocha whipped cream. Starting 1/2 inch from the edge, pipe a circle of cream around the top of the layer. Fill center of the circle with additional cream, smoothing surface with a large metal offset spatula. Repeat with the second and third layers, placing them cut side up. Arrange the top layer cut side down, aligning layers so the sides of the cake are even.

2. Empty the remaining whipped cream into the pastry bag. Pipe 1/2-inch whipped cream dots on the top layer, beginning at the outer edge. Each dot should touch the preceding one, forming a ring. Continue working toward the center of the cake until the entire surface is covered.

3. Place 1/2 teaspoon cocoa in a very fine mesh strainer. Gently tap the strainer over the surface of the cake to give it a light dusting of cocoa. Place the cake in the refrigerator uncovered to chill, but remove from refrigerator at least 1 hour before serving.

STORAGE: Store leftover cake in the refrigerator under a foil tent. This cake will keep up to 3 days.

VARIATION

MOCHA PRUNE WHIPPED CAKE

1. Follow recipe for Mocha Whipped Cream Filling, substituting Armagnac for Kahlúa. In a food processor, purée about 12 well-drained, pitted, stewed prunes. You should have about 1/2 cup purée. Reserve 1/4 of the whipped cream for decorating top layer. Fold the prune purée into remaining cream. Fill the cake as described in master recipe.

CREOLE PECAN CAKE

AT A GLANCE

SERVES: 10 to 12
PANS: Two 9″ layers
PAN PREP: Butter/
waxed paper/butter
OVEN TEMP: 350°
RACK LEVEL: Lower
third
BAKING TIME: 30 to
35 minutes
METHOD: Electric
mixer

This cake is my adaptation of a recipe from Katherine H. Long, Senator Russell Long's first wife, that appeared in a local Baton Rouge, Louisiana, cookbook. It is made with egg whites and an abundance of finely chopped pecans. These flavorful nuts are a variety of hickory nut that is native to the Louisiana lowlands as well as many other southern states. This luscious cake evokes the wonderful Creole flavors of Louisiana.

2¹/₂	cups sifted cake flour
1	tablespoon baking powder
¹/₄	teaspoon salt
¹/₂	teaspoon cinnamon
¹/₂	teaspoon nutmeg
1	tablespoon freeze-dried coffee
6	tablespoons boiling water
¹/₂	cup milk
³/₄	cup (1¹/₂ sticks) unsalted butter
²/₃	cup plus ¹/₄ cup superfine or strained sugar
³/₄	cup dark brown sugar, firmly packed
1	teaspoon vanilla extract
1	teaspoon maple extract
1¹/₃	cups finely chopped pecans (reserve 1 tablespoon to garnish cake)
6	large egg whites
¹/₂	teaspoon cream of tartar
1	recipe Penuche Frosting (page 449)

1. Position rack in the lower third of the oven and preheat to 350°. Butter two 9-inch layer pans. Line the bottoms and sides with waxed paper and lightly butter the waxed paper (page 66).
2. Sift together the flour, baking powder, salt, and spices, using a triple sifter. Set aside.
3. Dissolve the coffee in boiling water. Stir in the milk. Set aside.
4. Cut the butter into 1-inch pieces and place in the large bowl of an electric mixer fitted with beaters or paddle attachment.

Soften on low speed, then increase mixer speed to medium-high and cream until smooth and light in color, about 1½ to 2 minutes.

5. Add ⅔ cup superfine sugar, 1 tablespoon at a time, taking 3 to 4 minutes to blend it in well. Add the dark brown sugar over an additional 3 to 4 minutes. Scrape the sides of the bowl occasionally. Blend in the vanilla and maple extracts.

6. Reduce mixer speed to low. Add dry ingredients alternately with coffee mixture, dividing the flour into four parts and the liquid into three parts. Mix only until incorporated after each addition. Scrape the sides and mix for 10 seconds longer. Remove bowl from mixer, stir in the pecans, and set aside.

7. Wash and dry the beaters or whip attachment. In a separate large bowl, whip the egg whites on medium speed until frothy. Add the cream of tartar. Increase the mixer speed to medium-high and beat until the whites form soft peaks. Add ¼ *cup* of sugar, 1 tablespoon at a time, over about 20 seconds. Whip 10 seconds longer, until whites are shiny and stand in firm peaks.

8. Fold ⅓ of the whites into batter, taking about 20 turns. Fold in the remaining whites, taking an additional 20 turns.

9. Spoon batter into the prepared pans, smoothing the surface with the back of a tablespoon. Bake in the preheated oven 30 to 35 minutes, or until cake begins to come away from the sides of the pan and is brown on top and springy to the touch.

10. Remove from the oven. Set the pans onto cake racks for 10 minutes to cool and set. Then invert onto the racks sprayed with nonstick coating. Lift off the pans and peel off the waxed paper. Continue to cool to room temperature.

11. Prepare the frosting.

TO ASSEMBLE THE CAKE:

1. Place one layer on a serving plate, top side down. Cut four 4-inch strips of waxed paper and push them under the edges of cake to keep the plate clean. Using the back of a tablespoon, spread the top with a ½-inch layer of frosting, leaving a ½-inch unfrosted border around the edge. (Frosting may be difficult to spread as it is sticky.) Place the second layer top side up on top of the first, aligning the layers evenly. Cover the sides and top of the cake with the remaining frosting, swirling it on with the back of a tablespoon. Garnish top with the 1 tablespoon reserved nuts.

2. Remove the waxed paper strips. Chill for 30 minutes to set the

frosting. When ready to serve, dip a sharp knife into warm water and cut straight down to make neat slices.

STORAGE: Store at room temperature under a glass dome left slightly ajar to allow air to circulate freely. This cake will keep up to 3 days.

🌰 DOUBLE TROUBLE FUDGE CAKE

AT A GLANCE

SERVES: 10 to 12
PANS: Two 9-inch layers
PAN PREP: Butter/parchment/butter
OVEN TEMP: 350°
RACK LEVEL: Lower third
BAKING TIME: 30 to 35 minutes
METHOD: Electric mixer/food processor

Here's one that is absolutely addictive. A delicious candy-like filling baked into the cake creates a chewy contrast to the melt-in-your-mouth *chocolate layers and silky frosting. This is a winner for chocoholics—kids will love it too.*

THE CHOCOLATE-NUT FILLING:
- ¼ cup unsweetened dutch-process cocoa
- ⅓ cup sugar
- ¾ cup walnuts
- 2 tablespoons melted butter

THE CAKE:
- 3 ounces unsweetened chocolate, broken into small pieces
- ¾ cup hot water
- 1 tablespoon freeze-dried coffee crystals
- 2 cups sifted cake flour
- 1¼ teaspoon baking soda
- ½ teaspoon salt
- ½ cup (1 stick) unsalted butter
- 1½ cups superfine or strained sugar
- 3 large eggs
- 1 teaspoon vanilla extract
- ½ cup sour cream

- 1 recipe Chocolate Custard Frosting (page 454)

1. Position a rack in the lower third of the oven and preheat to 350°. Butter two 9-inch layer pans. Line the bottoms with parchment and butter again.

2. To make the chocolate-nut filling: Place the cocoa, sugar, and walnuts in the container of a food processor fitted with steel blade. Process until the nuts are medium-sized, add melted butter, and pulse *just* until crumbs are coated. Set aside.

3. To make the cake: In a small saucepan, combine the chocolate, water, and coffee. Stir over low heat until chocolate is completely melted and mixture is smooth. Set aside.

4. Sift together the flour, baking soda, and salt using a triple sifter. Set aside.

5. Cut the butter into 1-inch pieces and place in the large bowl of an electric mixer fitted with beaters or paddle attachment. Soften on low speed. Increase speed to medium-high and cream until smooth and light in color, about 1½ to 2 minutes.

6. Add the sugar, 1 tablespoon at a time, taking 6 to 8 minutes to blend it in well. Scrape the sides of the bowl occasionally.

7. Add the eggs, 1 at a time at 1-minute intervals, scraping the sides of the bowl as needed. Reduce mixer speed to medium. Blend in chocolate, then the vanilla.

8. Reduce mixer speed to low. Add the flour mixture alternately with the sour cream, dividing the dry ingredients into three parts and sour cream into two parts, and starting and ending with the flour. Mix only until incorporated after each addition. Scrape the sides of the bowl.

9. Divide ⅔ of the batter between the two prepared pans, smoothing the surface with the back of a tablespoon. Sprinkle half of the chocolate/nut mixture into each pan. Dab the remaining batter over the top of each layer, spreading it lightly over crumbs with the back of the spoon. It is not necessary for batter to cover crumbs completely. Bake in the preheated oven for 30 to 35 minutes, or until cake begins to come away from the sides of the pan and is springy to the touch.

10. Remove from the oven. Place the pans on cake racks for 10 minutes to cool and set the layers, spray the rack with nonstick coating, then invert and lift off pans. Continue to cool to room temperature.

11. Prepare the frosting.

TO ASSEMBLE THE CAKE:

1. Place one layer on a plate, top side down. Cut four 4-inch strips of waxed paper and slide them under the edge of the layer to protect the plate. Spread the layer with icing, leaving a 1/2-inch unfrosted border around the edges. Place the second layer top side up on the first. Using a long metal spatula, spread a thin layer of frosting around sides of cake.
2. Cover top of cake with icing, swirling it with the rounded bottom of a tablespoon. Recoat sides of cake with the remaining frosting.

STORAGE: Store at room temperature under a glass cake cover or in an airtight container for up to 5 days.

🐚 LADY BALTIMORE CAKE

▽ ....
AT A GLANCE

SERVES: 10 to 12
PANS: Two 9″ layers
PAN PREP: Butter/waxed paper/butter
OVEN TEMP: 350°
RACK LEVEL: Lower third
BAKING TIME: 30 to 35 minutes
METHOD: Electric mixer

....

Lady Baltimore Cake is one of the most festive of the great American party cakes. Traditionally made with egg whites, which give it a fine texture and a soft milky hue, it is subtly flavored with orange juice and rind. The frosting is full of raisins, figs, and walnuts.

When purchasing the dried figs for this frosting, look for the Calamyrna variety from California. These are plentiful during the holiday season from Thanksgiving through Christmas, but can be difficult to find the rest of the year. Those that are available have hardened and lost their flavor. An alternative would be Smyrna dried figs from a Middle Eastern store or a specialty food or nut shop. Whichever fig you select, be sure they are soft. Give the package a slight squeeze to test for freshness. If you cannot find ones that are soft, steam them briefly (page 63).

If you have trouble chopping the dried figs, try snipping them first into smaller pieces with a pair of scissors. Take care not to chop the nuts too fine.

This cake first appeared in a book entitled Lady Baltimore, by Owen Wister, as the creation of the character Alicia Rhett Mayberry, who was in real life a Southern belle. Mrs. Mayberry had invented the recipe years before, but after the book was published the cake became a sensation.

3¼   cups sifted cake flour
3½   teaspoons baking powder
 ½   teaspoon salt
  1   cup (2 sticks) unsalted butter
  1   teaspoon grated navel orange rind
1½   cups superfine or strained sugar, divided
  2   teaspoons vanilla extract
 ¾   cup water
 ½   cup orange juice
  6   large egg whites
 ¼   teaspoon cream of tartar

  1   cup coarsely chopped walnuts
 ½   cup coarsely chopped dried figs
 ½   cup coarsely chopped yellow raisins
 ½   cup sweet sherry
  1   recipe 7-Minute Frosting (page 448)

1. Position a rack in the lower third of the oven and preheat to 350°. Butter two 9-inch layer pans; line the bottom and sides with waxed paper and lightly butter the waxed paper.
2. Sift together the flour, baking powder, and salt in a triple sifter. Set aside.
3. Cut the butter into 1-inch pieces and place in the large bowl of an electric mixer fitted with the beaters or paddle attachment. Add the orange rind and soften on low speed. Increase the mixer speed to medium-high and cream until smooth and light in color, about 1½ to 2 minutes.
4. Add *1 cup* sugar, 1 tablespoon at a time, taking 6 to 8 minutes to blend it in well. Scrape the sides of the bowl occasionally. Blend in the vanilla.
5. Combine the water and orange juice. Reduce mixer speed to low. Add the dry ingredients alternately with the liquid ingredients, dividing the flour into four parts and the liquid into three parts, starting and ending with the flour. Mix only until incorporated. Scrape the sides of the bowl and mix for 10 seconds longer. Remove the bowl from the mixer and set aside.
6. Wash and dry the beaters. In a large separate bowl fitted with beaters or whip attachment, beat the whites on medium speed until frothy. Then add the cream of tartar and increase mixer speed to medium-high. Continue beating until the whites form

soft peaks. Slowly add ½ *cup* sugar, 1 tablespoon at a time over 45 seconds. Whip 15 seconds longer.

7. Using a 2¾-inch-wide rubber spatula, fold ⅓ of the whites into the batter in about 20 turns. Fold in the remaining whites, taking about 30 additional turns.

8. Spoon the batter into the prepared pans, smoothing the surface with the back of a tablespoon. Bake in the preheated oven 30 to 35 minutes, or until the cake begins to come away from the sides of the pan and is golden brown on top and springy to the touch.

9. Remove from the oven. Set the pans onto cake racks for 10 minutes to cool slightly, then invert. Lift off the pans and carefully peel off the waxed paper and continue to cool completely.

10. To prepare Lady Baltimore Frosting: Combine the walnuts, figs, raisins, and sherry in a small bowl and macerate ½ hour or longer. Make the 7-Minute Frosting (page 448).

11. Drain the fruit/nut mixture and dry thoroughly on several layers of paper toweling. Fold into the icing by hand. If the frosting is still too soft, chill 30 minutes before using.

TO ASSEMBLE THE CAKE:

1. Place one layer on a serving plate top side down. Cut four 4-inch strips of waxed paper and slide them under the edges of the cake to keep the plate clean. Using the back of a tablespoon, spread the cake top with a ½-inch-thick layer of frosting, leaving a ½-inch unfrosted border around the edge. (The frosting may be difficult to spread as it is sticky and chunky.) Place the second layer, top side up, on top of the first, aligning the layers evenly. Cover the sides and top of the cake with the remaining frosting, swirling it on with the back of a tablespoon.

2. Remove the waxed paper strips. Chill the cake uncovered for 20 minutes to set the frosting. When ready to serve, dip a sharp knife into warm water and cut straight down to make neat slices.

STORAGE: Meringue icings should not be stored airtight as they accumulate moisture. Store at room temperature covered with a glass dome slightly ajar to allow air to circulate freely. The cake will keep up to 3 days.

❧ ALMOND NUT CRUST LAYER CAKE

Here the crushed almonds/sugar coating in the pans forms a crusty surface for a golden cake. The frosting is delicious, but if you need this cake in a hurry, slice one inverted layer into wedges and serve. The almond crust makes a wonderful topping. The second layer may be frozen for the future.

▽

AT A GLANCE

SERVES: 10 to 12
PANS: Two 9″ layers
PAN PREP: Well buttered
OVEN TEMP: 350°
RACK LEVEL: Lower third
BAKING TIME: 30 to 35 minutes
METHOD: Electric mixer

THE CRUST:

½	cup toasted sliced almonds
1	tablespoon sugar

THE CAKE:

2½	cups sifted cake flour
1½	teaspoons baking powder
½	teaspoon baking soda
½	teaspoon salt
½	cup (1 stick) unsalted butter, at room temperature
4	ounces cream cheese, softened
1	teaspoon freshly grated lemon rind
1½	cups superfine or strained sugar
4	large eggs
1	teaspoon vanilla extract
½	teaspoon almond extract
½	cup milk
1	recipe Almond Cream Cheese Frosting (page 451)
1	cup toasted sliced almonds for decorating cake (optional)

1. Position a rack in the lower third of the oven and preheat to 350°. Generously butter two 9-inch layer pans.
2. To make the crust: Combine the nuts and sugar in a small bowl. Crush the nuts between the palms of your hand into very small pieces. Sprinkle evenly over bottom of prepared layer pans. Set aside.
3. To make the cake: Sift together the flour, baking powder, baking soda, and salt, using a triple sifter. Set aside.

*Special
Occasion
Cakes*

335

4. Put the butter, cream cheese, and lemon rind in the large bowl of an electric mixer fitted with beaters or paddle attachment. Soften on low speed. Increase mixer speed to medium-high and cream until smooth and light in color, about 1½ to 2 minutes.

5. Add the sugar, 1 tablespoon at a time, taking 6 to 8 minutes to blend it in well. Scrape the sides of the bowl occasionally.

6. Add the eggs, 1 at a time at 1-minute intervals. Blend in the extracts. Scrape sides of bowl again.

7. Reduce mixer speed to low. Add the flour mixture alternately with the milk, dividing the flour into three parts and the milk into two parts, starting and ending with the flour. Mix only until incorporated after each addition. Scrape the sides of the bowl. Mix 10 seconds longer.

8. Spoon the batter around the sides, then into the center of the prepared pans. Then, using the back of a tablespoon, carefully spread the batter from the sides to the center of the pan, taking care not to disturb the nut crust. Bake in the preheated oven for 30 to 35 minutes, or until cake begins to come away from the sides of the pan and is golden brown on top and springy to the touch.

9. Remove from the oven. Set the pans on cake racks for 10 minutes to cool slightly. Invert, carefully remove the pans, and continue to cool to room temperature. When cake is cool, frost if you like. Carefully press toasted almonds generously onto the sides.

STORAGE: Store at room temperature under a glass cake dome or in an airtight container for up to 5 days.

🌰 BOSTON CREAM PIE

In the mid-1850s, a German pastry chef who worked at the Parker House Hotel in Boston served his rendition of a popular cake known as pudding-cake pie.

Traditionally, this "pie" consisted of a single sponge layer, split into two thin disks filled with a thick layer of vanilla custard and dusted with confectioners' sugar. The Parker House chef broke with tradition and replaced the confectioners' sugar with a thin chocolate icing. The sides were left unfrosted, exposing the custard filling. His version became the rage of Boston and for years it was called Parker House Cream Pie. Eventually, the name of the hotel was dropped and the cake became known simply as Boston Cream Pie. My version of this perennial favorite calls for dripping the chocolate icing down the sides. This is a bonus for chocolate-lovers and also makes a prettier presentation.

1   Hot Milk Sponge Cake (page 262), baked and cooled

THE VANILLA CUSTARD FILLING:
1⅓   cups milk, divided
⅓   cup sugar
2   tablespoons cornstarch
1   tablespoon flour
1   large whole egg
1   large egg yolk
1   tablespoon butter
1   teaspoon vanilla extract

THE CHOCOLATE ICING:
1   ounce unsweetened chocolate, coarsely chopped
1   ounce semisweet chocolate, coarsely chopped
1¼   cups strained confectioners' sugar
3   tablespoons boiling water, plus a few extra drops for thinning glaze
1   tablespoon light corn syrup
½   teaspoon vanilla extract

1. To make the filling: In a medium saucepan, combine *1 cup* of milk and the sugar, and bring to a slow boil over low heat. Set aside.
2. In a small bowl, combine the cornstarch and flour. Gradually stir in the remaining ⅓ *cup* milk, whisking until very smooth. Then whisk in the whole egg and the egg yolk. Add to the hot sugar/milk. Bring to a boil on low heat, whisking constantly, until the mixture is thick and smooth. Cook 30 to 45 seconds after the mixture reaches a boil, stirring gently with a wooden spoon to prevent scorching.
3. Remove from the heat and stir in the butter and vanilla. Press a piece of buttered waxed paper onto the filling to prevent a skin from forming. Refrigerate until filling is chilled.
4. To make the chocolate icing: Place the chocolates in a medium mixing bowl. Melt slowly over a low flame in a skillet containing ½ inch of hot water.
5. Remove the bowl from the skillet. Stir chocolate to blend. Add sugar alternately with hot water, four parts sugar to three parts water, beating well after each addition.
6. Beat in corn syrup and vanilla. Icing should be pourable, the consistency of chocolate syrup. If too tight, add a few drops of boiling water until the desired consistency is reached. The frosting will tighten as it cools. If you are making it ahead of time, place the bowl in skillet filled with ½ inch of hot water to keep warm.

TO ASSEMBLE THE CAKE:
1. Divide sponge cake horizontally into 2 layers. Set the bottom layer cut side up on a serving plate. Cut 4 strips of waxed paper, each 4 inches wide, and slide under edge of the cake to keep plate clean while you frost.
2. Cover cake with a ½-inch layer of custard. Then position second layer over the first, cut side down. Holding the bowl 10-inches over the center of the cake, pour on the chocolate icing. Using a 10-inch metal spatula, *quickly* ease frosting to edges of cake. Allow it to drip randomly down the sides; frosting will set almost immediately.

STORAGE: Store uncovered in refrigerator for 15 to 20 minutes to set. If you wish, the cake can be made ahead and refrigerated up to 6 to 8 hours before serving. Remove ½ hour before serving. Leftover cake should be stored in the refrigerator, loosely covered with a foil tent. The cake will keep up to 3 days.

🌾 BURNISHED SUGAR LAYER CAKE

*C*aramelized sugar is used in various ways for a large variety of pastries and desserts. Here caramel syrup is blended into a vanilla batter, giving the cake a wonderful golden brown color and a marvelous burnished sugar taste.

The syrup may be made many days in advance and stored in a jar at room temperature; however, it will harden upon standing. When ready to use it, reheat the syrup to about 100° in a microwave at medium setting or in a bain-marie. It should be the consistency of thick maple syrup.

A word of caution: Do not attempt to make caramel with young children or pets underfoot. While the end result is delicious, the procedure for making caramel is serious business.

AT A GLANCE

SERVES: 10 to 12
PAN: Two 9″ layer pans
PAN PREP: Butter/ waxed paper/butter
OVEN TEMP: 350°
RACK LEVEL: Lower third
BAKING TIME: 30 to 35 minutes
METHOD: Electric mixer

THE CARAMEL SYRUP:

1¹⁄₃	cups sugar
¹⁄₄	cup water
3 to 4	drops lemon juice
¹⁄₄	cup hot water

THE CAKE:

1	cup sour cream
¹⁄₂	cup warm caramel syrup
¹⁄₄	teaspoon baking soda
2¹⁄₂	cups sifted cake flour
2	teaspoons baking powder
³⁄₄	teaspoon salt
³⁄₄	cup (1¹⁄₂ sticks) unsalted butter
1¹⁄₃	cups superfine or strained sugar
3	large eggs
1	teaspoon vanilla extract

THE BURNISHED SUGAR FROSTING:

¹⁄₂	cup (1 stick) unsalted butter, at room temperature
3	cups strained confectioners' sugar
¹⁄₈	teaspoon salt
3	tablespoons warmed caramel syrup
2 to 3	tablespoons sour cream
1	teaspoon vanilla extract
3 to 4	drops maple extract (optional)

Special Occasion Cakes

339

1. To make the caramel syrup: Put the sugar in a heavy 2-quart saucepan. (Do not use a smaller pan.) Add ¼ cup water and bring to a slow boil. Simmer until the sugar is dissolved. Stir briefly only if undissolved sugar clings to the bottom of the pot. Brush the sides of the saucepan with water to remove any sugar crystals, then add the lemon juice. Cook until the mixture turns deep golden brown, about 320° to 330°. This will take from 10 to 20 minutes, depending upon the thickness of the saucepan. Watch carefully, as the sugar syrup burns easily. If it gets too black, it will taste bitter.

2. When the desired color and temperature are reached, *immediately* remove the pan from the heat and set in a sink filled to a shallow depth with cold water to stop the cooking. *At once* pour the ¼ cup hot water into the syrup. The caramel will bubble up.

3. Return the saucepan to low heat briefly, stirring until smooth and syrupy. Pour into a measuring cup. Scrape the drippings from the pan with a buttered spoon. (The butter keeps the syrup from sticking to the spoon.) This recipe yields about ¾ cup syrup, enough to prepare the cake and glaze.

4. Position the rack in the lower third of the oven and preheat to 350°. Butter two 9-inch layer pans. Line the bottom and sides with waxed paper and butter the paper lightly.

5. To make the cake: In a small bowl, combine the sour cream, ½ cup warm caramel syrup, and baking soda. Set aside.

6. Using a triple sifter, sift together the flour, baking powder, and salt. Set aside.

7. Cut the butter into 1-inch pieces and place in the large bowl of an electric mixer fitted with beaters or paddle attachment. Soften on low speed. Increase the speed to medium-high and cream until smooth and light in color, about 1½ to 2 minutes.

8. Add the sugar, 1 tablespoon at a time, taking about 6 to 8 minutes to blend it in well. Scrape the sides of the bowl occasionally.

9. Add the eggs, 1 at a time at 1-minute intervals. Scrape the sides of the bowl as necessary. Beat for 1 minute longer. Blend in the vanilla.

10. Reduce the mixer speed to low. Add the dry ingredients alternating with the caramel-flavored sour cream, dividing the flour mixture into three parts and the sour cream into two parts, start-

ing and ending with the flour. Mix only until incorporated after each addition. Scrape the sides of the bowl and mix for 10 seconds longer.

11. Spoon the batter into the prepared pans and smooth the surface with the back of a tablespoon. Center the pans on the rack in the preheated oven and bake for 30 to 35 minutes, or until the cake is browned on top and springy to the touch.

12. Remove from the oven and place the pans on cake racks to cool for 15 minutes. Invert the pans onto the racks, and gently remove the pans and paper.

13. To make the frosting: In a medium-sized bowl, cream the butter with a wooden spoon until very smooth. Gradually add 1½ cups confectioners' sugar in 3 to 4 additions, blending well after each addition.

14. Blend in the caramel syrup, stirring until smooth. Add the remaining sugar and the salt, alternating with the sour cream. Flavor with vanilla and maple extracts. The frosting should be creamy, but do not overmix. If icing is too thin, chill it briefly in the refrigerator.

TO ASSEMBLE THE CAKE:

1. Place a layer on a plate top side down. Cut 4 strips of waxed paper, 4 inches wide, and slide under edges of layer to keep plate clean. Using a metal spatula, spread on frosting about ¼ inch thick, leaving a ½-inch unfrosted border all around. Place the second layer, top side up, on top of the first, aligning the layers evenly. Apply a thin layer of frosting to the sides with the spatula. Cover the top completely. Use remaining frosting for a second application around sides.

2. Gently press the bottom of a teaspoon into frosting, then pull it out to create little ¼- to ½-inch peaks. Continue on top and sides at ½-inch intervals. Chill in refrigerator for ½ hour or until peaks are set.

STORAGE: Store at room temperature under a glass dome or in an airtight container for up to 5 days.

🍂 MAJESTIC MANDARIN CAKE

If you wish to create a party cake that makes a statement, I can think of no better choice than this. It is dramatically high, feather-light, and has a heavenly orange cream frosting garnished with crunchy golden flakes of toasted coconut.

This cake is baked in an angel food pan. It is a nice touch to fill the center hole with an appropriate decoration. For bridal showers you may choose a miniature doll; for Christmas, try an arrangement of seasonal decorations, or at any time of year a cluster of fresh shrubbery greens.

1   Orange Sponge Cake (page 255),
     baked and cooled

THE MANDARIN FILLING AND FROSTING:

Three	11-ounce cans mandarin oranges
3/4	cup sugar
1/3	cup all-purpose flour
1/8	teaspoon salt
2/3	cup fresh orange juice, from navel oranges
2 to 3	tablespoons fresh lemon juice
2	large eggs, lightly beaten
1 1/2 to 2	tablespoons grated navel orange rind
1	teaspoon grated lemon rind
2 1/2	cups heavy cream, well chilled
3	tablespoons Grand Marnier, Cointreau, or Triple Sec
3 to 4	tablespoons Grand Marnier (optional)
One	3 1/2-ounce can shredded coconut, toasted (page 58)

1. Drain the oranges and set aside to dry thoroughly on several layers of paper toweling.
2. In top of double boiler, combine the sugar, flour, and salt. Slowly whisk in the juices, then blend in the eggs. Place the pan over 1 inch of simmering water and stir constantly with a wooden spoon until the mixture thickens, about 8 to 10 minutes. Remove from the heat and whisk briefly just to smooth mixture. Stir in the grated orange and lemon rinds. Place a buttered round of waxed

paper directly on surface to prevent a film from forming. Chill for 2 to 3 hours, or until very cold. This mixture can be made up to 3 days in advance.

3. Place the heavy cream in a large chilled bowl of an electric mixer fitted with chilled beaters or whip attachment. Whip on medium speed until it begins to thicken. Add liqueur and beat until cream forms firm peaks. Remove from machine and whisk 1/4 of the whipped cream into the orange filling, until smooth and well blended. Using a 2 3/4-inch-wide rubber spatula, fold the filling into the remaining cream. Divide the filling in half.

4. Set aside 40 of the nicest mandarin orange sections for garnish. Dice the remaining oranges and fold into 1/2 of the filling. The remaining filling will be used to frost the cake.

TO ASSEMBLE THE CAKE:

1. Place the cake on a serving plate bottom side up and cut horizontally into 4 layers (page 500). Set widest layer cut side up on a serving plate. Cut 4 strips of waxed paper, each 4 inches wide, and slip them under the cake to keep plate clean. If desired, brush layer lightly with Grand Marnier. Cover with 1/3 of the filling containing the diced orange segments. Position the second-widest layer over the first, narrowest side up. Brush with liqueur and cover with 1/3 of the filling. Repeat with the third layer. Place the top layer cut side down. Press cake gently to align the sides.

2. If you wish, set aside 1/4 of the reserved mandarin cream for piped decoration. However, this step is entirely optional. Cover the sides and the top of the cake with the cream, using a long metal spatula to smooth surface. Sprinkle the top and sides of cake with toasted coconut.

3. Fit a 14-inch pastry bag with a large #2 open star tube. Fill 1/3 full with remaining mandarin cream. Garnish the cake with rosettes spaced 1 inch apart, beginning with top outer edge, then inner edge, and finally the bottom edge.

4. Press reserved mandarin orange slices between rosettes. Chill uncovered in refrigerator for up to 8 hours. When ready to serve, arrange fresh lemon leaves (available at most florists) or other clean greenery in the center. To serve, slice with a serrated knife, using a gentle sawing motion.

STORAGE: Store in the refrigerator, lightly covered with an aluminum foil tent, for up to 4 days.

🌰 HAZELNUT BLITZ TORTE WITH PRALINE CREAM FILLING

▽················

AT A GLANCE

SERVES: 8 to 10
PANS: Two 9″ layers
with removable
bottoms (see Note)
PAN PREP: Well
buttered
OVEN TEMP: 325°
RACK LEVEL: Lower
third
BAKING TIME: 30 to
35 minutes
METHOD: Electric
mixer

·····················

During my childhood in the South, my mother frequently made a blitz torte. This unusual cake consists of two thin butter cake layers covered with a stiff meringue and topped with crushed hazelnuts. The meringue rises high above the sides of the pan during baking, but shrinks and forms a crusty, uneven surface as the cake cools.

The wonderful custard filling is flavored with praline paste, a delicious nut butter made from candied hazelnuts. Since the golden meringue crust is so pretty, frosting becomes unnecessary.

For a quick alternative to the praline filling, prepare an espresso-flavored filling by omitting the nut paste and adding 2 teaspoons of espresso zest (page 58) to the hot milk. When I use the espresso flavoring, I like to substitute pecans for the hazelnuts.

Whatever you choose to use as a filling, this torte is absolutely scrumptious, and I can assure you it will be a conversation piece every time you serve it.

THE CAKE:
- 1 cup sifted cake flour
- 1 teaspoon baking powder
- 1/8 teaspoon salt
- 1/2 cup (1 stick) unsalted butter
- 1/2 cup superfine or strained sugar
- 4 large eggs
- 1 teaspoon vanilla extract
- 3 tablespoons milk

THE MERINGUE:
- 1/2 cup superfine or strained sugar
- 1/3 cup strained confectioners' sugar
- 4 egg whites
- 1/2 teaspoon vanilla extract
- 1/2 cup hazelnuts, coarsely chopped
- 1 tablespoon granulated sugar

- 1 recipe Praline Cream Filling (page 442)

1. Position a rack in the lower third of the oven and preheat to 325°. Generously butter two 9-inch layer pans with removable bottoms.
2. To make the cake: Sift together the flour, baking powder, and salt, using a triple sifter. Set aside.
3. Cut the butter into 1-inch pieces and place in the small bowl of an electric mixer fitted with the beaters or paddle attachment. Soften on low speed. Increase mixer speed to medium. Cream until smooth and light in color, about 1½ to 2 minutes.
4. Add the sugar, 1 tablespoon at a time, taking 3 to 4 minutes to blend it in well. Scrape the sides of the bowl occasionally.
5. Add the egg yolks, 2 at a time at 1-minute intervals; beat 1 minute longer, scraping the sides of the bowl as necessary. Blend in the vanilla.
6. Reduce mixer speed to low. Add the flour mixture alternately with the milk, dividing the flour into three parts and the milk into two parts, starting and ending with the flour. Scrape the sides of the bowl. Mix 10 seconds longer.
7. Spoon the batter into the center of the prepared pans. Using the back of a tablespoon, spread the batter from the center out to the sides. This will be a very thin layer of batter. Set aside.
8. To make the meringue: Strain the superfine sugar and the confectioners' sugar together three times through a fine strainer. Place the egg whites in the large bowl of an electric mixer fitted with beaters or whip attachment. Beat on medium speed until the whites are frothy. Increase the speed to medium-high and continue to beat until the whites form firm moist peaks, but are not dry. Add the sugars, 1 tablespoon at a time, over 3 to 4 minutes. Blend in the vanilla and beat 1 minute longer, until you have a very stiff glossy meringue.
9. Spoon the meringue over the batter in the pans, making sure entire surface is covered and meringue clings to sides of pan. With the back of a tablespoon, swirl the meringue to form a few peaks. It should not be smooth. Sprinkle each layer with the hazelnuts, then top both with the *1 tablespoon* of granulated sugar. Bake in the preheated oven for 30 to 35 minutes, until the meringue is golden brown and feels dry to the touch.
10. Make the Praline Cream Filling.
11. Remove baked cakes from the oven and set the pans on cake racks to cool completely. Meringue will shrink and sink as it

stands. When the cake is completely cool, run a thin knife around the sides of pan to release any meringue that clings.

12. To remove the pans, place each layer on top of a coffee can—the outer ring will drop to the counter. Run a long sharp knife under bottom of cake to release the metal disk. Slide one layer gently onto a serving platter and the other onto a cake rack. If you have used springform or standard layer pans, cut a 12-inch piece of aluminum foil and place it gently over the meringue, molding the sides of the foil around the pan. Invert onto a second cake rack and carefully lift off the pan. Center a serving plate over the layer and invert again. The meringue side will be up. Do this carefully to avoid crushing the meringue. Repeat with the second layer; however, after removing the pan, turn the meringue right side up onto a cake rack instead of a plate.

13. Spoon filling over the bottom layer, leaving a ½-inch unfrosted border around the edges. Carefully slide the top layer from the rack onto the first layer. This cake is at its best served shortly after assembling. However, it can be filled and refrigerated, uncovered, up to 6 to 8 hours. Let stand at room temperature ½ hour before serving.

STORAGE: Cover loosely with aluminum foil and refrigerate for up to 3 days.

NOTE: If layer pans with removable bottoms are not available, you may substitute two 9-inch springforms or two 9-inch standard layer pans. However, special handling will be required to remove the cake.

CHEESECAKES

If one were to take a vote on the most popular cake served in this country, the cheesecake would probably be the winner. It is rich, high in calories, and beloved.

There are two main types of cheesecakes—what is commonly known as the New York type, made with cream cheese and sour or heavy cream, and the Italian or curd cheese variety, made with ricotta or, occasionally, cottage cheese.

New York cheesecake is the richer of the two, with a smooth, velvety texture. Italian cheesecakes are usually less creamy and somewhat lighter in texture. They can be tricky to make because the cheese often contains a great deal of moisture.

Most cheesecakes served in Italian restaurants are made with impastata. A commercial cheese available only to professionals, impastata has a drier texture and contains more fat than regular ricotta. To achieve a similar consistency, you would have to cook regular ricotta for many hours in a double boiler to remove the liquid, then drain it in cheesecloth. A more practical alternative is to purchase fresh ricotta in an Italian grocery store or specialty cheese shop. While not as satisfactory for baking as impastata, fresh ricotta is less moist than the varieties commonly found prepackaged in supermarkets, as well as other prepackaged curd cheeses such as cottage cheese.

Cheesecake crusts can range from cookie doughs to crusts made with graham crackers, zwieback, gingersnaps, at times mixed with chopped nuts, and chocolate wafers. Many cheesecakes are made with no separate crust at all, as the cheesecake itself forms a light outer crust as it bakes. Cookie dough crusts take a great deal of time to prepare, so with the exception of Pineapple Cheese Squares, I have stayed away from them. I either use a crumb crust or none at all.

Cheesecakes are not only delicious, they are quite simple to prepare. They are best made a day or two before you plan to serve them. The flavor improves as they mature, and they become easier to slice. They also have a very long shelf life. Whatever recipe you choose, you will never disappoint your guests when you offer a great cheesecake as the finale to your meal.

BEFORE YOU BEGIN . . .

▶ Be sure the cream cheese is very soft before you start mixing; lumps are very difficult to eliminate once they have formed. Blending the sugar into the cream cheese before adding other ingredients helps to smooth it out.

▶ Take care not to overbeat cheesecake batter. While the ingredients should be well blended, excessive beating creates too many air cells, which expand in the oven, causing the surface of the cheesecake to crack. This is especially true of the heavier cream-cheese-style batters.

▶ The texture of a cheesecake will be creamier if it is not overbaked. Remember, cheesecakes continue to bake as they cool down in the oven. Overbaking can also cause the top of the cheesecake to crack.

▶ Cheesecakes should mature in the refrigerator at least 24 hours before serving, and since most cheesecakes keep well, you can make them as much as 2 or 3 days ahead. Only the finishing touches, such as fruit toppings, should be completed shortly before serving.

▶ Cheesecake tastes best at room temperature. Remove the cake from the refrigerator at least 1 hour or more before serving, depending upon weather conditions.

▶ Cheesecakes that are baked in a waterbath or bain-marie will be creamier and moister. However, this method works well only for crustless cheesecakes or those that have only a thin crumb-type crust. This is because the waterbath also softens the exterior, which can make a crust too soggy.

▶ Springform pans are usually wrapped in heavy-duty aluminum foil when used in a bain-marie, to prevent leaks. You should also wrap any pan that has warped with age, because it, too, may leak.

▶ For many recipes that call for a waterbath, you can use an 8-inch (2-quart capacity) porcelain soufflé dish or a deep metal round pan without a removable bottom in place of a springform pan.

▶ Most cheesecakes are difficult to slice because of their creamy texture. To make clean slices, dip a sharp knife into warm water each time you make a cut. (If you are cutting the cake at the table, put the water in an opaque container so that the cloudy water will not show.) A wire cheese cutter also works quite well. You may also use a piece of dental floss pulled tightly through the cake. Needless to say, if you use this method, the cake should be cut in the kitchen.

🌾 ANN'S CHEESECAKE

AT A GLANCE

SERVES: 10 to 12
PAN: 9″ springform
PAN PREP: Butter
OVEN TEMP: 325°
RACK LEVEL: Lower third
BAKING TIME: 1 hour, plus 1 additional hour for oven cooling
METHOD: Electric mixer

Ann Amendolara Nurse teaches Italian cooking in the New York metropolitan area. Ann is an authority on fine food and I take special notice of any dish she prepares. Her cheesecake is one of the finest that I have ever tasted.

This crustless cake is made with a combination of cream cheese and ricotta and flavored with healthy amounts of lemon juice and pure vanilla extract. It is light and velvety, and impossible to stop eating. With each bite I tell myself, "This must be your last," but somehow it never is.

I have included Ann's recipe because if it is a collector's item with Ann, you know it is going to be exceptional.

½	cup (1 stick) unsalted butter
3	tablespoons all-purpose flour
3	tablespoons cornstarch
Two	8-ounce packages cream cheese, at room temperature
One	15-ounce carton whole milk ricotta cheese, liquid drained from the top
1½	cups sugar
4	large eggs
1½	tablespoons fresh lemon juice
1	tablespoon vanilla extract
1	pint (2 cups) sour cream

1. Position rack in the lower third of the oven and preheat to 325°. Butter a 9-inch springform pan.
2. In a small saucepan, melt the butter over low heat. Set aside to cool.
3. Mix together the flour and cornstarch and strain onto a sheet of waxed paper. Set aside.
4. Place the cream cheese and ricotta in the large bowl of an electric mixer fitted with beaters or paddle attachment. Mix on medium speed until smooth and creamy.
5. Add the sugar in 3 additions over 1 minute, scraping the sides of the bowl as necessary. Beat for 30 seconds longer.

6. Add the eggs, 1 at a time at 30-second intervals, mixing well after each addition. Blend in the flour/cornstarch mixture, lemon juice, and vanilla.
7. Add the melted butter and sour cream. Continue beating for 30 seconds or until all ingredients are well blended. Scrape the sides of the bowl and mix for 10 seconds longer.
8. Set the pan on an 18-inch square of heavy aluminum foil. Mold foil snugly around the pan to catch any batter that might leak. Pour the batter into the pan and bake in the preheated oven for 1 hour.
9. At the end of the hour, turn off the heat and, without opening the oven door, leave the cake in the oven for 1 additional hour. Remove from the oven. Set the pan on a cake rack to cool completely. Refrigerate. Remove from the refrigerator 1 hour before serving. Run a thin knife around edge of pan to loosen the cake, and carefully remove the rim. Transfer to a cake platter.

STORAGE: Store in refrigerator covered with aluminum foil for up to 5 days.

🌰 MANHATTAN CHEESECAKE

▽ ....
AT A GLANCE

SERVES: 10 to 12
PAN: 9″ springform
PAN PREP: Heavily
buttered
OVEN TEMP: 325°
RACK LEVEL: Lower
third
BAKING TIME: 40
minutes, plus 1
additional hour for
oven cooling
METHOD: Food
processor/electric
mixer

....

New York–style cheesecake has a luscious, dense consistency and a very creamy texture. This type of cheesecake is often called Lindy's cheesecake, named after the famous Broadway restaurant. While researching recipes for this book, I came upon no less than a dozen lists of similar ingredients claiming to be the original.

This recipe varies from traditional versions in that the pan is lined with a quick-to-make crumb crust instead of the more time-consuming sweet pastry dough. Tiers of sliced strawberries arranged on top make it picture-perfect.

....

THE CRUST:

10	double graham crackers, or enough to make about 1½ cups of crumbs
2	tablespoons sugar
⅓	cup (⅔ stick) unsalted butter, melted

THE CAKE:

1½	pounds cream cheese, at room temperature
1¼	cups sugar, divided
5	large egg yolks
½	cup heavy cream
2	teaspoons vanilla extract
1½	teaspoons freshly grated lemon rind
1½	teaspoons freshly grated orange rind
3	large egg whites

THE STRAWBERRY TOPPING:

¾	cup apricot preserves
1	tablespoon kirschwasser or Grand Marnier
3 to 4	cups large, deep red strawberries

1. Position rack in the lower third of the oven and preheat to 325°. Generously butter a 9-inch springform pan.
2. To make the crust: Break the crackers into the container of a food processor fitted with a steel blade. Add the sugar and pulse until you get fine crumbs. Pour in the melted butter, pulsing just to blend.

3. Empty the crumbs into the prepared pan. Using a spoon, press a thick layer (about ¹/₈ to ¹/₄ inch) of crumbs against the sides, extending about ²/₃ of the way up. Using a flat-bottomed glass, press the remaining crumbs evenly over the bottom of the pan. Be sure to flatten the crumbs where the sides meet the bottom. Refrigerate.

4. To make the filling: Wash the processor bowl and steel blade. Put the cream cheese and *1 cup* sugar in processor and process for 15 seconds, then scrape down the sides of the bowl and process 5 seconds longer. While the machine is running, pour the egg yolks through the feeder tube and process 10 seconds. Add the cream, vanilla, and the lemon and orange rinds. Process 10 seconds longer.

5. In the large bowl of an electric mixer fitted with beaters or whip attachment, beat the egg whites to soft peaks. Add ¹/₄ *cup* sugar, 1 tablespoon at a time, beating until the whites are shiny, about 45 seconds. With a 2³/₄-inch-wide rubber spatula, fold ¹/₄ of the cheese mixture into the whites, taking about 10 turns to lighten. Fold in the remaining cheese mixture, taking an additional 30 turns.

6. Pour the batter into the prepared pan. Set the pan on an 18-inch square of heavy-duty aluminum foil. Mold it around the sides of the pan to catch any batter that might leak. Bake in the preheated oven for 40 minutes.

7. At the end of the baking time, turn off heat and prop the oven door ajar with the handle of a wooden spoon. Cool the cake in the oven for 1 additional hour. Remove from the oven, discard the foil, and place the pan on a cake rack to cool for at least 3 hours. Refrigerate until ready to prepare strawberry topping.

8. To make the strawberry topping: In a small saucepan, combine the apricot preserves and liqueur, bring to a slow boil over low heat, and continue to cook until the preserves are completely melted. Remove from the heat. Strain through a fine strainer to remove the large pieces. Return to the saucepan. Set aside.

9. Wash, hull, and dry the berries well on several layers of paper toweling. Slice them in half lengthwise.

10. Arrange the berries cut sides down around the edge of the cheesecake with the points of the berries facing outward. Arrange a second circle inside the first, with points of the berries extending inward. The bottoms of the berries should touch. Fill in the center randomly.

11. Arrange a second layer of berries on top of the first, beginning ½ inch from the edge of the cake. Extend the points outward, placing them in the spaces between the points of the first layer of berries. Arrange the second layer with points extending outward also. Fill in the top with berries' points extended outward. Continue circling the top with the points of the berries outward, making a third and fourth layer if necessary. The design will resemble a rosette (see illustrations). The cake may now be refrigerated up to 4 or 6 hours, covered loosely with a strip of waxed paper.

12. Remove the cake from the refrigerator 1 hour before serving. Shortly before you are ready to serve it, warm the apricot preserves over low heat. (Do not glaze the berries until just before serving or they will become soft and runny.) With a pastry brush, lightly coat the berries, taking care not to disturb the design. If the preserves are too thick, thin them with a few drops of hot water.

STORAGE: Refrigerate covered loosely with a foil tent for up to 3 days.

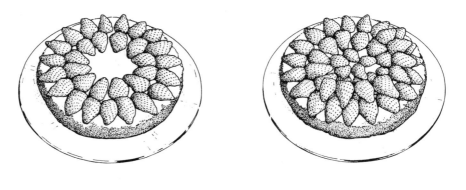

🍂 A GREAT ITALIAN CHEESECAKE

talian cheesecakes are prepared with ricotta, a high-moisture cheese made from milk or a combination of milk and whey, which is heated to extract the proteins.

When ricotta is baked it releases a substantial amount of liquid, which will make the filling watery if not dealt with in some fashion. Many recipes call for adding generous amounts of flour or cornstarch to absorb the moisture. However, this can make the cheesecake rather heavy and dry. A better method is to drain the ricotta in linen towels before using it, as specified in this recipe.

I created this creamy Italian cheesecake with the help of two fine Italian cooks, Joanne Roppate, who learned the secret of removing the water from the cheese from her Sicilian mother, and Sarah Melillo, whose contribution was to add a puréed whole navel orange to the batter, giving the cheesecake a refreshing citrus taste. The smooth texture comes from the use of confectioners' sugar in place of granulated.

Unlike most cheesecakes, this cake does not have to stand overnight. In fact, it's fabulous when freshly made. Try it and see if you don't agree.

▽

AT A GLANCE

SERVES: 8 to 10
PAN: 9″ springform
PAN PREP: Butter
OVEN TEMP: 325°
RACK LEVEL: Lower third
BAKING TIME: 70 to 75 minutes, plus an additional 1/2 hour for oven cooling
METHOD: Food processor

THE CRUMB CRUST:
- 18   Amaretti biscuits
- 2   tablespoons unflavored dried bread crumbs
- 3   tablespoons unsalted butter, melted and cooled

THE CAKE:
- 3   pounds fresh whole-milk ricotta
- 1   medium-sized navel orange (about 6 ounces)
- 8   large eggs
- 2   cups strained confectioners' sugar
- 3   tablespoons all-purpose flour
- 2   teaspoons vanilla extract
- 1/4   teaspoon salt
- 2/3   cup heavy cream

Special Occasion Cakes

1. To extract the excess water from the ricotta: Arrange two linen or 100% cotton dish towels (do not use terrycloth) on top of each other on the kitchen counter. Spread the cheese lengthwise on the doubled towels into a rectangle measuring about 14 × 5 inches. Bring the sides of the towels to the center and roll the cheese tightly in the towels, jelly-roll fashion. Let the cheese stand 1/2 hour. Unroll the towels and replace them with two clean, dry towels. Repeat the procedure, letting the cheese stand for another 1/2 hour.

2. Butter a 9-inch springform pan.

3. To make the crust: Break the biscuits into pieces and add with the bread crumbs to the container of a processor fitted with the steel blade. Pulse 6 to 8 times or until fine crumbs form. You should have 3/4 cup crumbs. Stop the machine and pour in the melted butter. Pulse 3 times just to blend.

4. Empty the crumb mixture into the prepared pan. With the bottom of a glass, press the crumbs evenly onto the bottom of the pan. (Do not extend the crumbs up the sides.) Refrigerate while you prepare the filling.

5. Position rack in the lower third of the oven. Preheat the oven to 325°.

6. To make the cake: Cut the entire orange, including rind and pith, into 2-inch chunks. You should have about 2 cups. Place the eggs and orange chunks into the container of a food processor fitted with the steel blade. Process for 2 minutes, until the mixture is thick and light in color and the orange pieces are finely chopped.

7. Stop the machine and add the ricotta and all of the remaining ingredients except the heavy cream. The volume of the ingredients will reduce in mixing. Process for 10 seconds, or just until smooth and creamy. Scrape down the sides and process for 5 seconds longer.

8. With the machine running, pour in the cream through the feeder tube. Immediately pour the filling into the pan.

9. Set the pan on a 12-inch square of aluminum foil, molding the foil around the sides of the pan to catch leakage. In the preheated oven, bake for 70 to 75 minutes, or until the top of the cake is golden brown. Turn off the heat and prop the oven door ajar with the handle of a wooden spoon. Cool the cake in the oven for an additional 1/2 hour.

10. Remove the cake from the oven. Set the pan on a cake rack to cool completely. Refrigerate at least 3 to 4 hours to set, but remove the cake from the refrigerator at least 1 hour before serving. Run a thin knife around the sides of the pan and carefully remove the rim.

STORAGE: Refrigerate, covered loosely with aluminum foil, for up to 1 week.

PINEAPPLE CHEESE SQUARES

AT A GLANCE

SERVES: 8 to 10

PAN: 8″ × 12″ × 2″ heatproof oblong glass

PAN PREP: Buttered

OVEN TEMP: Crust and filling—350° Topping—400°

RACK LEVEL: Lower third

BAKING TIME: Crust—16 to 18 minutes; Cheese filling—30 minutes, plus an additional 1 hour for oven cooling; Topping—8 to 10 minutes

METHOD: Food processor

Here a buttery shortbreadlike cookie dough crust is spread with a crushed pineapple mixture before the cheesecake ingredients are poured in. The baked cake is coated with a sour cream topping and briefly returned to the oven until the topping sets. These cheese squares are best served just slightly warm, but I find it difficult to resist eating them straight from the oven.

THE CRUST:

- 1¼ cups all-purpose flour
- ¼ cup sugar
- ¼ teaspoon salt
- ½ cup (1 stick) cold unsalted butter, cut into ¼-inch cubes
- 1 large egg

THE PINEAPPLE LAYER:

- One 20-ounce can crushed pineapple in light syrup
- 1 tablespoon sugar
- 1 tablespoon cornstarch
- ½ cup reserved pineapple juice
- 2 teaspoons lemon juice

THE CHEESE LAYER:

- 1 pound cottage cheese
- 8 ounces farmer cheese, at room temperature
- ¾ cup sugar, divided
- 3 tablespoons all-purpose flour
- 2 teaspoons grated lemon rind
- 1 teaspoon vanilla extract
- ⅔ cup heavy cream
- 4 large eggs

THE SOUR CREAM TOPPING:

- 1 cup sour cream
- 2 tablespoons sugar
- ½ teaspoon vanilla extract

Great Cakes

1. Position rack in the lower third of the oven and preheat to 350°. Butter an 8″ × 12″ × 2″ oblong ovenproof glass dish.

2. To make the crust: Place the flour, sugar, and salt into the bowl of a food processor fitted with the steel blade. Pulse 3 to 4 times. Add the butter, then process 10 seconds, or until fine crumbs form.

3. In a small bowl, beat the egg lightly with a fork. Add to the processor, and pulse only until the mixture begins to form a ball. Remove and shape the dough into a flat rectangle. Wrap in waxed paper and chill for 10 minutes.

4. Press the dough evenly over the bottom of the ovenproof glass dish. In the preheated oven, bake 16 to 18 minutes, or until the edges begin to brown. Remove the crust from oven and set aside.

5. While the crust is baking, prepare the pineapple filling: Drain the pineapple well, reserving ½ cup of the juice. In a medium-size saucepan, combine the sugar and cornstarch. Blend in the pineapple juice and drained pineapple. Bring to a slow boil and cook, stirring constantly, until the mixture thickens. Remove from the heat and stir in the lemon juice. Set aside to cool 5 minutes.

6. Spoon the pineapple filling over the crust, spreading it evenly with the back of a spoon. Set aside.

7. To make the cheese filling: Press the cheeses through a food mill or a colander into a large mixing bowl. Stir in *½ cup* sugar, flour, lemon rind, and vanilla, blending well. Slowly pour in the heavy cream.

8. Place the eggs in the container of a food processor fitted with the steel blade. Process 1 minute. With the machine running, pour remaining *¼ cup* sugar through feeder tube and process 1 minute longer. Stop the machine and add the cheese mixture, ½ at a time if container is small. Pulse 3 or 4 times just to blend. *Do not overprocess.*

9. Pour the cheese mixture over the pineapple filling. In the preheated oven, bake for 30 minutes.

10. Turn off the heat and prop the oven door open with the handle of a wooden spoon. Continue to cool in the oven for 1 hour. Remove from the oven and cool for ½ hour on a rack while you prepare the topping. The cake will sink slightly as it cools.

11. Preheat the oven to 400°.

12. Put the sour cream in a medium-size bowl. Whisk in the sugar and vanilla. Spread on the top of the cheesecake, leaving a ¼-

inch margin of cheese filling showing around edge. In the pre-heated oven, bake 8 to 10 minutes. Serve slightly warm.

STORAGE: Refrigerate, covered loosely with aluminum foil, for up to 4 days.

🔖 PROMENADE CHEESECAKE

This is one of my favorite cheesecake recipes. It's my rendition of one that was served at the Promenade Cafe, which overlooked the skating rink at Rockefeller Center in New York City. This recipe, which has been in my collection for years, was the first that I had ever made using a bain-marie, a method of baking cheesecakes that has become increasingly popular in recent years.

I like to bake this cake in a porcelain soufflé dish lightly coated with graham cracker crumbs, and serve it bottom side up. The crumbs give the cake an attractive golden brown finish, but they may be omitted if you like. Either way, this cheesecake is outstanding, especially when served with a topping of Marinated Tropical Fruits (page 481).

(page 481)

THE CRUMB COATING:
  3 double graham crackers
  1 tablespoon unsalted butter, melted

THE FILLING:
  2   pounds cream cheese, at room temperature
  1⅓ cups sugar
  1   teaspoon freshly grated lemon rind
  2   tablespoons lemon juice
  1   teaspoon vanilla extract
  4   large eggs

▽

AT A GLANCE

SERVES: 8 to 10
PAN: 8″ soufflé dish (2-quart capacity)
PAN PREP: Heavily buttered/bain-marie
OVEN TEMP: 325°
RACK LEVEL: Lower third
BAKING TIME: 1 hour, plus an additional ½ hour for oven cooling
METHOD: Electric mixer/food processor

Great Cakes

1. To make the crumb coating: Generously butter a 2-quart soufflé dish. Break the graham crackers into a food processor fitted with a steel blade. Pulse until you get fine crumbs. Add the melted butter, pulsing just to blend. Empty the contents into the prepared pan and press the crumbs onto the sides and bottom. Refrigerate while preparing the filling.
2. Position the rack in the lower third of the oven and preheat to 325°.
3. To make the filling: Place cream cheese, sugar, rind, lemon juice, and vanilla into the large bowl of an electric mixer fitted with beaters or paddle attachment. Mix on low speed for 1 minute, or until the cheese is smooth and all of the ingredients are well blended. Scrape the sides of the bowl occasionally.
4. Add the eggs, 1 at a time every 30 seconds, scraping the sides of the bowl as necessary. Mix until the batter is very smooth but *do not overbeat.*
5. Pour the batter into the prepared dish. Place the soufflé dish inside a larger pan and set both pans in the oven. To make the bain-marie (waterbath), pour very hot water into the larger pan up to a level of 1 inch. Bake in the preheated oven for 1 hour. Then turn off the heat and let the cake stand in the oven for an additional ½ hour. Remove from the oven and set the soufflé dish on a cake rack to cool to room temperature. When the cake is completely cool, run a thin knife around the edge of the dish to loosen the sides and invert onto a serving platter. If the cake does not release immediately, dip the soufflé dish into hot water for a few minutes to warm up the bottom. Invert the cake again and gently shake the dish to release the cake. Serve accompanied with Marinated Tropical Fruits if you like.

STORAGE: Refrigerate, covered with aluminum foil, for up to 1 week.

🌰 PRALINE CHEESECAKE

AT A GLANCE

SERVES: 10 to 12
PAN: 9″ springform
PAN PREP: Heavily
buttered/parchment
disk/bain-marie
OVEN TEMP: 325°
RACK LEVEL: Lower
third
BAKING TIME: 70
minutes, plus an
additional 1 hour
for oven cooling
METHOD: Food
processor

Here a delicious mixture of chopped toasted pecans and brown sugar bakes on the bottom of the cake to become a terrific crunchy topping when the cake is inverted.

When peaches are in season, this cheesecake is sensational served with Brandy Peach Topping (page 483). Or try Spiked Honey Bell Orange Topping (page 485), or just sliced fresh peaches or navel orange sections.

1½   cups toasted pecans
2   zwieback crackers, broken into pieces
1¼   cups light brown sugar, lightly packed, divided
¼   cup (½ stick) unsalted butter, melted
2   pounds cream cheese, at room temperature
⅓   cup granulated sugar
4   large eggs
1   cup sour cream
1½   teaspoons vanilla extract
½   teaspoon maple extract
1   teaspoon freshly grated lemon rind
1   teaspoon freshly grated navel orange rind

1. Position rack in the lower third of the oven and preheat to 325°. Generously butter a 9-inch springform pan and line the bottom with a parchment circle. Butter the parchment.

2. Put the pecans, zwieback, and *¼ cup* of light brown sugar in the bowl of a food processor fitted with the steel blade. Process until the nuts are ground medium-fine. Stop the machine and pour in the melted butter, then pulse just to combine. Empty the crumb mixture into the prepared pan. Press the nut mixture thickly up the sides with the back of a spoon, making a 1½- to 2-inch border. Use a glass to press the remaining nut mixture onto the bottom of the pan, being sure to press into the corners of the pan to get an even layer. Refrigerate the pan while you prepare the filling.

3. Wash and dry the processor bowl and steel blade. Place the cream cheese, the remaining *1 cup* of light brown sugar, and the white

sugar into the processor container and process with the steel blade for 30 seconds. Scrape the bowl and process 10 seconds longer. Add the eggs 1 at a time through the feeder tube and process for 10 seconds longer. Stop the machine.

4. Add the sour cream, extracts, and rinds. Process for 10 seconds longer. *Do not overprocess.* Pour into the prepared pan.

5. Cut an 18-inch square of heavy-duty aluminum foil and set the pan on the foil. Bring the edges of the foil up and mold it around the pan.

6. Place a larger and wider shallow pan onto the oven shelf and set the foil-lined pan into it. Fill the larger pan with 1 inch of boiling water. Bake the cake in the preheated oven for 70 minutes.

7. Turn the oven off and prop the door open with the handle of a wooden spoon. Cool the cheesecake in the oven for an additional hour. Remove the cake, still wrapped in aluminum foil, from the oven and set the cake on a rack to cool completely. When the cake is cool, change the aluminum foil to a clean piece, as it will be oily. Refrigerate the cake for 4 to 6 hours or overnight.

8. To unmold the cake: Dip a sharp, thin-bladed knife into hot water and run the knife around the edge of the pan to loosen the crust. Remove the side of the springform pan and invert the cheesecake onto a cake plate. Carefully ease the metal disk off the cake, using the tip of a sharp knife, and remove the parchment. If any of the nut crust sticks to the parchment, scrape it off with a metal spatula and press onto the cake. Dipping the spatula into hot water will help to smooth the surface. Refrigerate, covered with aluminum foil. Remove the cake from the refrigerator 1 hour before serving. When ready to serve, dust the top lightly with confectioners' sugar.

STORAGE: Refrigerate, covered with aluminum foil, for up to 1 week.

🌱 CHOCOLATE MARBLE CHEESECAKE

Marbleizing a cheesecake batter is fun. You may also experiment with patterns. Try alternating patches of vanilla and chocolate batter instead of the typical swirled effect. For best results, the batter should be very thick. Do not make this in a food processor as it overthins the batter so that it will not hold its design.

For hard-core chocophiles, this recipe is easily turned into a fabulous chocolate cheesecake. See the variation recipe on page 365.

See the variation recipe on page 365.

AT A GLANCE

SERVES: 10 to 12
PAN: 9″ springform
PAN PREP: Butter/
bain-marie
OVEN TEMP: 325°
RACK LEVEL: Lower
third
BAKING TIME: 1 hour,
plus 1 additional
hour to cool in
oven
METHOD: Electric
mixer

3	ounces imported bittersweet chocolate, such as Lindt Courante, Tobler, or Poulain
1	ounce unsweetened chocolate
1/2	cup heavy cream
1	teaspoon coffee zest (page 58)
2	pounds cream cheese, at room temperature
1 1/3	cups sugar
4	large eggs
1	cup sour cream
1 1/2	teaspoons vanilla extract

1. Position rack in lower third of the oven and preheat to 325°. Butter a 9-inch springform pan.

2. Break the chocolates into pieces and place in a small heatproof bowl. Set bowl in a pan of shallow simmering water and stir until melted, or melt in a microwave at medium setting. Blend in the cream. Add the coffee zest and stir until smooth. Set aside.

3. Place the cream cheese in the large bowl of an electric mixer fitted with beaters or the paddle attachment. Mix on medium speed for 30 to 45 seconds, until smooth and creamy.

4. Add the sugar in a steady stream, taking about 45 to 60 seconds. Scrape the sides of the bowl as necessary. Mix for 1 minute longer.

5. Reduce mixer speed to medium-low. Add the eggs, 1 at a time at 30-second intervals, mixing well after each addition. Add the sour cream and vanilla and mix for 30 seconds longer. Scrape the sides of bowl again.

6. Measure out 2 cups of the batter and transfer to a separate bowl. Add to it the chocolate mixture, stirring until thoroughly blended.

7. To marbleize the batter: Spoon ¼ of the vanilla batter over the bottom of the pan. Then, working from the edges to the center, circle the pan with alternating spoonfuls of chocolate and vanilla batters. Reserve ¼ of the vanilla batter and ½ cup of the chocolate batter to finish off the top. To complete the top, smooth on the reserved vanilla batter, working from the edges to the center, then dab on the remaining chocolate batter at random. Insert the handle of a wooden spoon into the batter and gently swirl around the pan to create an attractive marbleized surface. Center the pan on an 18-inch square of heavy-duty aluminum foil and mold the foil around the sides of the pan.

8. Select a pan large enough to allow at least 1 inch of water to circulate around the batter-filled pan. A shallow stainless steel roasting pan or a disposable aluminum foil roasting pan measuring about 12″ × 17½″ × 2″ is ideal. Pull out the oven rack to its full extension and set the empty pan on the rack. Place the batter-filled pan in the larger pan. Using a kettle or a 1-quart measuring cup, carefully pour very hot water into the larger pan to a level of about 1 inch. Gently ease the rack holding the pans into the preheated oven and bake for 1 hour.

9. Turn off the heat and prop the oven door open with the handle of a wooden spoon. Leave cake undisturbed for an additional hour. Remove the cake from the oven, discard the foil, and set the pan on a cake rack to cool completely. Refrigerate the cooled cake at least 24 hours before serving. To unmold the cake, run a thin knife around the edge of the pan and carefully remove the rim. Place the cheesecake on a cake platter. Let the cake stand at room temperature until ready to slice.

STORAGE: Refrigerate, covered with an aluminum foil tent, for up to 1 week.

VARIATION

CHOCOLATE CHEESECAKE

1. Increase the bittersweet chocolate to 6 ounces, the heavy cream to 1 cup, the coffee zest to 2 teaspoons, and the sugar to 1½ cups.
2. At Step 6, add the chocolate mixture to the vanilla batter, stirring until thoroughly blended. Omit marbling and proceed with recipe.

❦ BLACK BOTTOM MINT CHEESECAKE

Here cream cheese batter is flavored with Vandermint liqueur and baked in a candy-coated chocolate wafer crumb crust. When the cake is unmolded from the pan, the dark chocolate crust forms a beautiful contrast to the pale creamy top. Chocolate crème de menthe wafers inserted at angles around the edge of the cake make a dynamite presentation. (The classic procedure would be to prepare chocolate triangles from scratch; however, these candies offer a quick and tasty substitute.) This is one recipe that makes even a novice look like a real pro.

AT A GLANCE

SERVES: 10 to 12
PAN: 9″ springform
PAN PREP: Heavily buttered
OVEN TEMP: 325°
RACK LEVEL: Lower third
BAKING TIME: 50 minutes, plus an additional hour for oven cooling
METHOD: Electric mixer/food processor

THE CRUMB CRUST:
    One   9-ounce box chocolate wafers
    ⅓   cup (⅔ stick) unsalted butter, melted and cooled

THE FILLING:
    1   cup mint chocolate chips
    3   tablespoons water
    1½ to 2   tablespoons Vandermint liqueur
    1½   pounds cream cheese, at room temperature
    1   cup sugar
    4   large eggs
    2   teaspoons vanilla extract
    2   cups sour cream

    16   Andes Daydreams Crème de Menthe wafers by Suchard, for garnish

1. To make the crust: Generously butter a 9-inch springform pan. Break the chocolate wafers into a food processor fitted with the steel blade. Pulse until you have fine crumbs. Add the melted butter, pulsing just to blend. Empty contents into the pan and press the crumbs onto the sides with the back of a spoon, making a 1½- to 2-inch border. Use a flat-bottomed glass to press the remaining crumbs onto the bottom of the pan, being sure to press firmly into the sides. Refrigerate while you prepare the filling.

2. Position rack in the lower third of the oven and preheat to 325°.

3. To make the filling: Place chocolate chips and water in a small heat-proof bowl. Set the bowl in a pan of simmering water and stir until melted, or melt in a microwave on medium setting. Blend in the liqueur. Spoon the chocolate over the cooled crust, spreading it evenly with the back of a spoon. Set aside.

4. Put the cream cheese in the large bowl of an electric mixer fitted with beaters or paddle attachment. Mix for 30 to 45 seconds on medium speed, until smooth and creamy.

5. Add the sugar in a steady stream, taking about 30 to 45 seconds. Scrape the sides of the bowl as necessary. Mix 1 minute longer or until very smooth.

6. Reduce mixer speed to medium-low. Add the eggs, 1 at a time at 30-second intervals, mixing well after each addition. Add the vanilla and sour cream and blend for 30 seconds longer, scraping the sides of the bowl again as necessary.

7. Pour the cheese filling over the chocolate, starting around the sides, then filling in the middle. Smooth surface with the back of a spoon. Be careful not to disturb the crumb crust. Bake in the preheated oven for 50 minutes.

8. Turn off the heat and *without opening* the oven door, leave the cake in the oven for an additional hour. Remove from oven. Set on a cake rack to cool 3 hours or longer. Refrigerate at least 24 hours before serving.

TO SERVE: About 1 hour before you are ready to serve, run a thin knife around the edge of the pan and carefully remove the rim. Transfer the cheesecake to a cake platter and if you wish, garnish as follows.

Imagine that the surface of the cake is the face of a clock. Starting at 12 o'clock, press the long side of the candy gently against the cake. Push the inner end of the mint all the way into the cake so that the edge is completely flush with the surface, while the outer end of the mint is standing high. The mint will form an elongated triangle. Continue with 3 more mints, inserting them at 3, 6, and 9 o'clock. Then insert the remaining mints evenly around the top of the cake. Leave the cake at room temperature until ready to serve.

STORAGE: Refrigerate, covered with aluminum foil, for up to 1 week.

EUROPEAN TORTES and GATEAUX

These luxurious cakes are finished with mirrorlike glazes, rolled fondants, marzipan, and smooth buttercreams. Most seem more elegant than American-style party cakes.

Tortes are commonly Middle European, coming from such countries as Austria, Germany, and Hungary. In Austria and Germany they are called torten, and in Hungary, torta. They often contain whole or puréed dried fruits, fresh fruits, poppy seeds, and liqueurs. Because these ingredients contain a lot of moisture, the cakes mellow with age and are frequently better when eaten at least a day or two after baking. They are generally richer than American-style cakes, and tight-grained.

Gateaux, the French versions, are lighter in texture than tortes and are made primarily of a sponge-style cake called a genoise. A genoise contains little or no butter but, like a torte, is made with a large quantity of eggs and no chemical leavening.

Gateaux are generally assembled from several components, starting with genoise split into thin layers. The layers are saturated with liqueur syrup, filled with mousses, and covered with fruit glazes and buttercreams or other finishes. They can be garnished with chocolate curls, candies, crumbs, nuts, fruits, silver or gold dragées, and so on.

Tortes and gateaux are sometimes constructed from the same type of cake, such as a genoise. If this is the case, whether the cake is called a torte or a gateau depends on the country of origin. For example, if the French strawberry gateau were prepared in Vienna, it would be called a strawberry torte.

When making tortes or gateaux, it is wise to plan ahead, because some have many steps. Since these cakes freeze beautifully, you can make them up as the spirit moves you and freeze whole or split layers for future use. When you have a variety of different genoise layers on hand, you can mix them creatively. Liqueur syrups and fruit glazes will keep for weeks in the refrigerator. Since buttercreams also freeze quite well, you can whip up a professional-looking cake on very short notice.

The recipes in this section have been tailored for time and ease of preparation. I have attempted to keep them simple while maintaining their authenticity. I have provided quite detailed instructions for making genoise, as these cakes take a certain amount of skill to prepare.

This chapter is a roundup of grand selections for international tastes. Actually, your most difficult task will be trying to decide which one to make first.

BEFORE YOU BEGIN . . .

▶ Genoise batters deflate very quickly; therefore it is essential to have all your ingredients and utensils ready before you start.

▶ Baking pans must be more heavily buttered for genoise than for regular cake batters, as genoise batter can easily stick to the pan.

▶ Do not attempt to increase the base recipe for a genoise because the bowls of most standard-size electric mixers do not have the capacity for the increased volume.

▶ For a genoise, the eggs and sugar are combined and then heated to dissolve the sugar. The easiest way to do this is in the mixer bowl elevated over a saucepan slightly smaller than the bottom of the bowl, to keep the bottom of the bowl from touching the water. If the base of the bowl does touch the water, watch the mixture carefully and keep it in constant motion to prevent it from becoming too hot.

▶ First beat the egg/sugar mixture on medium-high speed to create a foam that triples in volume, then reduce the mixer speed to medium to stabilize the foam.

▶ Since you must work quickly when making a genoise, do not use a triple sifter for sifting flour into the batter. Use a single-mesh sifter or strainer instead; it's faster. Adding the flour too slowly can cause the egg/sugar foam to deflate.

▶ When folding flour into a genoise batter, be sure to use a 2³/₄-inch-wide rubber spatula. If you don't have one, fold using your cupped hand. Smaller spatulas are not satisfactory; they cover less surface and will quickly deflate the batter.

▶ When clarifying butter for a genoise, bear in mind that the flavor of the butter will vary according to the method of clarification. With the quick microwave method (page 43), the butter has a yellow color and a mild buttery taste. Using the longer method over direct heat (page 43), the butter turns golden and has a more intense flavor. If you cook the butter until it browns, the flavor will be even more intense and the batter will have a delicious browned butter taste.

▶ The temperature of the clarified butter should be between 100° and 110° when it is added to the batter. If the butter is too hot, it will immediately sink to the bottom of the bowl, making incorporation difficult. If it is too cold, the butter will not distribute evenly throughout the egg/sugar foam.

▶ Use a container with a pouring spout to add the butter to the batter. A glass measuring cup is ideal. If the container has no spout, the butter pours too quickly, giving you less control when distributing it over the batter.

▶ To help prevent the clarified butter from sinking to the bottom of the bowl, reserve a small amount of flour from the base recipe. When almost all the butter has been added, immediately sprinkle the remaining flour over the batter. As this flour is folded through the batter with the butter, it will help to keep the butter more evenly dispersed.

▶ To avoid oily streaks in the batter, be sure to sweep the spatula all the way to the bottom of the bowl as you fold the butter and flour together. Since the fat is liquid and heavy, it sinks quickly.

▶ Do not scrape any melted butter that has settled at the bottom of the mixing bowl into the cake pan. This residue will retard the parts of the cake it touches from rising.

▶ Unlike other types of cakes, genoises should always be baked until completely released from the sides of the pan.

▶ You may invert the baked genoise onto a cake rack or onto baking parchment lightly dusted with granulated sugar. The sugar method is best for short-term cooling; do not leave the cake on the sugar for hours or the sugar will melt and the cake will stick to the paper.

▶ Plain genoise cakes freeze very well (page 77) except for thin versions, such as those baked in a jelly roll pan. Do not freeze a thin genoise unless you can leave it in the pan; it is easily damaged unless well protected.

▶ Tortes or gateaux are usually placed on a cardboard disk before frosting for easier handling. These disks are available at many party or stationery shops, bakery supply houses, and from mail order sources (page 531), or you can make your own. To anchor the cake, either dab light corn syrup in several places around the disk or spread the disk with a 2-inch strip of frosting. Then press the layer on top. For further information, see pages 500–502.

▶ Genoise layers are always saturated with sugar or liqueur syrup to moisten the crumb. The best way to apply the syrup is to *dab* it onto the cut surface of the cake with a pastry brush about 1¼ inches wide. Do not brush the surface or too many crumbs will be loosened.

▶ An average genoise will absorb as much as 1 cup of syrup. This makes the sides of the cake swell, so it is necessary to trim them with a sharp knife if you want sides to be straight. Chill the genoise before cutting to prevent tearing.

▶ Gateaux or tortes that are finished with a smooth icing

such as a chocolate ganache or fondant are often coated with a thin apricot or other jam glaze on the surface in preparation for the final frosting. The glaze acts as a seal to allow for a smoother finish.

▶ Many gateaux and tortes are refrigerated for 3 to 4 hours to set. This standing time makes the cake easier to cut. However, when a cake is too cold, the flavor is impaired, so it is best to bring the cake back almost to room temperature before serving. Depending on weather and room temperature, this can take up to 3 hours for a whole cake frosted with buttercream. A cake coated with whipped cream will have to stand only from $1/2$ to 1 hour. In any event, while gateaux and tortes may be served a few hours after making, most are best if allowed to mature 24 hours.

🌿 CLASSIC GENOISE

....

lassic genoise is the foundation on which a variety of exciting past- ries are created. The clarified butter imparts a mellow flavor that gives this European-style sponge its distinctive taste.

....

BATTER WILL FILL:
9″ × 3″ round
10″ × 2″ round
Two 9″ × 1½″ layers
10-cup ring
10½″ × 15½″ × 1″, thick
  sheet cake
11″ × 17″ × 1″, thin sheet
  cake

BAKING TIME:
35 to 40 minutes
30 to 35 minutes
20 to 25 minutes
30 to 35 minutes
20 to 25 minutes

18 to 20 minutes

▽..

AT A GLANCE

SERVES: 10 to 12
PAN PREP: Very well
greased/flour
OVEN TEMP: 350°
RACK LEVEL: Lower
third
METHOD: Electric
mixer

....

5	large eggs (1 to 1¼ cups)
⅔	cup sugar
1½	teaspoons vanilla extract
½	teaspoon fresh grated lemon rind
3	tablespoons warm (100° to 110°) clarified butter
1	cup plus 2 tablespoons sifted cake flour

1. Position rack in the lower third of the oven and preheat to 350°. *Generously* grease the selected cake pan and lightly dust with all-purpose flour.

2. Select a saucepan that will suspend the large bowl of an electric mixer at least 2 inches above the pan's bottom. Fill the pan with 2 inches of water, bring to a boil, reduce heat, and maintain at a simmer.

3. Put the eggs in the mixing bowl. Whisk in the sugar, mixing briefly just to blend. Do not beat. Place the bowl over the simmering water and slowly stir continuously for about 3 to 5 minutes until:
   a. color darkens to a deep gold;
   b. the mixture is runny when allowed to flow from the whisk;
   c. the sugar is completely dissolved when rubbed between two fingers;
   d. the temperature is quite warm, between 110° and 120°.
   Alternatively, set the bowl directly into a 10-inch skillet filled

*Special
Occasion
Cakes*

with 1 inch of simmering water and proceed as above, watching carefully to prevent overheating.

4. Remove the bowl from the pan and dry the bottom. Fit an electric mixer with the beaters or whip attachment and beat the egg mixture on medium-high speed until cool, about 4 to 5 minutes. The mixture should triple in volume and become thick and light in color. To test, run your finger across the egg foam; it should leave a canal that holds its shape.

5. Reduce the mixer speed to medium. Add the vanilla and grated lemon rind. Whip 2 to 3 minutes longer to stabilize the eggs. Do not overbeat or the mixture will begin to deflate.

6. Remove the bowl from the mixer. Place the warm butter in a measuring cup for liquids, or any other container with a spout. Put the flour in a large fine strainer or single-mesh sifter and sprinkle it over the egg mixture 2 to 3 tablespoons at a time. Fold the flour in, using a 2¾-inch-wide rubber spatula, taking 10 to 12 turns, and making sure to reach the bottom of the bowl as you fold. Do not worry about incorporating all the flour until the last addition since too much handling will deflate the batter. Add the flour quickly, in about 5 to 6 additions.

7. Before the last addition of flour, quickly pour the warm butter in a steady stream over the batter. *Immediately* sprinkle in the remaining flour, folding it in with about 12 to 15 turns. This entire procedure should be done in 15 to 20 seconds.

8. Using the rubber spatula, *immediately* push the batter into the prepared pan. If any butter has collected on the bottom of the bowl, *do not* add it to the batter in the pan or it will retard the rising of the cake.

9. Tap the pan on the counter to remove air bubbles and quickly place in the preheated oven. Bake according to the time appropriate to the pan you have chosen. Cake is done when it is golden brown on top, springy to the touch, and has completely come away from the sides of the pan.

10. Remove the cake from the oven and let stand 10 minutes. Invert onto a cake rack sprayed with nonstick coating, remove the pan, and cool cake completely. If the cake sticks, run a thin, sharp knife around the side of the pan to loosen.

STORAGE: If you won't be using the cake immediately, wrap it in plastic wrap and place inside a plastic bag, secure well, and refrigerate for up to 3 days. For longer storage, freeze (page 77).

❧ CHOCOLATE GENOISE

Dutch-process cocoa is used for this chocolate genoise. Baking soda acts not as a leavener, but to give the cake its depth of color. Chocolate genoise, except for sheet cake versions, requires a slightly longer baking time than a cake without chocolate.

▽
AT A GLANCE

SERVES: 10 to 12
OVEN TEMP: 350°
PAN PREP: Very well greased/flour
RACK LEVEL: Lower third
METHOD: Electric mixer

BATTER WILL FILL:	BAKING TIME:
9″ × 3″ round	40 to 45 minutes
10″ × 2″ round	35 to 40 minutes
Two 9″ × 1½″ layers	25 to 30- minutes
10-cup ring	35 to 40 minutes
10½″ × 15½″ × 1″, thick sheet cake	20 to 25 minutes
11″ × 17″ × 1″, thin sheet cake	18 to 20 minutes

- ¾ cup strained cake flour
- ⅓ cup strained dutch-process cocoa
- ⅛ teaspoon baking soda
- 5 large whole eggs (1 to 1¼ cups)
- 2 large egg yolks
- ¾ cup plus 2 tablespoons sugar
- 2 teaspoons vanilla extract
- ¼ cup warm (100° to 110°) clarified butter

1. Position rack in the lower third of the oven and preheat to 350°. *Generously* butter the selected pan and dust with all-purpose flour.
2. Strain the cake flour, cocoa, and baking soda together 4 times. Set aside.
3. Select a saucepan that will suspend the large bowl of an electric mixer at least 2 inches above the pan's bottom. Fill the pan with 2 inches of water, bring to a boil, reduce heat, and maintain a simmer.
4. Put the whole eggs and yolks in the mixing bowl. Whisk in the sugar, mixing briefly just to blend. *Do not beat.* Place the bowl over the simmering water and stir slowly and continuously 3 to 5 minutes until:

Special Occasion Cakes

375

a. the color darkens to a deep gold;

b. the mixture is runny when allowed to flow from the whisk;

c. the sugar is completely melted when rubbed between two fingers;

d. the temperature is quite warm, between 110° and 120°.

Alternatively, set the bowl directly into a 10-inch skillet filled with 1 inch of simmering water and proceed as above, watching carefully to prevent overheating. Either procedure should take from 3 to 5 minutes.

5. Remove the bowl from the saucepan and dry the bottom. Fit an electric mixer with the beaters or whip attachment and whip the egg mixture on medium-high speed until cool, about 4 to 5 minutes. Mixture should triple in volume and be thick and light in color. To test, run your finger across the egg foam; it should leave a canal that holds its shape.

6. Reduce the mixer speed to medium and add the vanilla. Whip 2 to 3 minutes longer to stabilize the eggs. Do not overbeat or the mixture will begin to deflate.

7. Remove the bowl from the mixer. Pour the warm butter into a measuring cup for liquids or any other container with a spout. Place the cocoa and flour in a strainer and sprinkle it over the egg mixture 2 to 3 tablespoons at a time. Fold it in using a 2³/₄-inch-wide rubber spatula, taking about 10 to 12 turns and making sure to reach to the bottom of the bowl as you fold. Do not worry about incorporating all the flour until the last addition, as too much handling will deflate the batter. The flour should be added quickly in about 5 to 6 additions.

8. Before the last addition of cocoa/flour, quickly pour the warm butter in a steady stream over the batter. *Immediately* sprinkle in the remaining cocoa/flour mixture. Fold into the batter, taking about 12 to 15 turns. This entire procedure should be done in 15 to 20 seconds.

9. Using the rubber spatula, *immediately* push batter into prepared pan. Leave any butter that has collected on the bottom of the bowl. *Do not* add it to the pan or it will retard the rising of the cake.

10. Tap the pan on the counter to remove air bubbles and quickly place the pan in the preheated oven. Bake according to the time indicated for the pan you are using. Cake is done when it is springy to the touch and has completely come away from the

sides of pan. While the cake is baking, coat a fine-mesh cake rack with Pam or another nonstick cooking spray.

11. Remove the cake from oven and let stand 10 minutes. Run a thin sharp knife around edge of the pan to release and invert onto a cake rack sprayed with nonstick coating, remove the pan, and let cake cool completely. If the cake sticks, run a thin, sharp knife around the side of the pan to loosen.

STORAGE: If you won't be using the cake immediately, cover it with plastic wrap and place inside a plastic bag. Secure well and refrigerate for up to 3 days. For longer storage, freeze (page 77).

🌿 FILBERT GENOISE

AT A GLANCE

SERVES: 10 to 12
PAN: 10″ × 2″ round
PAN PREP: Very well greased/flour
OVEN: 350°
BAKING TIME: 30 to 35 minutes
RACK LEVEL: Lower third
METHOD: Electric mixer/food processor

This is an adaptation of a recipe taught to me by my friend and teacher, Chef Albert Kumin of the Pastry Arts Center in Elmsford, New York. Albert, who shares his extraordinary knowledge so generously, is the eminent dean of pâtisserie.

The method for preparing this batter differs from the classic genoise because of the large amount of nuts it contains. Rather than beating the whole eggs and the sugar together, you separate the eggs. The yolks are beaten with part of the sugar and the whites are stabilized with more sugar, then beaten into the yolk mixture. This forms a strong framework to support the weight of the nut/flour. The filberts must be ground to a powdery nut meal; you may do this in a food processor.

This is my favorite of all genoise cakes. After you taste it, you'll know why!

1½	cups toasted skinned hazelnuts (page 58)
⅔	cup unsifted cake flour
2	tablespoons cornstarch
7	large egg yolks
1	cup superfine sugar, divided
1	teaspoon vanilla extract
½	teaspoon grated lemon rind
5	large egg whites
¼	cup warm (100° to 110°) clarified butter

1. Position rack in the lower third of the oven and preheat to 350°. Generously grease a 10″ × 2″ round cake pan and dust with all-purpose flour.

2. Place the nuts, cake flour, and cornstarch in the container of a food processor fitted with a steel blade. Process for 30 seconds, then pulse 10 times, until very fine and powdery. The nuts are ready when they begin to cake or clump together around the sides of the bowl. If any large pieces remain, pulse further, but watch carefully to avoid overprocessing. Set aside.

3. Put the yolks in the small bowl of an electric mixer fitted with the beaters or whip attachment. Beat on medium-high speed 3 to 4 minutes or until thick and light in color. Add ¾ *cup* of sugar,

1 tablespoon at a time, taking about 3 to 4 minutes. Mixture should be ribbony. Blend in the vanilla and grated lemon rind, remove from mixer, and set aside.

4. Place the whites in the large bowl of an electric mixer and whip on medium speed until they form soft peaks. Increase speed to medium-high and add the remaining $1/4$ *cup* sugar over about 15 seconds. Whip 30 seconds longer.

5. Add the yolk mixture and whip 1 minute longer. Remove the bowl from the mixer. Pour the warm butter into a measuring cup for liquids or any other container with a spout. Put the nut meal in a coarse-mesh strainer* and sprinkle it in about 2 tablespoons at a time, folding with a 2¾-inch-wide rubber spatula. It will take 40 turns. Be sure to reach deep into the bottom of the bowl as you fold and work quickly, as too much handling will deflate the batter.

6. When 2 tablespoons of nut meal remain, quickly pour the warm butter in a steady stream over the batter. Quickly fold in the remaining nut meal, taking 10 to 15 turns. Discard any large pieces of nuts from the strainer.

7. Immediately push batter, using the rubber spatula, into the prepared pan and smooth the surface with the back of a spoon. If any butter has collected on the bottom of the bowl, *do not* add to the batter in the bowl or it will retard the rising of the cake.

8. Tap the pan on the counter to remove air bubbles and place the cake in the preheated oven and bake 30 to 35 minutes. The cake is done when it is springy to the touch and completely leaves sides of pan.

9. Remove the cake from the oven and let stand 5 minutes. Invert onto a cake rack sprayed with nonstick coating, remove the pan, and let cake cool completely.

STORAGE: If you will not be using the cake immediately, wrap it in plastic wrap, place it inside a plastic bag, secure well, and refrigerate for up to 3 days. If the cake is to be frozen, see page 77.

---

*If you do not own a strainer with large holes, sprinkle the nut meal over the batter with your hand, working as quickly as you can.

🌾 STREUSEL LEMON TORTE

▽
AT A GLANCE

SERVES: 10 to 12
PAN: 10-cup savarin
or fluted ring for
the buttersponge; 9-
inch layer for the
streusel
OVEN TEMP: 350°

I created this several years ago for a brunch course I was teaching. It was such a hit that I have since used it for my most elegant dinner parties.

This cake is most attractive when the genoise is baked in a large savarin ring mold. However, a fluted ring may be used instead. The advantage of the savarin mold is that it has a wide opening that can be filled with fresh strawberries.

1   Classic Genoise (page 373), baked in a 10-cup savarin or fluted ring mold

THE LEMON CREAM FILLING:
1   cup sugar
1/3   cup cornstarch
1/8   teaspoon salt
2/3   cup water
2/3   cup orange juice
4   large egg yolks
1 1/2 teaspoons grated lemon rind
1/4   cup freshly squeezed lemon juice
2   tablespoons soft unsalted butter
1   tablespoon Grand Marnier
1/2   cup heavy cream

THE COOKIE STREUSEL:
1/4   cup sugar
2/3   cup unsifted all-purpose flour
3   tablespoons finely chopped almonds
1/4   cup (1/2 stick) unsalted butter, melted

1/2   recipe Sugar Syrup made with Grand Marnier (page 467)
1   pint large unhulled strawberries, rinsed and well dried

1. To make the filling: Combine the sugar, cornstarch, and salt in a small heavy saucepan. Whisk in the water and orange juice,

blending until the dry ingredients are completely dissolved. Cook over medium heat, stirring continuously until the mixture comes to a boil and thickens. Simmer for a few moments. Remove from the heat to cool slightly.

2. Put the egg yolks in a small bowl and whisk lightly. Stir a small amount of the hot sugar/cornstarch mixture into yolks to temper them. Then whisk the yolk mixture back into the sugar/cornstarch mixture, blending well. Cook over low heat, stirring slowly with a wooden spoon, until filling comes to a full boil and is smooth and thick.

3. Remove from the heat and blend in the grated lemon rind, lemon juice, and butter. Transfer into a medium-sized bowl. Press a piece of buttered waxed paper directly onto the surface of the filling. Chill until quite cold, about 1 hour.

4. When the filling is chilled, stir in the Grand Marnier. In a medium-sized bowl, whip the heavy cream to soft peaks and fold in 1/2 of the cream, reserving the rest in the refrigerator for the lemon sauce.

5. Chill the filling again for at least 1/2 hour while you make the cookie streusel.

6. To make the cookie streusel: Preheat the oven to 350°. Add the sugar, flour, and nuts to the melted butter. Stir with a kitchen fork until small crumbs form. Take a handful of crumbs and make a fist to form a large clump. Then break each clump into coarse crumbs. Repeat, making several clusters and breaking them until a nice streusel is formed.

7. Place the streusel crumbs in a 9-inch layer pan. Bake in the preheated oven for about 8 to 10 minutes, or until lightly browned and hardened. Toss with a fork occasionally for even toasting. Remove from the oven and set aside to cool.

TO ASSEMBLE THE CAKE:

1. Slice the cake into 3 even layers (page 500). Place the bottom layer on a serving plate. Line the edge of the plate with strips of waxed paper. Brush the layer with warm sugar syrup and spread with the lemon cream to about 1/8-inch thickness. Repeat with the middle layer, moistening it with sugar syrup and covering it with additional filling to the same thickness.

2. Brush the cut side of the top layer with sugar syrup and arrange it on top of the cake, cut side down. Align the layers. Using a small spatula, spread the sides and top with a 1/8-inch coating of

lemon cream. Reserve leftover filling for the sauce. Place the cake in the refrigerator and chill ½ hour.

3. Break up large pieces of streusel and sprinkle the crumbs thickly over the sides and top of the cake, pressing them gently into the lemon cream. Using a sugar shaker, dust the entire cake generously with confectioners' sugar. Carefully remove the waxed paper strips and chill uncovered in the refrigerator for at least 3 to 4 hours to set.

4. To make a lemon sauce for garnish, fold remaining whipped cream into the leftover lemon cream filling. If desired, flavor with an additional tablespoon of Grand Marnier. Chill until ready to serve.

TO SERVE: Remove the cake from the refrigerator 30 to 60 minutes before serving, depending on weather conditions. Fill the center with bright red unhulled strawberries. Or place a spoonful of lemon cream sauce at the side of each slice of the torte and nestle 2 or 3 strawberries into the cream.

STORAGE: Store in the refrigerator, lightly covered with a foil tent, for up to 3 days.

🔥 LE GRAND PETIT FOUR CAKE

Great Cakes

When I think of French pastries, I envision a tray filled with fancy pastries and petits fours in a variety of shapes and flavors, richly laden with all types of wonderful trimmings. This beautiful cake is fashioned after one of those miniature creations.

For a stunning presentation, arrange a nosegay of fresh violets or pansies on top of the cake, off to one side.

One 3½-ounce can shredded coconut, lightly toasted
1 cup walnuts, chopped medium-fine
1 Classic Genoise (page 373), baked in a 10″ × 2″ round layer pan
1 recipe Liqueur Syrup (page 468)
1 large recipe Orange Buttercream (page 459)
Confectioners' sugar, for garnish

1. Spread the toasted coconut in the jelly roll pan, breaking it up gently with your hands. Add the walnuts and toss the coconut and nuts together. Set aside.
2. Divide the cake round into 3 layers (page 500). Place the first layer top side down on a cardboard disk cut slightly smaller than the cake. Brush with 4 to 5 tablespoons of liqueur syrup to moisten well. Spread with ¼ of the orange buttercream, then sprinkle with ⅓ cup of the coconut/nut mixture.
3. Place middle layer over the first, brushing again with liqueur syrup and spreading with another ¼ of the buttercream and ⅓ cup of the nut mixture.
4. Moisten the cut side of the third layer with additional liqueur syrup and turn, cut side down, onto the cake. Press the sides gently to align the layers. Spread the remaining buttercream over the sides and top.
5. Slide your hand underneath the cardboard disk and lift the cake. Hold the cake over the jelly roll pan and gently press a generous coating of the coconut/nut mixture onto the sides and then on top.
6. Put confectioners' sugar in a sugar shaker and sprinkle the sides and top generously. (A sugar shaker is essential here as this is the easiest way to dust the sides successfully.) If you wish, garnish with a nosegay of soft-petaled fresh flowers. Refrigerate uncovered for 3 to 4 hours to allow the cake to set. Remove the cake from the refrigerator up to 3 hours before serving to soften the buttercream.

STORAGE: Store leftover cake in the refrigerator, lightly covered with a foil tent, for up to 5 days.

✿ STRAWBERRY GATEAU

This is a European version of our strawberry shortcake. A genoise layer is heavily coated with whipped cream and halved strawberries. The second layer is thickly covered with whipped cream. Strawberry halves and piped whipped cream shells decorate the top. The sides remain unfrosted to expose the colorful filling. This is a visual masterpiece.

1½	teaspoons unflavored gelatin
3	tablespoons cold water
3	cups heavy cream, well chilled
⅓	cup strained confectioners' sugar
2	tablespoons Grand Marnier
1½	teaspoons vanilla extract
1	Classic Genoise (page 373), baked in a 10″ × 2″ round layer
1	recipe Sugar Syrup (page 467), flavored with Grand Marnier
1	quart medium-sized fresh strawberries, lightly rinsed and dried well on paper toweling

1. Place the cold water in a small ovenproof glass dish and sprinkle in the gelatin. Let stand 5 minutes. Set the dish in a skillet filled with ½ inch of hot water and heat, stirring occasionally, until the gelatin is dissolved and the mixture is clear. Remove from the heat and cool to tepid.
2. Place the chilled cream in the large chilled bowl of an electric mixer fitted with beaters or whip attachment. Beat on medium speed until it begins to thicken. Add the confectioners' sugar, gelatin, liqueur, and vanilla and beat until the cream begins to hold its shape. Finish beating by hand using a wire whisk.

TO ASSEMBLE THE CAKE:

1. Slice the genoise into 3 layers (page 500). Put the first layer top side down on a serving plate. Using a pastry brush, moisten with 3 to 4 tablespoons of sugar syrup. Fit a 14-inch pastry bag with a #4 large open star tube. Fill to ⅓ capacity with the whipped

cream and pipe a shell border (page 517) around the sides of the first layer. Spoon additional whipped cream in the center, level with the shell border. Smooth the surface with an offset metal spatula, being careful not to disturb the decorative border.

2. Hull half the strawberries. Reserve the remainder, stems attached, for garnish. Cut the hulled strawberries in half and arrange the berries on the cream, 1/4 inch from the edge, with the points facing out. Fill in the center with additional cut strawberries. Using the metal spatula, fill in the spaces with a thin layer of whipped cream.

3. Place the middle layer over the filling and brush with sugar syrup. The strawberries on the bottom layer should be visible between the layers. Pipe another shelled border around the sides, then spoon additional cream in the center and smooth the surface, but do not add strawberries. The cream should be about 1/2 inch thick.

4. Moisten the cut side of the third layer of cake with additional sugar syrup and place it, cut side down, on the gateau. Press the sides of the cake gently to align the layers. Fill the pastry bag with the remaining whipped cream and pipe a shell pattern in lines on top of the gateau, making about 8 to 10 strips.

5. Cut the unhulled strawberries in half, and place them cut side up, between the strips of whipped cream. Prop the berries slightly so the stems are up and the tips are pointed down. Refrigerate. Remove the gateau from the refrigerator 30 to 60 minutes before serving, depending upon weather conditions.

STORAGE: Cover the leftover cake lightly with a foil tent and refrigerate up to 3 days.

FILBERT GATEAU WITH PRALINE BUTTERCREAM

This gateau is packed full of chopped filberts. A filbert genoise is filled and frosted with a praline buttercream flavored with filbert paste. The intensely nutty taste of the filberts in the cake and the frosting is simply sensational.

1 Filbert Genoise (page 378), baked in a 10-inch round layer pan
1 recipe Sugar Syrup (page 467), flavored with dark rum
1 recipe Praline Buttercream (page 458)
1/2 cup heavy cream, whipped to soft peak stage (optional)
1 recipe Apricot Glaze (page 467), warmed
1 recipe Ganache Glaze (page 464), prepared just before using
3 tablespoons coarsely chopped toasted filberts, for garnish

TO ASSEMBLE THE CAKE:

1. Cut a cardboard disk slightly smaller than the cake. Divide the cake into 3 layers (page 500). Place the first layer top side down on the disk. Using a pastry brush, moisten the layer with 3 to 4 tablespoons of warm sugar syrup. Measure out 1 cup of the praline buttercream and set aside.

2. Spread the bottom layer with a 1/4-inch thickness of the remaining buttercream. Cover with 1/2 of the whipped cream, leaving a 1/4-inch border around the edge of the cake. Place the middle layer over the first, brushing with the sugar syrup and spreading with praline buttercream. Cover with the remaining whipped cream.

3. Moisten the cut side of the third layer with additional sugar syrup and place cut side down on the cake. Press the sides of the cake gently to align the layers. Put in the refrigerator to chill and set for 1/2 hour.

4. Lift the cake by sliding your open palm under the cardboard disk. Holding a serrated or very sharp knife with an 8-inch blade held parallel to the sides of the cake, trim the sides until they are perfectly straight. Cut a slight bevel at the top to help the glaze

drip over the edge. Brush the top and sides of the cake with warm apricot glaze, sealing the cut areas thoroughly. Chill while you prepare the ganache glaze.

5. Place a rack over a large shallow pan or skillet to catch the drippings. Remove the gateau from the refrigerator and set it on the rack. Have ready a metal spatula with a blade at least 8 to 10 inches long. Hold the saucepan containing the ganache glaze 10 inches above the cake and immediately pour the glaze onto the center. To achieve a smooth, mirrorlike finish, quickly pass the spatula four times over the top of the cake (page 414). (The glaze should cover the top and run down the sides.) Then lift one side of the rack and bring it down with a hard bang. This helps to spread the glaze more evenly. Work quickly before the glaze sets. Patch the bare spots on the sides with a smaller metal spatula, but do not touch the top again, as the glaze firms immediately. Let the cake stand 15 minutes to set after glazing.

6. To garnish the cake, fit a 12- or 14-inch pastry bag with a #114 large leaf tip. Fill with the reserved 1 cup of praline buttercream. Starting 1/2 inch from the outer edge of the cake, position the pastry tube at a 90° angle with the tip almost touching the top of the cake. Apply pressure to the pastry bag, moving it slightly toward the center of the cake. As the buttercream flows onto the cake, reverse the movement backward toward the edge of the cake and finish by pulling the bag again to the center. Stop applying pressure and press the bag downward, then swiftly pull it up to break the flow of frosting. Moving the bag back and forth builds a base of buttercream, which gives height to the top of the leaf. Repeat, making 12 leaves evenly spaced around the surface of the cake.

7. Make a second row of leaves on top of the first row, moving the pastry bag about 3/4 inch closer to the center. The leaves should be overlapping. Then make a third row on top of the second, again moving closer to the center. If space permits, you can make a fourth row (see illustration). However, leave a 2-inch space in the center to garnish with chopped filberts. Refrigerate uncovered for 3 to 4 hours to allow the cake to set. (Leftover buttercream may be frozen for another use.) Remove cake from the refrigerator up to 3 hours before serving.

STORAGE: Refrigerate leftover cake, lightly covered with a foil tent, for up to 5 days.

VIENNESE HAZELNUT TORTE WITH APRICOT BUTTERCREAM

A delectable orange-scented syrup gives this torte a wonderful melt-in-your-mouth consistency. The buttercream is flavored with puréed apricot and laced with Grand Marnier, surely one of the most complementary flavor combinations around.

1 Filbert Genoise (page 378), baked in a 10″ × 2″ round layer pan
1 recipe Sugar Syrup (page 467) flavored with Grand Marnier
8 canned apricot halves, drained very well on several layers of paper toweling

THE APRICOT BUTTERCREAM:
　　4 ounces (1 scant cup) dried apricots
1¼ cups water
⅔ cup confectioners' sugar
　　1 recipe Swiss Buttercream (page 456)
½ teaspoon grated navel orange rind
　　2 tablespoons Grand Marnier, Cointreau, or Triple Sec

1. To make the apricot buttercream: In a small heavy saucepan, combine the dried apricots and water. Cover and bring to a boil over high heat. Reduce the heat to low and simmer 20 to 25 minutes or until the apricots are *very* soft and the liquid is almost completely absorbed.
2. Off the heat, add the sugar. Whip with a fork until very smooth. You should have about ⅔ cups purée. Chill until completely cold.
3. To make the Swiss buttercream: After the final addition of butter in Step 5, reduce the mixer speed to medium-low. Blend in the chilled apricot purée, grated orange rind, and liqueur. Set aside.

TO ASSEMBLE THE CAKE:
1. Cut a cardboard disk slightly smaller than the cake. Divide the cake into 3 equal layers (page 500). Place the first layer top side

down on the disk. Using a pastry brush, moisten with 4 to 5 tablespoons of warm sugar syrup. Spread on ¼ of the apricot buttercream, leaving a ¼-inch unfrosted rim around the edge of the layer.

2. Place the second layer over the first, brushing again with the sugar syrup and spreading with ¼ of the frosting.

3. Moisten the cut side of the third layer with additional sugar syrup and place cut side down on the cake. Press the sides of the cake gently to align the layers.

4. Measure out ½ cup of the apricot buttercream and set aside for decorating the cake. Using a metal spatula, spread the remaining buttercream over the sides and top of the cake. Smooth the surface.

5. Fit a 14-inch pastry bag with a large #4 open star tube. Fill the bag with the reserved buttercream. Pipe eight 2-inch circles around the top of the cake, spacing as evenly as you can (seventh item, *Finishing Touches*, pages 491–92).

6. Place one apricot half, round side up, in the center of each circle. For a more professional finish, lightly brush the top of the apricots with Apricot Glaze (page 467). Refrigerate uncovered for 3 to 4 hours to set. Remove the cake from the refrigerator up to 3 hours before serving.

STORAGE: Refrigerate leftover cake, lightly covered with a foil tent, for up to 5 days.

🌰 BLACK FOREST CHERRY TORTE

This torte derives its name from the type of kirschwasser it contains rather than from the type of cherry. The kirsch most preferred is fine-quality imported brandy from the Alte Schwarzwalder, or Black Forest region, of Germany. Domestic kirsch may be substituted, but the flavor of the torte will not be the same.

The morello cherry is the best choice here. This thick-skinned, dark red cherry has a pleasant tart flavor that works beautifully in all kinds of wondrous desserts. Morello cherries are available at premium food stores or shops that carry fine imported products from Hungary or Central Europe. If you can't find them, you may substitute the sweeter Bing cherry, but avoid water-packed canned sour cherries because they are not presweetened.

1 Chocolate Genoise (page 375), baked in a 10″ × 2″ round layer pan
1 recipe Sugar Syrup (page 467), flavored with kirschwasser

THE CHERRY FILLING:

One 30-ounce jar morello cherries, or two 17-ounce cans Bing cherries packed in syrup
2 tablespoons cornstarch
2 tablespoons kirschwasser
1/2 teaspoon fresh lemon juice
1/8 teaspoon almond extract

THE WHIPPED CREAM:

2 cups heavy cream, well chilled
1/4 cup strained confectioners' sugar
1 teaspoon vanilla extract

12 red glacé cherries
Quick Chocolate Shavings (page 496) made from two 1-ounce squares of semisweet chocolate

1. Drain the morello cherries well, reserving ¾ cup of the juice.
2. In a heavy saucepan, dissolve the cornstarch in a small amount of the reserved cherry juice, then blend in the remaining juice. Stir over low heat until the mixture thickens and reaches a slow boil.
3. Remove from the heat and blend in the kirschwasser, lemon juice, and almond extract. Gently fold in the drained cherries and set aside to cool completely.
4. In a chilled bowl with chilled beaters, whip the cream until it begins to thicken. Add the confectioners' sugar and vanilla, and continue beating until the cream forms soft peaks. Finish beating by hand, using a wire whisk, whipping until the cream stands in firm peaks. Do not overbeat or the cream will become grainy. Set aside.

TO ASSEMBLE THE CAKE:
1. Divide the cake into 3 layers (page 500). Place the first layer cut side up on a serving plate. Moisten with 4 to 5 tablespoons warm sugar syrup. Fit a 14-inch pastry bag with a large #4 open star tube. Fill the bag about ⅓ full with whipped cream. Pipe a circle around the edge of the cake.
2. Spoon the cherry filling into the center of the circle, spreading it to the edge of the whipped cream.
3. Place the middle layer over the first and brush with 4 to 5 more tablespoons sugar syrup. Pipe a circle around edge, and fill with additional whipped cream to a thickness of ½ inch. Smooth the surface with an offset metal spatula.
4. Moisten the cut side of third layer with additional sugar syrup and place cut side down on the torte. Frost the sides and top with the remaining whipped cream, reserving ¾ cup for decorating cake.
5. To decorate the torte, run a pastry comb or tines of a fork around the sides. Beginning 2 inches from the edge, make 12 large rosettes around the top of the torte (seventh item, *Finishing Touches*, pages 491–92). Place a glacé cherry on top of each rosette.
6. Make the chocolate shavings according to instructions on page 496.
7. Fill in the middle of the torte with a generous amount of choc-

olate shavings. You may also scatter a light dusting of smaller chocolate shavings around the edges and sides of the cake if you wish. Chill the cake uncovered in the refrigerator for 3 to 4 hours to set. Remove from the refrigerator 30 to 60 minutes before serving, depending upon weather conditions.

STORAGE: Refrigerate leftover cake, lightly covered with a foil tent, for up to 3 days.

🌰 CHOCOLATE STRATA

AT A GLANCE

SERVES: 10 to 12

For this cake, chocolate genoise baked in a jelly roll pan is divided into fourths and layered with mocha buttercream filling. The entire loaf is swathed in additional buttercream and the sides are coated with toasted almonds. This is easy to make, and the oblong shape makes it an interesting addition to a buffet table.

1   Chocolate Genoise (page 375), baked in an 11″ × 17″ × 1″ jelly roll pan
1   recipe Sugar Syrup (page 467) flavored with Tía María or Kahlúa
1   recipe Mocha Buttercream (page 458) flavored with Tia María or Kahlúa
1   cup sliced toasted almonds (page 58)
½   small recipe Quick Chocolate Glaze (page 462), optional

1. Prepare the Chocolate Genoise according to the instructions. Dust a 20-inch piece of parchment with ½ teaspoon sugar. Invert the hot cake onto the paper and tap the pan to release. Set aside to cool.

2. Trim ¼ inch from the sides of the cake to remove the crusty edges. Cut the sheet lengthwise into three 3½" × 16½" strips. Use the center strips for the bottom and second layers. These are more uniform in height and will give the loaf a more even base.

TO ASSEMBLE THE CAKE:
1. Cut 4 strips of waxed paper, 2 long and 2 short, and place on an oblong serving platter or breadboard to keep the area under the cake clean.
2. Place the first cake strip top side down on the platter and moisten with 2 to 3 tablespoons of warm sugar syrup. Spread on a ⅜-inch layer of mocha buttercream. Repeat with the second and third layers. Brush fourth layer with sugar syrup and invert syrup side down onto the torte.
3. Spread the sides and top with the remaining buttercream, reserving 1 cup for decorating. Using the palms of your hands, gently press the toasted almonds around the sides of the torte. Fit a 14-inch pastry bag with a coupler (page 508) and small #34 star tube. Fill with the reserved buttercream. Pipe a shell border (page 517) around the top edge of the torte.
4. If you like, decorate the top with about 7 large chocolate stars (see illustration) or a design of your choice. To make the stars, use ½ the recipe of quick chocolate glaze in an 8-inch pastry bag fitted with a small #3 plain tube. Refrigerate the torte uncovered for 3 to 4 hours to set the frosting. Remove the cake from the refrigerator up to 3 hours before serving.

STORAGE: Refrigerate leftover cake, lightly covered with a foil tent, for up to 5 days.

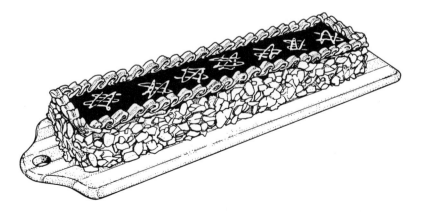

CHOCOLATE GATEAU WITH WHITE CHOCOLATE BAVARIAN CREAM

F *anciers of white chocolate swoon over desserts made with this mellow, creamy confection. Although its flavor may seem bland or overly sweet to some, it is heavenly paired with a robust bittersweet chocolate.*

1   Chocolate Genoise (page 375), baked in a 10″ × 2″ round layer pan
1   recipe Sugar Syrup (page 467), flavored with dark Jamaican rum

THE WHITE CHOCOLATE BAVARIAN CREAM:
- 5   tablespoons sugar
- 1½   tablespoons cornstarch
- ¾   teaspoon unflavored gelatin
- 3   large egg yolks
- ¾   cup milk
- 3   tablespoons light rum
- 1½   teaspoons vanilla extract
- 6   ounces imported white chocolate, broken into small pieces
- 1½   cups heavy cream, well chilled
- ½   cup lightly toasted slivered almonds, finely chopped
- 2   ounces (about ⅓ cup) coarsely chopped white chocolate
- 2   ounces (about ⅓ cup) coarsely chopped bittersweet chocolate

THE CANDY NUT CLUSTERS:
- 4   ounces (about ⅔ cup) coarsely chopped white chocolate
- ¾   cup lightly toasted slivered almonds
- 1   ounce bittersweet chocolate, chopped in small barley-size pieces
- 4   teaspoons imported dutch-process cocoa

1. To make the Bavarian cream: In a medium-sized saucepan off heat, whisk together the sugar, cornstarch, and gelatin. Add the egg yolks and whip until the mixture lightens in color. Stir in the milk, scraping the sides and corners of the saucepan with a rubber spatula. Whisk briefly until the mixture is completely smooth.

2. Cook over low heat, stirring constantly with a wooden spoon, until the mixture thickens and comes to a boil. Whisk briefly to smooth. Off the heat, stir in the rum and vanilla. Lightly butter a 12-inch square of waxed paper and place the paper, buttered side down, directly on the custard to prevent a film from forming. Set aside to cool to *tepid*.

3. Place the white chocolate in a medium-sized bowl and set in a 10-inch skillet filled with ½ inch hot water. Do not place the skillet over a flame, as white chocolate should not get too hot. When the white chocolate is completely melted, add the tepid custard and stir until smooth.

4. In a chilled bowl with chilled beaters or whip attachment, beat the cream to soft peak stage. Remove from the mixer and fold about ¼ of the cream into the custard. Then fold in the remaining cream along with the chopped almonds and coarsely chopped white and dark chocolates. Chill in the refrigerator for ½ hour or longer. The cream can be made 1 day in advance, if you wish.

TO ASSEMBLE THE CAKE:

1. Divide the cake into 3 layers (page 500). Cut a cardboard disk slightly smaller than the cake. Place the first layer top side down on the disk and brush with 3 to 4 tablespoons of warm sugar syrup. Spread on ⅓ of the Bavarian cream, leaving a ¼-inch unfrosted rim around the edge.

2. Place the middle layer over the cream filling, brushing with sugar syrup and spreading with another ⅓ of the cream filling.

3. Moisten the cut side of the third layer with additional sugar syrup and turn cut side down onto the cake. Press the sides gently to align the layers.

4. Spread the remaining Bavarian cream around the sides and top of the cake. Chill.

5. To make the candy nut clusters: Fill an 8-inch skillet with ½ inch of water. Heat the water until very hot, but not boiling, then turn off the burner. Put the white chocolate in a small bowl and set the bowl in the hot water. Let stand about 1 minute to soften.

Stir the chocolate with a rubber spatula until it is almost melted, then remove the bowl from the water and continue stirring until the chocolate is completely melted.

6. Fold the slivered almonds into the melted chocolate, thoroughly coating the nuts. Place the mixture in the refrigerator for 1 to 2 minutes, just to cool the chocolate slightly, then fold in the chopped bittersweet chocolate, taking just 2 or 3 turns. Do not overmix or the chocolate will bleed.

7. Cut an 8 × 12-inch piece of waxed paper and lay it on a flat plate. To form the candy nut clusters, drop teaspoons of the chocolate-coated nuts onto the paper, mounding them in the center. You should have 12 candy nut clusters. Refrigerate until set, about 5 minutes.

8. Using an extra-fine strainer, sprinkle the cocoa over the top of the cake, completely covering the Bavarian cream. Starting ½ inch from the edge, arrange the candy clusters evenly around the cake. Refrigerate the cake uncovered for 3 to 4 hours to allow it to set. Remove from the refrigerator up to 2 hours before serving.

STORAGE: Refrigerate leftover cake, lightly covered with a foil tent, for up to 5 days.

❧ CHOCOLATE GLACÉ WITH MASCARPONE PISTACHIO FILLING

Though long used in Italian cuisine, mascarpone cream cheese has just recently become popular in the United States. Its slightly tangy flavor bears a resemblance to English clotted cream. To make it, sweet cream is soured, the watery liquid drained off, and the rich curd then beaten until thickened. Galbani is the brand I prefer. It is packaged in small containers and has a surprisingly long shelf life of 4 months if kept refrigerated at 35° to 40°. It is available at most quality Italian grocery stores or specialty cheese shops.

If you become passionate about this wonderful cheese, you may omit the ganache glaze and instead double the recipe for the filling and use it to cover the entire cake. Either way, with just one mouthful of this deliciously decadent cake, all thoughts of calorie-counting will disappear.

1	Chocolate Genoise (page 375), baked in a 10-inch round layer pan
1	recipe Sugar Syrup (page 467)
1	recipe Apricot Glaze (page 467)

THE MASCARPONE FILLING:

1	large egg yolk
⅔	cup mascarpone cream cheese, preferably imported
1	tablespoon water
½	teaspoon unflavored gelatin
1	cup heavy cream, well chilled
½	cup strained confectioners' sugar
2	tablespoons dark rum
3 to 4	tablespoons chopped fine-quality bittersweet or semisweet chocolate (see step 5)
2	tablespoons plus 1 teaspoon chopped pistachios (see step 6)
1	recipe Ganache Glaze (page 464), prepared just before using

Special Occasion Cakes

397

1. To make the filling: In a medium-sized bowl, blend the egg yolk into the cheese.
2. Put the water in a small ovenproof glass dish. Sprinkle the gelatin over the top and let stand for 5 minutes to soften. Set the dish into a skillet filled with ½ inch boiling water and stir until the gelatin is dissolved and completely clear. Remove from the skillet and cool to *tepid*.
3. In a chilled bowl fitted with beaters or whip attachment, beat together the cream and sugar at medium speed. When the mixture begins to thicken, quickly add the gelatin and rum. Beat until the cream is thick and holds its shape.
4. Remove the bowl from the mixer. Stir ¼ of the cream into the cheese to lighten. Then add the cheese mixture to the remaining cream, gently folding the two together.
5. Using a very sharp knife, chop the chocolate into fine pieces. Set aside.
6. Rub the pistachios between two sheets of paper toweling to remove the salt. (It is not necessary to remove the skins.) Chop into small pieces. Reserve 1 teaspoon for garnish.
7. Fold the chocolate and pistachios gently into the filling. *Do not overmix.* Chill at least 1 hour until firm. This can be made a day in advance.

TO ASSEMBLE THE CAKE:

1. Divide the cake into 3 layers (page 500). Cut a cardboard disk slightly smaller than the cake. Place the bottom layer top down on the disk, and brush with about 3 to 4 tablespoons of warm sugar syrup.
2. Reserve ¼ cup of mascarpone filling for garnish. Spread the layer with ½ of the remaining filling, leaving a ½-inch unfrosted border around the edge. Place the middle layer over the filling. Brush with sugar syrup and spread with the remaining filling.
3. Brush the cut side of the third layer with sugar syrup and turn cut side down onto the cake. Press the sides of the cake gently to align layers. Chill in the refrigerator for ½ hour to set.
4. Lift the cake by placing your open palm under the cardboard disk. Holding a serrated or very sharp knife with an 8-inch blade parallel to the side of the cake, trim the sides until they are perfectly straight. Cut a slight bevel at the top to help the glaze drop over the edge. Brush the top and sides of the cake with warm

apricot glaze, sealing the cut areas thoroughly. Chill while you prepare the ganache glaze.

5. Place a rack over a large shallow pan or skillet to catch the drippings. Remove the gateau from the refrigerator and set it on the rack. Have ready a metal spatula with a blade at least 8 to 10 inches long. Hold the saucepan containing the ganache glaze 10 inches above the cake and immediately pour the glaze onto the center. To achieve a smooth, mirrorlike finish, quickly pass the spatula four times over the top of the cake (page 466). (The glaze should cover the top and run down the sides.) Then lift one side of the rack and bring it down with a hard bang. This helps to spread the glaze more evenly. Work quickly before the glaze sets. Patch the bare spots on the sides with a smaller metal spatula, but do not touch the top again, as the glaze firms immediately. Let the cake stand 15 minutes to set after glazing.

6. To garnish the cake, place the remaining filling in a 14-inch pastry bag fitted with a large #6 plain tube and make a pattern similar to a plus sign with an open space in the middle. To accomplish this, mark the top of the torte where you plan to make the plus sign with the tip of a toothpick to guide you. Holding the pastry bag straight up, place the tip directly onto the spot where you plan to make your first decoration. Starting from the outer perimeter of the plus sign, pipe 4 lines of 3 dots each, leaving about a 1-inch opening in the center. Fill the opening with the 1 teaspoon of reserved chopped pistachios. Refrigerate the cake uncovered for 1 to 2 hours to set. Remove the cake from the refrigerator up to 3 hours before serving, depending upon weather conditions.

STORAGE: Refrigerate leftover cake, lightly covered with a foil tent, for up to 5 days.

🍃 PAVLOVA MERINGUE TORTE

AT A GLANCE

▽

SERVES: 12 to 14
PAN: 10″ springform
(ring only)/12″ ×
15½″ cookie sheet
PAN PREP: Butter/
parchment
OVEN TEMP: 250°
RACK LEVEL: Lower
third
BAKING TIME: 1½
hours
METHOD: Electric
mixer

Pavlova is a light meringue-style cake, made principally with sugar and egg whites, that is native to Australia. It has a thin, crisp exterior with a soft center similar in texture to marshmallows.

This recipe is my dressed-up version of one given to me by my friend Nance Littlewood, of Melbourne. I've embellished the meringue layer with whipped cream and added a topping of marinated tropical fruits. Pavlovas are simple to prepare and can be made in a variety of shapes by changing the pans. These airy cakes melt in your mouth.

6	large egg whites
⅛	teaspoon salt
1	cup strained superfine or strained sugar
1	teaspoon cornstarch
1½	teaspoons vanilla extract
1	teaspoon fresh lemon juice
1	large recipe Whipped Cream (page 486)
	Wedges of figs or kiwis, or halved strawberries, for garnish
1	recipe Marinated Tropical Fruits (page 481) (optional)

1. Position the rack in the lower third of the oven and preheat to 250°.
2. Butter a 12″ × 15½″ cookie sheet and line it with parchment. Butter a springform ring very well and center it on the cookie sheet. Set it aside while you prepare the meringue.
3. Put the egg whites in the large bowl of an electric mixer fitted with beaters or the whip attachment. Beat on medium speed until frothy, add the salt, and continue beating until they reach the soft peak stage.
4. Increase mixer speed to medium-high. Add the sugar, 1 tablespoon at a time, taking about 4 minutes, to form a meringue. Scrape the sides of the bowl occasionally. Beat in the cornstarch, vanilla, and lemon juice. The mixture should be very thick and glossy.

5. Spoon the meringue into the prepared pan, spreading from the center to the outer rim. (Take care not to jar the pan.) Using the back of a tablespoon, press gently to remove any air pockets, and smooth the surface.

6. In the preheated oven, bake 1½ hours, or until the top of the torte sets slightly. The inside will remain moist. Remove from the oven. Immediately run a thin sharp knife around the edge of the pan to release the torte. Place on a cake rack to cool completely.

7. Remove the ring and invert the cake onto a cake rack. Carefully peel off the paper. Turn the torte right side up onto a serving platter.

8. To garnish the cake, spread the sides and top with the whipped cream, reserving ⅓ for decoration.

9. Fit a 14-inch pastry bag with a large #4 open star tube. Fill the bag with the reserved whipped cream. Evenly space 12 to 14 large rosettes around the top of the torte. Center wedges of figs, kiwis, or halved large strawberries on top of each rosette. Refrigerate, uncovered, until ready to serve.

TO SERVE: Slice the cake into wedges and top each slice with a spoonful of marinated tropical fruits if you like.

STORAGE: Refrigerate leftover cake, lightly covered with a foil tent, for up to 2 days.

❧ LISE TORTE

several years ago while visiting Denmark my husband and I were invited to the home of Lise Helmgaard Aaroe, the daughter of very close friends and an aspiring and talented culinary student.

several years ago while visiting Denmark my husband and I were invited to the home of Lise Helmgaard Aaroe, the daughter of very close friends and an aspiring and talented culinary student.

On this particular evening she served us a Danish-style sponge cake filled with a layer of chocolate custard, another of raspberries mixed with whipped cream, a topping of more whipped cream, and a garnish of sliced toasted almonds.

I have taught this torte many times to my students and their reaction has been the same as mine, instant love! While almost any summer berry or soft fresh diced fruit will do, try Lise's version first.

AT A GLANCE

SERVES: 10 to 12
PAN: 10″ x 2″ round layer
PAN PREP: Butter/ parchment
OVEN TEMP: 350°
RACK LEVEL: Lower third
BAKING TIME: 30 to 35 minutes
METHOD: Electric mixer

3/4 cup sifted unbleached all-purpose flour
2 tablespoons cornstarch
1 teaspoon baking powder
1/8 teaspoon salt
4 large eggs
3/4 cup superfine or strained sugar
1/2 teaspoon freshly grated lemon rind
2 tablespoons warm (105°) melted unsalted butter

1 recipe Bittersweet Chocolate Filling (page 442)
1/2 dry pint fresh raspberries (1 1/2 cups), rinsed and well drained
1 large recipe Whipped Cream (page 486)
1 cup toasted sliced almonds (page 58)

1. Position cake rack in lower third of the oven and preheat to 350°.
2. Butter the bottom only of a 10″ x 2″ round layer pan and line with a parchment disk.
3. Sift together the flour, cornstarch, baking powder, and salt. Set aside.
4. Place the eggs in the large bowl of an electric mixer fitted with beaters or whip attachment. Beat on medium-high speed for 2 minutes. Add the sugar, 1 tablespoon at a time, taking about 3 to 4 minutes to blend. Add the lemon rind. Scrape the sides of bowl occasionally. The mixture will thicken and be light yellow in color.

5. Reduce the mixer speed to low. Add the dry ingredients all at once and mix until just blended. Pour in the warm butter and mix 10 to 15 seconds longer. Pour the batter into the prepared pan and bake in the preheated oven 30 to 35 minutes.
6. While the cake is baking, prepare and chill the filling.
7. The cake is done when it turns golden brown on the top and is springy to the touch. Remove the cake from the oven and immediately invert onto a rack to cool in the pan. When the cake is cold, turn it top side up. To release the cake from the pan, with a thin, sharp knife cut around the sides using an up-and-down sawing motion to prevent tearing. Invert the cake onto a rack and remove the pan and parchment. Then turn the cake top side up.

TO ASSEMBLE THE CAKE:
1. Slice the cake into 3 layers (page 500), handling gently as the cake is fragile. The layers will be quite thin. Place the bottom layer bottom side down on a cardboard disk cut slightly smaller than the torte. Spread with the chilled chocolate filling, leaving a 1/2-inch border around the edge. Place the middle layer on top.
2. Fold the raspberries into 1 cup of the whipped cream. Spread the raspberries and cream over the cake, leaving a 1/2-inch unfrosted border around the edge. Be careful not to bruise the berries. Put on the top layer, cut side down, and gently press the sides of the cake to align the layers.
3. Cover the sides and top with the remaining whipped cream. Sprinkle the entire cake with the toasted almonds, and using a sugar shaker, sprinkle the sides and top lightly with confectioners' sugar. Refrigerate uncovered until ready to serve. Remove from the refrigerator 1/2 hour before eating.

STORAGE: Refrigerate leftover cake, lightly covered with a foil tent, for up to 3 days.

🐚 HUNGARIAN MAGYAR TORTE

AT A GLANCE

SERVES: 10 to 12

PANS: Two 10" layer pans

PAN PREP: Butter (bottom only)/ parchment

OVEN TEMP: 350°

RACK LEVEL: Lower third

BAKING TIME: 30 to 35 minutes

METHOD: Electric mixer/food processor

I named this unusual torte after the Hungarian nomadic tribe, the Magyars, who roamed Central Europe gathering whatever foods they could find to feed their people. Since the torte is a mélange of many different flavors from that part of the world, I thought the name appropriate.

The baked layers shrink considerably upon cooling and are very fragile; handle carefully when assembling. While the shape of the layers may be somewhat irregular at this point, the generous covering of chocolate whipped cream ensures a glamorous presentation.

THE CRUMB MIXTURE:

1/2	cup chopped unsalted water biscuits, such as Carr's (dried unflavored bread crumbs or matzo meal may be substituted)
1	full cup walnuts
1/4	teaspoon cinnamon
1/8	teaspoon nutmeg

THE CAKE:

6	large egg yolks
1 1/3	cups superfine or strained sugar, divided
1/2	teaspoon grated navel orange rind
1/2	teaspoon grated lemon rind
2	tablespoons poppy seeds (optional)
4	ounces bittersweet or semisweet chocolate, broken into small pieces and very finely chopped in the food processor
1/2	cup finely shredded carrot
1/2	cup finely shredded Golden Delicious apple
6	large egg whites
1/4	teaspoon cream of tartar

4	cups (twice the small recipe) Chocolate Whipped Cream (page 488)
Two	1-ounce squares semisweet chocolate, such as Baker's
12	candied violets

1. To make the crumb mixture: Place the water biscuits in the container of a processor and chop fine with the steel blade. Add the walnuts and spices, and pulse until the mixture turns into fine crumbs. Set aside.
2. Position rack in the lower third of the oven and preheat to 350°. Prepare two 10-inch layer pans with butter and line the bottoms with parchment paper circles.
3. *To make the cake: Put the egg yolks in the large bowl of an electric mixer fitted with beaters or whip attachment. Beat on medium-high speed for 2 minutes. Add 1 cup sugar, 1 tablespoon at a time, taking about 3 or 4 minutes to blend well. Scrape the sides of the bowl occasionally. The mixture will thicken and be light yellow in color.
4. Reduce the mixer speed to low and add the grated orange and lemon rinds, poppy seeds, chocolate, carrot, apple, and nut/crumb mixture all at once. Mix until just blended.
5. Remove the bowl from the mixer and set aside. In a separate large bowl of an electric mixer fitted with clean beaters or whip attachment, beat the egg whites on medium speed until frothy. Add the cream of tartar and beat to the soft peak stage. Gradually add 1/3 cup sugar, 1 tablespoon at a time, taking about 30 seconds. Beat 15 seconds longer. Remove the bowl from the mixer.
6. With a 2³/₄-inch-wide rubber spatula, fold 1/4 of the whites into the yolk batter, taking about 10 to 12 turns. Add the remaining whites and fold the two together, taking about 40 turns in all.
7. Pour the batter into the prepared pans and bake in the preheated oven 30 to 35 minutes, or until the cake is lightly brown on top and springy to the touch. Remove the layers from the oven and set on cake racks to cool for 15 minutes.
8. To release the cakes from the pans, run a thin sharp knife around the edge of the layers and invert onto cake racks sprayed with nonstick coating. Remove the pan and carefully peel off the paper. Continue to cool completely.

TO ASSEMBLE THE TORTE:

1. Slide the first layer of cake, top side down, onto a cardboard disk cut slightly smaller than the layer. Set aside 2 cups of chocolate whipped cream. Spread with the remaining cream to a thickness

*Steps 3 and 4 can also be done in a food processor.

of ³/₈ inch. Reinvert the second layer onto a cake rack so the top side is up. Carefully slide it onto the torte. The sides of the cake may be indented.

2. With an offset metal spatula, thickly coat the sides of the torte with the chocolate whipped cream, filling in the spaces to make the sides straight. Spread the cream smoothly over the top.

3. Make chocolate shavings according to the instructions on page 496. Sprinkle shavings on the top and around the sides of the torte.

4. Fit a 14-inch pastry bag with a large #4 or #5 open star tube. Fill the bag ¹/₃ full with the reserved chocolate whipped cream. Decorate the top with 12 large, evenly spaced loops (see illustration). To make the loops, hold the pastry bag at a 90° angle; the decorating tube should almost touch the top of the cake. Starting ¹/₂ inch from the edge of the torte, in a continuous motion make 3 graduated loops. The first loop should measure about 1¹/₂ inches, with the following two each a little smaller. Press a candied violet into the tip of each loop. Refrigerate uncovered for 3 to 4 hours. Remove from the refrigerator ¹/₂ hour before eating.

STORAGE: Refrigerate leftovers, lightly covered with a foil tent, for up to 3 days.

❧ SWISS CHOCOLATE SILK

This has been a favorite with my students since I wrote it many years ago. I had been asked to develop a recipe for a 3-inch-deep round layer pan, a challenge because without a center hole to allow air circulation, the middle of a cake often does not bake through. I used a bain-marie to keep the torte moist, a technique that was uncommon at the time for a flourless chocolate torte.

The cornstarch used in place of flour gives this a wonderful smooth velvety texture made crunchy with walnuts.

A student once told me that she almost had an accident while driving her car because she was daydreaming about this luscious cake. Perhaps I should caution everyone not to drive while under the influence of Swiss Chocolate Silk.

▽
AT A GLANCE

SERVES: 10 to 12
PAN: 9″ springform
PAN PREP: Butter/parchment/butter/bain-marie
OVEN TEMP: 325°
RACK LEVEL: Lower third
BAKING TIME: 55 to 60 minutes
METHOD: Electric mixer/food processor

2	tablespoons dried bread crumbs
1½	cups walnuts
¾	cup cornstarch
9	ounces imported bittersweet chocolate, such as Lindt Excellence or Tobler Tradition
¾	cup (1½ sticks) unsalted butter, softened
6	large egg yolks
1	cup superfine or strained sugar
1½	teaspoons vanilla extract
1½	tablespoons hot water
9	large egg whites
⅛	teaspoon cream of tartar
1	recipe Ganache Glaze (page 464), prepared just before using
1	recipe Chocolate Caraque (page 497), using 3 ounces of chocolate
1	recipe Chantilly Whipped Cream (page 489)

1. Position rack in the lower third of the oven and preheat to 325°. Butter a 9-inch springform pan, line the bottom with parchment, and butter the parchment.
2. Sprinkle the dried bread crumbs over the bottom and around the sides of the pan. Invert and tap to remove any excess.

Special Occasion Cakes

3. Place the nuts and cornstarch in the container of a food processor fitted with the steel blade. Pulse 4 to 5 times, then process for 15 seconds to chop fine. Set aside.

4. Melt the chocolate slowly over hot water. Stir in the butter, 1 tablespoon at a time, blending well. Set aside.

5. Put the egg yolks in the large bowl of an electric mixer fitted with beaters or whip attachment. Beat on medium speed for 2 minutes, or until lightened in color. Gradually add the sugar, 1 tablespoon at a time, taking about 4 to 5 minutes. Blend in the chocolate mixture, vanilla, and hot water. Beat 1 minute longer. Scrape the sides of the bowl as needed. Reduce speed to low, add the nut mixture, and blend just until incorporated. Remove the bowl from the machine and set aside.

6. In a separate large bowl of a mixer fitted with clean beaters or whip attachment, beat the egg whites on medium speed until frothy. Add the cream of tartar. Whip the whites until they stand in firm peaks. Remove the bowl from the machine. With a 2³/₄-inch-wide rubber spatula, fold 1/3 of the whites into the chocolate mixture, taking about 40 turns. Fold in the remaining whites, taking an additional 60 turns. Pour into the prepared pan.

7. Place the pan on an 18-inch square of heavy-duty aluminum foil. Bring up the edges of the foil and mold snugly around the pan. Put the springform inside a larger pan, slide them into the oven, and pour in very hot water to a depth of 1 inch. Bake in the preheated oven 55 to 60 minutes, until a toothpick inserted in the center comes out almost clean. Do not overbake. The cake should remain slightly moist.

8. Remove the cake pan from the bain-marie and set on a cake rack. Take off the foil. Cool the torte 30 minutes, then carefully release sides of pan. Place a piece of foil over the top and invert onto a cake rack. Remove the metal disk and parchment, and allow the torte to cool.

TO GARNISH THE CAKE:

1. Set the torte top side up on a cardboard disk cut slightly smaller than the torte. Set on a cake rack. Make the ganache.

2. Place the rack over a large shallow pan or skillet to catch the drippings. Have ready a metal spatula with a blade at least 8 to 10 inches long. Hold the saucepan 10 inches above the cake and immediately pour the ganache glaze onto the center. To achieve

a smooth mirrorlike finish, quickly pass the spatula four times over the top of the torte (page 466). The glaze should cover the top and run down the sides. Then lift one side of the rack and bring it down with a hard bang. This helps spread the glaze more evenly. Work quickly before the glaze sets. Patch the bare spots on the sides with a smaller metal spatula, but do not touch the top again as the glaze begins to firm immediately. Let the torte stand 5 minutes.

3. Before the glaze has completely set, sprinkle the surface with chocolate caraque, mounding the longest curls and slivers in the center. Press the sides with smaller pieces. Just before serving, sprinkle a light dusting of confectioners' sugar over the top.

TO SERVE: Cut the cake into wedges and serve with chantilly whipped cream.

STORAGE: Store at room temperature under a glass dome for up to 3 days.

❧ CHOCOLATE PASSION

AT A GLANCE

SERVES: 8 to 10
PAN: 9″ springform
PAN PREP: Butter/
parchment/butter/
bain-marie
OVEN TEMP: 325°
RACK LEVEL: Lower
third
BAKING TIME: 1½
hours
METHOD: Hand/
electric mixer

y friend Sondra Ballin of Memphis and I share a passion for great desserts. After we tasted this fabulous torte in New Orleans, she traced down the recipe and enthusiastically mailed it to me so I could include it in this book. I have revised the original, but the concept remains the same. It is sublimely rich, with a smooth soufflélike center and a crusty top. The torte rises high as it bakes, then collapses into a heavenly chocolate mass. It is essential to use a fine-quality imported bitter chocolate.

Sondra and I love this torte served slightly warm, but it is also delicious eaten at room temperature.

9	ounces imported bittersweet chocolate, such as Lindt Excellence or Tobler Tradition
1	cup (2 sticks) unsalted butter, cut into 1-inch pieces
⅔	plus ½ cup strained or superfine sugar
8	large egg yolks, lightly beaten
6	large egg whites

1. Position rack in the lower third of the oven and preheat to 325°. Butter a 9-inch springform pan, line the bottom with a parchment circle, and butter the paper.
2. Break the chocolate into pieces and melt very slowly in a double boiler over low heat. Add the butter and stir until well blended and very smooth.
3. Add ⅔ *cup* sugar and continue stirring until it is completely incorporated.
4. Remove the top of the double boiler and blend in the egg yolks thoroughly off the heat. Set aside.
5. Place the egg whites in the large bowl of an electric mixer fitted with beaters or the whip attachment. Whip on medium speed until they reach the soft peak stage. Add the remaining ½ *cup* sugar gradually, taking about 30 seconds. Beat 15 seconds longer until whites form a glossy, firm meringue. Do not overbeat.
6. Whisk ¼ of the meringue into the chocolate mixture to lighten. *Do not fold.* Then using a 2¾-inch-wide rubber spatula, fold the

chocolate mixture into the remaining meringue, taking about 50 turns. Pour the batter into the prepared pan.

7. Set the pan onto an 18-inch square of heavy aluminum foil. Bring the sides of the foil up and mold snugly around the pan. Place springform inside a larger pan and set both pans in the oven. Pour in very hot water to a depth of 1-inch. In the preheated oven, bake 1½ hours.

8. Remove the torte from the bain-marie and place it on a cake rack. Torte will have risen to top of pan, but will sink dramatically upon cooling. This is okay. Carefully peel down the foil and *immediately* run a thin knife gently around the edge of the pan to release any crust that may cling, allowing the torte to sink naturally. After 10 minutes, release the sides to let the cake breath, but do not remove the ring. Cool 30 minutes.

9. Remove the outer ring and carefully invert the cake onto the cake rack. Lift off the bottom of the pan and peel off the paper. When the torte is cool, invert onto a cake plate.

TO SERVE: Serve at room temperature or, if you prefer, warmed slightly in a 300° oven for 10 to 15 minutes. Dust the top generously with confectioners' sugar just before serving. Accompany with Chantilly Whipped Cream (page 489) or, for a sensational presentation, garnish the plate with navel orange sections and accompany with Orange Crème Anglaise (page 476).

STORAGE: Store at room temperature, covered with aluminum foil, for up to 3 days or refrigerate for up to 1 week.

❧ SACHERTORTE

AT A GLANCE

SERVES: 10 to 12
PAN: 9″ springform
PAN PREP: Butter/
parchment
OVEN TEMP: 350°
RACK LEVEL: Lower
third
BAKING TIME: 40
minutes
METHOD: Electric
mixer

This is my rendition of the famous Sachertorte, a delicious, dense chocolate cake believed to have been created in 1832 by Franz Sacher.

Before I developed this recipe I tested at least nine other versions, each claiming to be the original, none of which I considered acceptable. The tortes puffed during baking but shrank as they cooled. The sides frequently collapsed and the centers sank slightly. The slices had a heavy damp line through the center.

Finally, two of the students in my Viennese pastry class at the New School in New York City gave me another recipe that also claimed to be the original from Vienna. While the ingredients were similar to those in the recipes I'd already tested, the eggs were incorporated differently. Instead of folding in the beaten egg whites after adding the flour, this recipe called for adding a bit of sugar to the whites, then folding them in alternately with the flour. To my delight the torte came out perfectly.

Great care should be taken not to overbeat the egg whites. It is crucial that they be whipped just to the soft peak stage.

In Vienna, Sachertorte is traditionally served with schlag, lightly sweetened whipped cream. Needless to say, using fine-quality imported chocolate is essential.

THE CAKE:

- ³/₄ cup (1¹/₂ sticks) unsalted butter
- ³/₄ cup superfine or strained sugar, divided
- 5 large egg yolks
- 5 ounces imported bittersweet chocolate, such as Lindt Excellence or Tobler Tradition, melted and cooled to tepid
- 7 large egg whites
- ¹/₈ teaspoon salt
- ³/₄ cup strained cake flour

- 1 recipe hot Apricot Glaze (page 467)

THE SACHERTORTE GLAZE:

    1/2 cup superfine or strained sugar
    2   tablespoons water
    2   tablespoons light corn syrup
    4   ounces imported bittersweet chocolate, finely chopped
        in a food processor

1. Position rack in the lower third of the oven and preheat to 350°. Butter a 9-inch springform pan. Cover the bottom with a parchment circle.

2. To make the cake: Place the butter in the large bowl of an electric mixer fitted with beaters or paddle attachment. Soften on low speed, then increase speed to medium-high and cream until smooth and light in color, about 1 1/2 to 2 minutes. Add *1/2 cup* sugar 1 tablespoon at a time, taking about 3 to 4 minutes to blend well.

3. Add the yolks alternately with the melted chocolate, taking 3 to 4 minutes, dividing each into three parts, starting with the yolks. Beat well after each addition. Transfer the mixture to a large bowl.

4. Wash and dry the beaters and mixer bowl well. In the large bowl, whip the egg whites on medium-low speed until frothy. Add the salt. Increase mixer speed to medium-high and continue whipping until they reach the soft peak stage. Add the remaining *1/4 cup* sugar over about 15 seconds, and beat for an additional 10 to 15 seconds to form a soft meringue. *Do not overbeat.*

5. Put the flour in a triple-mesh sifter. Using a 2 3/4-inch-wide rubber spatula, fold in the meringue and sift the flour alternately into the chocolate batter, dividing the meringue into four parts and the flour into three parts, starting and ending with the meringue.

6. Pour the batter into the prepared pan. Bake in the preheated oven 40 minutes, or until the torte begins to come away from the sides of the pan. Be careful not to overbake. The torte will puff during baking but will shrink as it cools.

7. Remove the torte from the oven and set on a cake rack for 30 minutes. Release the sides of the pan and invert the torte onto the rack, remove the bottom of the pan, and peel off the paper. Cool completely. Wrap in plastic wrap for 2 or 3 days to mature. (Authentic recipes require that the torte ripen; however, it is also delicious freshly made.)

TO ASSEMBLE THE CAKE:

1. Place the torte on a cardboard disk cut slightly smaller than the torte.
2. Lift the cake by placing your hand with your palm open under the cardboard disk. Holding a very sharp knife with an 8-inch blade parallel to the sides of the torte, trim the sides to make them as even as you can. If a few indentations remain, it is okay.
3. Level the top of the torte by cutting a slight bevel around the edges to help the glaze drip over the sides. To test if the surface is level, hold a long spatula or ruler on its side and place it flush against the torte. If any spaces are visible, continue to trim until the surface is perfectly level. Discard the selvage. Brush the top and sides with warm apricot glaze and chill the torte in the refrigerator 1/2 hour to set completely.
4. Place a rack over a large shallow pan or skillet to catch any drippings. Remove the torte from the refrigerator and set it on the rack.
5. To make the glaze: Place the sugar, water, and corn syrup in a small saucepan. Stir briefly. Cover and bring to a slow boil, brushing the sides of the pan occasionally with water to prevent crystals from forming.
6. Off the heat, add the chocolate. Let stand 1 minute, then stir until completely melted and smooth. For best results, use immediately.*
7. Hold the saucepan 10 inches above the torte and pour the glaze onto the center. To achieve a smooth mirrorlike finish, quickly pass a metal spatula with a blade at least 8 to 10 inches long four times over the top of the torte. The glaze should cover the top and run down the sides. Starting at the top of the torte, on the first sweep bring the spatula down the middle, on the second sweep, bring the spatula up on the right side of the torte. On the third sweep, bring it down the left side, and on the final sweep, back up over the middle. Then lift one side of the rack and bring it down with a hard bang. This helps spread the glaze more evenly. This procedure must be done quickly to ease the glaze evenly over the top and down the sides before it sets. Patch the bare spots on the sides with a small metal spatula, but do not touch the top again as the glaze sets immediately. Let the Sachertorte stand 15 minutes.

*For illustrations of the technique of applying the glaze, see page 465.

8. If you wish to write "Sacher" across the top of the torte, remove 2 to 3 tablespoons of glaze that have dropped into the pan. Thin with a few drops of water, then place in an 8-inch pastry bag fitted with a small #3 plain tube. You may also use a small paper cone (page 510).

9. Test for an even flow by writing "Sacher" on a piece of waxed paper (page 515). Then print "Sacher" across the top of the cake. Allow the glaze to set completely before covering with a glass cake cover. When ready to serve, slice the torte into wedges and serve with Chantilly Whipped Cream (page 489).

STORAGE: Store at room temperature under a glass cake cover for up to 3 days, or refrigerate for up to 1 week. Serve at room temperature.

PASSOVER SPONGE CAKES and TORTES

P assover sponge cakes and tortes differ from other cakes in that they are not made with flour and usually do not contain chemical leavening. While a few are completely flourless, most are made with matzo cake meal and/or potato starch in place of the flour.

Matzo cake meal is produced from finely ground matzo, the un-leavened bread that is the mainstay of the Passover holiday. Potato starch is a thickening agent manufactured from mashed potatoes. These products make delicious cakes that often taste and look the same as a sponge cake or torte prepared with regular flour. Matzo cake meal and potato starch are often used together, but when they are used alone they yield cakes with different textures. Sponge cakes made with matzo cake meal have a tender cakelike crumb. Those made with potato starch have more "pull" or elasticity to the bite, and more volume. When used in place of flour, potato starch gives a torte a smooth, velvety texture.

Both sponge cake and torte batters consist mostly of eggs, which are a primary source of leavening when air is beaten into them and also form a strong framework for the other ingredients. Sponge cakes contain flour and are always light and airy. Tortes made without flour do not rise as high and have a denser texture.

People who bake Passover sponge cakes have very strong opinions about what makes them great. Some judge solely on the basis of height; however, truly fine sponge cake should meet four requirements: volume, flavor, texture, and form.

This chapter begins with the two most popular Passover sponge cakes. The first, a classic Passover sponge cake, is made with half matzo cake meal and half potato starch. Feather Sponge, made only with potato starch, makes an impressive presentation due to its beautiful, majestic height.

In recent years, tortes have gained popularity as a Passover pastry. Their sturdier batters can be blended with chocolate, nuts, and fruits of all kinds to offer variety, making them a pleasant change from the familiar sponge.

This chapter highlights a few special Passover treats, but you'll find other cakes in the book that are also suitable. Choices include such tempting recipes as Hazelnut Torte with Meringue Topping (page 146), Flourless Chocolate Roulade (page 268), Nut Soufflé Roll (page 276), Hungarian Magyar Torte (page 404), Pavlova Meringue Torte (page 400), and Chocolate Passion (page 410). Many cheesecakes are flourless and may be used as well.

BEFORE YOU BEGIN . . .

▶ Matzo cake meal and potato starch can be found in the ethnic food section of a supermarket.

▶ Neither matzo cake meal nor potato starch needs presifting. However, if the potato starch is lumpy, strain first to remove lumps before measuring.

▶ When matzo cake meal and potato starch are used together in a recipe, they must be thoroughly blended before being added to a batter. Sift or strain the measured amounts together 4 times.

▶ Passover sponge cakes are especially sensitive to overbeating because they are not made with regular flour. When using a KitchenAid Mixer, *reduce the mixing time by one-half.*

▶ Take care not to overbeat the egg whites, as overbeating makes them dry and grainy and difficult to fold into the batter.

▶ Recipes that call for a 10-inch angel food pan with a 4-quart capacity can be easily baked in smaller pans. Simply cut the recipe in half and bake in an 8-inch tube pan (2-quart capacity) with a removable bottom.

▶ Since tortes contain a small amount of or no flour, it is normal for them to shrink somewhat after baking.

▶ For more information, refer to "Before You Begin" in the Sponge Cake section (pages 253–54). All of the information will apply to Passover sponge cakes.

🌾 PASSOVER SPONGE CAKE

This is my favorite all-purpose holiday sponge cake. It has beautiful volume and form, a delicious citrus flavor, and a crumb so light and tender that each mouthful melts on your tongue.

Another great feature of this cake is that the recipe is so nicely balanced that variations are a cinch to prepare. Two lovely selections follow at the end of this recipe. The cake is wonderful plain, used as a shortcake, or accompanied with fresh fruit. No matter which way you choose to serve it, I guarantee it will disappear in no time.

AT A GLANCE

SERVES: 14 to 16
PAN: 10″ angel food with removable bottom (4-quart capacity)
PAN PREP: Ungreased
OVEN TEMP: 350°
RACK LEVEL: Lower third
BAKING TIME: 50 to 55 minutes
METHOD: Electric mixer

¹/₂	cup matzo cake meal
¹/₂	cup potato starch
8	large egg yolks
1	large whole egg
1¹/₂	cups superfine or strained sugar, divided
¹/₄	cup fresh navel orange juice
4	teaspoons fresh lemon juice
1	teaspoon grated navel orange rind
1	teaspoon grated lemon rind
8	large egg whites
¹/₄	teaspoon salt

1. Position a rack in the lower third of the oven and preheat to 350°. Have ready an ungreased 10-inch angel food pan.
2. Using a fine-mesh strainer, strain together the matzo cake meal and potato starch 4 times. Set aside.
3. Place the egg yolks and the whole egg in the small bowl of an electric mixer. Beat on medium speed for 2 minutes. Add *1 cup* of sugar, 1 tablespoon at a time, taking 4 to 5 minutes to blend it in well.* Scrape the sides of bowl occasionally. The mixture will thicken and turn light yellow in color.
4. Reduce the mixer speed to medium-low. Add the juices and rinds; beat 1 minute longer.
5. Reduce speed to low. Gradually add the dry ingredients and mix for 10 to 15 seconds, or until the batter is smooth. Transfer to a large mixing bowl and set aside.

*If using a KitchenAid Mixer, reduce mixing time by one-half.

Special Occasion Cakes

6. Place the egg whites in the large bowl of the mixer. Using clean beaters or the whip attachment, beat the whites on medium speed until frothy. Add the salt. Increase speed to medium-high and beat until the whites form soft peaks. Toward the side of bowl, gradually add the remaining $1/2$ *cup* sugar over 30 seconds, to blend. Beat 15 seconds longer.
7. With a $2^{3}/_4$-inch-wide rubber spatula, fold $1/4$ of the beaten whites into yolk mixture, taking about 20 turns to lighten. Fold in the remaining whites, taking another 40 turns.
8. Gently spoon the batter into the pan and smooth the top with the back of a spoon. Bake in the preheated oven 50 to 55 minutes, or until the cake is golden brown and springy to the touch.
9. Remove the cake from the oven and *immediately* invert the pan onto a cake rack. Let the cake cool completely in the pan. To remove the pan, turn the cake upright and run a thin, sharp knife 2 or 3 strokes around the sides of the pan. Then run the knife around center tube. Lifting cake by center tube, remove the ring. To loosen the bottom, run the knife under the cake in 2 or 3 sweeps, then invert the cake and remove the tube section. Transfer to a cake platter, top or bottom side up.

STORAGE: Store at room temperature under a glass dome, or covered with aluminum foil, for up to 1 week.

VARIATIONS

CHOCOLATE FLECK CAKE

1. Grate 3 ounces of semisweet chocolate, using a hand grater to make very fine dustlike particles. Do not use a food processor. Set aside.
2. Omit the lemon rind and juice in Step 4, and add $1^{1}/_2$ teaspoons of vanilla extract with the orange rind and juice.
3. At the end of Step 5, fold in the grated chocolate after transferring the egg yolk mixture to a larger bowl. Do not overmix. Proceed with recipe.

NUT SPONGE

1. In Step 5, fold in 1 cup finely chopped walnuts or pecans after adding the dry ingredients. Proceed with recipe.

🌾 FEATHER SPONGE CAKE

....

*I f made up properly, this beautiful cake will rise to the heavens.
    Do not overhandle the batter; too much folding will deflate the
eggs. It is not necessary for the whites to disappear entirely, only the
larger pieces.*

....

▽ ....

AT A GLANCE

SERVES: 14 to 16
PAN: 10″ angel food
with removable
bottom (4-quart
capacity)
PAN PREP: Ungreased
OVEN TEMP: 350°
RACK LEVEL: Lower
third
BAKING TIME: 50 to
55 minutes
METHOD: Electric
mixer

....

8	large egg yolks (see Note)
1	whole large egg (see Note)
1 1/2	cups superfine or strained sugar, divided
2	tablespoons orange juice
1 1/2	tablespoons fresh lemon juice
1	teaspoon grated navel orange rind
2	teaspoons grated lemon rind
1	cup potato starch
8	large egg whites
1/4	teaspoon salt

1. Position a rack in the lower third of the oven and preheat to
   350°. Have ready an ungreased 10-inch angel food pan.
2. Put the yolks and the whole egg in the small bowl of an electric
   mixer. Beat on medium speed for 2 minutes. Add *1 cup* of sugar,
   1 tablespoon at a time, taking 4 to 5 minutes to blend it in well.*
   Scrape sides of bowl occasionally. The mixture will thicken and
   turn light yellow in color.
3. Reduce mixer speed to medium-low. Add the juices and rinds,
   and beat 1 minute longer.
4. Reduce speed to low. Gradually add the potato starch and mix
   for 10 to 15 seconds, or until the batter is smooth. Transfer the
   batter to a large mixing bowl and set aside.
5. Place egg whites in the large bowl of the mixer. Using clean beaters or the whip attachment, beat the whites on medium speed
   until frothy. Add the salt. Increase the speed to medium-high,
   and beat until the whites form soft peaks. Gradually add the
   remaining *1/2 cup* sugar over 30 seconds. Beat 15 seconds longer.
6. Using a 2 3/4-inch-wide rubber spatula, fold 1/4 of the beaten whites

*If using a KitchenAid Mixer, reduce mixing time by one-half.

*Special
Occasion
Cakes*

into yolk mixture, taking about 20 turns to lighten. Then fold in remaining whites, taking 40 additional turns.

7. Gently spoon the batter into the pan, smoothing the surface with the back of a spoon. Bake in the preheated oven 50 to 55 minutes, until cake is golden brown and springy to the touch.

8. Remove from the oven and *immediately* invert the pan onto a cake rack. Let the cake cool completely in the pan. To remove the pan, run a thin, sharp knife 2 or 3 times around the sides of the pan. Then run the knife around the center tube. Lift the cake by the center tube and remove the outer ring. To loosen the bottom, run the knife under the cake in 2 or 3 sweeps, then invert onto a rack and remove the tube section. Place on cake platter, top or bottom side up.

STORAGE: Store at room temperature under a glass dome or covered with aluminum foil for up to 1 week.

NOTE: If you are using a KitchenAid mixer, reduce the total number of eggs from 9 to 7 and the mixing time by one-half.

🌰 WINE NUT SPONGE CAKE

This is for those who love the distinctive flavor and texture of nuts. It has an intense nutty flavor and moist crumb that comes from the rich oils nuts exude when they are finely chopped. Sweet Passover wine, cinnamon, and tangy citrus rinds further enhance the flavor.

This is a very fragile cake, so take care when removing it from the pan to avoid tearing it, and use a deft hand when inverting the cake onto a cake platter.

▽
AT A GLANCE

SERVES: 14 to 16
PAN: 10″ angel food with a removable bottom (4-quart capacity)
PAN PREP: Ungreased
OVEN TEMP: 325°
RACK LEVEL: Lower third
BAKING TIME: 50 to 55 minutes
METHOD: Electric mixer/food processor

1¼	cups pecans or walnuts
½	cup matzo cake meal
½	cup potato starch
1	teaspoon cinnamon
7	egg yolks
1⅓	cups superfine or strained sugar, divided
⅓	cup sweet Passover wine
1½	teaspoons freshly grated orange rind
1	teaspoon freshly grated lemon rind
7	egg whites
¼	teaspoon salt

1. Position a rack in the lower third of the oven and preheat to 325°. Have ready an ungreased 10-inch angel food pan.
2. Place half of the nuts in the container of a food processor. Pulse 6 to 8 times with the steel blade to break up the pieces. Then process for 15 to 20 seconds or until the nuts are finely chopped. Empty the chopped nuts into a small bowl. Repeat with the other half of the nuts, then combine with the first batch and set aside.
3. Using a fine-mesh strainer, strain together the matzo cake meal, potato starch, and cinnamon 4 times. Set aside.
4. Put the egg yolks in the small bowl of an electric mixer fitted with beaters. Beat on medium speed for 2 minutes. Add *1 cup* of sugar, 1 tablespoon at a time, taking 4 to 5 minutes to blend it in well. Scrape the sides of the bowl occasionally. The mixture will thicken and turn light yellow in color. Drizzle in the wine and then add the orange and lemon rinds.

Special Occasion Cakes

5. Reduce the mixer speed to low and add the dry ingredients ⅓ at a time, mixing only until blended. Remove the bowl from the mixer and set aside.

6. Wash and dry the beaters. In the large bowl of the mixer, whip the egg whites on medium speed until frothy. Add the salt and increase the speed to medium-high. Whip until the whites form firm peaks when the beaters are lifted. Toward the sides of the bowl, gradually add the remaining ⅓ *cup* sugar, taking 30 seconds. Whip the mixture 45 seconds longer. *Note:* This cake is made with a stiff meringue.

7. Using a 2¾-inch-wide rubber spatula, fold ¼ of the beaten whites into the yolk mixture, taking 20 turns to lighten. Then fold the yolk mixture into the remaining whites. After about 20 turns, begin sprinkling in the chopped nuts and continue folding until all the nuts are added, taking about 40 additional turns.

8. Gently spoon the batter into the pan, smoothing the surface with the back of a spoon. Center the cake on the rack and bake in the preheated oven for 50 to 55 minutes, or until the cake is golden brown and springy to the touch.

9. Remove the cake from the oven and *immediately* invert onto a cake rack to cool completely in the pan. To remove, moisten a thin, sharp knife under very hot water and run the blade 3 or 4 times around the sides of the pan, moistening the knife each time. Then run the knife around the center tube. Lift the cake by the center tube and remove the outer rim. Run the knife under the cake in 2 or 3 sweeps and carefully invert the cake onto a rack. Remove the tube section. Then center a cake platter over the cake and turn the cake top side up onto the platter. Dust the top of the cake lightly with confectioners' sugar just before serving.

STORAGE: Store at room temperature under a glass dome or covered with aluminum foil for up to 1 week.

🍂 PASSOVER LEMON CHIFFON CAKE

....

This cake contains vegetable oil for moistness, but less than is in a traditional chiffon batter. The cake has a piquant lemony taste, but you can try any combination of juices and rinds that strikes your fancy.

....

▽..

AT A GLANCE

SERVES: 14 to 16
PAN: 10″ angel food with removable bottom (4-quart capacity)
PAN PREP: Ungreased
OVEN TEMP: 350°
RACK LEVEL: Lower third
BAKING TIME: 45 to 50 minutes
METHOD: Electric mixer

....

½	cup fresh lemon juice
4	teaspoons grated lemon rind (from about 2 medium lemons)
⅔	cup matzo cake meal
⅔	cup potato starch
8	large egg yolks
1	whole large egg
1⅔	cups superfine or strained sugar, divided
⅓	cup flavorless vegetable oil
8	large egg whites
¼	teaspoon salt

1. Place the lemon juice and rind in a small saucepan. Bring to a slow boil, then simmer 4 to 5 minutes. You should have about 6 tablespoons of liquid. Add a bit of water if there is not enough. Set aside to cool.
2. Position a rack in the lower third of the oven and preheat to 350°. Have ready an ungreased 10-inch angel food pan.
3. Using a fine-mesh strainer, strain together the matzo cake meal and potato starch 4 times. Set aside.
4. Place the yolks and the whole egg in the small bowl of an electric mixer. Beat on medium speed for 2 minutes. Add *1 cup* sugar, 1 tablespoon at a time, taking 4 to 5 minutes to blend it in well.* Scrape sides of bowl occasionally. The mixture will thicken and turn light yellow in color. *Slowly* pour in the vegetable oil in a steady stream, taking 15 seconds. Beat for 1 minute longer.
5. Reduce the mixer speed to medium-low. Add the cooled lemon juice and rind. Beat 1 minute longer.
6. Reduce speed to low. Gradually add the dry ingredients and mix

*If using a KitchenAid Mixer, reduce mixing time by one-half.

for 10 to 15 seconds, or until batter is smooth. Transfer to a large mixing bowl and set aside.

7. Wash and dry the beaters. Put the egg whites in the large bowl of the mixer. Using the beaters or whip attachment, beat on medium speed until frothy. Add the salt.

8. Increase the mixer speed to medium-high and whip until the whites form soft peaks. Gradually add the remaining ²/₃ *cup* sugar over 45 seconds. Beat the meringue 30 seconds longer.

9. Using a 2³/₄-inch-wide rubber spatula, fold ¼ of the meringue into the yolk mixture, taking 20 turns to lighten. Fold in the remaining whites, taking about 40 additional turns.

10. Gently spoon the batter into the pan, smoothing the top with the back of a spoon. Center the pan on the rack and bake in the preheated oven for 45 to 50 minutes until cake is golden brown on top and springy to the touch.

11. Remove from the oven and *immediately* invert onto a cake rack. Let the cake cool completely in the pan. To remove the pan, run a thin, sharp knife 2 or 3 times around the sides of the pan. Then run the knife around the center tube. Lift cake by the center tube and remove the outer rim. Run the knife under the cake in 2 or 3 sweeps. Invert and remove the tube section. Place the cake on a cake platter, top or bottom side up.

STORAGE: Store at room temperature under a glass dome or covered with aluminum foil for up to 1 week.

CRUNCHY MERINGUE TORTE

I have made this torte for years using crackers, but broken matzos make a delicious substitute. It differs from the usual Passover sponge in that it has a very chewy texture—almost like a meringue candy.

▽
AT A GLANCE

SERVES: 6 to 8
PAN: 9″ springform
PAN PREP: Very well greased/dusted with matzo cake meal
OVEN TEMP: 325°
RACK LEVEL: Lower third
BAKING TIME: 35 to 40 minutes
METHOD: Electric mixer

4	large egg whites
1/4	teaspoon salt
1	cup plus 2 tablespoons superfine or strained sugar, divided
1 1/2	teaspoons vanilla extract
2	plain matzos, broken into 1/4-inch pieces (about 1 1/2 cups)
3	ounces semisweet chocolate, broken into 1/4-inch pieces (about 1/2 cup)
1	cup coarsely chopped walnuts (reserve 2 tablespoons for topping)

1. Position a rack in the lower third of the oven and preheat to 325°. Generously grease a 9-inch springform and dust with matzo cake meal. Invert and tap lightly into sink to remove excess.
2. In the large bowl of an electric mixer fitted with beaters or whip attachment, beat the egg whites on medium speed until frothy. Add the salt. Increase speed to medium-high and continue to beat until whites stand in firm, moist peaks, but are not dry. Add *1 cup* of the sugar, sprinkling it in toward the side of the bowl, over 2 minutes, starting with 1 tablespoon and increasing to 2 tablespoons. Continue beating until the whites form a thick, shiny meringue. Add the vanilla and beat 15 seconds longer.
3. Remove the bowl from the mixer. Using a 2 3/4-inch-wide rubber spatula, fold in the matzo, chocolate, nuts, and remaining *2 tablespoons* of sugar.
4. Spoon the meringue into the prepared pan. Smooth the top with the back of a spoon and sprinkle with the reserved 2 tablespoons of walnuts. Cut a 12-inch piece of aluminum foil and place the cake pan on the foil, molding the edges around the pan. Bake in the preheated oven 35 to 40 minutes, until torte starts to come away from the sides of pan and begins to brown lightly on top.

Special Occasion Cakes

427

Remove the cake from the oven, discard the aluminum foil, and place cake on a rack to cool completely. Run a sharp knife around edge of pan and remove the metal rim. Cut the cake into wedges and serve with a dollop of whipped cream.

STORAGE: Store in the refrigerator, lightly covered with foil, for up to 4 days.

🍫 CHOCOLATE SPONGE LOAF WITH ORANGE WALNUT WHIPPED CREAM

This is a delicious Passover treat for those times when you wish to serve a very special holiday dessert. Since the batter is made with potato starch, it has a wonderful velvety texture.

▽
AT A GLANCE

SERVES: 6 to 8
PAN: 10½″ × 15½″ × 1″ jelly roll
PAN PREP: Butter/parchment/butter (bottom only)
OVEN TEMP: 375°
RACK LEVEL: Lower third
BAKING TIME: 12 to 14 minutes
METHOD: Electric mixer

THE CAKE:

⅓	cup strained unsweetened cocoa
1	tablespoon freeze-dried coffee
⅓	cup boiling water
4	large egg yolks, at room temperature
⅞	cup (1 cup less 2 tablespoons) superfine or strained sugar
1	teaspoon vanilla extract
¼	cup strained potato starch
4	large egg whites, at room temperature
	Pinch of salt
1½	teaspoons sugar for garnish
½	teaspoon cocoa for garnish

THE ORANGE WALNUT WHIPPED CREAM:

1	cup walnuts, coarsely chopped
2	cups heavy cream, well chilled
2 to 3	tablespoons confectioners' sugar
1	teaspoon vanilla extract
½	teaspoon grated navel orange rind, or to taste

1. Position a rack in the lower third of the oven and preheat to 375°. Butter the bottom of a 10½" × 15½" × 1" jelly roll pan, line the bottom of the pan with parchment, and butter the parchment.

2. To make the cake: Put the cocoa in a small bowl. Dissolve the coffee in boiling water and stir it into the cocoa in two additions, blending until very smooth. Set aside.

3. In a small bowl of an electric mixer, beat the egg yolks on medium speed until thickened and light in color. Add the sugar, 1 tablespoon at a time, taking 3 to 4 minutes to blend it in well.* Reduce speed to low and add the chocolate mixture and vanilla extract. Beat 1 minute. Blend in the potato starch.

4. In the large bowl of an electric mixer fitted with clean beaters or whip attachment, beat the whites on medium speed until frothy. Add the salt. Increase speed to medium-high and continue beating until the whites are firm and shiny, but not dry.

5. Using a 2¾-inch-wide rubber spatula, fold ¼ of the beaten whites into the chocolate mixture, taking 20 turns to lighten. Then fold the chocolate mixture into the remaining whites, taking about 40 additional turns.

6. Push the batter into the prepared pan with a rubber spatula. Using a tablespoon, carefully spread the batter evenly across pan and into the corners. Bake in the preheated oven 12 to 14 minutes, until cake is springy on top and comes away from sides of the pan.

7. While the cake is baking, cut a strip of baking parchment about 18 inches long and dust it with 4 teaspoons of granulated sugar.

8. When cake is done, remove it from the oven. Run a thin knife around the sides of the pan and *immediately* invert onto the sugared paper. Carefully lift off the pan. To loosen the parchment, brush with warm water, wait 30 seconds, and carefully peel off paper.

9. To make the orange cream filling: Spread the nuts in a shallow baking pan and bake in a 325° oven for 6 to 8 minutes or until lightly toasted. Cool and chop coarsely.

10. Place the cream in the large chilled bowl of an electric mixer fitted with chilled beaters or whip attachment. Beat on medium speed until the cream begins to thicken. Add the sugar, vanilla, and orange rind and continue to beat until the cream forms soft

*If using a KitchenAid Mixer, reduce mixing time by one-half.

mounds. Remove from the mixer. Using a wire balloon whisk, finish beating by hand until the cream is thick.

11. Remove ½ of the cream to a small bowl. Use this cream for frosting the sides of the loaf. Fold ½ cup chopped walnuts into the remaining cream for the filling, reserving the remainder of the nuts for garnish.

TO ASSEMBLE THE CAKE:

1. Combine the 1½ teaspoons sugar and the cocoa in a small bowl. Set aside.

2. Divide the sponge sheet into four 3½″ × 10″ strips. Cut 4 strips of waxed paper, 2 long and 2 short, and place on serving platter to protect it.

3. Position one of the strips from the middle section of the cake on the platter, top down. Spread with ⅓ of the walnut cream filling. Cover with a second strip from the middle section, top down, and spread with another ⅓ of the filling. Using one of the end pieces, arrange the third strip, top down, and cover with remaining filling. Place the last strip, top side up. Press the sides of the loaf gently to align the layers.

4. Using a fine-mesh strainer, dust the top of the cake heavily with the sugar/cocoa mixture by tapping strainer gently over surface of cake.

5. Spread the remaining cream on the sides of the cake. Garnish the sides with reserved coarsely chopped walnuts by pressing the nuts into the cream with the palm of your hand. Place the cake in the refrigerator at least 1 hour to set. Before serving, let stand 15 minutes at room temperature.

STORAGE: Refrigerate leftover cake covered loosely with a foil tent for up to 3 days.

❧ CHOCOLATE ALMOND TORTE

···

This dense, moist chocolate torte is rich with the flavor of toasted almonds, but its true charm lies in the fragile crust that forms across the top as the cake bakes. Although the crust flakes when the torte is sliced, I find the crumbs actually add to its appeal. A day's rest before serving mellows the chocolate flavor, making the torte even better.

···

▽··

AT A GLANCE

SERVES: 8 to 10
PAN: 9″ springform
PAN PREP: Greased/
matzo cake meal
OVEN TEMP: 350°
RACK LEVEL: Lower
third
BAKING TIME: 45 to
50 minutes
METHOD: Electric
mixer

························

7	ounces bittersweet or semisweet chocolate, melted
1	tablespoon freeze-dried coffee
1/4	cup boiling water
2/3	cup blanched, slivered almonds, lightly toasted (page 57)
1/4	cup potato starch
1/2	cup (1 stick) unsalted butter
1	cup plus 3 tablespoons superfine or strained sugar, divided
6	large egg yolks
1	teaspoon vanilla extract
6	large egg whites
1/8	teaspoon salt

1. Position a rack in the lower third of the oven and preheat to 350°. Butter a 9-inch springform pan and dust with matzo cake meal. Invert and tap to remove excess.
2. Dissolve the coffee in the boiling water. Add all at once to the melted chocolate, blending until completely smooth. Set aside.
3. Put the almonds and potato starch in the container of a food processor fitted with the steel blade. Process until the almonds are ground very fine, or chop very fine by hand, then combine with the potato starch. Set aside.
4. Cut the butter into 1-inch pieces and place in the small bowl of an electric mixer fitted with beaters or paddle attachment. Soften on low speed. Increase speed to medium and cream until smooth and light in color, about 1½ to 2 minutes.
5. Add *1 cup* sugar, 1 tablespoon at a time, taking 4 to 5 minutes to blend it in well. Scrape the sides of the bowl occasionally. Add the yolks, 2 at a time, at 1-minute intervals. Add the cooled choc-

*Special
Occasion
Cakes*

431

olate mixture and the vanilla and continue beating until blended. Scrape the bottom of the bowl as necessary.

6. Reduce mixer speed to low. Add the flour/nut mixture all at once and mix until just blended.

7. Wash and dry the beaters. Place the egg whites in the large bowl of an electric mixer and whip on medium speed until frothy. Add the salt. Increase the speed to medium-high and continue beating until the whites form soft peaks. Add the remaining 3 *tablespoons* sugar, 1 tablespoon at a time, over 30 seconds. Continue to beat 15 seconds longer.

8. Remove the bowl from the mixer. Using a 2¾-inch-wide rubber spatula, fold ¼ of the whites into yolk mixture, taking 20 turns to lighten. Fold in the remaining whites, taking about 40 additional turns.

9. Spoon the batter into the prepared pan, smoothing the top with the back of a spoon. Bake in the preheated oven for 45 to 50 minutes, or until the cake begins to leave sides of pan. Remove from the oven and place on a cake rack to cool completely. The cake will sink somewhat in the center as it cools and the top will form a fragile crust. Run a sharp knife around edge of pan, then remove the outer ring. Just before serving, dust the top generously with confectioner's sugar. Cut into wedges and serve with a dollop of whipped cream.

STORAGE: Store at room temperature under a glass dome or covered with aluminum foil for up to 3 days.

Part Four

SWEET ENDINGS

Fillings, Frostings, Glazes, and Syrups

illings, frostings, glazes, and syrups are the finishing touches that transform ordinary cakes into special treats. While many cakes are delicious plain, there are occasions when you may wish to serve a more dressed-up pastry. These preparations not only lend eye appeal, they perform a function. Fillings offer an opportunity to vary the flavor and texture, while frostings and glazes not only add taste, they form a protective shield that preserves freshness. Syrups add moistness.

In terms of flavor and texture, fillings and frostings should be compatible with each other as well as the cake they are decorating.

435

Also bear in mind the refrigeration issue. Cakes containing custard or pudding fillings made with eggs, and fresh fruit or whipped cream fillings, require refrigeration because these ingredients are more perishable. Generally, 3 days is the maximum storage time even under refrigeration. Cakes filled with jam are less perishable.

Frostings made with confectioners' sugar are good choices for butter cakes, since neither the frosting nor the cake requires refrigeration. If you do make a butter cake with a filling or frosting that requires cold storage, make the cake ahead, but do not assemble it until the day it is to be eaten. The cake will harden if chilled too long in the refrigerator.

European-style buttercream frostings are less sweet than confectioners' sugar frostings, but they are sinfully rich. They are made with a generous amount of butter, either egg yolks or whites, granulated sugar, and flavorings. While all buttercreams require refrigeration, they have a long shelf life and also freeze extremely well, making them a real advantage for spur-of-the-moment needs. Having a stockpile of buttercreams in the freezer also makes it easy to combine more than one flavor in a cake.

Buttercreams are most compatible with genoise or cakes such as sponge or chiffon. These cakes do not harden in the refrigerator and although the buttercream does harden, it softens upon standing at room temperature. Buttercream-frosted cakes should never be served directly from the refrigerator.

This chapter contains a recipe for a Swiss-style buttercream made with sugar, egg whites, and butter that is less rich than the classic French buttercream, which contains egg yolks. It can be made in a variety of flavors such as chocolate, mocha, praline, and orange. An easy-to-make variation on the European-style buttercreams is Quick Buttercream Frosting, a tasty light frosting that is a breeze to prepare.

Glazes, which are thinner coatings than frostings, are the least perishable. Generally, glazes are of three types: those that are spread, those that are drizzled, and those that are poured. Glazes that are spread and drizzled are the simple sugary types that are used to garnish such cakes as fluted or bundt styles. These glazes do not have to cover the entire surface of the cake and are easily applied with a spoon or pastry brush. The most common is vanilla glaze, made primarily from confectioners' sugar and water.

A poured glaze has a formal mirrorlike finish commonly identified with European-style tortes. The luxuriously rich ganache, a thick coating made from fine chocolate and heavy cream, is one of the most popular of these. Glazes such as ganache are often applied over a thin layer of strained preserves, which provides a very smooth surface upon which to pour the glaze.

Glazes have the best sheen if made shortly before using. Upon standing, they form a sugary crust and, because they thicken quickly, will require some thinning with liquid. They can be frozen but again the glossiness and fluidity will be affected. Syrups are used for genoise layers. They turn dry cakes into moist and flavorful creations.

Throughout the book are filling, frosting, and glaze recipes paired with appropriate cakes. However, many can be used with other cake recipes to suit your personal taste. The dried-fruit-and-nut-filled frosting that accompanies the recipe for the Lady Baltimore cake, for example, would be fabulous on the golden citrus chiffon cake.

Whether you choose to coat your cake with a simple glaze or a more intricate topping, frosting a cake is fun to do and the results are gratifying. Notice how the conversation stops as you set a beautiful cake on the table. Inevitably at least one of your guests will gasp in admiration and then say, "Oh no, I really shouldn't"—but, inevitably, they do.

Fillings

▶ Fillings made with egg yolks or fruit should be prepared in noncorrosive heavy saucepans such as stainless steel or enameled cast iron. Aluminum pans can interact with these ingredients, discoloring the filling or imparting a metallic taste.

▶ Fillings that are thickened with flour or cornstarch must be brought to the boiling point over *low* heat to prevent scorching, then cooked at least 1 minute so the starch can develop its full thickening power. Insufficient cooking may result in the filling thinning down upon cooling.

▶ Since fillings consist of few ingredients, it would seem they should be easy to make. In reality, they are a bit tricky until you've mastered the technique. Here are a few tips for avoiding lumps and breakdowns:

—Stir fillings continuously with a wooden spoon until they begin to thicken. Wooden spoons do not scratch the saucepan and reach easily into the edges of the pan to free any thickened substance that may accumulate. They also do not become hot, as a metal spoon would.

—Just as the mixture reaches the boil, change from a wooden spoon to a whisk and, using just a few back-and-forth motions, whisk the filling. This immediately smooths out any lumps that may have begun to form. Elevate the saucepan 2 to 3 inches above the flame while whisking. This slows down the cooking and further minimizes the risk of lumping. Return to the spoon and, gently stirring, continue to cook at least 1 minute longer.

—Do not vigorously stir cornstarch-thickened fillings after they reach the boiling point; overmixing causes them to

438

thin down. Stirring occasionally just to prevent the sauce from sticking to the bottom of the saucepan is sufficient.

▶ For the best vanilla flavor in custard fillings, use vanilla bean. One inch of vanilla bean is about equivalent to 1/2 teaspoon of vanilla extract. You may use vanilla extract along with the vanilla bean, reducing the amount of vanilla bean accordingly.

▶ Cut solid chocolate into pieces before adding to hot milk or cream. Otherwise, the chocolate takes so long to melt that it becomes too hot and the flavor is impaired.

▶ To prevent a film from forming on the surface of a filling as it cools, cover it with lightly buttered waxed paper or parchment. To hasten the cooling of a filling that is to be refrigerated, lift the paper up from time to time and give a gentle stir with a spoon.

▶ You can also speed the cooling by transferring the filling from the hot saucepan to a bowl and putting it in a larger bowl filled with ice cubes and a small amount of water. Or simply place the saucepan directly into the ice-cube-filled bowl.

▶ When you are blending cooked fillings with whipped cream and/or whipped egg whites, the consistency and temperature of both ingredients directly affect how smoothly they will combine. The whipped cream and the egg whites should be whipped just to the soft peak stage. The temperature of the filling must be *tepid*. If it is too hot, the filling will thin out when the ingredients are combined. If it is too cold, lumps will form.

▶ Since cooked fillings are not as sweet and sugary as frostings, they can be applied more thickly. Usually about 1/4 inch is sufficient, depending on personal preference and the requirements of the recipe.

▶ Cooked fillings have a short shelf life and are at their best when used the day they are made. They should not be frozen.

🌿 CLEAR LEMON FILLING

Makes about 1¹/₂ cups, enough to cover a 9- or 10-inch layer or two 8-inch layers

....

One of my favorite cake fillings, this is marvelous between layers of plain genoise, yellow or white butter cake. A simple white frosting such as a 7-Minute Frosting (page 448), Quick Buttercream (page 447), or Whipped Cream (page 486) is the most compatible with the refreshing citrus taste.

....

³/₄	cup plus 2 tablespoons sugar
3	tablespoons cornstarch
3	tablespoons unbleached all-purpose flour
³/₄	cup water
¹/₂	cup fresh orange juice
¹/₄	cup fresh lemon juice
2	large egg yolks
1 to 2	tablespoons soft unsalted butter
1	teaspoon grated lemon rind

1. In a 1¹/₂-quart saucepan, combine the sugar, cornstarch, and flour. Using a whisk, stir until thoroughly blended.
2. In a small bowl, combine the water, orange juice, and lemon juice. Gradually add the liquids to the dry ingredients, whisking until smooth. Bring to a gentle boil over low heat, stirring constantly with a wooden spoon. The mixture will be very thick. Simmer on *very low* heat 1 to 2 minutes longer, stirring gently.
3. Place the egg yolks in a small bowl and whisk lightly to blend. Gradually add ¹/₄ of the sauce to yolks, stirring, to temper them. Then whisk the yolk mixture into the saucepan. Cook over low heat until filling comes to a second boil. Be sure to stir into the edges of the saucepan with a wooden spoon to reach any sauce that might cling.
4. Off the heat, blend in the butter and lemon rind. Transfer the filling to a bowl, then butter a small piece of waxed paper and place it greased side down onto the surface of the filling to keep it from

filming. Put the filling in the refrigerator for at least 1/2 hour or until completely cool. Stir briefly to smooth out before using.

STORAGE: This filling is at its best when used the day it is made.

❧ VANILLA PASTRY CREAM FILLING

Makes about 1 1/3 cups, enough to cover a 9- or 10-inch layer or two 8-inch layers

....

This basic vanilla cream filling is lightened with whipped cream. Since it requires refrigeration, it is best used with sponge-style cakes.

....

1	cup milk
One	2-inch piece vanilla bean
3	large egg yolks
1/4	cup sugar
2	tablespoons cornstarch
1	tablespoon flour
1/3	cup heavy cream
1	teaspoon vanilla extract

1. Put the milk and vanilla bean in a 2-quart saucepan. Over *low* heat, bring to just below the boiling point. Set aside.
2. Place the egg yolks in a small mixing bowl. Gradually add the sugar, whisking until the mixture lightens in color. Blend in the cornstarch and flour.
3. Remove the vanilla bean from the milk and slit it lengthwise with the tip of a paring knife. Scrape the small black beans from inside the pod into the milk. Discard the pod.
4. Whisk 1/4 of the milk into the yolk mixture, mixing until smooth. Then add the yolk mixture to the remaining milk. Place over low heat, and continue to stir constantly around the sides of the saucepan with a wooden spoon, until the mixture comes to a gentle boil and is quite thick.

5. Using the whisk, stir the filling briefly just until lumps are removed and the mixture is smooth. Simmer on low heat for 1 minute, stirring occasionally with a wooden spoon. Be sure to scrape the sides. Place the saucepan in a bowl of ice filled with a small amount of water, and cool until *just tepid*. This will only take a few minutes.
6. While the filling is cooling, whip the cream to the soft peak stage. Fold the cream and vanilla extract into the tepid custard, incorporating until smooth.

STORAGE: Cover with a piece of buttered waxed paper or parchment and refrigerate for at least ¹/₂ hour. This filling is at its best when used the day it is made.

VARIATION
....

PRALINE CREAM FILLING

Substitute 2 tablespoons praline paste (page 498 or see Mail Order Sources) for the vanilla bean in Step 1, whisking it into the heated milk until smooth. If the praline paste does not readily dissolve, press it frequently against the sides of the saucepan with a spoon to soften. Strain the milk before adding to the yolk mixture to remove lumps. Proceed with recipe, reducing the vanilla extract to ¹/₂ teaspoon.

❧ BITTERSWEET CHOCOLATE FILLING

Makes about 1¹/₃ cups, enough to cover a 9 or 10-inch layer or two 8-inch layers

....

This chocolate filling has a puddinglike consistency and is a fabulous addition to layer cakes. The custard blends with the crumb of the cake to create a pleasant soft sensation for the palate. A sweeter version of this filling follows. Although that recipe yields slightly more, the two are interchangeable.

....

    1 cup milk
  1/4 cup heavy cream
    2 ounces unsweetened chocolate, finely chopped
    2 large egg yolks
  1/3 cup sugar
    1 tablespoon cornstarch
    1 tablespoon flour
  1/8 teaspoon salt
    1 teaspoon vanilla extract

1. Place the milk, cream, and chocolate in a heavy 2-quart saucepan and heat on a low flame almost to boiling, stirring with a whisk until the chocolate is completely melted and the mixture is smooth.
2. In a medium-sized mixing bowl, whisk the yolks until lightened in color. Gradually add the sugar, whisking until the mixture thickens like a batter. Blend in the cornstarch, flour, and salt.
3. Stir about 1/4 of the hot chocolate mixture into the yolk mixture to temper the eggs. Then add the yolk mixture to the remaining chocolate and stir thoroughly to blend.
4. Set the saucepan over low heat and, using a wooden spoon, stir constantly until the mixture begins to thicken. Just as the mixture reaches the boiling point, switch from the spoon to a whisk, stirring briefly just until smooth. Again using the wooden spoon, scrape into the corners of the pan and continue to cook over low heat for about 1 minute, stirring occasionally. If the filling is not completely smooth, whisk again briefly, but *do not overbeat*.
5. Remove the saucepan from the heat and stir in the vanilla. Transfer the filling to a bowl, cover with buttered waxed paper or parchment, and let stand at room temperature for 15 minutes, then refrigerate until cold.

STORAGE: This filling is at its best when used the day it is made.

🦢 CHOCOLATE CUSTARD FILLING

Makes about 2 cups, enough to fill two 9-inch layers

....

> 1½   cups milk
> ⅓   cup heavy cream
> 2   ounces unsweetened chocolate, finely chopped
> ½   cup sugar
> 2   tablespoons cornstarch
> 4   teaspoons flour
> ⅛   teaspoon salt
> 3   large egg yolks
> 1½   teaspoons vanilla extract

1. Fill the bottom of a double boiler with 1 to 1½ inches of water. Bring to a boil and reduce the flame to low.
2. Put the milk, cream, and chocolate in the top portion of a double boiler. Set over the boiling water and heat, stirring with a whisk, until the chocolate is completely melted and the mixture is smooth.
3. In a medium-sized mixing bowl, whisk together the sugar, cornstarch, flour, and salt. Whisk the dry ingredients rapidly into the hot milk, blending until smooth.
4. Stir constantly with a wooden spoon and, as the mixture thickens to the consistency of warm chocolate pudding, use the whisk again to remove any lumps that may have formed, but do not overmix. Cover the pot and cook the filling 10 to 12 minutes, stirring occasionally. Be sure to reach into the corners of the saucepan to remove any lumps that may have accumulated.
5. In a small bowl, lightly beat the egg yolks. Add about ⅓ cup of the hot filling to the yolks to temper them. Then return the yolk mixture to the remaining hot filling and stir thoroughly with a wooden spoon. Continue to cook over low heat for 2 to 3 minutes, stirring occasionally. The custard will thicken further. If the filling is not smooth, whisk again briefly.
6. Remove the custard from the top of the double boiler and blend in the vanilla. Empty the filling into a bowl, cover the top with buttered waxed paper or parchment, and let stand at room temperature for 15 minutes. Then refrigerate until cold.

STORAGE: This will keep 3 days tightly covered in the refrigerator.

Frostings

▶ The texture of the cake should be compatible with a glaze or frosting. Fillings and frostings that require refrigeration work best with sponge-style cakes. Since butter cakes harden when they are chilled, nonrefrigerated frostings are your best choice.

▶ Always brush excess crumbs from the sides of a cake with a soft pastry brush before applying a frosting or glaze.

▶ Many cakes are easier to frost when the cake is supported by a cardboard disk cut to size. The disk enables you to hold the cake in your hand while frosting it. Disks are especially useful for European tortes that receive glazes, since the cardboard base simplifies moving the cake from a rack to a serving platter.

▶ Cakes are secured to plates or cardboard disks with dabs of light corn syrup. A thin smear of icing spread onto the plate or disk will also do the trick.

▶ Double layer cakes should be positioned with the bottom layer top side down and the top layer top side up. This not only makes the frosting easier to spread; since there are no crumb surfaces exposed to the frosting, it gives the cake a more even shape. If the layers are not the same thickness, place the thinner layer on top. The thicker bottom will support the cake better.

▶ When assembling cakes with more than two layers, place the first layer top side down on a cake plate or cardboard disk and continue to position the layers top side down until you reach the top layer. The final layer is almost always positioned top side up. If the layers have not been evenly cut, build up the lowest side of the bottom layer with frosting so that the top of the cake will be even.

▶ For best results, beat confectioners' sugar frostings by hand. An electric mixer breaks down the butter and also whips too much air into the frosting, creating air bubbles that prevent the icing from spreading smoothly.

▶ It is best to use confectioners' sugar icings immediately because they thicken and form a crust as they stand. If this happens, thin with drops of hot water.

▶ On larger cakes, the consistency of the confectioners' sugar icing between the layers should be slightly thicker than on the top and sides. After the layers are assembled, thin the remaining frosting with drops of the liquid used in your icing recipe or with hot water before proceeding.

▶ Buttercream frostings are sensitive to heat. If the day is very humid or your kitchen very warm, the butter breaks down too quickly. Working in an air-conditioned kitchen is advisable.

▶ It is best to use an electric mixer when making buttercreams because the eggs require lengthy beating.

▶ If a buttercream frosting becomes too soft, refrigerate it for 5 to 10 minutes to firm. However, do not leave it in the refrigerator too long or the buttercream will harden.

▶ If a cake is to be dusted with confectioners' sugar, do so just before serving; otherwise it will be absorbed into the surface of the cake.

▶ Very fresh cakes can be difficult to frost because they are very soft and the frosting often tears the cake. Placing the cake in the freezer for 5 to 10 minutes will firm the outer surface.

🍂 QUICK BUTTERCREAM FROSTING

*Makes about 3 cups, enough to fill and frost two 9-inch layers;
three 8-inch layers; the top and sides of a 9″ × 13″ × 2″
oblong cake; or a 10-inch tube cake*

....

I came upon this wonderful buttercream through my friend, Sherry
Nashmy, whose grandmother made it for all special family occasions.
*It is a quick and delicious alternative to a classic buttercream. The
consistency is not as refined as that of a traditional buttercream, but
is light and fluffy, making it seem less rich.*

....

3	tablespoons all-purpose flour
1	cup milk
1	cup (2 sticks) unsalted butter
1	cup superfine or strained sugar
1½	teaspoons vanilla extract

1. Place the flour in a small saucepan. Whisk in the milk slowly, until the mixture is smooth and free of lumps. Over low heat, stir constantly until mixture comes to a boil and thickens to a thick white sauce.
2. Remove the saucepan from the heat and continue to whisk until the sauce is very smooth. Set aside to cool to tepid, about 5 to 10 minutes. The sauce should not be too warm when it is added to the butter, or the butter will melt. However, do not allow the sauce to become too cold or it will not blend smoothly into the butter/sugar mixture.
3. While the custard is cooling, cut the butter into 1-inch pieces and place in the large bowl of an electric mixer fitted with the beaters or whip attachment. Soften on low speed, then increase the speed to medium-high and cream until light and smooth, about 1½ to 2 minutes.
4. Reduce mixer speed to medium. Gradually add the sugar, 1 tablespoon at a time over 3 minutes. Then add the sauce 1 tablespoon at a time over 30 seconds. Blend in the vanilla and continue to beat for about 20 to 30 seconds or until the frosting is somewhat fluffy.

QUICK CHOCOLATE BUTTERCREAM FROSTING

In a small heatproof container, slowly melt 2 ounces of bittersweet or semisweet chocolate. Cool to tepid. Add to the buttercream just before the vanilla extract in Step 4.

❧ 7-MINUTE FROSTING

Makes about 4 cups, enough to fill and frost two 9-inch layers; three 8-inch layers; the top and sides of a 9″ × 13″ × 2″ oblong cake; or a 10-inch tube cake

. . . .

The name of this heavenly frosting refers to the length of time that the ingredients must be beaten while cooking. A hand-held electric mixer is best to use, as the frosting must be whipped continuously over simmering water to achieve a thick, fluffy consistency. The end result is a light and luscious classic American frosting.

. . . .

3	large egg whites
1½	cups superfine or strained sugar
½	teaspoon cream of tartar
⅓	cup water
1	tablespoon light corn syrup
1½	teaspoons vanilla extract

1. Fill the bottom of a double boiler with 1 inch of water. Bring rapidly to a boil, then reduce heat to maintain a simmer.
2. Place the egg whites, sugar, cream of tartar, and water in the top of double boiler, stirring to blend the ingredients. Set over the bottom of the double boiler, cover, and cook for 1 minute. Remove the lid and stir again briefly. Using a pastry brush, brush sides of saucepan with water to prevent crystals from forming, cover, and heat 30 seconds longer.
3. Using a hand-held electric mixer, beat over the simmering water for a minimum of 7 minutes, or until thick and fluffy.
4. Add the corn syrup and vanilla and beat on medium speed 2 minutes longer. Remove from the heat. Empty into a stand mixer and beat on medium speed until the frosting cools and is very thick. If the frosting is still too soft, refrigerate for 30 minutes, then beat again.

NOTE: If the weather is very humid, additional beating time may be required. This frosting is best used the day it is made.

VARIATION

PENUCHE FROSTING

A brown sugar rendition of 7-minute frosting:

1. Instead of the superfine sugar called for in Step 2, use 1½ cups firmly packed dark brown sugar.
2. Add ½ teaspoon maple extract along with vanilla extract in Step 4.

CREAM CHEESE FROSTING

Makes about 3 cups, enough to fill and frost two 9-inch layers;
three 8-inch layers; the top and sides of a 9″ × 13″ × 2″
oblong cake; or a 10-inch tube cake

....

T his creamy, slightly tangy frosting is the traditional topping for carrot
cakes, but it is also scrumptious on most chocolate cakes.

To maintain the beautiful creamy texture, it is best to prepare this
frosting by hand. An electric beater will overmix the frosting and cause
it to become too thin.

....

$2/3$ cup (1$1/3$ sticks) unsalted butter, at room temperature
Two 8-ounce packages cream creese, at room temperature
$1/2$ teaspoon freshly grated navel orange rind
$21/2$ cups strained confectioners' sugar
2 tablespoons sour cream
1 teaspoon vanilla extract

In a medium-sized mixing bowl, combine the butter and cream
cheese. Using a wooden spoon, cream until very smooth. Blend in
the orange rind. Add the sugar alternately with the sour cream, about
three additions of sugar to two additions of sour cream. Beat until
smooth and creamy. Stir in the vanilla extract. Swirl the cream
cheese frosting onto the cake with the back of a tablespoon.

❧ ALMOND CREAM CHEESE FROSTING

*Makes about 3 cups, enough to fill and frost two 9-inch layers;
three 8-inch layers; the top and sides of a 9″ × 13″ × 2″
oblong cake; or a 10-inch tube cake*

....

*The almond flavor can be enhanced with a garnish of toasted sliced
almonds. About 1/2 cup chopped toasted almonds mixed into the
frosting is an appealing alternative.*

....

1/3	cup (2/3 stick) unsalted butter, at room temperature
One	3-ounce package cream cheese, at room temperature
3 3/4	cups strained confectioners' sugar, or more as needed
3	tablespoons heavy cream
1/4 to 1/2	teaspoon almond extract
1/8	teaspoon salt
2	tablespoons amaretto liqueur

1. Put the butter and cream cheese in a medium-sized mixing bowl. Using a wooden spoon, cream until smooth and well blended.
2. Add 2 cups of the sugar, 1/2 of the heavy cream, and salt. Beat with a wooden spoon until smooth. Add the remaining sugar, heavy cream, almond extract, and liqueur. Blend until smooth and creamy, but do not overmix or the frosting will break down. If the frosting is too thick, add a few drops of heavy cream.

❧ CREAMY PEANUT BOURBON FROSTING

Makes about 3 cups, enough to fill or frost two 9-inch layers; three 8-inch layers; the top and sides of a 9″ × 13″ × 2″ oblong cake; or a 10-inch tube cake

....

This frosting is the perfect complement for Georgia Peanut Cake (page 323). It is also a smashing success on any chocolate cake.

....

¹/₂	cup smooth peanut butter
¹/₄	cup (¹/₂ stick) unsalted butter, at room temperature
One	3-ounce package cream cheese, at room temperature
3	tablespoons bourbon whiskey
1 to 2	tablespoons milk or cream, plus additional milk or cream for thinning frosting, if necessary
1	teaspoon vanilla extract
4 to 4¹/₂	cups (1 pound) strained confectioners' sugar
3 to 4	tablespoons coarsely chopped peanuts, for garnish

1. Place the peanut butter, butter, and cream cheese in a medium-sized bowl. Blend with a wooden spoon until very smooth.
2. In a small bowl, combine the bourbon, milk or cream, and vanilla. Add the sugar to the peanut butter mixture alternately with the liquids, about four additions of sugar to three additions of liquid, mixing until smooth and creamy. If the frosting is too stiff, add additional drops of milk or cream until desired spreading consistency is reached. After frosting, sprinkle the chopped peanuts over the top of the cake.

❧ ....

SOUR CREAM CHOCOLATE FROSTING

Makes 1¼ cups, enough to cover the top of a 9″ × 13″ × 2″ oblong cake

....

Sour cream and chocolate make a sensational frosting that is not too sweet. The slightly tangy flavor adds a delicious zing to any vanilla or chocolate cake. Double the recipe if you wish to frost a layer cake.

....

1½	ounces unsweetened chocolate, coarsely cut
1½	ounces semisweet chocolate, coarsely cut
2	tablespoons unsalted butter
¼	cup sour cream
1⅔	cups strained confectioners' sugar
2 to 3	teaspoons hot water
¾	teaspoon vanilla extract
1	tablespoon honey

1. Place chocolates and butter in a medium-sized bowl. Melt in a bain-marie or in a microwave at medium setting. Remove from the heat and cool for 2 or 3 minutes. Gently stir in the sour cream.
2. Add the sugar alternately with 2 teaspoons of hot water, blending until smooth. Stir in the vanilla and honey. If the frosting is too stiff, add about 1 additional teaspoon of hot water.

Sweet Endings

🐚 CHOCOLATE CUSTARD FROSTING

Makes about 3 cups, enough to fill and frost two 9-inch layers;
three 8-inch layers; the top and sides of a 9" × 13" × 2"
oblong cake; or a 10-inch tube cake

....

This cooked chocolate frosting is soft and creamy and complements
most any layer cake.

....

2	ounces unsweetened chocolate, coarsely chopped
2	ounces semisweet chocolate, coarsely chopped
1	tablespoon freeze-dried coffee
1/2	cup boiling water
1	cup sugar
3	tablespoons cornstarch
1/8	teaspoon salt
1	cup half-and-half
1	tablespoon unsalted butter
1 1/2	teaspoons vanilla extract

1. In a small heavy saucepan, combine the chocolates, coffee, and boiling water. Stir until the chocolate is completely melted and the coffee dissolved. In a separate small bowl, combine the sugar, cornstarch, and salt and add to chocolate mixture, stirring until blended. Slowly add the half-and-half, whisking gently until well combined.

2. Bring to a boil over low heat, stirring continuously with a wooden spoon. Cook gently about 1 minute longer, stirring occasionally, then remove from the heat. Off the heat, blend in the butter and vanilla. To cool quickly, set saucepan in cold water. Stir gently, do not beat, until icing is thick enough to spread. This will only take a few minutes.

🐚 ....

❧ SHINY FUDGE FROSTING

Enough to fill and frost top and sides of two or three 9-inch layers

....

1/2	cup sugar
1/4	cup water
2	tablespoons light corn syrup
4	ounces unsweetened chocolate, coarsely chopped
3	tablespoons unsalted butter, softened
2	cups strained confectioners' sugar
2	tablespoons very hot water
1	teaspoon vanilla extract

1. Combine the sugar, water, and corn syrup in a medium-sized saucepan. Stir briefly, cover, and bring to a slow boil. Brush sides of saucepan occasionally with clear water to prevent crystals from forming. When sugar is completely dissolved, simmer syrup about 3 minutes.

2. Remove the sugar syrup from the heat and add the chocolate all at once, stirring continuously with a metal spoon until the chocolate is dissolved. Beat the butter into the chocolate mixture, then add the confectioners' sugar alternately with the hot water, dividing the sugar into two parts and the water into two parts. Blend in the vanilla and beat again until smooth and shiny.

3. Set the pan in a shallow saucepan filled with 1/2 inch to 1 inch hot tap water until ready to use. This frosting tightens quickly, so it must not be prepared too far in advance, and then should be kept slightly warm to keep it pourable. If icing is still too thick, add a bit more hot water. Do not let the icing become excessively hot, or it will be too fluid.

🌀 SWISS BUTTERCREAM

Makes 3¹/₂ to 4 cups, enough to generously fill and frost the top and sides of two 9-inch layers; three 8-inch layers; one 10-inch layer; or a 9″ × 13″ × 2″ oblong cake

....

This Swiss-style buttercream is the easiest to make and the least rich of all the classic buttercream frostings. It is made with egg whites instead of yolks, and does not contain a cooked sugar syrup as do the French-style buttercreams. The frosting is creamy and not too sweet.

All buttercreams, even this simpler one, can be tricky. To ensure success, it is essential that the butter be the proper temperature, neither too soft nor too firm. The best way to determine correct temperature is to hold the wrapped bar of butter in your hand and press with your thumb and forefinger. The butter should feel cool in your hand and show slight indentations from your fingers. If you wish to test the temperature, insert an instant thermometer into the butter; it should read about 68°.

Mastering buttercreams is not as difficult as it may appear. In the beginning you may feel intimidated, but after 2 or 3 times, you should feel comfortable with the procedure. Swiss buttercream lends itself to many delicious flavorings and is a wonderful frosting to use for cake decorating. So, if your first efforts are less than perfect, be persistent; it is well worth the effort.

....

4	large egg whites
³/₄	cup strained superfine sugar
1¹/₂	cups (3 sticks) unsalted butter, slightly firm
1¹/₂ to 2	tablespoons Grand Marnier or another liqueur of your choice
1	teaspoon vanilla extract

1. Place the egg whites in the large bowl of an electric mixer. Using a wire whisk, beat until the whites are very foamy and begin to thicken, just *before the soft peak stage.*
2. Set the bowl over a saucepan filled with about 2 inches of simmering water. The bottom of the bowl should not touch the water. Whisk in the sugar, 1 to 2 tablespoons at a time, taking about 30 to 45 seconds. Continue beating 2 to 3 minutes or until the

whites are warm (about 120°) and the sugar is dissolved. The mixture will be thick and resemble whipped marshmallow.

3. Remove the bowl from the pan. In an electric mixer fitted with the beaters or whip attachment, beat the whites and sugar on medium-high speed for 5 to 7 minutes, or until the mixture forms a very thick meringue and is cool. Do not overbeat. Set aside.

4. Place the butter in a separate clean mixing bowl. Using the beaters or paddle attachment, cream the butter on medium speed for 45 to 60 seconds, just until it is smooth and creamy. *Do not overbeat* or the butter will become too soft. Set aside.

5. On medium-low speed blend the meringue into the butter, 1 to 2 tablespoons at a time over about 1 minute. Add the liqueur and vanilla and beat 30 to 45 seconds longer until thick and creamy. Refrigerate for 10 to 15 minutes before using.

    If the buttercream fails to come together: Reheat the buttercream briefly over simmering water for about 5 seconds, stirring with a wooden spoon. Be careful not to overheat. The mixture should look broken and there will be some liquid at the bottom of the bowl; however, it will rebind upon beating. Return the bowl to the mixer stand, and whip on medium speed just until the mixture rebinds and is creamy.

    If the buttercream is too soft: Chill the buttercream in the refrigerator for about 10 minutes and rewhip. If this doesn't work, cream an additional 2 to 4 tablespoons of butter, but *do not make it as soft as the butter you originally used.* It must be smooth but still cool. On low speed, quickly add the creamed butter to the buttercream, 1 tablespoon at a time.

STORAGE: Refrigerate in an airtight container for up to 5 days. The buttercream may also be frozen at 0° or below for up to 6 months. For best results, pack the buttercream in two 16-ounce plastic containers. Thaw in the refrigerator overnight or for several hours at room temperature before using.

(variations follow)

VARIATIONS

MOCHA BUTTERCREAM

  1½   teaspoons espresso zest (page 58)
   2   ounces bittersweet chocolate, melted and cooled to
       tepid
   2   tablespoons coffee liqueur, such as Tía María

Blend ½ cup of the buttercream into the melted chocolate. Stir in
the espresso zest, then add to the remaining buttercream. Whip
briefly on medium-low speed to combine. Blend in the liqueur.

CHOCOLATE BUTTERCREAM

   6   ounces imported semisweet chocolate, melted and
       cooled to tepid
  ½   teaspoon espresso zest (page 58)
   2   tablespoons Grand Marnier or dark Jamaican rum

Blend 1 cup of the buttercream into the melted chocolate. Stir in
the espresso zest, then add to the remaining buttercream. Whip
briefly on medium-low speed to combine. Blend in the liqueur or
rum.

PRALINE BUTTERCREAM

      ⅓   cup praline paste (page 498 or see Mail Order Sources)
  1½ to 2   tablespoons dark Jamaican rum

Blend ½ cup of the buttercream into the praline paste, then add to the
remaining buttercream. Whip briefly on medium-low speed to combine. Blend in the rum.

ORANGE BUTTERCREAM

      2   tablespoons grated navel orange rind
      1   teaspoon grated lemon rind
1 to 2   additional tablespoons Grand Marnier, Cointreau,
           or Triple Sec

Add the orange and lemon rinds to the butter during the creaming in Step 4 of the master recipe. Blend in the liqueur. If you prefer a stronger orange flavor, add more rind after the liqueur has been added.

LEMON BUTTERCREAM

Omit orange rind. Increase lemon rind to 4 teaspoons.

Glazes and Syrups

BEFORE YOU BEGIN . . .

- ▶ Thin sugary glazes that are spread rather than poured go on a cake more smoothly if the cake is still warm. The hotter the cake, the more thinly the glaze can be spread.
- ▶ Use the back of a tablespoon to spread a glaze made with confectioners' sugar, as it is easier to maneuver than a spatula. A thinner coating can be made by brushing on the glaze with a pastry brush.
- ▶ Glazes that are to be drizzled on should be applied after the cake has cooled. The best ways to drizzle are from the pointed tip of a teaspoon, the spout of a measuring cup, an 8-inch pastry bag fitted with a small #2, #3, or #4 plain tube, or a paper parchment bag.
- ▶ If you wish, you may glaze a cake twice. This gives an extra-smooth finish. It is also desirable if the first application did not go on well. Simply double the recipe for the glaze.
- ▶ Apply trimmings such as chopped nuts as soon as the glaze begins to set. If the glaze hardens, the trimmings will not stick.
- ▶ Do not cover a glazed cake with a glass dome until the glaze has completely hardened.
- ▶ If a glaze must stand for a short while, place it in a pan of *warm* water to prevent its becoming too thick. Do not let the glaze get too hot or it will thin down.
- ▶ When thinning a glaze that is too thick, add the liquid sparingly. A few drops of water go a long way.
- ▶ Leftover glazes can be frozen, but the sheen may be affected. After thawing, reheat the glaze over hot water, adding drops of hot water as needed.

🌺 VANILLA GLAZE

This thin confectioners' sugar glaze gives cakes an attractive finish and adds a touch of sweetness. Because it is so versatile, amounts are given for both small and large cakes. The smaller quantity will glaze the top of a 9″ × 13″ × 2″ oblong cake, or partially cover the top and sides of a fluted cake. If you wish to glaze the entire cake, use the larger amount.

SMALL CAKE

Makes about ¹/₃ cup

1	cup strained confectioners' sugar
4	teaspoons boiling water
1	teaspoon corn syrup
¹/₂	teaspoon vanilla extract

LARGE CAKE

Makes about ¹/₂ cup

1¹/₂	cups strained confectioners' sugar
2	tablespoons boiling water
1¹/₂	teaspoons corn syrup
³/₄	teaspoon vanilla extract

1. In a small bowl, combine the confectioners' sugar, water, corn syrup and vanilla. Blend with wire whisk until smooth.
2. This glaze may be applied with the back of a tablespoon or a fine pastry brush, or drizzled from the tip of a teaspoon, depending on your recipe.

Sweet Endings

🔥 QUICK CHOCOLATE GLAZE

....

*T his chocolate glaze has been a favorite of mine for years. It has won-
derful flavor, is quick to whip up, and holds its gloss under refrigeration. It also freezes well. This recipe includes amounts for both small
and large cakes, with about the same coverage as the preceding vanilla
glaze.*

....

SMALL CAKE

Makes about ¹/₂ cup

....

1	ounce unsweetened chocolate, coarsely chopped
1	ounce semisweet chocolate, coarsely chopped
2	teaspoons unsalted butter
²/₃	cup strained confectioners' sugar
2	tablespoons boiling water (about)
2	teaspoons light corn syrup
¹/₂	teaspoon vanilla extract
2	teaspoons dark Jamaican rum (optional)

....

LARGE CAKE

Makes about ³/₄ cup

....

1¹/₂	ounces unsweetened chocolate, coarsely chopped
1¹/₂	ounces semisweet chocolate, coarsely chopped
1	tablespoon unsalted butter
1	cup strained confectioners' sugar
3	tablespoons boiling water (about)
1	tablespoon light corn syrup
³/₄	teaspoon vanilla extract
1	tablespoon dark Jamaican rum (optional)

1. Place the chocolates and the butter in a small glass bowl. Set the bowl in a pan filled with 1 inch of hot water and stir until the ingredients are melted and smooth, or melt in a microwave. Off the heat, stir in the sugar and water alternately, beating well. Blend in the corn syrup, then the vanilla. Stir in the rum.
2. At this point the glaze should be glossy and pourable. If it is too thick, beat in drops of hot water to thin.

🍂 LEMON GLAZE

Makes about ¹/₂ cup, enough to cover a 9″ × 13″ × 2″ oblong cake

....

Here is a wonderful glaze with the piquant taste of citrus. Be sure to coat the cake while it is still warm. If the glaze needs thinning, add the water very sparingly.

....

2 tablespoons unsalted butter, at room temperature
1 cup strained confectioners' sugar
2 teaspoons fresh lemon juice
1 teaspoon hot water
¹/₂ teaspoon vanilla extract

In a small bowl, cream the butter with a wooden spoon. Add the confectioners' sugar alternately with the lemon juice and water, three additions of sugar to two additions of liquid. Beat until smooth, then blend in the vanilla. The glaze should be pourable. If not, thin with drops of hot water.

❧ BROWN SUGAR GLAZE

Makes about ¹/₂ cup, enough to glaze a 9-inch fluted ring cake

....

This caramel-flavored glaze is delicious on cakes made with brown sugar, spices, or nuts. Or try it on chocolate- or coffee-flavored cakes and top with chocolate shavings.

....

3	tablespoons butter
3	tablespoons light brown sugar
3	tablespoons heavy cream
³/₄	cup strained confectioners' sugar
¹/₂	teaspoon vanilla extract

1. In a small saucepan, melt the butter and sugar together over low heat. Stir in the heavy cream and cook slowly until the mixture comes to a gentle boil. Simmer 1 to 2 minutes.
2. Off the heat, gradually add the confectioners' sugar in three additions, whisking until smooth. Blend in the vanilla. The icing should be pourable. If it is too thick, thin with drops of extra cream.

❧ GANACHE GLAZE

Makes about 1 cup, enough to cover the top and sides of a 9- or 10-inch layer, or a 9- or 10-inch tube cake

....

Ganache is a blend of chocolate, heavy cream, and sometimes butter and corn syrup that is heated together. As the mixture cools, it thickens and can be put to various uses at different stages. While it is still warm it can be used as a delicious fudge sauce. As it cools to tepid, it becomes this classic European semisweet glaze.

Slightly chilled ganache can be whipped to make a marvelous chocolate filling and frosting. If it becomes very cold, it will solidify. Solid ganache becomes the basis for chocolate candy truffles. A small amount of the solid chocolate mixture is gently rolled into a ball, dusted with unsweetened dutch-process cocoa, and allowed to set.

The consistency of a ganache glaze should be similar to thin chocolate pudding, firm enough to coat the surface without exposing the cake. Take care not to stir a ganache too much or air bubbles will form, and will show on the finished cake.

This recipe can easily be increased or reduced using a ratio of 1 ounce (2 tablespoons) of heavy cream to 1 ounce of chocolate. You may use either semisweet or bittersweet chocolate or a blend of both, but whatever your choice, a fine imported chocolate is essential.

Ganache is a versatile and marvelous medium to become acquainted with.

....

6 ounces imported semisweet or bittersweet chocolate, such as Lindt Excellence or Tobler Tradition
6 ounces (3/4 cup) heavy cream
1 tablespoon light corn syrup
1 tablespoon Grand Marnier, Cointreau, or dark Jamaican rum
3/4 teaspoon vanilla extract
1/2 to 1 teaspoon hot water, if needed

1. Break the chocolate into 1-inch pieces and place in the basket of a food processor fitted with the steel blade. Process until the chocolate is finely chopped. Empty the chocolate into a medium-sized bowl and set aside.
2. In a small saucepan, heat the heavy cream and corn syrup on low heat until it comes to a gentle boil. Immediately pour the hot cream over the chopped chocolate. Let it stand for about 1 minute, then stir the chocolate and cream together, slowly mixing until all the chocolate is melted.
3. Blend in the liqueur or rum and vanilla. If the surface is oily, stir in 1/2 to 1 teaspoon of hot water. The glaze should thicken as it stands, but remain pourable. If the ganache fails to thicken, chill it in the refrigerator for 4 to 5 minutes. Watch carefully, as it must not be too cold.

Sweet Endings

1.

The technique of applying the ganache for a smooth, mirror-like finish is as follows:

a. Place the torte on a cardboard disk cut slightly smaller than the cake. Transfer to a rack set over a pan large enough to catch the excess glaze.

b. Hold the saucepan 10 inches above the torte and pour the glaze onto the center (fig. 1). Quickly pass a metal spatula with a blade at least 8 to 10 inches long four times over the top of the torte (fig. 2). The glaze should cover the top and run down the sides.

c. Starting at the top of the torte, on the first sweep bring the spatula down the middle (fig. 3), on the second sweep, bring the spatula up on right side of the torte (fig. 4). On the third sweep, bring it down left side (fig. 5), and on the final sweep, back up over the middle (fig. 6).

d. Lift one side of the rack and bring it down with a hard bang to force the glaze to spread evenly. This procedure must be done quickly to ease the glaze over the top and down the sides before it sets.

e. Patch any bare spots on the sides using a small metal spatula, but do not touch the top again as the glaze sets immediately. If the ganache becomes too firm to spread on the sides, reheat it for a few seconds.

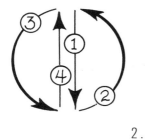

2.

STORAGE: Ganache can stand several hours at room temperature, but it must be warmed on low heat before using. It can also be made ahead and stored in the refrigerator in an airtight container for up to 2 weeks. It can be frozen at 0° or below for up to 9 months. If frozen, reheat the ganache in a bain-marie or double boiler. It does not have to be thawed first.

3.

4.

5.

6.

❧ APRICOT GLAZE

Makes enough for one 10-inch layer

....

2/3 cup thick apricot preserves
1   tablespoon water

1. Place the apricot preserves and water in a small heavy saucepan. Stir and bring to a slow boil, then simmer 2 to 3 minutes. If the mixture begins to stick to bottom of pan, add more water as needed.
2. Remove from the heat and push through a fine-mesh strainer. Discard the residue from the strainer. Using a fine pastry brush, apply the glaze to the cake while it is still warm. If the glaze becomes too thick, thin it down with a few drops of water. You may use this glaze at whatever consistency you wish. (My preference is to apply it thinly, but a thicker coating may be used if you prefer.)

❧ SUGAR SYRUP

Makes 1 cup, enough for one 10-inch layer, split into 3 disks

....

1   cup water
1/4 cup sugar
2   tablespoons dark rum or orange-flavored liqueur

Place the water and sugar in a small heavy saucepan. Bring to a slow boil and simmer 5 minutes. Off the heat, add the liqueur. Allow to cool slightly before applying to the cake. This may be made in advance. *Rewarm before using.*

Sweet Endings

🌰 LIQUEUR SYRUP

Makes 1 generous cup, enough for one 10-inch layer, split into 3 disks

....

³/₄	cup water
¹/₄	cup sugar
2	slices navel orange, cut ¹/₄ inch thick
One	2-inch piece vanilla bean
2	tablespoons dark rum
2	tablespoons Grand Marnier

Place the water, sugar, orange slices, and vanilla bean in a small heavy saucepan. Bring to a slow boil and simmer 5 minutes. Off the heat, add the rum and liqueur, and set aside to cool slightly before applying to cake. Squeeze the juice from the orange slices back into the syrup. Discard the slices and vanilla bean. This may be made in advance. *Rewarm before using.*

Sauces, Toppings, and Whipped Creams

Sauces, toppings, and whipped creams give homespun cakes more pizzazz. Simple and quick to make, they are perfect when you need a last-minute dessert for spur-of-the-moment entertaining.

Fruit sauces add a touch of color to spark up a plate. Toppings can be used to dress up any plain cake. The uses of whipped creams are almost limitless. Flavored whipped creams can accompany a variety of cakes, and whipped cream is also the easiest medium to work with when using a pastry bag (pages 508–18).

Most of the sauces are best when served slightly warmed to bring out their flavor.

▶ Cook sauces that contain lemon juice, egg yolks, or other acidic ingredients in noncorrosive, heavy saucepans such as stainless steel or French enameled cast iron. These ingredients will interact with aluminum pans to acquire a metallic taste or discolor. Heavy saucepans are advisable anyway, to avoid overheating.

▶ As for fillings, a flour- or cornstarch-thickened sauce must be brought to a full boil and then allowed to simmer at least 1 full minute to develop the starch fully. Undercooking results in a too-thin sauce.

▶ Wooden spoons are best for stirring sauces. They won't scratch the pan and they easily reach into the edges to free any thickened sauce that accumulates. To smooth out any lumps that may have formed, switch to a wire whisk just before the sauce reaches the boiling point and whisk lightly using just a few back-and-forth motions. Then return to the wooden spoon.

▶ Do not vigorously stir sauces thickened with cornstarch after the sauce has reached the boiling point, as overmixing causes the sauce to thin down. Stir occasionally just to prevent the sauce from sticking to the bottom of the saucepan.

▶ When washing fresh fruit for sauces, dry it thoroughly. Wet fruit will make the sauce watery.

▶ Stir fresh fruit sauces gently to avoid bruising the fruit.

▶ Avoid overcooking fruit sauces. It is actually preferable to undercook them slightly as the fruit will continue to cook as the sauce cools. In any event it is wiser to transfer the cooked sauce to another container to cool, so the fruit doesn't overcook in the hot pan.

▶ It is best to whip cream just before it is needed. It has a tendency to break down or separate and become watery if it stands too long.

▶ Properly whipped cream should look smooth and glossy, not dry and grainy. When whipped cream is spread on a cake, it has more body than you realize and often becomes thicker as it is worked with a spatula.

🌿 WARM LEMON SAUCE

Makes 1 full cup

....

This sauce is one of my favorites. It transforms almost any plain cake into something special.

....

1/2	cup sugar
1	tablespoon cornstarch
1	tablespoon unbleached all-purpose flour
1/8	teaspoon salt
3/4	cup water
1/4	cup fresh lemon juice
1	large egg yolk
1	teaspoon freshly grated lemon rind
1	tablespoon unsalted butter

1. In a small saucepan, combine the sugar, cornstarch, flour, and salt. Add the water and lemon juice. Cook over low heat, stirring constantly with a wooden spoon. When the sauce reaches the boil, stir with a whisk to smooth out any lumps, then simmer 1 minute, stirring occasionally with the wooden spoon.
2. In a small dish, lightly beat the egg yolk. Pour about 1/4 cup of hot sugar/lemon mixture into the yolk to temper. Then add the yolk mixture to the saucepan, stirring until blended. Bring to a slow boil and simmer for 1 minute longer, stirring occasionally.
3. Remove from the heat and blend in lemon rind and butter. Serve warm with any plain cake of your choice.

STORAGE: Refrigerate in a covered container for up to 3 days. Reheat before serving.

🌰 HOT FUDGE SAUCE

Makes about 1 1/3 cups

....

T his sauce has a glossy lavalike consistency and a rich chocolate flavor that comes from using a fine imported chocolate. Be sure to use a heavy saucepan when preparing the sauce to prevent the chocolate from burning.

Although the name of this sauce implies that it is served hot, I usually serve it warm to prevent ice cream or whipped cream from melting too quickly.

....

6	ounces imported bittersweet chocolate, such as Lindt or Tobler
3/4	cup heavy cream
1/4	cup sugar
2	tablespoons light corn syrup
2	tablespoons water
1	teaspoon vanilla extract

1. Break the chocolate into small pieces and place in a heavy 1-quart saucepan with the cream, sugar, light corn syrup, and water.
2. Cook over low heat, stirring constantly with a wooden spoon, until the chocolate is completely melted and the mixture is very smooth. Bring to a gentle boil and continue to cook for about 2 minutes.
3. Off the heat, stir in the vanilla extract. Set aside to cool. When ready to serve, reheat to lukewarm. If the sauce becomes oily, stir in a few drops of hot water.

STORAGE: The sauce can be made several days ahead and stored in the refrigerator in a covered container. Reheat to lukewarm in a double boiler, stirring until smooth.

🌰 RASPBERRY SAUCE

Makes 1 cup

....

This is an easy-to-make, no-fail raspberry sauce. Although it may be made in a food processor, the sauce maintains its consistency with less separation when made in a blender.

....

1 box frozen raspberries in syrup, thawed
1 to 2 tablespoons framboise or kirschwasser, to taste

1. Purée the raspberries until very smooth in a blender or food processor. Strain through a fine strainer, pressing through as much pulp as possible with the back of a spoon. Discard the seeds.
2. Add the liqueur and refrigerate until ready to use. Let stand for 1/2 hour at room temperature before serving.

STORAGE: Refrigerate in a covered container for up to 3 days.

🌰 CRÈME ANGLAISE

Makes 1 full cup

....

Crème anglaise is a delicate sauce classically made only with egg yolks, sugar, and milk. Heavy cream is sometimes added as an enrichment. On its own it is a delicious accompaniment to cakes and pastries. It also is a base for a number of custard-type desserts. When thickened with starch, it becomes a pastry cream. If gelatin and whipped cream are added to the pastry cream, it becomes a Bavarian cream. When made with a mixture of milk and heavy cream and then frozen, it becomes ice cream. The more cream it contains, the richer and smoother the ice cream will be.

The recipe for crème anglaise can be easily doubled or even tripled and is convenient to have on hand because it can be used in so many ways. The basic sauce is flavored with vanilla and liqueur or rum and is also wonderful when made into such flavors as chocolate, coffee, or orange. You can also make it into a cream sauce by folding in a small amount of whipped heavy cream to give it more body.

The key to making crème anglaise successfully is to cook the sauce in a heavy stainless steel or enameled saucepan almost to the boiling point while keeping the mixture in constant rapid motion with a wooden spoon. Watch for steam to swirl around the top of the sauce. Within seconds, the sauce gains the desired consistency—that of heavy cream.

The common mistakes in making crème anglaise are not cooking it long enough for the sauce to thicken or overcooking it to the boiling point, causing the egg yolks to curdle. If in doubt, overcooking is probably preferable. Incipient curdling can usually be salvaged by quickly passing the sauce through a strainer into a chilled metal mixing bowl, or by whirling it briefly in a blender. Do not scrape the bottom of the pot as the most curdling is present there.

With a little practice, in no time you will be able to make perfect crème anglaise.

....

4	large egg yolks
1/4	cup sugar
3/4	cup milk
1/4	cup heavy cream
1 to 1 1/2	teaspoons vanilla extract
1	tablespoon Grand Marnier or dark Jamaican rum

1. In a medium-sized bowl, using either a whisk or hand-held electric beater, whip the egg yolks until they begin to lighten in color. Gradually add the sugar and whisk until the mixture thickens, and becomes light in color, about 2 minutes.
2. Chill a medium-sized bowl by setting it over a larger bowl filled 1/3 full of ice cubes and water. Place a fine strainer over the medium-sized bowl. Set aside.
3. In a heavy medium-sized saucepan, scald the milk and cream over low heat. Gradually add the scalded milk and cream to the yolk mixture, whisking until well blended. Return the egg mixture to the saucepan. Cook over medium-low heat, stirring constantly with a wooden spoon. Do not use a whisk; the mixture will become too foamy.
4. As the mixture nears the boiling point, begin to stir the sauce vigorously while *lifting the saucepan up and down over the flame to prevent the bottom from becoming too hot*. Shortly after the steam begins to form, the consistency of the sauce should begin to resemble heavy cream. When bubbles begin to form around the edge of the pot, *immediately* pour the sauce through the strainer into the chilled bowl to stop the cooking. Stir for a minute or two to cool, then blend in the vanilla and liqueur or rum. Cover the sauce and place in the refrigerator to chill. The sauce will thicken further when cold.

STORAGE: Refrigerate in an airtight container for up to 4 to 5 days.

(variations follow)

CHOCOLATE CRÈME ANGLAISE

Makes 1¹/₄ cups

....

Add 2 ounces of finely chopped bittersweet chocolate to the scalded milk and cream in Step 3. Off the heat, stir until the chocolate is melted. Proceed with the recipe. The addition of chocolate makes this sauce somewhat thicker.

COFFEE CRÈME ANGLAISE

Makes 1 full cup

....

Stir 1 teaspoon espresso zest (page 58) into the scalded milk and cream in Step 3. Proceed with the recipe. Use a coffee-flavored liqueur such as Kahlúa or Tía María.

ORANGE CRÈME ANGLAISE

Makes 1 full cup

....

Add 1¹/₂ teaspoons grated navel orange rind to the scalded milk and cream in Step 3. Let steep off the heat 15 minutes. Rescald before using. Proceed with the recipe. Omit the vanilla extract called for in Step 4 and add Grand Marnier to taste.

VANILLA CREAM SAUCE

Makes about 1½ cups

....

Whip ¼ cup heavy cream to soft peak stage. Fold into the chilled crème anglaise.

CHOCOLATE CREAM SAUCE

Makes about 1⅔ cups

....

Whip ¼ cup heavy cream to soft peak stage. Fold into the chilled chocolate crème anglaise.

COFFEE CREAM SAUCE

Makes about 1½ cups

....

Whip ¼ cup heavy cream to soft peak stage. Fold into the chilled coffee crème anglaise.

ORANGE CREAM SAUCE

Makes about 1½ cups

....

Whip ¼ cup heavy cream to soft peak stage. Fold into the chilled orange crème anglaise.

CRÈME FRAÎCHE

....

Crème fraîche is a very thick French-style cream with a slight tangy flavor. The touch of sour used in combination with sweets is very refreshing to the palate. It can be used as a topping for fresh fruit or with almost any dessert. The cream is a mainstay in French restaurant kitchens, where it is used as an enrichment for sauces.

Crème fraîche is similar to sour cream, but has a more delicate flavor. Its butterfat content is about 40 percent, as compared to heavy cream with about 36 percent. When whipped, it is thicker and has more body than whipped cream. Adding a few spoonfuls of crème fraîche to heavy cream adds a nice touch to ordinary whipped cream.

Although crème fraîche is now manufactured in the United States, it may be difficult to find, so it's nice to know how to make your own. If you have access to a whipping cream that has a higher butterfat content than heavy cream, it will be thicker and better. Also, try to use heavy cream that has not been ultrapasteurized. This type of cream can take twice as long to develop a culture.

....

1   cup heavy cream
1   tablespoon buttermilk

In a small saucepan, heat the heavy cream until tepid. Stir in the buttermilk. Pour the mixture into a clean jar, securing the lid tightly. Shake the jar a few times to blend the cream and buttermilk together well. Allow the mixture to stand in a warmish place from 12 to 18 hours, or until it begins to thicken. The tang intensifies as the mixture stands. Stir briefly and refrigerate overnight. It will thicken further as it ages.

STORAGE: Crème fraîche will keep about 1 week in the refrigerator.

❧ YOGURT TOPPING

Makes 1 cup

....

Yogurt topping is a refreshing alternative to cream-based sauces and
is the ideal choice for those who wish to keep their calories down.
The topping is at its best used shortly after it's made.

....

      1/2   pint low-fat unsweetened yogurt
  2 to 3   tablespoons strained confectioners' sugar
      1/2   teaspoon vanilla extract

In a small bowl, combine the yogurt and the sugar, stirring briefly
to blend. Stir in the vanilla. Cover and store in the refrigerator until
ready to use. Serve within 1 hour.

🍃 BROILED TOPPING

Makes about 2 cups

....

Plain cakes baked in shallow pans are delicious when finished with a caramelized broiled topping made from chopped nuts, coconut, brown sugar, and butter.

....

3/4   cup pecans
1/2   cup shredded or Angel Flake coconut
1/3   cup (2/3 stick) unsalted butter
1/2   cup light brown sugar
1/3   cup heavy cream
  1   large egg yolk

1. Put the pecans and coconut in the container of a food processor fitted with the steel blade. Pulse 4 to 6 times or until the pieces are medium-size. Set aside.
2. In a medium skillet, melt the butter over low heat, and blend in the sugar, cream, egg yolk, and nut mixture. Heat briefly, stirring to combine. The mixture may be made ahead, but must be warmed before using.
3. Before applying the topping, let the finished cake stand 10 minutes to set. Then distribute the warm pecan/coconut mixture over the top of the hot cake and gently spread with the back of a tablespoon, taking care not to tear the cake.
4. Set the oven temperature to broil and return the cake to the oven. Broil for 45 to 60 seconds, or until the topping bubbles and turns a golden brown. Watch carefully to avoid burning.

🌿 MARINATED TROPICAL FRUITS

Makes about 3 cups (12 servings)

....

⌈ *xotic fruits such as papaya, kiwi, prickly pear, and mango, once rarely*
⌊ *seen in grocery stores, are now easily obtainable. Because they are
soft-fleshed and do not hold up well under extreme heat, these tasty,
colorful fruits are more commonly used in cold desserts, sorbets, and
fruit garnishes than in cakes. However, they make a grand topping
that is delicious on cakes or with a scoop of ice cream, or a delightful
addition to cake à la mode.*

    *I like to add fresh pineapple; its sweet pungency blends well with
the more delicate varieties.*

....

½	cup sugar
1	cup water
1- to 1½-inch	piece of vanilla bean
4 to 5	cups assorted cut fruit, in ¼- to ½-inch pieces (papaya, kiwi, prickly pear, mango, or pineapple)
3 to 4	tablespoons Chartreuse or Strega
3	tablespoons fresh lemon juice

Combine the sugar, water, and vanilla bean in a medium-sized
saucepan. Bring to a boil over medium heat, simmer for 5 minutes,
and set aside to cool to room temperature. Add the liqueur and
lemon juice. Remove the vanilla bean. Strain the syrup through a
fine strainer over the fruit, cover, and refrigerate for 3 to 4 hours
before serving.

STORAGE: Refrigerate in a covered glass container for up to 2
days.

🐦 STRAWBERRY TOPPING

Makes about 2¹/₂ cups (6 to 8 servings)

....

This vibrant red strawberry topping dresses up any plain cake it is paired with. I like to serve the sauce in a glass bowl or sauceboat. If the sauce has been refrigerated, it tastes better if you let it stand at room temperature for about 15 minutes before serving.

....

1	quart fresh strawberries
¹/₄ to ¹/₃	cup superfine sugar
2	tablespoons seedless black raspberry preserves
2	tablespoons orange juice
1 to 2	teaspoons lemon juice
2	tablespoons Grand Marnier

1. Put strawberries in a bowl filled with cold water. Change water until free of sand. Drain well. Remove the stems and lay berries on several layers of paper toweling to drain further.
2. Measure 2 cups of the strawberries, cut them into quarters, and place the berries in a medium-sized bowl. Set the remainder aside for later use. Sprinkle the superfine sugar over the quartered berries, cover the bowl, and allow the berries to stand 30 to 45 minutes or until the sugar has extracted some juice. Stir the berries occasionally.
3. Empty the berries and juice into the container of a food processor fitted with the steel blade. Add the raspberry preserves and the juices and process until smooth. Pour the purée into a saucepan and bring to a boil on a low flame. Simmer for 5 minutes. Remove the sauce from the heat, stir in the Grand Marnier, and empty the sauce into a bowl to cool.
4. Thickly slice the remaining berries and fold into the cooled sauce just before serving. Serve at room temperature.

STORAGE: The sauce and the cut strawberries may be prepared ahead and stored separately in the refrigerator up to 1 day before using. Do not assemble until shortly before serving; the sliced berries will become too soft.

🌿 BRANDY PEACH TOPPING

Makes 2 cups

....

1½	pounds firm, ripe peaches
½	cup water
⅓	cup sugar, or to taste
1	slice lemon, cut ⅛ inch thick
2-inch	piece cinnamon stick
1	tablespoon cornstarch
1	tablespoon water
2	tablespoons peach brandy, Grand Marnier, or Cointreau

1. Pour enough boiling water over peaches to cover the fruit by ½ inch and let stand 2 minutes. Drain the peaches and rinse with cold water to stop the cooking. Cut the fruit in half, remove the pits, and peel. The skin will slide off easily. Cut each half into quarters and taste for sweetness. Set aside.

2. In a medium-sized saucepan, combine the water and sugar. Bring to a boil over medium heat, stirring continuously until sugar is dissolved. Add the lemon slice and cinnamon stick, cover, and simmer for 2 to 3 minutes.

3. Add the peaches and bring to a second boil. Partially cover the pot and simmer about 7 minutes, or until peaches are translucent but still firm.

4. Dissolve the cornstarch in the water and gently stir into the peaches, taking care not to break the fruit. On low heat, bring to a gentle boil and simmer 1 minute. Off the flame, blend in liqueur to taste. Serve warm.

STORAGE: Store in a lidded glass jar in the refrigerator for up to 7 days. Reheat gently before serving.

(variation follows)

BING CHERRY TOPPING

Makes 2 cups

· ·

    1   pound pitted Bing cherries

Wash cherries and dry well on several layers of paper toweling. Remove the pits with a cherry pitter. Proceed with recipe starting at Step 2. Watch the cooking time so the cherries do not overcook. Flavor with Cherry Heering or kirschwasser.

❧ BLUEBERRY TOPPING

Makes 2 cups

· ·

    1   pint (about 3 cups) blueberries
  1/3 cup sugar
    4   teaspoons cornstarch
  1/2 cup water
    1   teaspoon fresh lemon juice
    2   tablespoons Cherry Heering or kirschwasser

1. Rinse berries with cold water. Pick off any stems and dry well on several layers of paper toweling. Set aside.
2. In a medium-sized skillet, combine the sugar and cornstarch. Stir in the water, then add the berries and lemon juice. Stir briefly just to coat berries with the liquid. Cover, on low heat, bring to a gentle boil, shaking the pan frequently. Do not stir or berries will break. As soon as the berries look translucent and glazed, they are done.
3. Scrape the sides of the pan with a rubber spatula, easing off the clinging fruit. Remove from heat. *Immediately* sprinkle with spirits and carefully transfer to a bowl to cool to room temperature.

STORAGE: Store in a lidded glass jar in the refrigerator for up to 7 days. Reheat gently before serving.

❧ SPIKED HONEYBELL ORANGE TOPPING

Makes 2 cups

....

These sweet, flavorful oranges, available only in January, make a wonderful topping combined with orange marmalade and just a bit of dark rum or liqueur. During the rest of the year, navel or blood oranges make a satisfactory substitute.

....

1.

2.

6   honeybell, navel, or blood oranges
½   cup orange juice, reserved from the oranges
⅓   cup sweet orange marmalade
1   tablespoon honey
1   tablespoon cornstarch
2   tablespoons dark rum, Grand Marnier, or Cointreau

1. Cut the oranges into sections: Slice off the top and bottom of each orange, cutting deep enough to reach the flesh. Hold the cut side of the orange flat against the work surface. Using a very sharp knife, cut down the side of the orange to expose the flesh (fig. 1). Continue until the orange is completely peeled, then cut on either side of the membranes and remove the orange sections (figs. 2, 3). (You should have about 1¾ to 2 cups sections.) Squeeze the membranes, reserving ½ cup of juice.
2. In a small, heavy saucepan, combine the orange juice, marmalade, and honey. Bring to a boil, then reduce heat and simmer for 1 to 2 minutes, or until the sauce is reduced to about ⅔ cup.
3. Meanwhile, dissolve the cornstarch in the rum. Add to the reduced syrup and stir continuously until the mixture returns to a boil. Simmer for 15 seconds.
4. Remove from the heat and set aside to cool for 5 minutes. Fold in the orange sections. Serve at room temperature.

3.

NOTE: This topping can be made up to 3 hours ahead of time, but it thins out as it stands. If it becomes too thin, reheat over low heat and add 1½ to 2 teaspoons of cornstarch dissolved in 1 tablespoon of orange juice, bring to a boil, simmer 15 seconds, and cool.

🍃 WHIPPED CREAM

P ure heavy cream with at least 36 percent butterfat is the best cream to use for whipping. However, pure cream is increasingly difficult to obtain. You will have to shop around in order to locate it, as most supermarkets stock the now ubiquitous ultrapasteurized heavy cream.

Ultrapasteurization is a process by which the cream is heated to a higher temperature than normal to kill certain strains of bacteria that cause the cream to deteriorate more rapidly. Heating the cream to this higher temperature lengthens the shelf life from 5 to 7 days to several weeks. Because of the increased heat, it is necessary to add stabilizers and emulsifiers, so it is not considered a "pure" cream.

When this process was first introduced, the cream was difficult to whip and at times had a burned or cooked taste. Over the years, the technology has improved; I no longer have difficulty whipping it, but occasionally I can still detect a cooked flavor.

A few essential steps should be taken to prepare whipped cream. Avoid using cream that is too fresh; it will not whip as easily as more mature cream. Check the date on the carton of cream before using. Generally, if the expiration date is soon, but has not passed, the cream should be fine for whipping.

Always begin with well-chilled cream, bowl, and beaters or whip attachment. Placing them in the freezer for about 10 minutes before using will do the trick. If you are using ultrapasteurized cream, a straight-sided bowl is a good choice if you have one. Begin beating on medium speed and maintain this speed throughout the process. This minimizes the danger of overbeating, creates the smoothest consistency, and stabilizes the cream. Heavy cream more than slightly doubles in volume when whipped.

When the cream has reached the soft peak stage, I recommend finishing the whipping by hand using a balloon whisk. This only takes a few twists, results in a more even consistency, and avoids overbeating. It has been my experience that cream reaches the stiff peak stage too quickly by machine. The cream becomes grainy and sometimes it will curdle and begin to turn into butter.

For those with patience, the ultimate procedure would be to whip the well-chilled cream over a bowl of crushed ice, using a large chilled balloon whisk. This produces a whipped cream that can stand over a longer period of time with the least amount of separation or breaking down.

INGREDIENTS	*Makes 2 cups* SMALL CAKE	*Makes 3 cups* LARGE CAKE
Heavy cream, well chilled	1 cup	1½ cups
Strained confectioners' sugar	2 tablespoons	3 tablespoons
Vanilla extract	1 teaspoon	1½ teaspoons

1. Put the cream in the small chilled bowl of an electric mixer fitted with beaters or chilled whip attachment. Beat on medium speed until the cream begins to thicken, then add the sugar and vanilla, or any other flavoring of your choice.
2. Continue to whip until sugar and vanilla are blended and the cream falls in soft mounds when the beaters are lifted. Remove from the mixer. With a hand-held balloon whisk, whip until the cream thickens, is smooth, and holds its shape. *Do not overbeat or the cream will become grainy.*

VARIATION
· · · · · · · · · · · · · · · · ·

FORTIFIED WHIPPED CREAM

A *small amount of gelatin added to the cream helps stabilize it and enables it to hold its shape. Use this when preparing cakes ahead of time, and in hot weather. The following ingredients should be added to the preceding recipe.*

· ·

INGREDIENTS	SMALL CAKE	LARGE CAKE
Cold water	1 tablespoon	1½ tablespoons
Unflavored gelatin	½ teaspoon	¾ teaspoon

1. Put the water in a small custard dish. Sprinkle the gelatin over the water and allow to stand 5 minutes. Set the dish into a skillet

filled with ½ inch of hot water. Heat, stirring constantly, until gelatin is clear and completely dissolved. Set aside to cool to *tepid*. (Do not allow gelatin to become too cool or it will begin to solidify.) Slowly pour into the cream as it starts to thicken. Proceed as described in preceding recipe.

🍫 CHOCOLATE WHIPPED CREAM

....

Unlike plain whipped cream, which is frequently used as an accompaniment, chocolate whipped cream generally fills and frosts cakes. Therefore, the measurements listed reflect the amount required for this use.

....

INGREDIENTS	*Makes 3 cups* SMALL CAKE	*Makes 4 cups* LARGE CAKE
Heavy cream, well chilled	1½ cups	2 cups
Strained confectioners' sugar	¼ cup	⅓ cup
Strained unsweetened cocoa	2 tablespoons	3 tablespoons
Liqueur: Kahlúa, dark Jamaican rum, or Grand Marnier	1½ tablespoons	2 tablespoons

1. Put the cream, confectioners' sugar, and cocoa in the large bowl of an electric mixer. Using a wire whisk, stir just to blend. The sugar and cocoa will not dissolve completely. This is okay. Cover and chill in the refrigerator for 1 hour.

2. Remove from the refrigerator and whip on medium speed with chilled beaters or whip attachment until the cream begins to thicken. Add the liqueur and beat until the cream falls in soft mounds when the beaters are lifted.
3. Remove from the mixer. With a hand-held balloon whisk, whip until the cream thickens, is smooth, and holds its shape. Do not overbeat, or the cream will become grainy.

❧ CHANTILLY WHIPPED CREAM

Makes about 1 cup (6 servings)

....

Chantilly cream is heavy cream that has been whipped to form soft mounds when you lift the beaters or whisk. The cream is not whipped any more; it should remain soft to be used as a light topping for cakes or desserts.

....

    1   cup heavy cream, well chilled
    2   tablespoons strained confectioners' sugar
    1   teaspoon vanilla extract
    1   tablespoon Grand Marnier or other liqueur or rum (optional)

Put the cream in the small chilled bowl of an electric mixer fitted with beaters or chilled whip attachment. Beat on medium speed until the cream begins to thicken. Add the sugar, vanilla, and the optional liqueur or rum, and continue to whip, just until the cream falls in soft mounds when the beater is lifted.

STORAGE: Cover and refrigerate until needed. The cream is best if it is used shortly after whipping. It may begin to thin down or separate when standing. If this happens, rewhip briefly with a wire whisk.

Sweet Endings

The Finishing Touches

beautifully decorated cake is festive, celebratory—but to me, the most appealing decorations are the most natural. Brightly colored frostings trimmed with gumdrops, animal crackers, and so on are not my style. I like to keep things simple. There are exceptions, of course, as when a formal cake is required for a wedding or anniversary, but unless you have a true passion for the cake decorator's art, it is best to leave these elaborate cakes to the professional or a highly skilled amateur. Since there are many fine publications available that are devoted exclusively to cake decorating, this chapter mainly covers the kind of work that is appropriate to the cakes in this book.

Achieving stylish decorations is not as difficult as you may think. A fine presentation can be made without using a pastry bag at all. I love to garnish cakes with edible fresh flowers or fresh fruits. Candies and nuts used with a little imagination can perform wonders, as can chocolate shavings or caraque, the dramatic larger pieces. Even an unfrosted cake can be pretty when the plate is trimmed with fresh violets.

Using a pastry bag is not difficult, but it does take practice. In this chapter are illustrations to guide you through a few simple decorating techniques, along with helpful hints to overcome decorating pitfalls. Two or three pastry bags and a few tubes are enough to get you started. For your first efforts, try piping with whipped cream; it is very easy to work with. Confectioners' sugar frostings, though a bit sweet, are easy to manage too.

This chapter features two master recipes for pastry bag use, decorators' Buttercream Frosting and Decorators' Flower Cream. Both are easy to use and have a pleasant flavor. For simple decorations, buttercreams are also wonderful.

After you have spent money, time, and effort preparing a cake, you'll want it to look as appealing as possible, especially if you plan to serve it to guests. I like a cake to look so inviting that people can't wait to eat it, not so stiff and unreal that you don't want to touch it. For me decorating and garnishing a cake is "playtime"—I hope it will be for you as well.

BEFORE YOU BEGIN . . .

▶ Placing the unfrosted cake in the freezer for a few minutes will help to firm the soft edges, making it easier to apply a frosting without tearing.

▶ If a cake is very uneven, level the top with a serrated knife.

▶ Avoid overmixing Decorators' Buttercream and Flower Cream. Excessive mixing produces air pockets, which prevent a smooth application. Keep these buttercreams covered as much as possible when using so they don't dry out or crust on the surface. A damp HandiWipe placed on top of the bowl is perfect. If the frosting firms too quickly to finish smoothly as you apply it, wet the spatula with warm water and then complete the application.

▶ Assemble all your equipment before you begin to work— large and small straight and offset icing spreaders, serrated knife, waxed paper, cake decorating equipment, food coloring, toothpicks, and a paring knife.

▶ If you are a novice, you might want to try decorating a cake in the same color as the frosting. This makes mistakes less obvious. Gorgeous cakes can be made with pink on pink, white on white, or chocolate on chocolate.

▶ The cake should be as close to eye level as possible when you decorate the sides, so you can comfortably see what you're doing. Rotate the cake as you decorate.

▶ To space a design evenly on a cake, make tiny holes with a toothpick, using an imaginary clock face as your guide. First make the holes at 12, 3, 6, and 9 o'clock. Then mark the spaces in between with 1 or 2 more holes around the top, depending on how much space you need between the decorations.

▶ When trimming the narrow opening of a new pastry bag to fit a coupler or tube, be careful not to cut too much off the bag. Check the size of the opening after each cut.

▶ Avoid piping top borders on the edge of the cake; this creates a framed or still look. You can create more interesting designs by piping 1 to 1½ inches in from the edge.

▶ Cake garnishes should indicate the flavor of the cake. Nut cakes should be trimmed with nuts, gingerbread is nice with bits of candied ginger, and so on. Avoid such incompatible pairings as maraschino cherries on a lemon cake. Candied lemon peel would be a better choice.

▶ A cake is more interesting if the decorations on the top have some height. Build up your designs to have some dimension.

▶ Do not use script for your first attempts to write on a cake. Printing is easier.

▶ Apply garnishes such as chopped nuts, coconut, and chocolate shavings before the frosting has set, while it is still soft. Press the trimmings gently into the frosting with the palm of your hand.

▶ For an especially pretty chocolate garnish, try mixing three colors of shaved chocolate—dark, milk, and white.

❧ DECORATORS' BUTTERCREAM

Makes 3 cups, enough to fill and frost two 9-inch layers; three 8-inch layers; a filled 10-inch layer; a 9" × 13" × 2" oblong cake; or a 10-inch tube cake

···

This is my choice whenever I want to make an elaborately decorated cake. It spreads easily and stays fresh for a long time, a real advantage since most cakes should be decorated well ahead of using.

Unlike the European buttercreams made with large amounts of butter, eggs, and granulated sugar, this contains confectioners' sugar, vegetable shortening, and only a bit of butter, making it characteristically American. Although its color is not true white, it is whiter than a classic European buttercream. I do not recommend making it with butter only, because the butter will give it a yellowish hue and an oilier consistency.

This frosting forms a beautiful background for festive scrolls and flourishes made with a pastry tube.

Decorators' Buttercream has a pleasant taste and a lovely natural appearance, two qualities that I especially favor for fancy decorated cakes.

···

1/2	cup solid vegetable shortening
2	tablespoons soft unsalted butter
1/2	teaspoon salt
1	pound (4 to 4 1/2 cups) strained confectioners' sugar
1/3	cup milk
1	teaspoon vanilla
1 to 2	tablespoons Grand Marnier or other orange liqueur (optional)

1. In the large bowl of an electric mixer fitted with beaters or the paddle attachment, cream together the shortening and butter on medium-low speed until completely blended.
2. Stir the salt into the confectioners' sugar. Add the sugar alternately with the milk to the shortening/butter mixture. Starting

Sweet Endings

493

with the sugar, add four parts sugar to four parts milk. Mix together until smooth, but *do not overmix*. Blend in the vanilla and liqueur.

STORAGE: Place in an airtight container and refrigerate. For easy spreading, remove from the refrigerator at least 1 hour before using and allow it to come to room temperature. For longer storage, freeze. Thaw in the refrigerator for 24 hours, then let stand at room temperature for at least 1 hour before using.

VARIATION
. . . .

CHOCOLATE DECORATORS' BUTTERCREAM

2/3	cup strained unsweetened cocoa
1/4	cup light corn syrup
1 to 2	tablespoons Kahlúa or Tía María liqueur, instead of orange liqueur (optional)

Strain the confectioners' sugar and cocoa together. Then add to the shortening/butter mixture as directed in the master recipe. Add the corn syrup simultaneously with the milk. Blend in the optional Kahlúa or Tía María with the vanilla, as per master recipe.

🌿 DECORATORS' FLOWER CREAM

Makes about 3 cups, enough to decorate an 8- or 9-inch layer cake; a 10″ × 2″ round cake; a 9″ × 13″ × 2″ oblong cake, or a 10-inch tube cake

....

ven a novice can transform a simple cake into a frosted fantasy with this. As you'll see, with just a little practice you can easily perform the magic.

Decorators' flower cream is prepared in various degrees of stiffness depending upon the design you wish to create, so it is best to plan your pattern in advance.

A firm frosting is used for shaping flowers. Borders and scrolls require a medium consistency, and for lettering or line patterns the frosting should be the thinnest. Fluidity is achieved by adding additional milk in very small amounts. Take great care not to overhandle the frosting. Too much mixing causes it to break down.

Refer to "Before You Begin" for further tips.

....

- ³/₄ cup vegetable shortening
- ¼ cup soft unsalted butter
- ½ teaspoon salt
- 1 pound (4 to 4½ cups) strained confectioners' sugar
- 1 teaspoon vanilla extract
- 2 tablespoons milk

1. In the large bowl of an electric mixer fitted with beaters or the paddle attachment, cream together the vegetable shortening and soft butter on low speed until completely blended.
2. Stir the salt into the confectioners' sugar. Add half the sugar to the shortening/butter mixture, blending just until incorporated. Add the remaining sugar, the vanilla, and the milk. Mix just until incorporated. *Do not overmix.* Remove the bowl from the mixer. If the frosting is too thick, stir in a few drops of milk. Test the consistency by placing a small amount of frosting in a pastry bag. If the frosting still seems too thick, add droplets of milk as needed.

Sweet Endings

🌰 QUICK CHOCOLATE SHAVINGS

Put two or three 1-ounce squares of semisweet chocolate wrapped in paper in the microwave oven. Microwave for 10 seconds on the defrost cycle. Turn the squares over and microwave again for 10 seconds. Repeat 2 or 3 more times, then unwrap the chocolate and test the temperature. It should still be firm and feel slightly cooler than body temperature when held to the inside of your wrist. (This cannot be done in the oven; the outside of the chocolate square melts too quickly.)

Handle the chocolate with a piece of paper toweling so that it doesn't touch your hands. Place one square on a cutting board. Using a sharp knife with at least an 8-inch blade, make thin slices across the chocolate. The slices should break apart into long shavings. If the chocolate still seems too hard and the shavings too fine, return the chocolate to the microwave for a few seconds longer.

🌰 CHOCOLATE CARAQUE

....

Put 2 or 3 ounces of broken semisweet chocolate pieces in a small bowl and set in a skillet filled to a depth of ½ inch with very hot, but not boiling, water. Stir until the chocolate is almost melted, then remove the bowl from the water. Continue stirring until the chocolate is completely melted.

Immediately pour the chocolate onto a clean marble slab if you own one, or a 17- × 14-inch cookie sheet. Using a 10-inch metal spatula, spread the chocolate back and forth (fig. 1). As it begins to thicken, shape it into a thin rectangle about 16 inches long and 6 to 7 inches wide. Allow the chocolate to stand for a few minutes to set but not harden.

The chocolate is ready when it begins to lose its sheen and no longer feels tacky to the touch. Holding a 10-inch thin-bladed knife such as a meat slicer at a 45° angle, scrape along the chocolate slowly to the right and then to the left in a zigzag fashion to form rolls and long slivers (fig. 2). As each roll is shaped, remove it to a separate plate (fig. 3).

Initially, you may have to make a couple of sample curls to see if the chocolate is at the correct temperature. If the chocolate becomes too cold, it will not curl. You will have to scrape it up, remelt it, and start again.

When you've worked all the chocolate, arrange the rolls and slivers in a decorative mound on top of the cake using a metal spatula or gentle hand. Scrape up any remaining chocolate slivers from the board and sprinkle them over the cake.

....

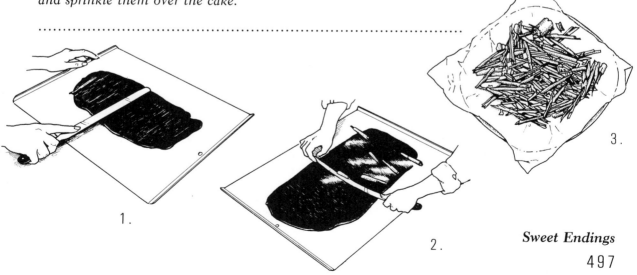

1.

2.

3.

🍂 PRALINE

Makes 1 cup

....

*P*raline is not as difficult to make as you may think. It contains two ingredients, sugar and nuts. When sugar is heated, it melts and turns into syrup; the syrup is heated through various stages from the thread stage at 215° to the blackjack stage at 415°. Hundreds of confectionery items are made at different points in between.

This is a classic recipe for praline, in which skinned hazelnuts are added to the sugar syrup at the hard crack stage, a temperature of 300° to 310°. The mixture is quickly turned onto buttered parchment. After it cools it becomes a brittle candy. You may also use skinned almonds or pecans, but I prefer the distinctive flavor of hazelnuts.

Hard praline can be used in many ways. It can be chopped for a crunchy topping for cakes. When pulverized into a powder, it becomes a flavoring for desserts, pastries, fillings, and frostings. If praline is whirled in a processor for several minutes, it will turn into a paste that can be used for many of the same purposes as praline powder.

....

1	cup (4½ ounces) hazelnuts
⅔	cup sugar

1. Toast the hazelnuts in a 300° oven for 12 to 15 minutes or until the skins begin to pop. Remove the nuts from the oven and turn them onto a clean dish towel or several layers of paper toweling. While they are still hot, rub them briskly back and forth to remove their skins. It's okay if a small amount of skin remains.
2. Line a jelly roll pan with parchment and lightly butter the parchment.
3. Put the sugar in a heavy 10-inch skillet. Heat on a low flame for about 10 to 20 minutes, or until the sugar begins to melt around the edges. Sugar heated in a thin metal skillet will melt faster, but slower cooking in a heavy pan will prevent scorching and ensure better flavor. *Do not stir the sugar.* Swirl the pan as necessary to keep the melted sugar from burning. Brush the sides of the pan with water to remove any sugar crystals. If the sugar in the center of the skillet does not dissolve, stir *briefly.*

4. When the sugar is completely melted and caramel in color, re- move the skillet from the heat. Stir in the nuts with a wooden spoon and separate the clusters. Return to low heat and stir to coat the nuts on all sides. Cook until the mixture starts to bubble. Take care when working with the syrup at this point, as it is dangerously hot.
5. Turn the mixture into the parchment-lined jelly roll pan, spread- ing evenly as best you can. As it cools, it will harden into a brittle.
6. Break the candied nuts into pieces and place them in the con- tainer of a food processor. Pulse to a medium-fine crunch or pro- cess until the brittle turns into a powder. If you wish to make a nut paste, process for several minutes.

STORAGE: Store in an airtight container in a cool dry place com- pletely free of humidity. Do not refrigerate.

🪶 EDIBLE FLOWERS

....

The soft texture and natural colors of edible fresh flowers are lovely, with a delicate look that is very appealing against a frosting. Not only are edible flowers beautiful in their natural state, but they achieve another dimension when glazed with sugar, a procedure that is easily accomplished using a small paintbrush. Gently apply frothy beaten egg white onto the surface of the petals, leaves, or stem. Sprinkle gran- ulated sugar over the top of the flowers, giving a dusting of sparkling sugar to the surface. Set the glazed flowers onto waxed paper to air- dry. If any touch-up is required, repeat the procedure. Before using, gently shake the flower to remove any excess sugar crystals.

The following flowers are good choices because they are quite com- monly available: mums, carnations, roses, pansies, lilacs, nasturtiums, lavender, tulips, and squash blossoms. Select blossoms that are appro- priate to the size of your cake.

❧ TIPS FOR FINISHING CAKES LIKE A PRO

HOW TO SPLIT ROUND AND OTHER CAKES

Splitting a cake into thin disks is called "torting." There are many gadgets available that help perform this job, but it is a good idea to learn to do it by hand. As with most techniques, practice makes perfect, and if your first attempts are not exactly even, it really won't matter as a little extra frosting spread between the layers will help to level the cake.

These directions are written for a round cake; if you are splitting a square cake, the procedure is the same. If you wish to cut a loaf cake, position the cake with the long side in front of you. Insert the knife on the right side of the cake and cut across. Since the cake is narrow, there is no need to rotate it while cutting.

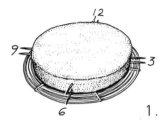

1.

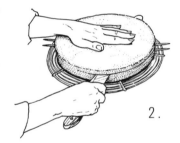

2.

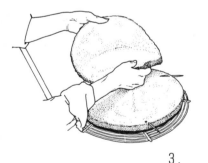

3.

1. First mark off each disk by inserting toothpicks into the sides at 12, 3, 6, and 9 o'clock (fig. 1). If you are slicing a layer into two disks, insert the toothpicks halfway up the side of the layer. If you are making three disks, insert two rows of toothpicks around the layer, 1/3 and 2/3 of the way up the side. If you wish, use a ruler held upright to make sure the toothpicks are evenly spaced.
2. Choose a serrated knife with a blade long enough to reach across the entire cake. Holding the knife at 3 o'clock if you are right-handed and 9 o'clock if you are left-handed, saw across the first layer using a gentle back-and-forth motion as you rotate the cake in a complete 360° circle (fig. 2). Just the cake is turned, not the knife. Use the toothpicks as your guide and keep your eyes only on the side of the cake you are cutting.
3. After you have cut completely through the cake, remove the first thin layer and place it on a piece of waxed paper (fig. 3). Continue with the next layer(s).

HOW TO ASSEMBLE CAKE LAYERS

1. Select the thickest and most even layer for the bottom and center it top side down on the platter. If you are

lining the plate with waxed paper, slide it under the layer at this point.

2. For a two-layer cake, position the second layer top side up. If you are working with three or more layers, place each layer except the final layer top side down, aligning the sides carefully.

3. If cake disks are uneven, reverse the thick and thin sides as you stack them, placing a thin side over a thick side and vice versa, to ensure an even cake. If the cake is still uneven, it can usually be leveled by spreading more frosting on the lower side. If the cake is very uneven, level the top with a serrated knife before frosting.

HOW TO PREPARE THE CAKE PLATE

WAXED PAPER METHOD WITHOUT CARDBOARD DISK:
This technique is used with American-style cakes to keep the plate free of icing and spills when chopped nuts, coconut, or crumbs are pressed on the sides. Be sure to remove the waxed paper before piping a frosting border around the bottom; otherwise the decorative edge will come off the cake when the paper is removed.

1. If you are using a doily, dab the bottom of the cake plate in several places with light corn syrup or frosting. Alternatively, cut three or four 4-inch strips of Scotch tape. Turn each strip into a circle by joining the ends. Press the tape circles onto the plate. Center the doily on the plate, pressing gently so it adheres.

2. Tear off 4 pieces of waxed paper, each approximately 4 inches wide. Place one at the top and one at the bottom of the plate, one to the left and one to the right. Position the strips roughly at the circumference of the cake. Do not slide them too far under the layer or the cake may tear when you remove the paper. Center the layer on the plate on top of the paper, making sure that no part of the plate and/or doily is exposed. Remove the strips of paper by easing them gently to the left and to the right. Slide each strip out to the side rather than pulling it toward you, going in the same direction each time.

Sweet Endings

501

CARDBOARD DISKS: Cardboard disks are used to support cakes when they are to be glazed, if they must be held in the palm of your hand for side applications of icings and trimmings, or to permit transporting them without a plate. They come in standard cake pan sizes in round, oblong, and square shapes, and are available in stores that specialize in cake decorating equipment and party supplies, in the cake decorating centers or housewares sections of department stores, or through mail order sources (page 531)

Select a disk approximately 1 inch smaller than the size of the cake to allow for shrinkage of the cake. If you are using a 10-inch pan, use a 9-inch disk. You may also cut a cardboard disk to the desired size, but be sure to trim it slightly smaller (about 1/4 inch) than the bottom of the baked cake so the disk is not visible.

To secure the cake, dab a little light corn syrup or spread a teaspoon or two of frosting onto the disk. Center the layer on the disk and press gently.

If the cake is to be glazed, place it on a rack and set it over a pan to catch the drips. If it is to be frosted, set it on a turntable if you own one. Otherwise, a rack, preferably round, will be fine.

TURNTABLES AND ALTERNATIVES

A decorator's turntable has a heavy base and a flat metal top that rotates to make it easy to decorate the sides of the cake. It is an essential piece of equipment for professionals; however, for home use a substitute can be easily devised. I use an inexpensive round aluminum broiling pan commonly available in supermarkets or discount stores. It is about 1 1/2 inches high and measures 11 inches in diameter. It comes with a rack, which I do not use.

I set the cake on a cardboard disk on the 12-inch round cake rack and place it over the broiler pan. Because the pan is lightweight, it is easy to turn. This contraption actually has one advantage over a turntable; it can also be used when you are applying a glaze since it will catch drips, while a turntable cannot be used for this purpose. Another option is simply to use an inverted large layer pan, but you must be sure to keep the cake centered on the pan so it will not tip.

HOW TO TINT FROSTINGS

Vegetable food dyes are available in two forms, liquid and paste. Liquid colors give a more delicate hue; for deeper tones, use the paste. The most important colors to purchase are red, yellow, green, and blue. With these primary colors, commonly sold in sets, you can create almost any color you wish.

Always use the tip of a toothpick to tint the frosting, as a little coloring goes very far. As much as a single drop of coloring could be far too much. It is a good idea to make a small sample first and, after you arrive at the color you desire, tint the rest of the frosting to match.

A toothpick is also helpful when you wish to blend colors. To create lavender, for example, you would blend red and blue together; yellow with a touch of red will give you peach. Again, work with only a tiny bit of coloring at a time.

HOW MUCH FROSTING TO USE

Although the quantity will vary according to the size of the layers and the thickness with which icing is applied, I estimate that you will need 3 cups of frosting to fill and cover the top and sides of two 9-inch layers. This is especially true of thick, creamy frostings. It takes about ³/₄ to 1 cup to cover the bottom layer, the same amount for the top layer, and about 1 to 1¹/₄ cups to go around the sides.

Buttercreams and other rich frostings may be used more sparingly, according to taste. Since whipped cream coatings are aerated, they can be applied more generously. My preference is to spread frosting thickly on unlayered cakes, such as those baked in oblong pans. Spread the frosting more thinly on cakes that are cut into thin disks, to avoid excessive richness.

After you fill a cake, it is wise to frost the sides first. This makes for easier patching between layers and/or leveling uneven layers. The sides take more frosting than you realize. If you run short you can finish the top of the cake with a piped border of frosting or swirl the frosting on the edges with the back of a spoon.

The unfrosted center can be spread with seedless jam and sprinkled with nuts or coconut, or even topped with fruit. Or, you can always whip up some heavy cream and pipe whipped cream rosettes on top of the cake, or use another compatible frosting. Two kinds of frostings on a cake can be delicious.

Sweet Endings

503

HOW TO FROST A LAYER CAKE

1. Sweep off excess crumbs with a pastry brush, and place the bottom layer top side down.
2. Using a long metal spatula, cover the bottom layer with frosting, leaving a 1/2-inch border around the edge.
3. Continue with successive layers as described on page 501.
4. When you have added the final layer, cover the sides of the cake with a thin layer of frosting, extending it slightly higher than the top of the cake. Fill in any spaces in the frosting that may appear between the layers.
5. Spread a thin layer of frosting over the top of the cake. If one side of the cake is higher than the other, build up the lower side with additional frosting until the cake is perfectly even. If necessary, use a ruler to measure the height from the bottom to the top of the cake.
6. Allow the frosting to set for 2 to 3 minutes. Then refrost the cake, again starting with the sides, but this time apply a thicker layer of icing, making the surface as smooth as possible. If you warm the blade of the spatula by running it under hot water just before completing the application, it will help to smooth uneven spots. Allow the frosting to set until firm, about 15 minutes. You are now ready to decorate the cake. To frost cakes that are not layered, use the same technique, starting with Step 4.

1.

2.

EASY AND PRETTY FROSTING DESIGNS

A few ordinary kitchen utensils can be used with imagination to create beautiful cakes, as long as the frosting is stiff enough to hold its shape. Generally confectioners' sugar frostings work best. Here are some quick ideas to fancy up an ordinary cake.

SWIRLS AND CIRCLES (fig. 1): After applying the second coat of frosting, make half-circles by moving the tip of the spoon first to the left side at the top, then to the right, starting at 12 noon and finishing at 6 o'clock. To make full circles simply connect the half circles.

PEAKS (fig. 2): After you have applied the second coat of frosting, press the back of a teaspoon or the tip of a small metal spatula gently into the frosting, then pull the utensil out toward you. Repeat this at least every 3/4 inch randomly over the surface of the cake.

FORK LINES (fig. 3): Following the same procedure as for peaks, use a table fork, bringing the fork toward you for about 1 inch while curving it slightly to the left, then to the right, to the left, to the right, and so on, to make half-moon-shaped lines. Make the fork marks at random over the top and sides of the cake.

RIDGES (fig. 4): Place the cake on a turntable or an inverted layer tin. Holding your hand as steady as possible, press a pastry comb into the frosting and rotate the cake to form a line of ridges around the sides of the cake. After you've done the sides, position the pastry comb on top of the cake with the inside tip exactly in the middle of the cake and the other side on the edge, like a sundial. Holding the pastry comb at a 90° angle and keeping your hand very steady, rotate the cake until the top has a complete circle of ridges.

WAVES (fig. 5): Place the cake on a turntable or an inverted layer tin. Press a pastry comb into the sides of the cake at a 90° angle, moving it up and down around the sides. You will have to do this several times to go around the entire cake. The wider sweeps you make with the comb, the bigger the waves will be. Across the top repeat the same pattern of waves you did on the sides. A saw-tooth bread knife also works very well to make wavy lines on the top of the cake.

RIPPLES (fig. 6): Using an 8-inch offset metal spatula, apply the frosting thickly on the sides and top of the cake, making it very smooth. Then hold the spatula vertically against the side of the cake. Gently press it into the frosting while twisting your wrist slightly toward you to make an indentation in the frosting, then relax the pressure. A ripple of frosting should appear down the side of the cake. Continue around the sides of the cake, spacing the ripples about 1 inch apart. To finish the top, hold the spatula almost flat and weave the tip back and forth, forming ripples across the top, starting at the rim of the cake.

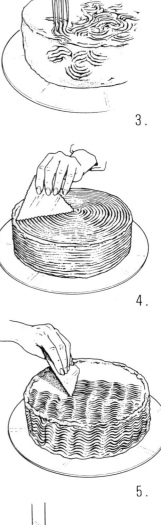

3.

4.

5.

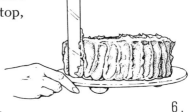

6.

QUICK CAKE DECORATIONS AND TRIMMINGS

Ideas are endless when you use your imagination. Take a serious look at your cupboard, your garden, and your household accessories. In most instances, you have more resources at your fingertips than you realize. Listed below are a few ideas to get you started.

1. Cut a round piece of paper the size of the top of the cake. Fold the paper into eighths and cut a few 1-inch designs—hearts, circles, diamonds, or flowers—into the paper along the fold. Open the paper and place it over the top of an unfrosted cake. For dark chocolate or spice cakes, dust the surface heavily with confectioners' sugar, then carefully lift up the paper. For light-colored cakes, use cocoa powder.

2. Buy a ready-made stencil or make your own by drawing an object such as a flower, a heart, or a guest of honor's initials on lightweight cardboard. Cut out the pattern with a single-edge razor blade. Place the stencil on top of the unfrosted cake and dust the surface with confectioners' sugar or cocoa powder.

3. Chocolate shavings (page 496), caraque (page 497), chopped nuts, coconut, or toasted cake crumbs accumulated from trimmings of cakes make great cover-ups for frosted cakes, especially when your frosting does not quite meet your expectations. If you wish to cover the top and sides, place the cake on a cardboard disk. Lift the cake with the palm of your hand and hold it over a shallow pan to catch the excess. Gently press the trimmings into the sides and top of the cake. Repeat to make sure all bare spots are covered.

4. Decorate cakes with small pieces of such fresh fruit as wedges of figs, sliced kiwis, and fresh berries. Strawberries cut into fans, halves, or quarters make beautiful garnishes, or try making strawberry roses. Select a few extra-large well-shaped berries, and cut each berry as you would a radish rose. Start with five slits on the bottom to resemble petals, make four slits in the next layer, and three slits in the third layer. Three of these berries clustered toward the side of a cake make a very striking presentation, as does a single huge berry.

5. Glazed edible flowers (page 499) and grapes make cakes sparkle with a professional look. Select an assortment of green, purple, and black grapes, rinse, and gently dry. Place the grapes on a sheet of waxed paper. Using a kitchen fork, lightly beat an egg white until it is frothy and brush the white on all sides of the well-dried grapes. Sprinkle them generously with sugar. Let stand at room

temperature for $\frac{1}{2}$ hour, then resugar them. Let stand for 2 or 3 hours or until the surface hardens.

6. For a romantic touch, make a tiny floral nosegay, using such delicate flowers as baby roses, pansies, or violets. Tie several together with thin wire or dental floss. Cover the stems with a small piece of moistened paper toweling and then wrap them in aluminum foil. Stick the stem into the top of the cake, slightly off center. If the cake does not require refrigeration, simply refrigerate the nosegay until serving time.

7. Slivers of candied lemon or orange rind make attractive and tasty garnishes. Use two lemons or one navel orange for one cake. Remove the rind with a lemon zester or a vegetable peeler, cutting it into paper-thin strips. On a cutting board, cut the strips into tiny slivers as thin as you can make them. In a small heavy saucepan on medium heat, blanch the slivers in 1 cup of water for 4 to 5 minutes to remove the bitterness. Drain. Add $\frac{1}{4}$ cup water and 2 tablespoons of sugar to the pot. Bring to a gentle boil over low heat and simmer 5 minutes. Add the rind and continue cooking over low heat until the rind is glazed and transparent and the liquid is syrupy. Using a kitchen fork, lift the rind from the syrup and spread it on a double thickness of paper toweling, separating the pieces with the fork. Sprinkle the slivers with 2 to 3 teaspoons of sugar and toss them with the fork to coat them on all sides. Let stand for 2 or 3 hours, tossing occasionally with the fork, until thoroughly dried.

8. A variety of ready-made cake trimmings are available in specialty food shops, candy stores, or through the mail order sources listed on page 531. Crystallized violets and roses; crushed crystallized ginger; silver and gold dragées; angelica; candies such as chocolate truffles, nonpareils, liqueur-filled chocolate candies, chocolate jimmies; whole nuts, such as hazelnuts, blanched almonds, pecans, and walnuts dipped in chocolate—all add interest and flavor when teamed with a compatible cake.

Decorating with Pastry Bags and Tubes

If you have been bitten by the cake decorating bug and wish to advance beyond the simple techniques to fancier decorations, then try your hand at decorating with a pastry bag. The following pages will introduce you to the basics of working with pastry bags and tips. You will learn how to make simple borders, rosettes, drop flowers, leaves, or anything else your imagination dictates.

To get started, you'll need to invest in a few pieces of equipment. I recommend Ateco's plastic-coated canvas pastry bag or Wilton's Featherweight bag. Do not use a nylon bag unless you are working with savory ingredients; the nylon conducts heat from your hand, causing the icing or whipped cream to become too soft or break down.

The 14-inch bags are perfect for most all-purpose decorating. This is the recommended size for whipped cream and meringue, because these ingredients are aerated. Larger bags tend to flop over at the top and get in the way. The 8-inch bag is useful for small amounts of frosting and for delicate work and is best for beginners who find it difficult to make a parchment cone (page 510). Also, since a parchment cone is stiff, you will find a canvas bag easier to maneuver, especially if decorating is new to you.

Pastry bags are used either with or without a coupler, a two-piece part that consists of a round head to which the tip is attached, and a ring that screws over the tip to secure it. Couplers are used with small decorating tubes. Large tubes don't require them. The tapered end of a new pastry bag usually must be trimmed with scissors to accommodate a coupler or large pastry tube. The bag may also require trimming if the tube does not fit tightly. Be careful when trimming not to cut away too much of the bag.

The advantage of the coupler is that it allows you to change tips without emptying the bag. However, many beautiful effects can be created using only one tip. For instance, a leaf tube can be used for a pretty design on top of a cake as well as for a border. When I plan to do more intricate or dainty work, I usually select the smaller tubes. The larger tubes are good for bolder designs. Pastry tubes come in a wide range of styles and sizes, but unless you are a serious decorator, only a few are essential. After reading this section, you will have a good idea of which sizes to buy and how to use them.

Another piece of equipment commonly used for cake decorating is a parchment cone. The cone is primarily used for such line work as writing with icing, or for making pinhead-size dots.

Disposable heavy-duty plastic decorating bags have become very popular. These bags, which can be found in most cake decorating departments, are suitable for quick decorating jobs or when you are working with a range of colors. A quick way to make your own disposable pastry bag comes from Rose Levy Bernbaum, author of *The Cake Bible*. She forces icing down into one of the corners of a "zippered" plastic bag. After pressing out the air, she twists the bag tightly and cuts off the tip to the desired size. Both of these types of plastic bags can be used with or without the coupler.

HOW TO SELECT A TIP
....

The size of the pastry tube you use is determined by frosting type and cake size. You would not want to use a large tip with a thick buttercream, as the richness is overwhelming. However, if you are frosting with whipped cream, which is aerated and not overly sweet, a large tube is preferable. Furthermore, piping whipped cream through a small tube overworks the cream to a point where it becomes watery. Generally you should choose dainty decorations for small cakes, saving larger ones for big cakes.

Although there are dozens of tips to choose from, four of the most popular are the *plain* or *round* tube for lettering and line work, the *open star* for borders, the *closed star* for making starlike drop flowers,

Sweet Endings

509

and the *leaf*, which is not only used with flowers, but makes lovely borders and designs as well.

The open and closed star tips can often be used interchangeably, but the open star gives wider coverage and is better when you are making overlapping borders. The closed star is preferable for drop flowers. For beginners, a drop flower border is one of the easiest to make.

Small and large tubes are not interchangeable, but you may use the next closest number, such as a #3 plain tube instead of a #2. The opening is a bit wider, but it will give a similar effect. The selection of star tubes also refers to the size of the opening, as well as how many facets it has (some have six, others eight and so forth). In all instances, the bigger the tube, the larger the number.

HOW TO MAKE PARCHMENT CONES

Parchment cones are used when you are working with small quantities of frosting. They are handy for touch-up work or lettering, or when you wish to change colors quickly. You can make any size cone you wish, from very tiny ones that hold only a tablespoon of frosting to larger ones that hold up to ½ cup. It takes practice to make them, but their convenience makes the effort worthwhile. If you run out of parchment, you may substitute waxed paper, but it is thinner and harder to work with.

To make a parchment cone, fold and cut a 15-inch square of parchment diagonally to make two 15-inch triangles (fig. 1). (Triangle measurements are calculated along the short edge. If you fold one of the parchment triangles again, you will have two 10½-inch triangles.) If you wish to make smaller triangles, cut the paper in half again. If you are using waxed paper, cut a 12-inch square and fold it point to point. Keep the paper double thickness to give it more body.

"Ready to fold," precut 15-inch parchment triangles for making cones are available at stores that specialize in cake decorating equipment.

To fold a triangle into a cone, place it on the counter with the wide side away from you. The paper should look like an open fan. The lower point of the fan is Point A, the right upper tip is Point B, and the left upper tip is Point C. Hold the paper at Point A with

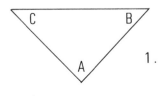

1.

your thumb on top pointed toward the wide edge of the paper and your fingers underneath (fig. 2).

Bring Point B over Point A, sliding the paper under your thumb and pressing it down to hold it in place. The tips of Points A and B should line up exactly. Then wrap Point C around the top of the partial cone, bringing the paper under (fig. 3). Turn the cone over by turning your wrist out. Your fingers are now on the bottom and the seams should be visible. Pull the cone tight until Point C aligns perfectly with Points A and B.

When all three points meet, slide Point C to the left and Point B to the right, about 1 inch in opposite directions, and pull the paper toward you as tight as you can (fig. 4). The tip of the cone should be completely closed. If not, working from the inside point, pull tightly until it does close. To secure the cone, staple it on the inside seam first, then staple it again where the outside seam meets. You will have three points protruding out.

Fold the points inside the cone to round off the top. For larger bags, tape the outside seam to secure the cone (fig. 5). Snip a minute piece off the bottom, but do not trim away too much (fig. 6). If you are inserting a pastry tube, cut the cone to fit the tube.

When the tip of the cone is prepared, fill the cone no more than one-third to one-half full. Press the air from the top of the cone, fold the left and right corners to the middle, and roll the paper down until it meets the frosting. If you are filling the bag with a thin frosting or glaze, fill the cone first and then snip the bottom tip, otherwise the frosting will ooze from the end of the cone.

HOW TO FILL A PASTRY BAG

Fold the edge of the bag to form a cuff about ¼ to ⅓ down its length. You are now ready to fill the bag.

If you are using a coupler: Separate the two pieces and drop the wide head down into the bag. For a proper fit, the end should extend out about halfway up the ring threads. Place the tip you wish to use over the head of the coupling base. Screw the ring onto the head to secure the tip.

If you are not using a coupler: Drop the decorating tip down into the bag, aiming at the hole. Pull the tip through the hole, extending it out about half the length of the tip. It should fit tightly.

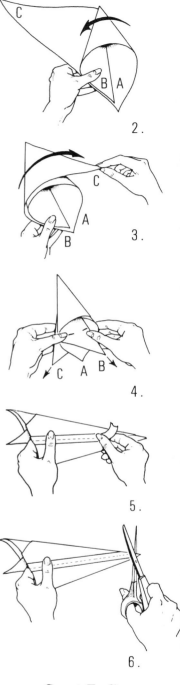

2.

3.

4.

5.

6.

Sweet Endings

511

You are now ready to fill the bag. For easier handling, stand the bag in a container such as a tall jar or a glass. Using a large metal spatula, fill the bag no more than $1/3$ to $1/2$ full with frosting. Do not try to put too much frosting in at once or it will ooze out the top of the bag when you start to decorate. It also makes the bag harder to squeeze. After each addition of frosting, press your thumb and forefinger against the bag to clean off the spatula as you withdraw it.

Turn up the collar and twist the bag several times to force the icing down to the tip and to secure the top opening. You can also close the bag by flattening the top, turning the corners in toward the center, and folding the bag down from the top. Squeeze the bag gently until the icing flows smoothly through the tip to release air pockets. You are now ready to begin to decorate the cake.

HOW TO HOLD THE PASTRY BAG

Grip the pastry bag between your thumb and forefinger at the level of the filling. Your fingers should be wrapped around the front of the bag; your thumb should be positioned across the twisted opening to hold in the filling. To squeeze, exert pressure on the bag by pressing with your fingers and thumb. Use the thumb and forefinger of the other hand to steer the bag. Never squeeze the bag with both hands, only with your dominant hand. Squeezing with both hands will inevitably cause the frosting to ooze out of the top of the bag.

If, like most novice decorators, you can't resist squeezing the bag with both hands, try placing your other hand behind you. Simple decorations can easily be done with one hand.

One other key point: Keep your hand relaxed. You are not holding a time bomb.

DECORATING HINTS

With pastry bag in hand, confronting a blank cake, almost everyone who has ever decorated a cake has wondered, "What do I put on this cake?" How you choose to decorate your cake is always a matter of preference and imagination. Here are a few of my thoughts on what makes a pretty cake.

▶ I like to avoid cake borders on the top and bottom. They are boring. If I do a bottom border, I usually decorate the top without a border. If I do choose to do a border on the top and bottom, I like to start the top border about 1 to 1½ inches in from the edge.

▶ For a birthday or anniversary cake, I prefer not to letter a message. Lettering requires an especially steady hand and a good eye. There are many other ways to express your good wishes without risking an error. Here are a few suggestions:

—Write the "year" of the occasion instead. For a 25th anniversary, make a double row of drop flowers about 3 inches high in the shape of the numbers, using a small #34 drop flower tip. A third row of drop flowers can be placed on top in between the two lower rows if you wish.

—Place a miniature easel next to the cake holding a hand-written card saying, for instance, "Happy 21st Birthday, Bob."

—Use a symbol that is appropriate to the event. If the occasion is a baby shower, pink and blue diaper pins pressed vertically into the frosting around the base of the cake make an adorable presentation.

—If you do wish to write a message on the top of a cake, write the message first before you do any other design. That way, if you make a mistake centering the letters, you can fill in the open space with a cluster of drop flowers, stars, or whatever suits you. Placing candles in this area is another idea.

▶ Patterns on top of cakes are often more attractive if they are done in a half moon or arch placed closer to the edge than the center of the cake.

▶ Cake decorations are more eye catching if you vary the height of the frosting. High and low points create more interest.

BASIC DESIGNS

Here are some easy basic designs to get you started. You may make them using either large or small tubes. To determine which size tip is appropriate for your cake, refer to page 509.

Since the numbers you want to buy are not always available when you go to buy them, I have indicated more than one tip number for each design. The tip numbers marked with an asterisk are the preferable sizes, but if the store is out of those sizes, you may substitute the others.

OVERLAPPING BORDERS

Suggested tips:
- Small size: Star—#29, *#34
- Leaf—*#68, #70
- Large size: Open star—*#2, *#4, *#6
- Plain tip—#2, *#4
- Leaf—*#114

Use a medium-consistency frosting. Hold the pastry bag at a 45° angle with the tip about ¼ inch from the top of the cake, and squeeze using moderate pressure. As the frosting comes through the tip, move the bag away from you slightly and increase the pressure, then pull the pastry bag toward you in a steady motion. Relax the pressure and press the tip down, then quickly lift the pastry bag up to break the flow of the frosting. The design should resemble a teardrop. Just before the point of the teardrop, begin the second application of frosting. It should overlap the tail of the first teardrop. Repeat the procedure around the cake, making a continuous overlapping border. Be sure to rotate the cake as you decorate.

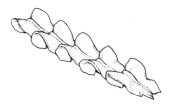

DROP FLOWER BORDERS

Suggested tips:
- Small size: Star—#29, *#34
- Large size: Open and/or *closed star—#2, *#4, #5, *#6

Use medium-consistency frosting. Holding the pastry bag at a 90° angle with the tip about ¼ inch from the top of the cake, squeeze using moderate pressure to make a single drop flower. The more pressure you apply, the wider the flower will be. When the flower reaches the size you wish, decrease pressure and press the tip down against the flower. Lift the bag up immediately and give it a slight twist to break the flow of frosting. If the flower measures about ½ inch across, start the next flower ¼ inch from the edge of the first. The flowers should join but not overlap. Repeat the procedure around the cake making a continuous border. Be sure to rotate the cake as you decorate.

DOTS AND LINE WORK

Suggested tips:
    Small size: Plain—*#2, *#3, #4
    Large size: Plain—#2, *#4, *#5, *#6

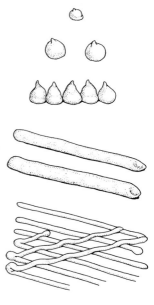

For dots and line work, use thinner frosting. Hold the pastry bag at a 90° angle with the tip almost touching the top of the cake.

To make the dots: Squeeze using light pressure. When the dot is the size you wish, immediately lift the pastry bag to break the flow of frosting.

To make lines: Squeeze using light pressure and pull the bag toward you with a steady hand. When the line is as long as you want it, drop the tip of the bag down slightly, then immediately lift to break the flow of frosting. Lines can be short, the full length of the cake, or zigzagged.

To make scrolls: Simply form a figure S, making as many as you wish in a pattern around the cake. Arches, stems, or any outlined silhouette can also be used.

LETTERS

Suggested tips:
    Small size: Plain—*#2, *#3

For lettering, the frosting should be quite thin so that it flows easily through the tube. Before you start, practice writing the name or message you are going to use on a piece of paper exactly as you plan to write it on the cake, or use the bottom of the cake pan. The

Sweet Endings

shorter the message, the better your chances of not making an error.

Holding the pastry bag at a 90° angle with the tip almost touching the frosting, print each letter using light pressure. Do not use script; the flow of the frosting is difficult to control. If you wish, you can use a toothpick to place a pinhead-size mark where you plan to place each letter. Form each line of the letter separately. For example, if you were drawing the letter "H," you would make two vertical lines and join by one horizontal line. As each line of the letter is completed, press the tip down, then quickly lift the pastry bag up to break the flow of frosting.

DROP FLOWERS

Suggested tips:
    Small size: Star—#29, *#34
    Large size: Open and/or *closed star—#2, *#4, #5, *#6

The simplest kind of drop flowers are made from closed star tips. The star is called a drop flower. Use medium-consistency frosting. Hold the pastry bag at a 90° angle with the tip about ¼ inch from the top of the cake. Squeeze using moderate pressure. When the drop flower is as big as you want it, press the tip down slightly, then immediately lift the pastry bag up to break the flow of frosting. Small clusters of drop flowers make dainty accents; when scattered over a large area, they form an eye-catching overall pattern. Drop flowers are also nice around the base of candles. These are very attractive when stems and leaves are attached.

ROSETTES

Suggested tips:
    Small size: Star—#29, *#34
    Large size: Open and/or *closed star—#2, *#4, #5, *#6

Use medium-consistency frosting. Hold the pastry bag at a 90° angle with the tip about ¼ inch above the top of the cake. Squeeze the bag using moderate pressure and move the tip in a circle. When you have completed one full turn, drop the tip slightly into the rosette, then immediately lift it up to break the flow of the frosting.

Great Cakes

516

If you wish, you can make two graduated circles, the bottom one slightly larger than the top. Instead of stopping the flow of the frosting at the end of the first full circle, swirl the frosting around a second time, then drop the tip slightly into the rosette and immediately lift it up to break the flow of the frosting. To give the rosette a finished look, make a small drop flower on top of the rosette using the same tip.

SHELLS AND SWIRLS

Suggested tips:
    Small size: Star—#29, *#34
    Large size: Open and/or *closed star—#2, *#4, #5, *#6

Use a medium-consistency frosting. Holding the pastry bag at a 45° angle with the tip about ¼ inch above the top of the cake, squeeze the bag, increasing pressure as the frosting flows through the tip. Move the bag slightly away from you, then toward you, to form a shell or teardrop shape. To break the flow of the frosting, drop the bag down slightly, then quickly pull it away. If you wish to make a curved shell, give the bag a slight twist to the left or the right before you break the flow of frosting.

FLAT AND STANDING LEAVES

Suggested tips:
    Small size: Leaf—*#68, #70
                #352 (closed-tip leaf)
    Large size: Leaf—*#114

Use a medium-consistency frosting. Hold the pastry bag at a 45° angle with the tip about ¼ inch above the top of the cake. To make a flat leaf, squeeze the bag using moderate pressure, allowing a little frosting to fall onto the cake to build a base for the leaf. As you are squeezing, move the bag away from you slightly and then overlap the strip of frosting you have just made by pulling the bag toward you, continuing to extend the frosting until you reach the size leaf you desire. Pinch the end of the leaf gently between your thumb and forefinger to form a point.

Sweet Endings

To make a stand-up leaf, follow the directions for a flat leaf, but when the leaf is the size you want it, lift the bag, giving it a slight twist as you do so. Pinch the end of the leaf gently between your thumb and forefinger to form a point.

HOW TO CLEAN PASTRY BAGS & TUBES

Pastry bags should be turned inside out and washed in warm soapy water. Rinse well and wipe partially dry with a towel. Stuff a couple of pieces of paper toweling in the center of the bag and stand on the counter to dry completely. If the pastry bag has a metal ring, you can also hang it to dry.

Wash pastry tips well with a pastry tube brush, a tiny brush made especially for this purpose, or a cotton swab or pipe cleaner.

Pastry bags have to be replaced after a period of time as they go rancid and develop a sour odor. Let your nose be the judge. Decorating tubes will last indefinitely if they are not bent out of shape.

APPENDIXES

EQUIVALENTS AND SUBSTITUTIONS

....

AMOUNT AND INGREDIENT	EQUALS
1 cup sifted cake flour	1 cup less 2 tablespoons sifted all-purpose flour
1 cup sifted all-purpose flour	1 cup plus 2 tablespoons sifted cake flour
1 ounce unsweetened chocolate	3 tablespoons cocoa plus 1 tablespoon vegetable oil, or shortening (see page 19 for semisweet chocolate substitutions)
1 cup sour milk	1 cup less 1 tablespoon regular milk plus 1 tablespoon white vinegar or strained lemon juice, set aside for 5 minutes
1 cup buttermilk	1 cup plain or low-fat yogurt
1 cup whole milk	$\frac{1}{2}$ cup evaporated milk mixed with $\frac{1}{2}$ cup water
1 tablespoon cornstarch (for thickening purposes)	2 tablespoons all-purpose flour
1 tablespoon potato starch (for thickening purposes)	2 tablespoons all-purpose flour
1 teaspoon double-acting baking powder	$\frac{1}{2}$ teaspoon baking soda
1 teaspoon baking soda	2 teaspoons double-acting baking powder
1 teaspoon single-acting baking powder	$\frac{1}{2}$ teaspoon cream of tartar plus $\frac{1}{4}$ teaspoon baking soda plus $\frac{1}{4}$ teaspoon cornstarch
2 egg yolks	1 whole egg

AMOUNT AND INGREDIENT	EQUALS
1 cup granulated sugar	1 cup firmly packed light or dark brown sugar
1 cup granulated sugar	1 cup superfine sugar
1 cup granulated sugar	7/8 cup honey less 3 tablespoons liquid plus 1/4 teaspoon baking soda per 2 cups flour
1 cup light brown sugar	1 cup granulated sugar plus 1/4 cup unsulphured light molasses

STICK OR SOLID
MEASURING CHART BY WEIGHT

....

(Applies to butter and/or other solid fats)

4 sticks =	16 ounces =	32 tablespoons =	2 cups =	1 pound =	454 grams
2 sticks =	8 ounces =	16 tablespoons =	1 cup =	1/2 pound =	227 grams
1 1/2 sticks =	6 ounces =	12 tablespoons =	3/4 cup =	3/8 pound =	169 grams
1 1/3 sticks =	5 1/3 ounces =	10 2/3 tablespoons =	2/3 cup =	1/3 pound =	151 grams
1 stick =	4 ounces =	8 tablespoons =	1/2 cup =	1/4 pound =	113 grams
3/4 stick =	3 ounces =	6 tablespoons =	3/8 cup =	3/16 pound =	84 grams
2/3 stick =	2 2/3 ounces =	5 1/2 tablespoons =	1/3 cup =	1/6 pound =	76 grams
1/2 stick =	2 ounces =	4 tablespoons =	1/4 cup =	1/8 pound =	56 grams
1/4 stick =	1 ounce =	2 tablespoons =	1/8 cup =	1/16 pound =	28 grams

Great Cakes

DRY MEASURING CHART BY VOLUME

(For raw fruits and vegetables)
(Rounded Off)

4 pecks = 1 bushel
1 peck = 8 quarts   2,000 grams = 2 kilograms
1 quart = 4 cups = 2 pounds = 908 grams   1,000 grams = 1 kilogram
1 pint = 2 cups = 16 ounces = 454 grams   500 grams = ½ kilogram

DRY MEASURING CHART BY VOLUME

(For dry ingredients)

16 tablespoons	= 1 cup	=	8 ounces
14 tablespoons	= ⅞ cup	=	7 ounces
12 tablespoons	= ¾ cup	=	6 ounces
10⅔ tablespoons	= ⅔ cup	=	5⅓ ounces
8 tablespoons	= ½ cup	=	4 ounces
5⅓ tablespoons	= ⅓ cup	=	2⅔ ounces
4 tablespoons	= ¼ cup	=	2 ounces
2 tablespoons	= ⅛ cup	=	1 ounce
1 tablespoon	= 3 teaspoons	=	½ ounce
½ tablespoon	= 1½ teaspoons	=	¼ ounce
⅓ tablespoon	= 1 teaspoon		

Pinch or dash = the amount caught between two fingers

METRIC EQUIVALENTS OF MEASURES BY WEIGHT

·····································

(Rounded off)

2³/₁₆ pounds			=	1 kilogram
2 pounds	=	32 ounces	=	908 grams
1 pound	=	16 ounces	=	454 grams
¹/₂ pound	=	8 ounces	=	227 grams
¹/₄ pound	=	4 ounces	=	113 grams
¹/₈ pound	=	2 ounces	=	57 grams
		1 ounce	=	28 grams
		¹/₂ ounce	=	14 grams
		¹/₄ ounce	=	7 grams

FLUID MEASURING CHART BY VOLUME

(Rounded off)

1 gallon =	4 quarts =	4 liters
1/2 gallon =	2 quarts =	2 liters
1 quart =	4 cups =	1,000 milliliters (1 liter)
1 pint =	2 cups =	500 milliliters (1/2 liter)
1/2 pint =	1 cup =	250 milliliters (1/4 liter)
1 quart =	32 ounces =	.946 milliliter
1 fifth =	25 ounces =	(4/5th quart)
2 cups =	16 ounces =	.473 milliliter
1 cup =	8 ounces =	.236 milliliter
1/2 cup =	4 ounces =	.118 milliliter (1 gill)
1/4 cup =	2 ounces =	.059 milliliter
1 jigger =	1 1/2 ounces =	.045 milliliter
(3 tablespoons)		
2 tablespoons =	1 ounce =	.030 milliliter
1 tablespoon =	1/2 ounce =	.015 milliliter
Dash =	a few drops	

GLOSSARY

·····················

BAIN-MARIE: A waterbath; a large open vessel, partially filled with hot water, holds a smaller pan.

BATTER: A mixture thin enough to pour or drop from a spoon.

BEAT: A rapid motion used to incorporate air into a batter or dough.

BLANCH: To drop into boiling water for 1 to 2 minutes, generally to remove thin skin without cooking food.

BOIL: To cook until bubbling (212°).
   a. *Slow boil*—To bring to boil on low flame to avoid scorching; a few bubbles appear on surface.
   b. *Rapid boil*—To bring to boil on high flame with many bubbles on surface.

BREAKDOWN: The separation of butterfat from milk solids that results in a curdled appearance.

CARAMELIZE: To cook sugar slowly until it turns to liquid and color changes to dark amber (310°).

CLARIFIED BUTTER: Butter that is slowly cooked to a point where the whey and milk solids separate from the fat.

COAT A SPOON: A thin film adheres to the back of a spoon dipped into a mixture such as custard.

CREAM: To beat solid fats such as butter until well blended, with smooth texture, increase in volume, and a lightened color.

CRISP: To heat until crunchy.

CUT IN: To blend fats into dry ingredients with two knives or a pastry blender, forming small particles of fat coated with flour.

DÉGOURAGE: A salting procedure used to extract liquid from watery vegetables, such as zucchini.

DOT: To scatter small bits over a surface.

527

DOUBLE BOILER: A doubled or nested pot; the bottom is filled with a water level low enough so the top portion does not touch the water underneath. Its use prevents scorching of foods that burn quickly.

DOUGH: Dry ingredients that are bound with liquid to form a mass stiff enough to hold in your hand.

DUST: A thin, fine-textured covering of powdery ingredients such as flour, sugar, crumbs, or nuts sprinkled over a surface.

FILM: A thin covering that forms on the surface of cooked custards when exposed to air.

FOLD IN: To combine two substances of different densities, to maintain air and/or volume.

FROTHY: Showing a surface of light, foamy bubbles.

GANACHE: A blend of semisweet chocolate and heavy cream that performs different functions at various temperatures.

GARNISH: Trim or adornment of foods to enhance appearance.

GENOISE: A type of sponge cake usually containing melted butter. The cake is the basis for many elaborate preparations.

GLAZE: A thin covering.

GRATE: To make thin, flakelike particles.

HULL: To remove stems from berries.

LIAISON: To bind or thicken one substance with another; the thickening agent can be a starch, egg yolks, and/or heavy cream.

LIGHTEN: To add a light substance, such as beaten egg whites or whipped cream, to a thick batter to decrease the density of the batter.

MACERATE: To soften or draw out liquid by soaking in liquer or sprinkling with sugar, usually applies to fruit.

MARBLEIZE: To combine two or more flavors or colors of batter to create a mottled effect, or to vein a textured filling through a batter.

MARINADE: An acidic liquid in which food is soaked for flavor, enrichment, or tenderization.

MARINATE: To soak in liquor, marinade, or brine.

MERINGUE: A mixture formed by adding sugar to whipped egg whites, then beating until it holds its shape.

MINCE: To chop into very tiny pieces.

PARE: To peel off skin and otherwise make ready for use.

PEAK STAGE: A condition, usually of beaten egg whites or heavy cream, in which the whipped substance holds a peak.

PITH: The white, spongy tissue that lies between the outer skin and the pulp of citrus fruit.

PLUMPING: Process of softening dried fruit such as raisins by immersion in hot water or by steaming.

POACH: To cook foods slowly in a covered saucepan or skillet with just enough simmering liquid to cover.

PRALINE: A hardened candy made of caramelized sugar and nuts, usually pecans, almonds, or hazelnuts.

PURÉE: A smooth, thick mixture, usually made from fruits or vegetables.

REDUCE: To cook until a specified amount of liquid has evaporated.

REFRESH: To renew by exposing food to either hot or cold temperature.

RIBBON: A very thick stage of a beaten mixture, usually eggs and sugar. When poured from a height, the substance makes thick, ribbony waves.

RIND: The firm outer covering of fruit, also called zest.

SAUTÉ: To fry in small amount of fat or oil.

SCALD: To heat slowly under boiling point until bubbles appear around outer rim of saucepan and a thin film forms over top surface.

SCORE: To make overlying horizontal and vertical lines across a surface in a tic-tac-toe pattern.

SCRAPE DOWN: To push ingredients clinging to the sides of a mixing bowl toward the center with the aid of a rubber spatula.

SCUM: A film formed over certain foods when heated.

SHRED: To cut on a shredder into thin flat strips.

SIFT: To strain or sieve to remove lumps.

SIMMER: To cook on low flame so the liquid shows little surface movement.

SKIM: To remove an unwanted substance from the surface of a liquid.

SLIVER: To cut into thin slices.

STABILIZE: To fortify a delicate substance like beaten egg whites or whipped cream with an ingredient that strengthens it.

STEAM: To cook foods elevated above boiling hot vapors, such as plain or seasoned water.

STEEP: To soak, usually in a hot liquid, to extract an essence.

TEMPER: To modify one substance with another, often to adjust temperature.

TEPID: Moderately or slightly warm.

TORTE: A cake, usually made with beaten eggs and little or no flour, that is generally dense and rich.

ULTRAPASTEURIZING: A commercial process by which heavy cream is heated to a high temperature to increase shelf life. Stabilizers and emulsifiers are added.

UNHULLED: For berries, stem intact.

WEEPING: Exuding watery liquid, as when uncooked beaten egg whites break down from standing, or when baked meringues are tightly covered.

WELL: Parting dry ingredients from the center out to form a depression.

WHIP: To beat air into a substance with beater or whisk until volume is achieved.

ZEST: The colored pared skin of a citrus fruit.

MAIL ORDER SOURCES

·····································

GENERAL

The Baker's Catalogue
King Arthur Flour Company
P.O. Box 876
Norwich, VT 05055
(800) 827-6836

Extensive line of specialty flours, baking ingredients, specialty pans, utensils, and accessories.

Bridge Kitchenware
214 East 52nd Street
New York, NY 10022
(212) 688-4220

Extensive selection of domestic and imported cake pans, French wire cake racks, cake decorating equipment, baking accessories, porcelain cake platters for roulades, domed cake covers, baking parchment (packaged in sheets) sold in bulk. Commercial equipment available. Catalog available.

Cooktique
9 Railroad Avenue
Tenafly, NJ 07670
(201) 568-7990

Broad selection of baking pans and baking accessories, gadgets, cookbooks, cake decorating equipment, quality chocolate and flavorings, praline paste, unusual china, glass and hand-crafted cake plates, domed cake covers, and cake service gifts. Catalog available.

Dean & DeLuca
560 Broadway
New York, NY 10012
(800) 221-7714

Select baking equipment, praline paste, premium flavorings, high-quality dried fruits and nuts, unusual jams and jellies, cocoas and chocolates. Catalog available.

Sweet Celebrations
7009 Washington Avenue, South
Edina, MN 55439
(888) 328-6722

Huge selection of unusual cake pans and accessories for baking and cake decorating, specialty flavorings, chocolates, colored sugars, cardboard cake disks, every frill imaginable. Catalog available—a must for all serious bakers.

Maison Glass, Inc.
P.O. Box 317–H
Scarsdale, NY 10583
(800) 822-5564

Praline paste, premium jams, jellies, syrups, flavorings, cocoas, chocolates, candies, confectionery fruits, dried fruits, crystallized flowers. Catalog available.

Williams-Sonoma
Mail-Order Department
P.O. Box 7456
San Francisco, CA 94120-7456
(415) 421-4555

High-quality baking pans and accessories, small kitchen appliances, flavorings, chocolates and cocoas, cake decorating equipment. Catalog available.

Zabar's
249 W. 80th Street
New York, NY 10024
(212) 787-2002

Large selection of baking pans and accessories, small appliances, coffee beans, quality specialty foods. Catalog available.

CHOCOLATES

New York Cake & Baking Distributors
56 West 22nd Street
New York, NY 10010
(212) 675-2253

Large selection of chocolates; also praline paste, extensive line of baking pans and decorating equipment, cardboard disks. Catalog available.

Ghirardelli Chocolate Manufacturing
1111 139th Avenue
San Leandro, CA 94578
(415) 483-6970

Good-quality domestic chocolates. Catalog available.

The Nestlé Co., Inc.
100 Manhattanville Road
Purchase, NY 10577
(914) 251-3000

Excellent-quality domestic chocolates, Burgundy dark chocolate especially recommended. Sold in bulk. No catalog.

SPECIALTY FLOURS

Arrowhead Mills
Box 866
Hereford, TX 79045
(806) 364-0730

El Molino Mills
P.O. Box 2250
City of Industry, CA
(818) 599-6096

White Lily Flour Company
Box 871
Knoxville, TN 37901
(615) 546-5511

Swans Down Cake Flour
Luzianne Blue Plate Foods
640 Magazine Street
New Orleans, LA 70130
(800) 692-7895

BIBLIOGRAPHY

Amendola, Joseph. *The Bakers' Manual.* Rochelle Park, NJ: The Hayden Book Company, 1972

Amendola, Joseph and Donald E. Lundberg. *Understanding Baking.* Chicago, IL: Medalist Publications, 1970

American Heritage Editors. *The American Heritage Cookbook.* New York: American Heritage Publishing Co., Inc., 1964

August Thomsen & Co. *Ateco Simplified Cake Decorating.* Glen Cove, NY: August Thomsen & Co., 1960

Beranbaum, Rose Levy. *The Cake Bible.* New York: William Morrow, Inc., 1988

Bianchini, F. and F. Corbetta. *The Complete Book of Fruits and Vegetables.* New York: Crown Publishers, 1976. (originally published in Italy as *I Frutti della Terra,* by Arnoldo Mondadori Publisher, 1973)

Braker, Flo. *The Simple Art of Perfect Baking.* New York: William Morrow, 1985

Brody, Jane. *Jane Brody's Nutrition Book.* New York: W. W. Norton & Company, Inc., 1981

Child, Julia, Louisette Bertholle, and Simone Beck. *Mastering the Art of French Cooking, Volume 1.* New York: Alfred A. Knopf, 1961

Cunningham, Marion. *The Fannie Farmer Baking Book.* New York: Alfred A. Knopf, 1984

D'Ermo, Dominique, *The Chef's Dessert Cookbook.* New York: Atheneum, 1976

Diccionario de Mejicanismos. Mexico City: Editorial Porrua, S.A., 1983

Dodge, Jim and Elaine Ratner. *The American Baker.* New York: Simon & Schuster, 1987

Dutton, Margit Stoll. *The German Pastry Bakebook.* Radnor, PA: Chilton Book Company, 1977

Fance, W. J. *The Student's Technology of Bread Baking and Flour Confectionery*. London: Routledge & Kegan Paul, 1981

Farm Journal Inc., edited by Nell B. Nichols. *Farm Journal's Country Cookbook*. Garden City, NY: Doubleday & Company, Inc., 1972

Fussell, Betty. *I Hear America Cooking*. New York: Viking, 1986

General Mills, Inc. *Betty Crocker's Picture Cook Book*. New York: McGraw-Hill Book Company, Inc., 1950

Gillette, F. L. *Mrs. Gillette's Cookbook*. Akron, OH: The Saalfield Publishing Company, 1908

Gilman, Marion Blatsos and Richard Gilman. *Desserts and Pastries*. New York: Van Nostrand Reinhold Company, Inc., 1984

Goodbody, Mary with Jane Stacey. *Pretty Cakes*. New York: Harper & Row, 1986

Gonzalez, Elaine. *Chocolate Artistry*. Chicago: Contemporary Books, 1983

Heatter, Maida. *Maida Heatter's Book of Great Desserts*. New York: Alfred A. Knopf, 1974

Hess, O. and A. *Viennese Cooking*. New York: Crown Publishers, Inc., 1952

Horry, Harriett Pinckney. *A Colonial Plantation Cookbook*. From an original work that began in 1770. Edited with an introduction by Richard J. Hooker. Columbia, SC: University of South Carolina, 1984

Jones, Evan. *American Food*. New York: Vintage Books, 1981

Lang, Jenifer Harvey. *Tastings*. New York: Crown Publishers, Inc., 1986

Lundberg, Donald E. and Lendal H. Kotschevar. *Understanding Cooking*. Holyoke, MA: Marcus Printing, 1985

Morton, Marcia and Frederic Morton. *Chocolate*. New York: Crown Publishers, Inc., 1986

Mariani, John F. *The Dictionary of American Food & Drink*. New Haven, CT: Tickner & Fields, 1983

McCulloch-Williams, Martha. *Dishes & Beverages of the Old South*. "A facsimile of the original, published in 1913" with a new introduction by John Egerton. Knoxville, TN: The University of Tennessee Press, 1988

McGee, Harold. *On Food and Cooking*. New York: Charles Scribner's Sons, 1984

Montagne, Prosper. *Larousse Gastronomique*. London: The Hamlyn Publishing Group, Ltd., 1972

Peck, Paula. *The Art of Fine Baking.* New York: Simon & Schuster, 1961

Pepin, Jacques. *La Technique.* New York: Quadrangle/The New York Times Book Co., Inc., 1976

Pritikin, Nathan with Patrick M. McGrady, Jr. *The Pritikin Program for Diet and Exercise.* New York: Grosset & Dunlop, 1979

Radecla, Helena. *The Fruit & Nut Book.* New York: McGraw-Hill Book Company, 1984

Rombauer, Irma S. and Marion Rombauer Becker. *The Joy of Cooking.* New York: Bobbs-Merrill Company, Inc., 1985

Seranne, Ann. *The Complete Book of Home Baking.* Garden City, NY: Doubleday & Company, 1950

Silverton, Nancy. *Desserts.* New York: Harper & Row Publishers, Inc., 1986

Simon, André L. and Robin Howe. *Dictionary of Gastronomy.* New York: McGraw-Hill Book Company, 1970

Sultan, William J. *Practical Baking.* Westport, CT: AVI Publishing Company, 1986

Tannahill, Reay. *Food and History.* New York: Stein & Day, 1973

Time-Life Techniques. *The Good Cook, Cakes Edition.* Chicago, IL: Time-Life Books, 1970

Wennberg, G. L. *Desserts, Pastries and Fancy Cakes.* Copenhagen: Ivar Forlag, 1964

Wilton Enterprises, Inc. *The Wilton Method of Cake Decorating, Course II.* Woodridge, IL: Wilton Enterprises, 1987

INDEX

....

and basic pastry bag designs for, 514–18
and chocolate buttercream for (variation), 494
and chocolate caraque for, 497
and decorators' buttercream for, 493–94
and decorators' flower cream for, 495
and decorator's turntable for, 502
and edible flowers for, 499
and frosting amounts needed for, 503
and frosting designs for, 504–5, 514–18
and how to frost layer cakes, 504
and how to split cakes for, 500
with pastry bags, 508–18
and praline for, 498–99
and preparing cake plates for, 501–2
and quick chocolate shavings for, 496
and quick decorations and trimmings for, 505–7
and staple decorations for, 82
and tinting frostings for, 503
tips, 491–92
Cake flour, 6
Cake pans: See Baking pans
Cake racks, 38
Cakes:
with brown spots on surface, xxviii
with collapsed sides, xxvi
and common mistakes made in baking, xxv
with crisp baked toppings, 145
crumbly, xxvi
with dense line at base, xxvii
dry, xxvii
freezing, 77–79
frozen, defrosting, 79
with moist line under top crust, xxvii
not rising well, xxv
with peaked or cracked surface, xxviii

with poor color or dark crust, xxviii
and preparing for freezing, 78
and releasing from pans, 74–75
sinking in center, xxvi
slicing, 191. See also How to slice cakes
splitting, 500
that stale quickly, xxvii
with sticky fillings, 145
storing, 75–77, 191
with streaks of uneven color, xxvii
with tacky or sticky texture, xxvi
and testing for doneness of, 73–74
with textured coatings, 145
with tough texture, xxvi
with tunnel-like holes, xxvii
types of, 39–41
see also Angel food cakes; Batters; Butter cakes; Cheesecakes; Chiffon cakes; Coffee cakes; Fruit cakes; Gateaux; Layer cakes; Pound cakes; Rolled cakes; Roulades; Sponge cakes; Tortes; Upside-down cakes; individual names
Cameron, Dolores, 98
Candied pepita seed cakes, 188–89
Candy nut clusters, 394–96
Caramel syrup:
about, 339
for burnished sugar layer cake, 339–40
Cardboard disks, 502
Carrot(s):
in Hungarian Magyar torte, 404–6
pineapple cake, 232–34
Chantilly whipped cream, 489
Cheese: See Cream cheese; Ricotta cheese
Cheesecakes:
about, 41, 347–48
Ann's, 350–51
black bottom mint, 366–67
chocolate (variation), 365
chocolate marble, 364–65
great Italian, 355–57
Manhattan, 352–54
pineapple cheese squares, 358–60

glacé with mascarpone pistachio
    filling, 397–99
glaze; quick, 462–63
in graham cracker cake, 325–27
in Hungarian Magyar torte, 404–6
icing, for Boston cream pie, 337–
    38
jimmy cake, 142–43
and keeping bits from sinking in
    batters, 145
in Lise torte, 402–3
macaroon cake, 176–78
marble angel food cake, 302–4
marble cake; Zach's, 122–24
marble cheesecake, 364–65
in marble pound cake, 104–5
melting, 54–55
    in liquids, 56
in mocha buttercream (variation),
    458
nut cake; chewy, 182–83
nut filling, 330–31
passion, 410–11
pear upside-down cake, 249–50
pecan roulade with mocha
    whipped cream, 278–80
prune cake; brandied, 225–26
pudding sauce; little tea shop cake
    with, 114–15
roulade with whipped apricot
    soufflé; flourless, 268–70
in Sachertorte, 412–15
and salvaging hard and grainy, 54
semisweet, 19–20
shavings; quick, 496
silk; Swiss, 407–9
sour cream cake, 134–35
sour cream frosting, 453
sponge loaf with orange walnut
    whipped cream, 428–30
staple, 82
storing, 57
strata, 392–93
in sweetmeat angel cake, 305–7
tempering, 56–57
unsweetened (bitter), 19–20
walnut pound cake, 106–7
whipped cream, 488–89
white, 21–22

Bavarian cream, 394–95
    in candy nut clusters, 394–96
    melting, 55
    zinger; black, 110–11
Chunky chocolate chip cake, 172–73
Cinnamon:
    chiffon cake (variation), 283
    swirl bundt (variation), 128
Citrus rinds:
    grating, 62
    see also Lemon(s); Lime; Orange(s)
Classic genoise, 373–74
Clear lemon filling, 440–41
Cocoa: See Chocolate
Coconut:
    in broiled topping, 480
    canned, 315
    in chocolate macaroon cake, 176–78
    desiccated
        about, 315
        in graham cracker cake, 325–27
    layer cake, 314–15
    in le grand petit four cake, 382–83
    lemon roulade with (variation),
        266–67
    pound cake; toasted, 100–101
    preparing fresh, 61
    toasting, 58, 100
    see also Coconut milk
Coconut milk, preparing, 61–62
Coffee:
    about, 17
    cream log, 270–72
    cream sauce (variation), 477
    crème anglaise (variation), 476
    marble cake (variation), 129
    zest
        in graham cracker cake, 325–27
        making, 58
        in mocha whipped cream,
            chocolate pecan roulade
            with, 278–80
        in royal chiffon (variation), 282–
            83
    see also Espresso
Coffee cakes:
    about, 153
    oatmeal, with crunchy broiled
        topping, 160–61